PIECEWORK

PIECEWORK

WRITINGS ON MEN AND WOMEN,

FOOLS AND HEROES, LOST CITIES, VANISHED

FRIENDS, SMALL PLEASURES, LARGE

CALAMITIES,

AND HOW THE WEATHER WAS

PETE HAMILL

LITTLE, BROWN AND COMPANY
BOSTON   NEW YORK   TORONTO   LONDON

FIRST EDITION

Library of Congress Cataloging-in-Publication Data

Hamill, Pete.
    Piecework : writings on men and women, fools and heroes, lost cities, vanished friends, small pleasures, large calamities, and how the weather was / Pete Hamill.
      p. cm.
    ISBN 0-316-34104-5
    I. Title.
    PS3558.A423P53   1996
    814'.54 — dc20   95-4738

10 9 8 7 6 5 4 3 2 1

HAD
Published simultaneously in Canada by Little, Brown & Company (Canada) Limited
Printed in the United States of America

This book is for
EDWARD KOSNER

CONTENTS

ACKNOWLEDGMENTS

As a writer for newspapers and magazines, I've been blessed by good editors. I've acknowledged elsewhere the inspiring influence of Paul Sann, who in my mind will always be the editor of the *New York Post*. At that newspaper, I was also guided by Fred McMorrow, Al Davis, Joe Rabinowitz, and Bob Friedman. At the *New York Daily News*, the late Sid Penner edited my columns with a master's precision, while Pucci Meyer refined and clarified the longer articles and short stories I wrote for that newspaper's Sunday magazine. At the *Village Voice*, Karen Durbin, Tom Morgan, and, later, Don Guttenplan were all fine editors of my pieces. At *Esquire*, Dave Hirshey has been ingenious at anticipating themes and stories that would remain fresh in spite of that magazine's long lead time.

Early on, I learned many things about craft from Jack Nessel, Clay Felker, and Milton Glaser, when they worked together at *New York* magazine. Nessel placed his loupe upon my texts (and those of others) and with humor and patience worked only to make them better. Felker was always bursting with ideas and discoveries and enthusiasms, but Glaser edited Felker; listening to their debates was essential to my education. Under a later regime at *New York*, I was fortunate to be edited by Peter Herbst and Dick Babcock; they maintained the high standards established by the founding editors.

In a long, varied career, there were many others: Steve Gelman, Ray Robinson, Bill Ewald, Don McKinney, Seymour Krim, Wayne Lawson, Myra Appleton, Barry Golson, Peter Moore, Harvey Shapiro, George Walsh, Richard Kluger, Linda Perney, Jeff Schaire, Peter Biskind, Harriet Fier, and, in a later enlistment at the *New York Post*, Jerry Nachman, Richard Gooding, Eric Fettman, John Cotter, and Lou Colasuonno. Even brief encounters with their skills have added to my craft. Directly or indirectly, their work is in this book too.

But across the years, one magazine editor has provided a special kind of continuity. Ed Kosner was assistant night city editor at the *New York Post* on my first night in the city room. He edited my first piece of copy. Later, as editor of *New York* magazine for twelve years, he assigned many of the articles in this book. A lifetime has passed, and we're still working together, now at *Esquire,* where Kosner is the editor. Hundreds of thousands of my words have come under his pencil. With his efficiency, clarity, and intelligence, he has always helped make them better. We communicate in a kind of intellectual shorthand, a few words here, a note there, and then back to the typewriter or computer. In a trade populated by prima donnas, we've never exchanged a harsh word. More important, we're friends. *Un abrazo, Eduardo.*

PIECEWORK

INTRODUCTION

For thirty-five years now, I have worked at the writing trade. Writing has fed me, housed me, educated my children. Writing has allowed me to travel the world and has provided me with a ringside seat at some of America's biggest, most awful shows. Writing has permitted me to celebrate and embrace many public glories and to explore the darkest side of my own personality. Writing is so entwined with my being that I can't imagine a life without it.

Usually, I work every day, seven days a week, at the tradesman's last. When I go three days without writing, my body aches with anxiety, my mood is irritable, my night dreams grow wild with unconscious invention. Because I write fiction *and* journalism, I follow no set routine. Struggling with a novel, I've spent months at my desk, a bore to those who live with me. But when laboring at journalism, the days are more jagged, the hours broken by telephone calls, interviews, research in libraries or newspaper morgues. The desk has its attractions, but I've also worked in parked cars, in a hotel lobby where the air burned with tear gas, in a tent under a mortar attack. In my drinking days, I wrote in the back rooms of bars, too. I've written longhand on yellow pads and restaurant menus. Feeding coins into a pay phone, I've dictated complete paragraphs from scribbled notes. I started with manual typewriters and now use a computer. The work does not get easier.

The older I get, the more I am humbled by the difficult standards of my trade. About many things, from the meaning of baseball to the nature of human beings, I was far more certain at thirty than I am at sixty. Each day I learn something new. This is not, of course, my hobby. It is my pride that I have been a professional from the beginning, paid for every published word, unsupported by foundation money or government grants. But although I'm a professional of my trade, I struggle each day to retain the innocent eye of the amateur. I do piecework, and with each piece, I'm forced to begin again, to try to find something fresh in the familiar, to look at my subjects as if they'd never been written about before.

What do you do? asks the stranger. *I'm a writer,* I answer. On some mornings, this reply can still astonish me. Like so many other writers, I wanted in my adolescence and young manhood to join an entirely different guild.

The craft of cartooning first grabbed my heart when I was eleven years old, and that adolescent passion gradually evolved into a desire to be a painter. My first short stories and essays were written at Mexico City College in 1956, when I was studying painting there on the GI Bill. My first published words were two poems that appeared in 1958 in the literary magazine of Pratt Institute, where I was a student in the art school. The first words I wrote for money appeared the following year in a Greek magazine named *Atlantis,* for which I worked as art director; the story was in English, and I was paid $25. On the night in 1960 when I walked into the city room of the *New York Post* to try to be a newspaperman, I was working days as a commercial artist. I was twenty-five years old, a high school dropout from a poor family in Brooklyn.

A few years earlier, the desire to be a painter had been derailed by several factors: a failure of will and the need to earn a living. I was uncertain of my talents as a painter, afraid of committing to a vocation that might give me a life of prolonged poverty. So I found work in an advertising agency, and though I was proud to be making my way in the world, I didn't much like the way I was doing it. There just wasn't much romance in designing letterheads or laying out catalogs. But within months of sitting down at a typewriter in a newspaper city room, even with a substantial cut in pay, I felt exuberant and free. The graphic arts were set aside; I went to work at mastering the writer's trade.

When I started writing for Dorothy Schiff's wonderful afternoon tabloid, I had no plans for the future, no certainties about a career. The *Post* was seventh in circulation among the city's seven dailies; we all knew it could fold the next morning, so it was imperative to live for tonight, for the next edition, even if that edition might be the last. I definitely wasn't there for the pension plan. Newspaper people were flamboyant, hard-drinking, bohemian anarchists, with great gifts for obscenity and a cynicism based on experience. Or so I thought. I loved being in their company, in city rooms, at murder scenes, or standing at the bar after work.

For me, the work itself was everything. I had grown up under the heroic spell of the Abstract Expressionist painters, and one of their lessons was that the essence of the work was the doing of it. At twenty-five, I thought I had started late and therefore had to hurl myself into the work — and the life that went with it. In my experience, nothing before (or since) could compare to walking into the *New York Post* at midnight, being sent into the dark, scary city on an assignment, and coming back to write a story for the first edition. No day's work was like any other's, no story repeated any other in its details. Day after day, week after week, I loved being a newspaperman, living in the permanent present tense of the trade. I had no idea as a young man that from my initiation into the romance of newspapers would flow novels, books of short stories, too many screenplays, a memoir, and millions of words of newspaper and magazine journalism. I didn't know that I was apprenticing to a trade that I would practice until I die.

This is not to claim that I've produced an uninterrupted series of amazements. Reading over a quarter-century of my journalism for this collection (my first since *Irrational Ravings* in 1970), I have often winced; if I'd only had another three inches of space, or another two hours beyond the deadline, perhaps this piece would have been better or that piece wiser. There were newspaper columns that I wish I'd never written, full of easy insult or cheap injury. There were many pieces limited by my ignorance. Too many lazily derived their energy from the breaking news to which they served as mere sidebars. Others were about figures who were once famous and are now obscure (and hence have been excluded from this collection — any footnotes of explanation would be longer than the originals). Sometimes I completely missed the point, or didn't see the truth of a story whose facts were evidently there in my notebook. But this is not an apology. It is the nature of such work that it is produced in a rush; the deadlines usually force the newspaper writer to publish a first draft because there is no time for a second or third. Once that piece is locked up in type and sent to the newsstands, there is no going back; the writer can correct the factual error, but it's too late to deepen the insight, alter the mistaken or naive judgment, erase the stale language that was taken off the rack. He or she can only vow never to make *that* error again and start fresh the next day.

Early on, I understood why these hurried writings were called pieces. The built-in limitations of the form were the enemies of thoroughness; the very best a journalist could hope for was to reveal fragments that stood for the whole, like an archeologist working in a ruined city. When I started writing magazine articles, with their longer deadlines and expanded space, some of those problems were solved. But I was still at the mercy of the people I interviewed. The journalist can prepare well, listen carefully, and, thanks to modern technology, record what he hears with absolute fidelity. But human beings lie. Cops lie. Lawyers lie. Actors lie. Victims lie. Statistics lie. The objective reporter writes down the lies and tries to check them against other sources. But sometimes one lie is merely countered with another lie and the reporter is forced by the standards of objectivity to print both.

To be sure, at the heart of every story there is a bald fact or two. The body of a man lies in an alley. The body can be measured and weighed and checked for scars or tattoos, thus providing new facts to the cop and his unofficial collaborator, the reporter. The dead man's wallet might reveal the facts of his identity: a name, an address, an age, his bank, the number of his driver's license. All facts, if the credentials are legitimate. Wives or lovers or rivals will speak about the dead man and add a few more small facts about his life and death. But the best detectives also know that the facts don't always reveal the truth, certainly about an entity as complicated as a human being. The facts can't record the dead man's final thoughts, or his dreams, desires, confusions and ambiguities. They can't explain the meaning of his life.

That's why so many journalists turn to writing novels: to get at the truth beyond the facts, about themselves and others. If reporters stick around long enough, if they see enough human beings in trouble, they learn that the guilty are sometimes innocent and the innocent probably have an angle. Things, as the philosopher said, ain't what they seem to be. Nor are people. I've known many newspaper reporters whose lives were permanently soured by what they had witnessed and their work ruined by a self-protecting indifference. Others survived, usually by fealty to the *dailiness* of the enterprise. They plunged into the moments of the story and its writing and left it all behind when they were finished. Or they distilled what they knew into fiction. The trick was to see the world as a skeptic, not a cynic, while allowing for the wan possibility of human decency.

After 1965, when I started writing a newspaper column, I was freed from the tyranny of an impossible objectivity. The facts were still the core of the work, of course, but in the column form I was able to express my feelings or ideas about those facts. From the beginning, the form felt natural to me; I was like a musician who had found at last the instrument that was right for him. My earliest columns echoed with the voices of those who came before me, from Murray Kempton and Jimmy Cannon to Robert Ruark and Westbrook Pegler; I watched carefully what my friend Jimmy Breslin was doing at the *New York Herald Tribune,* where he was inventing a new kind of newspaper column. In my early work, I can see the marks that all of them put on me. But I was writing too much, too quickly, to imitate any of them slavishly. For all writers, newspaper work is a valuable shortcut to finding style; its pressures force the writer to do what works most naturally.

In finding my own language, or style, the keys were tone and rhythm. The tone was a matter of understanding the story and being open to its essence; presented with the brayings of some obvious political fraud, the tone was mocking; witnessing some urban calamity, the tone was infused with a sense of tragedy. I thought of the process as "hearing the music." The rhythm of that music was inseparable from the tone. For one kind of story, simple declarative sentences, as blunt as axes, were best; for others, it was necessary to use longer lines, more complicated rhythms. The style was itself a form of comment or explanation.

I used everything I knew to express, or refine, both rhythm and tone. When I was a teenager, I wanted for a brief season to be a jazz drummer. In an old issue of *Down Beat,* I read an interview with Gene Krupa, one of the stars of the Benny Goodman band, and he was asked a smart question: Since the drummer was the metronome of the band, how did *he* keep time? What served as *his* metronome? Krupa answered that he kept chanting to himself one simple phrase: "lyonnaise potatoes and *some* pork chops." He would drag the word "lyonnaise" and emphasize the "some" to insure that the beat wouldn't become too mechanical. So in those first years, I often sat at a Royal Standard typewriter in the city room, writing about some fire or homicide or snowstorm, all the while humming under my breath, "lyyyyy-oh-naise-p'taytas an' *some* pork chops, yeah — lyy-yyy-oh-naise-p'taytas an' *some* pork chops," keeping time with my right foot, as if using a pedal on a bass drum. I wanted that rhythm

in the sentences. I wanted to add some gaudy word to serve for a splash on the cymbals. Even now, when a deadline is crashing upon me, I chant Krupa's mantra.

Over three decades, I've written newspaper and magazine columns for the *New York Post,* the *Village Voice,* the *New York Daily News, New York Newsday, Esquire,* and *New York,* along with freelance articles for these and other periodicals. In a way, these columns and articles make up a kind of public diary, a recording of where I was and what I saw and who I met along the way. In a meandering, unplanned way, they're about one American writer grappling with the meaning of the public events of his time: Vietnam and Watergate, riots, assassinations, scandals, murders, political betrayals. During the period covered by this collection, I chose my own subjects. Usually I thought of them myself; sometimes suggestions for pieces came from editors, but as a freelancer I was, of course, free to decline.

Many pieces originated in my personal history; when I wrote about New York or Mexico or Ireland, I brought to those pieces the kinds of knowledge that didn't always exist in books. Memory, myth, lore: all had their uses. But at other times, I often chose subjects about which I knew nothing. My ignorance would then force me to learn, to engage in a crash course of books, clippings, reporting. Gradually, I began to make connections among a variety of subjects; a civil rights story about Martin Luther King and Stokely Carmichael could also be informed by a knowledge of Faulkner and the blues. A murder at a good address might be written better with a knowledge of investment banking, real estate dealings, or the novels of Louis Auchincloss. I might more clearly understand the latest homegrown fascist if I knew about *volkische* nationalism, the history of Sparta, or the drawings of George Grosz. Specialization had no attraction for me; it would be like spending a life painting only roses. I wanted to be, and am, a generalist.

As a young man, my ambition was to embrace those general qualities that Ernest Hemingway, a former newspaperman, once said should be present in all good books: "the good and the bad, the ecstasy, the remorse and sorrow, the people and the places and how the weather was." That ambition was amazingly presumptuous, of course, and in some obvious ways, comic. No tabloid newspaperman would ever admit to an editor (or anyone else) that he was looking for "the ecstasy, the remorse and sorrow" in the streets of New York or believed he could fit them into 700 words. But as callow as I was,

that scrap of Hemingway rhetoric did help me to understand that even fragments could serve a larger purpose. His words were not inconsistent with what gradually became a more modest ambition: to understand the way the world worked and how I fit into it.

These pieces are products of that ambition. In each of them, I first wanted to know something about a person, a place, an event, or an idea. I wanted to hear their music. Then I wanted to pass on what I'd learned to others. Looking at many of them for the first time since they were written, I remembered who I was when I wrote them, the houses I inhabited, the people I loved, my large stupidities and small triumphs, and yes, how the weather was.

PETE HAMILL, 1995

PART I

THE CITIES OF NEW YORK

If I'd grown up in another city, I almost certainly would have become another kind of writer. Or I might not have become a writer at all. But I grew up in New York in the 1940s, when New York was a great big optimistic town. The war was over and the Great Depression was a permanent part of the past; now we would all begin to live. To a kid (and to millions of adults) everything seemed possible. If you wanted to be a scientist or a left-fielder for the Dodgers, a lawyer or a drummer with Count Basie: well, why not? This was New York. You could even be an artist. Or a writer.

As a man and a writer, I've been cursed by the memory of that New York. Across five decades, I saw the city change and its optimism wane. The factories began closing in the late 1950s, moving to the South, or driven out of business by changing styles or tastes or means of production. When the factories died, so did more than a million manufacturing jobs. Those vanished jobs had allowed thousands of men like my father (an Irish immigrant with an eighth-grade education) to raise families in the richest city on earth. They eagerly joined unions. They proudly voted for the Democratic ticket. They put paychecks on kitchen tables, asked their kids if they'd finished their homework, went off to night games at the Polo Grounds or Ebbets Field, and were able to walk in the world with pride. Then the great change happened. The manufacturing jobs were replaced with service work. Or with welfare. One statistic tells the story: In 1955, there were 150,000 New Yorkers on welfare; in 1995, there were 1.3 million.

With the jobs gone, the combined American plagues of drugs and guns came to the neighborhoods. New York wasn't the only American city to be so mauled; but because it was at once larger and more anonymous, a sense of danger bordering on paranoia became a constant in the lives of its citizens. This wasn't a mere perception; it could be measured. Throughout the 1950s, New York averaged 300 murders a year; by 1994, the city fathers were ecstatic when the number of homicides dropped to 1,600 after years hovering around the 2,000 mark. In my time, even the poorest New Yorkers learned to triple-lock their doors and bar the windows against the relentless presence of the city's 200,000 heroin addicts. The middle class (children of all those factory workers) began to hire private cops to patrol their streets. They avoided subways late at night. They paid for parking lots to protect their cars against the patrolling junkies. They bought very large dogs. After a while, they stopped sending their kids to the public schools, which had begun adding metal detectors to their doors. Finally, many of them began to move away.

These pieces reflect the yearning of an entire generation of New Yorkers for the city that changed forever when we weren't even looking. We're the New Yorkers who remember the city when it worked, in every sense of that word. No matter how we live now, we are hostages to that time when each of us lived in a neighborhood that was an urban version of the American hometown. My hometown was in Brooklyn, across the East River from haughty Manhattan; there are men and women who remember their hometowns in the Bronx and Queens and parts of Manhattan the way I remember mine. Some live on in the city. Others have scattered around the country. I know from my mail that they still measure all places by the New York they knew when young.

As I write, New York seems to be reviving again. The engine of this latest revival is the wave of new immigrants. We are in the midst of the greatest immigration wave since the turn of the last century, and the new arrivals have one huge advantage over old New Yorkers: they are free of the curse of memory. They might yearn for the countries they left behind, but they couldn't care less about the Dodgers or Luna Park or the street games of 1951. In *their* New York, they live in the present tense, working at the hardest jobs, but they have visions of the future. Everywhere a New Yorker turns, he encounters Koreans, Pakistanis, Dominicans, Palestinians, Russians, Mexicans, Haitians. And it was the places they remember that propelled them to New York. Back in their hometowns, the hope of a decent life was insupportable and so they chose exile. In New York, they drive the city's cabs. They wash the dishes of the city's restaurants. They sell the city oranges at midnight. They empty bedpans in the city's hospitals. They open little stores and small businesses and at night, exhausted, drained, they ask their children if they have finished their homework. Someday, the children of the newest immigrants also might write pieces like these, full of inconsolable memories. I hope I last long enough to read them, just to see what I had missed.

THE LOST CITY

Once there was another city here, and now it is gone. There are almost no traces of it anymore, but millions of us know it existed, because we lived in it: the Lost City of New York.

It was a city, as John Cheever once wrote, that "was still filled with a river light, when you heard the Benny Goodman quartets from a radio in the corner stationery store, and when almost everybody wore a hat." In that city, the taxicabs were all Checkers, with ample room for your legs, and the drivers knew where Grand Central was and always helped with the luggage. In that city, there were apartments with three bedrooms and views of the river. You hurried across the street and your girl was waiting for you under the Biltmore clock, with snow melting in her hair. Cars never double-parked. Shop doors weren't locked in the daytime. Bus drivers still made change. All over town, cops walked the beat and everyone knew their names. In that city, you did not smoke on the subway. You wore galoshes in the rain. Waitresses called you honey. You slept with windows open to the summer night.

That New York is gone now, hammered into dust by time, progress, accident, and greed. Yes, most of us distrust the memory of how we lived here, not so very long ago. Nostalgia is a treacherous emotion, at once a curse against the present and an admission of permanent resentment. For many of us, looking back is simply too painful; we must confront the unanswerable question of how we let it all happen, how the Lost City was lost. And so most of us have trained ourselves to forget.

And then suddenly, you hear a certain piece of music and you are once again at the bar of the Five Spot on St. Marks Place. You are listening to Monk, of course, and working hard at being hip. On another afternoon, you see the slanting yellow light on 125th Street, and abruptly you are again leaving Frank's restaurant in the early sixties after lunch with a politician and you walk down to Michaux's bookstore to find that rare poem by Countee Cullen or read the news from Africa. You flick on the television set late on an exhausting night, and in the silvery images of some forgotten forties movie, you glimpse the Brevoort Hotel on Fifth Avenue and 8th Street and then you are at one of its sidewalk tables again with an impossibly beautiful girl on a cloudless summer afternoon. All the wars are over, you have an entire $30 in your pocket, and the whole goddamned world seems perfect. Who then resident in the Lost City could dare imagine a day when the Brevoort would be gone, along with the Five Spot and Monk, Frank's and Michaux's, and even that impossibly beautiful girl?

In the cross-cutting of memory, the Brevoort leads you down 8th Street when it was the splendid Main Street of the Village. You have come up out of the subway from Brooklyn or Queens or the Bronx and are engulfed by swarming crowds, lining up for Bergman or Fellini at the 8th Street or the Art, and the very air seems thick with sensuality. Old men are selling lemon ices from carts. There's a Bungalow Bar truck down at the corner. Music is playing from upstairs apartments in this year before air-conditioning silenced the New York night: Symphony Sid or Jazzbo Collins, Alan Freed or Murray Kaufman *(Mee-a-zurry, Mee-a-zurray, all through the night)* . . . even, in memory, Jack Lacy on WINS before it became an all-news station *(Listen to Lacy, a guy with a style, of spinning a disk with finesse, yes, yes)*. If it's warm enough, and the right year, you can hear the ball games too: Ernie Harwell and Russ Hodges bringing us the Giants (with Frankie Frisch the Fordham Flash on the postgame show), or Red Barber and Connie Desmond with the Dodgers, or hear the simulated crack of a bat and the simulated roar of a crowd, and *Today's baseball, with Bert Lee and Marty Glickman, and the absent Ward Wilson, who is ailing.* . . . Ward Wilson was always absent. Ward Wilson was always ailing. And nobody listened to the Yankees.

Across the street is Hans Hofmann's art school, in the building that used to be the Whitney Museum. Upstairs, you can see easels and the backs of stretched canvases, the faces of people talking passionately about space and gesture, oblivious to the dense space and extravagant gestures of the street below them, but subliminally driven by its energy. There, wandering up from MacDougal Street: That's Joe Gould, who has translated Rimbaud into the language of seagulls and is writing the oral history of the world. You run into Hans Hess, the great émigré typographer from Huxley House, and he once more insists upon the obvious superiority of Caslon over Garamond, "except, of course, in boldface." Then you wander into the pulsing heart of the great crowded street: the Eighth Street Bookshop.

All here is intimidation, if you are young and recently arrived in the Village: Kafka and Brecht, Artaud and Ionesco glower from book jackets; the clerks look through you; Eli Willentz, the owner, sighs when you mispronounce a writer's name. But look: There is James Baldwin, home from Europe, talking near the counter to Eli — a man like any man, not a statue in the park; Robert Creeley is in from Black Mountain College; the small, dark man looking at the book of drawings by Heinrich Kley is Alfred Andriola, who draws "Kerry Drake" in the *Mirror;* the thick-bodied man with the face of a disappointed stevedore is Franz Kline; and walking past the store, waving diffidently to someone, or everyone, tall and fiercely mustached, is Harold Rosenberg. To make this a perfect New York evening, the next strolling New Yorker would have to be Sal Maglie.

They're all gone now. A Nathan's opened on the corner and the Eighth Street Bookshop closed and the street changed and everybody went away or died. They became part of the Lost City, along with the San Remo, where Maxwell Bodenheim wrote poems for bar change before he got himself murdered; the Rienzi; the Fat Black Pussy Cat; and the *old* Figaro, where the most beautiful waitresses worked and you read for hours over coffee or listened to old men with Austrian accents argue about Wittgenstein at the next table, without being pried from the chair. Maybe we broke them; we had no money then, and the owners didn't seem to care. Maybe the old refugees from Hitler made too much money and moved uptown; maybe the cops made life impossible; maybe the places just wore out. What matters is this: They are gone.

As are so many other things. No young New Yorker can ever go on a summer evening with a girl to listen to free concerts under the stars at Lewisohn Stadium. The young will not pay a dime to ride down Fifth Avenue in a double-decker bus (killed in '53) or race up Third Avenue on the el, gazing into living rooms out of John Sloan or Edward Hopper, propelled above Clarke's and Original Joe's and

Manny Wolf's and the High Hat. Once, King Kong himself had assaulted the el and it had survived, with its rusting potbellied stoves in the waiting rooms. But in 1955, the last great el in Manhattan (there were others on Second Avenue, Sixth Avenue, Ninth Avenue) was torn down, vanishing into the Lost City, to be replaced with still another bland arroyo of steel and glass.

On the most basic level, of course, these were simply means of transportation. When better methods were invented, they were replaced. But alas, the double-decker buses were more than just a means of moving people uptown or down; they were also a *ride,* adding an element of play to the task of going to work. And the el was more than a people-hauling machine; it was at once monument, curse, shelter, frontier, and a roaring example of energy made visible.

Perhaps most stupid of all the stupidities inflicted upon the city in the years after the war was the destruction of the trolley-car system. Every time I see a groaning bus coughing fumes as it lumbers across three traffic lanes, I long for the trolley cars. They were electric and therefore didn't poison the air. They ran on steel tracks and so were unable to bully their way across other traffic lanes; at the same time, they helped police that traffic, preventing by their implacable presence the infuriating double- and triple-parking that today clots so many of our streets. Some trolleys were chunky, square, steel-and-wood affairs that looked like the Toonerville Trolley in the comics; their geriatric cousins still live in San Francisco and New Orleans. Others were able to remove their side panels in the summertime. In the 1940s, the newest ones were sleek and "streamlined." And they seemed to go everywhere. Within the limits of my own Brooklyn hamlet, we had eleven separate lines: on Flatbush Avenue, Union Street, Bergen Street, Vanderbilt Avenue, Church Avenue, 9th Street, 15th Street, Fifth Avenue, Seventh Avenue, McDonald Avenue, and, most gloriously, on Coney Island Avenue. The last was "streamlined," all silver and green, and it carried us from Bartel-Pritchard Square all the way to Coney Island, past row houses and strange chalky neighborhoods, through the last of the Brooklyn vegetable farms and then into an immense brightness, the sudden odor of the sea air and the beach beyond. No wonder that lost baseball team was once called the Trolley Dodgers. No wonder nobody I knew drove a car.

Coney Island is still there, of course. But in the summertime now, the girls don't dance beside the pool at Oceantide or pick up boys at

Raven Hall. There is no line at Mary's Sandwich Shop. Nobody is at the bar at Scoville's, where my father and his friends did their drinking, or at McCabe's, where the younger crowd did theirs. Nobody listens to bands at Feltman's. You hear no laughter at Steeplechase the Funny Place, nor will you see sailors and squealing girls strapped together into the parachute ride. They're all dead or gone.

I remember being in Coney Island the day that Luna Park burned to the ground. The year was 1944. I was a boy. But there was a sudden stirring on the beach, a movement away from the surf to the boardwalk, and then great clouds of black smoke piling into the cobalt sky. You could hear voices: *Luna Park's on fire.* People were running then, and we could hear the sirens of the Fire Department and saw high arcs of water rising in a beautiful way and falling into the flames. Reporters were there and photographers with Speed Graphics, all of them wearing hats with press cards stuck in the rims, just as they did in the movies. We watched for hours, drawn as New Yorkers always are to the unity of disaster, and saw the rides and buildings collapse into black, wet rubble until there was no more Luna Park. The next day, we read all about it in the newspapers, and I felt for the first time that peculiar New York sensation: Something that was once in the world is now gone forever.

There is a photograph by Weegee, taken on V-E Day, 1945, that shows a man working at a newsstand. We can see three daily newspapers: the *Journal-American,* the *World-Telegram,* and *PM*; the magazines are *Liberty, Air News, Argosy, Song Parade, American, Judy's, Crack Detective, Phantom Detective, Cartoon Digest, American Astrology, White's Radio, Magazine Digest, Popular Science, Mechanix Illustrated, Die Hausfrau,* and *Die Welt* (must've been a Yorkville newsstand). We cannot see some other New York dailies that were publishing that year: the *Herald Tribune* and the *Mirror,* and in the outer boroughs, the Brooklyn *Eagle,* the Brooklyn *Times-Union,* the Bronx *Home-News,* the Long Island *Press,* the Long Island *Star-Journal.* They are now all dead, as is every other publication on that newsstand except *Popular Science* and *American Astrology.* It's one of the saddest photographs I've ever seen.

Around the time the newspapers began to die, the older New York started giving way to the new. Television was changing everything. Within a decade of its triumph in the mid-fifties, it killed the nightclubs and supper clubs: the Latin Quarter, the Stork, El Morocco, the Copa, Billy Rose's Diamond Horseshoe, the Astor Roof, Ben Maksik's out in Queens, the Elegante in Brooklyn (where I once saw a smashed Judy Garland perform for a roomful of gangsters), the Château Madrid, Sammy's Bowery Follies (which biographer Herbert Lottman tells us Albert Camus enjoyed so much, on his only trip to New York, that he had A. J. Liebling take him back twice), Nick's in the Village, Tony Pastor's, all the West 4th Street strip joints like the Heat Wave (run by Tony Bender), to mention only a few. Lindy's, made famous by Damon Runyon, wasn't a nightclub, but it was a night *place*, full of columnists (the old three-dotters), press agents, gangsters, and show-business people, and it survived into the early sixties. For a while near the end, I worked for the *Post* outside the place in a radio car with photographer Artie Pomerantz and once saw Walter Winchell do a tap dance on the sidewalk. The old bebop palaces on 52nd Street turned into strip joints (Ah, Lily St Cyr! O, Winnie Garrett! And where is Evelyn West and her Treasure Chest?) and then fell before the developers. Bill Miller's Riviera, across the North River under the George Washington Bridge, was locked up one morning, then had its doors nailed shut, and was finally torn down. Even Birdland closed. Many of these places were velvet-roped dives, run by wiseguy veterans of the Prohibition wars; to drop into the Copa upon a winter's eve was to risk an arrest for consorting. Some peddled junk and women; a few provided floating crap games in nearby hotels; they clipped customers, abused or exploited too many of the performers. But they had energy and color and a certain brutal style, and when they vanished, something went out of New York.

But television didn't just shutter nightclubs. The movie houses began closing, too. In my neighborhood, we had the RKO Prospect, the Venus, the Globe, the 16th Street, the Sanders, the Avon, and the Minerva: all gone. In downtown Brooklyn, the RKO Albee died along with the Fox (where Buddy Holly and Ritchie Valens and the Big Bopper played in the first huge New York rock-and-roll shows), the Brooklyn Paramount and the Duffield and the Terminal up on Fourth Avenue, beside the Long Island Rail Road, where you could see three movies for a half-dollar. Wandering through the *souk* of the Lower East Side, you could find the Palestine, the Florence, the Ruby, and the Windsor (among many others, most of which were nicknamed The Itch); they, too, died, driven into the Lost City with the great Yiddish theaters: the Grand, the Orpheum, the Yiddish

Arts. Out in Queens, around 165th Street, the Loew's Valencia closed, along with the Alden, the Merrick, the Jamaica, the Savoy, and the Hillside. On East 14th Street in Manhattan, there was a place called the Jefferson, where we went to see the Spanish movies and vaudeville acts, improbably trying to learn the language from Pedro Infante and Jorge Negrete, lusting for Sarita Montiel, laughing at the comedy of Johnny El Men, while ice-cream vendors worked the aisles. Gone. In Times Square, the Capitol disappeared, the Roxy, the Criterion, the Strand. The Laffmovie on 42nd Street played comedies all day long, but now, where Laurel and Hardy once tried to deliver Christmas trees, the movies are about ripped flesh. Who now can verify the existence of the old Pike's Opera House on 23rd Street and Eighth Avenue (converted first to vaudeville and then to movies after the Metropolitan Opera established itself at 39th Street and Broadway)? It was torn down to make way for the ILGWU houses, thus eradicating the building where Jay Gould once had his office and where Fred Astaire learned to dance. And most astonishing and final of all, the Paramount itself was murdered in its sleep.

None of this was new. In Nathan Silver's elegiac 1967 book, *Lost New York,* we can see photographs of many of the vanished ornaments of our city: the beautiful Produce Exchange at Beaver and Bowling Green, destroyed in the mid-fifties; the three Brokaw mansions at 79th and Fifth, two of which were smashed into rubble in 1965, to be replaced by an ugly high rise; Rhinelander Gardens on 11th Street between Sixth and Seventh Avenues, with their cast-iron filigreed balconies and deep front gardens, demolished in the late fifties; the splendid Studio Building at 51-55 West 10th Street, designed by Richard Morris Hunt, inhabited by a string of artists, including John La Farge and Winslow Homer, until it was demolished in 1954; the elegant, high-ceilinged cast-iron buildings on Worth Street between Church and Broadway, torn down in 1963 to make way for a parking lot; the old Ziegfeld Theater at 54th and Sixth; the Astor Hotel on Broadway between 44th and 45th; dozens of others. A city is always more than its architecture, but to destroy the past that is expressed by enduring architecture is an assault on history itself. Growing up here, you learned one bitter lesson: Whenever something was destroyed for the crime of being old, what replaced it was infinitely worse.

All along, there were complaints from architects, historians, and a few concerned citizens about this municipal vandalism. Usually, they were dismissed as the sentimentalities of cranks. But after a group of dreadful men ordered the destruction of Pennsylvania Station in 1963 to make way for the equally dreadful new Madison Square Garden (they subsequently brought their gift for ruin to the railroad itself), there was a widespread sense of horror and fury. Outraged citizens fought for and won the establishment of a Landmarks Preservation Commission. Many buildings have been saved, including Grand Central Terminal and Radio City Music Hall. But when it was decided to slam the Marriott Marquis Hotel into Times Square a few years ago, it was still impossible to save the Astor theater (opened in 1906), the Bijou (1917), the Gaiety/Victoria (1909), the Helen Hayes (1911), and, most heartbreaking of all, the Morosco, which had survived wars, depression, and turkeys since 1917. They're gone. Forever.

But listen: someone out in the street is playing an old tune. We are in a white, silent house in Gramercy Park in winter or out upon the granite cliffs of Fort Hamilton. Snow is falling. It is almost midnight. Listen: It's the sound of an organ-grinder. And if you surrender to the sound, you can go back. . . . You can still call down to a neighbor through the dumbwaiter shaft. You can go to Grand Central and pick up the *20th Century Limited* for Chicago on Track 34. You can sip coffee at the Cafe Royal on 12th Street at Second Avenue and listen to the sound of Yiddish. You can celebrate St. Patrick's Day at Moskowitz & Lupowitz. You can gaze up at the Stuyvesant building at 142 East 18th Street and know that here Richard Widmark kicked that old lady down the stairs. You can go to a rent party on a Saturday night and then go to Minton's Playhouse and hear Art Tatum. You can shop at the Hester Street market or at Wanamaker's, at Namm's or Loeser's or Mays or Martin's in Brooklyn, at Gertz in Jamaica, at Best and Company or Ohrbach's, at Masters or Korvette's. You can still go to Gimbel's. If you are poor, you can go to S. Klein on Union Square and battle for bargains with the toughest women in the history of New York.

If it's very late and you are hungry, you can take a cab to the Belmont Cafeteria downtown or the Garfield on Flatbush Avenue. Better: Wait till tomorrow; there's a 99-cent hot lunch at the Tip Toe Inn on 86th and Broadway. Have the brisket and then drop a nickel in the subway and go downtown and take a walk. The old socialists are still discussing the imminent collapse of capitalism with the writers from the *Forvetz* at the Garden Cafeteria. In Union Square, they are arguing about surplus value, the Spanish Republic, and the true meaning of Marx's *Grundriss*.

Or wander through midtown. That's Frankie Carbo, the gangster, at the bar of the Neutral Corner, up the block from Stillman's Gym, and if you don't like his company, and you've already seen the fighters work out at Stillman's, you can go up to Harry Wiley's in Harlem and catch Sugar Ray Robinson or go down to 14th Street, where Cus D'Amato has a kid named Patterson in the Gramercy Gym. You can get into a big old Packard, as I did with my father and his friends once during the war, and ride out to the Gym at Georgia and Livonia in Brownsville, where Bummy Davis trained under the agate eyes of the hoods from Murder Incorporated. You can see fights at the St. Nicholas Arena on West 66th Street, at the Eastern Parkway Arena, the Ridgewood Grove, the Coney Island Velodrome, Fort Hamilton Arena, the Broadway Arena, the Star Casino in the Bronx, or the Jamaica Arena. Or if it's a Friday night, you can go through the lobby of the old Garden at Eighth Avenue and 50th Street, past the detectives and the wiseguys and the fight managers, past the bronze statue of Joe Gans, and into the great smoky arena.

In the Lost City of New York, the subway will be a nickel forever, and if you fall asleep and travel to the end of the line, you will still have your wallet and your life. In the Lost City, you can still go to Dexter Park on Eldert's Lane on the Brooklyn-Queens border and see the amazing players from the Negro Leagues, maybe even Josh Gibson, who once hit a ball out of there that traveled more than 600 feet; you can see the Bushwicks play baseball, hoping for a call from Branch Rickey; you can watch the House of David baseball team and the best of the immigrant soccer teams. We still have the Polo Grounds. We still have Ebbets Field. We still have Willie Mays.

If it's a sultry August evening, you will be able to hurry down to Sheepshead Bay and step up to the Clam Bar at Lundy's. Or you can drive out to Rockaway, get on the rides at Playland, drink cold beer and eat pig's feet at Fennessey's, Gildea's, or Sligo House, McGuire's or the Breakers, and look at the girls outside Curly's Hotel at 116th and the ocean.

If that is too long a journey, you can ride one of the many ferries that cross the Hudson each day to Jersey. You can swim in the rivers without fear of disease, and even swim at night with the seals in the Prospect Park Zoo. You can trust the oysters from Long Island

Sound. You can spend an entire Saturday among the used bookshops along Fourth Avenue. You can watch seaplanes flying down the East River, dipping elegantly under the bridges and out to the vast harbor. Listen: You might even hear the Pan Am Clipper leaving from Floyd Bennett for Lisbon.

The Lost City is full of forgotten common and proper nouns: Red Devil paint, Cat's Paw soles and heels, Griffin All-Black polish might still exist, but I don't see them anymore. Nor do I see beers called Trommer's White Label, Ruppert's, and Rheingold, candies called Sky Bars, Houten's, and B-B Bats. And for young men going out on dates, a repulsively flavored package of licorice microchips called Sen-Sen that is guaranteed to keep your breath sweet while kissing. In some lost year, Junior Persico is in Rosie's Royal Tailors next to the 72nd Precinct in Brooklyn, being measured for pants with a three-inch rise, pistol pockets, saddle stitching, a balloon knee, and a thirteen peg. He will walk home looking like an Arabian prince.

Meanwhile, the eternal New York war against the cockroach is being waged with J-O Paste and Flit. The men are smoking Fatimas and Wings. In the candy stores, they are selling "loosies" (2 cents a cigarette, two for 3), mel-o-rolls, Nibs, hard car'mels, Bonomo Turkish taffy, long pretzels, Mission Bell grape and Frank's orange soda, twists, egg creams, lime rickeys, and a nice 2-cents plain. Everybody knows what a skate key is and what it means when your wheels get "skellies." A pound of butter is carved from wooden tubs. Here, your only jewelry is a Captain Midnight code-o-graph or a Tom Mix whistling ring. And here you always have spaldeens. An endless supply. Pink and fresh and beautiful. Spaldeens: made no longer by the A. G. Spalding Company; street kids now would rather smoke crack than hit a ball three sewers. But we still have them here in the Lost City. Spaldeens: traveling high into the sky of a thousand neighborhoods in the game called stickball. The game is almost never played anymore, except by aging men. In the Lost City of New York, we will play it forever.

In this New York, you can still wander through the stalls of the Washington Market. You can get your hair cut for a quarter at the barber schools on Third Avenue and the Bowery. You can watch the leather-workers ply their trade at the foot of the Manhattan Bridge or watch the old craftsmen roll cigars on Astor Place or see an old Italian shoemaker working in a window with his mouth full of nails.

You can bring your kitchen knives down to the truck to be sharpened. You can watch the iceman make his deliveries, stronger than any other man on earth. You can wait for the "rides" to come around in the evening: the Whip and the Loop-the-Loop. You can hang out at the pigeon coop on the roof. You can put your groceries "on the bill." If you get sick, the doctor will come by in an hour. You can sit at the Battery and watch the ocean liners cleave through the harbor, powerful and regal among their court of tugboats, heading for berths on the North River (the reporters have arrived on the launch, with their press cards in their hats, and they are interviewing the Duke and Duchess of Windsor, or propping a movie star on top of a steamer trunk). You can walk out on the white porch of the Claremont Inn on Riverside Drive and 125th Street and watch the cruise boats move north to Bear Mountain. On Sunday nights, you will almost certainly turn on the radio and hear that staccato voice: "*Goodevening Mr.andMrs. NorthandSouthAmerica andalltheships-atsea. . . . ThisisWalterWinchellandtheJergensJournal — let's go to press. . . .*"

Or you can meet that girl in the polo coat who is arriving at Penn Station from college in Vermont or Ohio or Philadelphia. And if you're lucky, if all goes well at Seventeen Barrow Street or the Bijou or the Olde Knick or the Fleur de Lis, if you have enough money and courage, you might succeed in taking her to the old Ritz Carlton and wake up with her in the bright, snowy light of New York. If it isn't that easy, you will postpone everything. You will take her to Condon's. Or to hear Miguelito Valdes sing "Babalu" in the club at the Great Northern Hotel, knowing that upstairs in 1939 William Saroyan wrote *The Time of Your Life* in five days and maybe the two of you could find the room (in the interests of literature, of course). Maybe you'll get a sandwich at Reuben's or stroll through Times Square and look at the Camel sign with the guy blowing smoke rings into the night or the two huge nude statues flanking the waterfall of the Bond Clothes sign and then slip into Toffenetti's for coffee or head east to Glennon's for a few final beers. Take your time. All of this will be here tomorrow too. Yeah.

I suppose that 30 years from now (as close to us as we are to 1958), when I've been safely tucked into the turf at the GreenWood, someone will write in these pages about a Lost New York that includes Area and the Mudd Club and Nell's, David's Cookies and Aca Joe and Steve's ice cream. Someone might mourn Lever House or

Trump Tower or the current version of Madison Square Garden. Anything is possible. But if so, I hope that at least one old and wizened New Yorker will reach for a pen and try to explain about *our* lost glories: and mention spaldeens and trolleys and — if he can make it clear, if he has the skill and the memory — even Willie Mays.

NEW YORK,
December 21–28, 1987

THE SECRET CITY

Every day, we move through the giant city on the sad or preposterous or exhilarating errands of our lives. Most of the time, we see little. We are New Yorkers, after all, and it is our pride that we think we know the city. Certainly each of us is outfitted with an interior map, a template of the city's geography. The sun rises in Brooklyn and sets in New Jersey. The Bronx is up and the Battery's down. We know where the bridges are, and the tunnels; we understand how they lash together the stony islands of the New York archipelago. We are aware of the great markers — the Empire State Building and Central Park, the Brooklyn Bridge and City Hall, Wall Street and Yankee Stadium, all those and a few dozen more. We are filled with information about our restaurants, theaters, museums, bookstores, music, scandals, celebrities, gangsters, and home-run hitters. We are from here. We know.

And yet, if we stay around long enough, if we try to see without the blinders imposed by work and fear and habit, we discover one terrible fact: We know almost nothing. New York can serve as home, workshop, prison, or bazaar. It can dazzle or defeat us. But it never yields up all of its secrets. In the end, the only thing the true New Yorker knows about New York is that it is unknowable.

Obviously, all attempts at imposing symmetry are doomed. But it can be said with some modest confidence that for each of us there are two New Yorks: the city we think we know and the Secret City. The first is inhabited by friends and enemies, relatives and acquaintances, and to some extent by the public figures of the time; we understand its rules and protocols; we discuss it at dinner or on the telephone or in bed.

But the Secret City is barely glimpsed. Often it is as different from the familiar city as the New York of Louis Auchincloss is from the New York of John Gotti. There are some doors in this city that are forever closed to strangers; some are among the satrapies of the Upper East Side; some are in Ridgewood. You see a New Yorker who has established dominion over one of the great Wall Street firms; he has done his work with honor and responsibility, and now he and his family lead gilded lives. In the precincts where he works, he is treated with respect, a certain awe, and even, among those who depend upon him for advancement, a small amount of fear. But his accomplishments, his reputation, his existence mean nothing at all to this other New Yorker, a good carpenter from Fort Greene, who makes objects of wood that might be around long after the first man is dead. For each man, the other lives in the Secret City.

Each day, the citizens of these hidden worlds pass one another in the street and almost never connect. Here we are on West 47th Street on a Tuesday afternoon plump with spring. Out on the sidewalks are the grandees and supplicants of the world of diamonds, gold, precious stones; they deal, trade, bargain with one another; they decode fresh news from Antwerp and the Urals. And moving among them is a professor of Romance languages, now turning, abruptly adjusting his stride, then angling through traffic toward the Gotham Book Mart. He sidesteps the elated young accountant from Forest Hills who is carrying on his shoulder a brand-new VCR from 47th Street Photo.

As he enters the splendid old bookstore, he is brushed by the messenger from the commercial-art studio, rushing to pick up photostats. He doesn't even see the professional wrestler who is going to consult his back doctor. All inhabit separate worlds, different cities. And if it's impossible even to know 47th Street between Fifth and Sixth, how could anyone ever hope to know the great sprawling anarchic city itself?

One can't. Sometimes I wander the city without plan or destination, cooling out after a prolonged bout of work. And if I'm now too old to be surprised, I can be intrigued. More than once, I've found myself on West End Avenue, staring up at the old pre-war buildings. They are like vertical neighborhoods, the most obvious symbols of the vertical city, with their penthouses snug and distant at the apex. And I try to imagine the lives lived within their walls.

Who is the man with the white hair and the grave manner standing at that sixth-floor window? His hands are behind his back. He looks down into the avenue, but occasionally his mouth moves, he glances behind him. I imagine the air thick with Freudian orthodoxies, and some troubled human being supine upon a couch, while lacerated murmurs beg for peace.

Two floors above, there are four windows so filthy that the glass resembles membrane. I conjure an atmosphere of retreat and withdrawal, some final decision to avoid all further disappointment, to move until the end through loveless rooms full of shrouded furniture, dusty books, and old newspapers, like the Collyer brothers when I was young. On such days, I never investigate; sometimes the most terrible thing of all is to confirm what you have only imagined.

Those apartments are part of the Secret City, a place that is a part of New York, and therefore dense and layered and always plural. But that very density is always changing, those layers shifting, new elements being added to the pluralism. As soon as you think you have figured out New York, have located its poles and its center of gravity, the city's axis shifts again. A disco or restaurant is suddenly hot; a year later, it's in Chapter 11. You read learned treatises about white flight, the triumph of the suburbs, the end of middle-class New York; within months, white families are contending with black families for the same run-down real estate and, hey, where did all those Koreans come from? The place is simply too large, too dynamic, too infinitely various and mysterious. Almost all of us live with what Alvin Toffler might have more properly called present shock.

That might be why there has never been a great novel about New York. The best New York novels have been fragments, pieces about the garment district, Wall Street, the lives of the rich, the agony of the slums, the treacheries of the theater or the Mob or the magazine business. They are often as brilliant as tesserae, and as incomplete. The New Yorks described by Scott Fitzgerald and Jerome Weidman, Truman Capote and Norman Mailer, E. L. Doctorow and William Styron, Jimmy Breslin and Henry James, Jay McInerney and John Cheever, Edith Wharton and John O'Hara, John Dos Passos and Daniel Fuchs and Mario Puzo (to name only a few), simply have nothing in common with one another. Forget literary mastery, craft, the sense of place. It's the *vision* of each writer that is completely different. Each sees a certain New York and reveals it to the rest of us. But it's usually not *our* New York. We can go to London and still see Dickens. Balzac's ghost prowls Paris. Raymond Chandler seems to have invented Los Angeles. But we never see one writer when we look at New York. The great novel of twentieth-century New York might be the *Daily News*.

There are, of course, a number of forces that sometimes unify the city we know and the Secret City: weather, sports, television. But when you see the children of the rich prancing like Lippizaner stallions through the Upper East Side, you do not need a degree in anthropology to realize that they are different from the people on the corner of 5th Street and Avenue C. Not better or worse. Simply different. Separated by money, history, and unearned privilege from their fellow citizens. The woman in Crown Heights, her husband gone, struggling to keep off welfare and send her children each morning to school, inhabits a universe different from that of those women with predatory faces that you see in Bendel's. I know second-generation New Yorkers who have never been to Brooklyn; I know Brooklynites who have never been to Radio City Music Hall. Class separates us. And rank, identity, esteem, and prestige.

All such distinctions express themselves in a variety of ways, and many of them can seem alien. Young black kids in the Secret City of Bed-Stuy or Brownsville talk endlessly about "my image." Not about the self. Nor about a true understanding of one's strengths and limits. No: They preen and pose and brag about their elaborately constructed masks. They aren't alone. The white kids downtown spend endless hours creating punk uniforms to trundle off to that week's rock club. The rest of us stand off and watch, usually amused, almost always separated from any true contact because of the impenetrability of the masks. Look (we say): inhabitants of the Secret City. Sometimes we can marvel at their amazing labors and ferocious choices: They have decided to perform their lives instead of living them. But after the glance and the wisecrack, we move on. That's *their* New York; it's not ours. And, of course, they are making similar judgments about us.

Sometimes the appearance of people from the Secret City can be disturbing. Most New Yorkers succumb easily to the instinct to make the world smaller and therefore more manageable. We construct our own parishes. Here are our friends. There are our restaurants and shops and the movie house. This is our favorite bar. There is the church or synagogue. Here, among these familiar streets and places, we are known. We are safe. We hope such places will last a lifetime. And, of course, they don't. One morning the butcher dies and his children sell the place and move to Florida. The condominium racketeers show up and soon Mrs. Flanagan and Mrs. Moloff are no longer on the bench beside the park across the street and we've lost a piece of the intricate mesh of daily life. A nameless developer alights on the block and a few months later the earthmovers and cranes are pummeling away, and two bars vanish, and a bodega, and the barbershop where the bookmaker took bets.

Now there are new people on the block. And new buildings. And the parish has permanently changed. Who *are* these people, asks the old New Yorker, and where did they all come from?

They came from the Secret City. That is, they came from beyond the parish. Their vision of New York is not ours. And often the older New Yorker closes up, denies the new, retreats into those entombed cities of memory and loss. Many of the young can't understand the almost permanent nostalgia of older New Yorkers.

Why are the middle-aged always talking, at the risk of maudlin cliché, about the Old Neighborhood, about places gone and buried, about Ebbets Field and Birdland, the Cedar Tavern and the old Paramount? The reason is probably simple: In those places, they were happy. Sentimentality is almost always a form of resentment.

But in a very important way, this is terribly sad. By retreating from the new or the foreign or the strange, the New Yorker cuts himself off from the throbbing engine of the city itself. The city's fabled energy is the result of millions of small daily collisions: the push and shove followed by resistance or collapse. That remorseless process often affects individual lives; it alters entire neighborhoods; and without it, we would be dead.

So the other New York, the Secret City, shouldn't really be a blank on the maps, marked with the legend DRAGONS LURK HERE. Whether we accept it or not, the unknown, remote, and alien city is there, all around us, relating to the city we know the way anti-matter relates to matter. There are zones of the Secret City that can provoke rage; you must enter them with a patient fatalism. In New York, there will never be an end to self-importance, malice, the iron heart, so you learn to cherish the latest exhibits.

After a while, you smile in appreciation of the idiotic snobberies that so many people embrace as substitutes for thought. You await with enthusiasm this year's Golden Couple — there is one every year, in every set — and watch them migrate as if they were the center of the population, serene, self-absorbed, supremely blessed. Then you wait for the line in the gossip columns announcing the final rupture. The details don't really matter. For the time that the Golden Couple was everywhere in the hamlet of society, they offered delicious entertainment. That is the way to see them. Not with envy or spite or some nagging sense that you are missing something by not moving in their orbit. Such people exist in a New York of their own making; next year, their successors will unfurl their diaphanous flags.

You can maintain some distance by looking at another Secret City: that of the mendicants, the poor and homeless, that squalid Calcutta of the New York heart. This is most certainly not entertainment; these people are not mere performers. Most are trapped in a permanent indigence, steady reminders that there is nothing ennobling about poverty. It is a simple matter to look away from them, to ignore their desperate marginality. But to do so is to live an illusion, to invent a New York that doesn't exist. These people, along with the almost 900,000 men, women, and children on welfare, are part of a city that doesn't read the New York *Times,* doesn't think about takeover bids, the hot new restaurants, the bond market, the next Democratic candidate, nuclear war, or nuclear disarmament. They are not waiting for tickets to *Les Misérables.* They have more elemental concerns: food, drink, shelter, survival.

Such people give us perspective about our own lives, serving as heartbreaking reminders that living in this city can be precarious at best but that even our most fruitless encounters and dispiriting defeats are as nothing compared to the life of the man living each night in a cardboard box on the street. Our relative freedom from want should encourage mobility, propel us into small adventures. In New York, we don't have to go far. On almost any given day, we can face grotesqueries; the next day might be riddled with ambiguity; and even for those of us trapped in offices, stamping away at a million documents like the man in Kurosawa's *Ikiru,* there is the possibility of surprise.

You walk down an avenue in Chelsea and hollow-eyed men in filthy coats implore you to grant them alms; two blocks later, every other woman is beautiful, with dark, flirting eyes; at the next corner, a religious lunatic pursues you, flaying you for your sins, preaching your doom in capital letters. At lunch, a friend's wife starts blabbing on about channeling and past-life experiences and the joys of life in dear old Atlantis; the waiter tells you that the Mets have scored two runs in the bottom of the second; word arrives that a guy you knew has died of AIDS. In a little over an hour, you have experienced pity, lust, anger, incomprehension, elation, loss. At last you leave, and at the corner, a group of hustlers, peddling crack, fake Rolexes, used books, sees you and is suddenly tense, poised for action, like an orchestra awaiting a downbeat.

And all around you lies the Secret City. Forgotten alleys, houses with lost histories, streets turbulent with the emanations of power. Places so new the odor of paint stains the air; others so old that they are to a neophyte explorer incredibly new and surprising. There are places only a few know about; others that are so commonplace we forget they exist. All are there to be savored, enjoyed, rejected. Some of my own favorites are those monuments to the great swaggering days of nineteenth-century capitalism, whispering to us across the decades. The shades of old brigands seem to be looking on in judgment from these places, mocking the arrogant ziggurats of the Trumps, sneering at the assorted felonies of their successors on the Street. But surely if they could look down from the ramparts of those old fortresses, they would also be comforted. Certainly the rampaging ferocity of the present crop of the newly rich makes the old robber barons look nearly austere. You see the new crowd all over the city now, feverishly spending, talking ceaselessly about money, being cruel to waiters and rude to their neighbors. They are citizens of that Secret City whose only fulcrum is greed.

But it's still possible to move around New York without being appalled by either hollow grandeur or unspeakable degradation. There are other places, too, along with the unpredictable people who make them possible. Most often, they don't have a line of stretch limousines double-parked outside. They are on streets where the sky is not yet blocked by the extravagant dwellings of coke dealers and Euro-trash. They permit intimacy. They adhere to the emotional codes of the parish. They are not retailed in the shrill treble of the huckster. They certainly can't be found by staying home.

But they are there, they are there. . . . It's still possible, whether you are native or stranger, equipped with a guidebook or only the senses, to go forth on a glorious New York morning, turn a sudden corner and discover with astonishment that you are capable of surprise. On such days, you can then surrender to the most romantic and tragic emotion of all: You want to live forever.

NEW YORK,
May 4, 1987

ON THE STREET / I

This was at two in the morning on Columbus Avenue, with a cold wind blowing from the river. I came out of an all-night deli with some coffee and the papers. On the corner, a black man in a filthy down jacket was poking around in a garbage can. There was a large brown plastic bag beside him on the sidewalk. He found a piece of uneaten bagel and four empty Diet Pepsi cans. He slipped the bagel in his jacket pocket. The cans went in the plastic bag. He glared, his yellow eyes peering at me from above a mask of thick wiry beard. Then he spit toward me. At last, I was home.

"Choo lookin' at, man?" he said. "Never seen no homeless person before?" He glanced at the window of a boutique. "Miss Ethel sprayed the sink," he said, lifting his bag, rattling the cans. "They all down by the creek, where the ballfield be." Then he was off, talking to himself as he loped toward Broadway, carrying a bag of cans whose redemption would be easier than ours.

I was back in the New York of the '80s. And, of course, that hostile man with the plastic bag on his shoulder and the split screen in his head wasn't alone, wasn't some municipal oddity. If you have been away for a while, as I have been, such people are the first you see: without jobs or families or shelter. This defeated army of mendicants seems made up of winos and junkies and the quite literally insane, but many of its unwilling recruits have simply run out of luck.

There are other signs of barbarism here too: the scarred lumpy streets (the great civic monument of the Koch administration might be the steel plate covering the hole in the street); the need for the stupefaction of drugs among all social classes; fear and tension in the subways; and the continuing scandal of housing. Shelter is one of the most elemental human needs but in New York now it is largely beyond the means of many people. Some end up homeless. Others must settle for less than they need. God help the man or woman grown old in this city, heavy with books, records, the valued accumulations of a lifetime, and forced suddenly to move. There is nowhere to go.

What is extraordinary is that the general population hasn't risen in outrage. A major reason for this passivity in the face of torment is the deepening cynicism and fatalism of most New Yorkers. Again, this is most clear if you have been away awhile. The administration of poor Ed Koch has been the most corrupt since Jimmy Walker, but not a single figure has risen from the general muck to challenge him, as La Guardia rose from the Seabury investigations. For the last decade, our politicians cheated, lied, plundered the town; now a few of them are on the way to the pen. But who would turn to another politician for aid against the corrupt flood? Not a New Yorker.

But for a returned pilgrim, the worst single change in the last year is the racism — black and white — unleashed since a black man was chased to his death by a young white mob in Howard Beach. In subways, on buses, in casual encounters on the street, I've seen more antiwhite hostility than at any time since the months following the murder of Martin Luther King in 1968. Many young blacks seem to be spoiling for a fight; to some extent this need to strike back is understandable; but the level of racism isn't lowered by such collisions. This form of the black response is itself racism; nobody wants to be beaten or killed because of the color of their skin. It's disgusting when whites do it to blacks; it is equally disgusting when blacks do it to whites, and to recite the history of slavery and oppression in America to justify it is itself a condescending form of racism.

In this city, racism is not an abstraction to be discussed in a sociology class; usually the virus comes from concrete experience. Many blacks can cite a catalogue of insults and injuries, from the refusal of a cab driver to stop on a rainy night to the white policeman using his baton as if he were judge, jury, and executioner. But this is also true of those who are victimized by blacks. The other day I saw four well-dressed black teenagers coming along Broadway. It was midafternoon. School was just out. They went past a Korean fruit and vegetable store, and then, all at once, darted back. Each stole something: an orange, a cantaloupe, an apple, some grapes. They began to run, and a Korean man in his forties ran after them in vain. But when he came back he was still seething with fury.

"*I work, I work!*" he shouted in a thin, high, frustrated voice. "I work all day, all night. And they *steal*. They just steal. They don't work. It's not fair!" The man said he just didn't understand. This happens three, four times a week; never the same young men; always blacks. Would four Koreans come down the street and steal from a black grocer? "Why don't they work?" After six years in this country, and two years in business, "they" had become a loaded word in his vocabulary. And probably a permanent one.

Driving through central Brooklyn one afternoon, through mile after mile of men clustered together on street corners while women without men were engulfed by children, driving through blasted streets smelling of defeat and abandonment, I remembered a scene I had witnessed many times last year in the cities of the American South: black families dining together in restaurants. Children. A mother. A father. I've been back in New York now for five weeks and haven't seen such an event yet. Thirty years after the freedom rides, the North might now have much to learn from the South.

Squalor is, of course, only part of the city. This remains a city of enormous energy, great museums and theaters, generosity and wit, splendid architecture. But in my half-century here, I've never seen social disparity as violently drastic as it is now. In the evenings in Manhattan, you often pass among people who look like drawings by George Grosz. Suddenly and ferociously rich, the men eat their way through the city, consuming food, wine, art, real estate, companies, stores, neighborhoods. They are all appetite and no mind, no heart. During the day the women prowl Madison Avenue or 57th Street as if searching for prey, buying clothes, buying breasts, buying paintings, buying status. In a city where human beings struggle for the privilege of sleeping over subway grates, these people even have money to hire "art advisers"; this is like hiring a fuck adviser.

One day, soon after I was back, I wandered around Wall Street to look at the inhabitants. Every other person seemed high, either on cocaine or the platinum roar of the stock market. In one of the restaurants, I struck up a conversation with a broker. I asked him if any of the immense transactions in the bull market would produce either goods or jobs. "No, just money," he said and laughed. But when I asked him if the sight of the homeless disturbed him, the grin turned to a sneer: "Hey, man, there's nothing *I* can do about that. That's an old movie. That's the '60s, pal."

Well, no, not the '60s. The '80s. But for all of that it was good to be home.

VILLAGE VOICE,
May 5, 1987

GOD IS IN THE DETAILS

The wonder is that there is any beauty left at all. The century's assault has been relentless. Every year, another fragment of grace or style or craft is obliterated from New York, to be replaced by the brutally functional or the commercially coarse. Vandalism is general. I don't mean only those morons with spray cans, whose brainless signatures now mar even the loveliest old carved stone. There are corporate vandals, too, political vandals, and vandals equipped with elaborate aesthetic theories. They never rest, and when they strike, their energy is ferocious.

And yet, beauty persists — scattered across the city, the beauty of nature, and of things made by men and women. There is beauty above as people hurry through the city streets. It nestles behind the fortress walls of banal structures, and sometimes stands unrevealed before our eyes. In recent years, the Landmarks Preservation Commission, the Municipal Art Society, and other groups have done splendid work preserving what remains of the past, but much is already lost, and everywhere there are valuable and beautiful creations under threat. Still, there are places whose value need not be ratified by a committee; they are hidden islands of the marvelous, capable of evoking emotional, even mysterious, responses.

I don't know the name of the sculptor whose flowers, cupids, and ornamental letters adorn the façade of the Stuyvesant Polyclinic, on Second Avenue between St. Marks Place and 9th Street, but I love his excess, the showering extravagance of his talent. The man who wrought the iron steps and balconies of the townhouse at 328 East

18th Street is unknown to me, but although he did his job in 1852, his work is here today to pleasure the eye. The Montauk Club, in Brooklyn, has always been part of my life; as a child, I'd gaze up at the frieze of Indians around the top of the building and invent tales to go with those faces and figures; today, I marvel at the audacity of the men who made the building, shamelessly lifting the basic design from a Venetian palace and then localizing it with a narrative of the first Americans.

All such places have a personal meaning. Why do the sprawling Victorian houses in Clinton Hill seem so melancholy now? Powerful men once lived in this Brooklyn neighborhood, in the area around Pratt Institute, raising huge families far from the congestion of Manhattan; in summer now I expect to see Mark Twain emerge onto a porch in a white suit to hector the millionaires who are his hosts, or I envision Jack Johnson walking defiantly on these streets with his white wife. The Billopp House, on Staten Island, can summon a more remote era; built in 1680 by the British military man who won Staten Island from New Jersey in a boat race, this austere and serene building stands at one end of Hylan Boulevard like a reproof. In front of such a house, or on Grace Court, in Brooklyn, or along some of the elegant streets of Bedford-Stuyvesant, there comes the urge to be still.

Stillness, in fact, is probably the only condition that will allow the city's beauty to reveal itself. You can't experience it from the window of a careening taxi, or rushing from subway to office. Time must be taken, imagination engaged. I'm convinced that one of this city's greatest architects was a Brooklynite named Ernest Flagg, who died in 1947 at age 90. He designed the old Mills hotel, on Bleecker Street (the Village Gate is on the ground floor), St. Luke's Hospital, and the Flagg Court housing complex, in Bay Ridge. He had a long, productive career, living in a house of his own design at 109 East 40th Street and on an estate on Staten Island.

Today, he is almost completely forgotten — except for two masterpieces. One is the "little" Singer building, at 561 Broadway, near Prince Street, complete with wrought-iron railings, its façade sheathed in orange and blue terra-cotta. The other is the Scribner bookstore, at 597 Fifth Avenue. His greatest masterpiece, however, is gone. This was the Singer tower, at 149 Broadway, a Beaux-Arts extravaganza full of decoration and briefly the tallest building in the world when it went up in 1908. I used to visit there when I worked downtown at the old New York *Post;* the building was a romantic affront to all the reigning dogmas of the Bauhaus. I loved it. Then it fell into the hands of United States Steel and was, of course, demolished.

And yet the eclectic, imperialist confidence of that old building made it part of New York in a way that many newer buildings will never be. Sometimes I go downtown to look at the "little" Singer building (now the Paul Building), which is a more handsome example of Flagg's work than the tower, and I wonder what New York would be like today if his vision (and those of his contemporaries) had prevailed, instead of the bullying blankness of the International Style. Certainly this would be a more visually interesting city. Flagg's buildings have detail, ornament, proportion, and, most important, surprise. The eye can move from floor to roof of the Singer/Paul building and be at once assured by the proportions and surprised by the decoration. Are Flagg's buildings functional? I don't really know; I've never worked in one of them. But if the function of a bookstore is to sell books, then the Scribner shop is certainly functional; I can never enter that store without buying a book.

The great triumph of the International Style gave us an architecture of planes, textures, proportions, devoid of ornament. Form must follow function, we were told, over and over and over again. Conveniently, this message coincided with the desire of real-estate men to get maximum bang for the buck. Ornament, stonework, detail cost money; get rid of them, create an aesthetic that makes such cost cutting appear to be a form of modernism, and the result could be an instant fortune. In schools of art and architecture after World War II, an entire generation was instructed to bow before the creations of Ludwig Mies van der Rohe and Walter Gropius. Today, I'm convinced that the entire movement was a gigantic mistake. No wonder that the graffiti artist gazes at the dull, blank, almost totalitarian surfaces of the International Style and begins to decorate. His decorations may be ugly, acts of vandalism, but the urge to impose a human presence can be understood.

I realize that I'm speaking here for unfashionable values. Yes, I can look at the Seagram Building and realize what Mies was driving at. On rainy days, I can enjoy the atrium of the Ford Foundation, and I've even spent some pleasant hours among the lavish Vegas-isms of the Trump Tower. But nobody can tell me that the latest version of Madison Square Garden is an improvement on the old Penn Station any more than I can be convinced that the mucky color and primitive draftsmanship of Willem de Kooning are an improvement over, say, John Singer Sargent. The new is different, but it isn't better; to say it is, given the evidence, is preposterous. Less is rarely more. Less is more often merely less.

Forgive the arrogance, but I believe that most New Yorkers share those sentiments. One reason we live here, instead of Los Angeles or Phoenix or Houston, is that the past is intricately involved in our lives. Like some residents of New Orleans or San Francisco, among American cities, we feel personally damaged when a hunk of the past is removed. We don't like change. We want the places we loved when we were growing up to be there for our children. Yes, everything changes; this is one reason nostalgia corrodes so many New Yorkers and always has. The anonymous author of the 1866 guide to New York called *New York as It Is* begins his book with these words:

"The denizens of New York are such utilitarians that they have sacrificed to the shrine of Mammon almost every relic of the olden time. The feeling of veneration for the past, so characteristic of the cities of the Old World, is lamentably deficient among the people of the New."

The condition and the protest remain essentially the same. But it is no accident that so many of the unseen beauties of New York are survivors from the past. Most New Yorkers have their own private places. Those places most often evoke the past. For example, I sometimes enjoy visiting the traffic island in Grand Army Plaza, in Brooklyn, with its dumb modern monument to John F. Kennedy and its wonderful Bailey Fountain (all Neptunes and Tritons and memories of the Piazza Navona). I walk around the Soldiers' and Sailors' Memorial Arch, with its evocations of the Etoile, in Paris, and look at the fine bas-relief of Lincoln by Thomas Eakins, and then stare up at the rest. I know that the heroic statuary at the top of this and similar monuments is essentially rhetoric; it propagates patriotic myths; it glorifies values I don't share. And yet, I prefer looking at it to gazing at Calder or Donald Judd. I not only think about the formal values of the work, the craft, the belief in the well-made thing, but also imagine the artist's studio, his rough hands, his friends dropping in to chat, the delivery of the great piece to its present site. I wonder who was president at the time, and what the newspapers said, and what happened to the models.

Those are, of course, impure reactions. But in some peculiar way the work that provokes them is doing what great art does: It invokes a sense of continuity with the past, joining us to the generations that came before ours, forcing an obligation to the generations that will follow. When I show my daughters Nathan Silver's *Lost New York*, or the "then" and "now" photographs in various books from Dover Publications, they are angry that they'll never have the chance to see any of those vanished places. And I'm angry because in nearly every case the building that replaced the old was inferior in style, craft, and even function to the thing removed.

If there is a lesson in those pictures of the hidden beauty of New York, it may be this: Leave things alone. Give up the idea of constant renewal, that variation on the dream of perpetual youth. Seek what is truly valuable. Embrace it. Protect it. Love it.

NEW YORK,
December 26, 1983–January 2, 1984

ON THE STREET / 2

This is how a life can end: It is the tail end of the lunch hour, Tuesday, March 4, and I'm in a taxi with my daughter, moving downtown on Seventh Avenue. The sky is sullen, the color of gruel. In the garment district, traffic inches along, blocked by double-parked trucks, men pushing carts, buses heaving their great bulk across lanes. Horns blare; men curse. A tractor-trailer stands across 34th Street like a wall.

This is how a life can end: The huge truck moves, and the blocked downtown traffic begins at last to move. Usually, it's like water rushing from a burst dam. Today, the rush doesn't happen. The lights are blinking green all the way to 23rd Street, but there is no clear passage for traffic. On every street, pedestrians are crossing the avenue, ignoring red lights, jaywalking in the center of the block. A mustached young man comes close, allows the taxi to pass within inches, performs a capeless veronica, matador of Seventh Avenue. A black man snarls angrily as if the taxi were challenging his right to jaywalk. A sockless man with a Jesus beard stands in the middle of the avenue looking at the sky. Our taxi is at the front of the knot of traffic; the driver is in his thirties, lean and dark, anxious. He is beeping his horn, riding his brake pedal.

This is how a life can end: We slow down at 31st Street as a dozen jaywalkers hurry to safety. "These people are nuts," I say. The cab driver shakes his head: "Now you know why cab drivers go crazy." Dark laughter. A man eating a hot dog in the middle of our lane jumps back and curses. Then up ahead, we see a dense group of people crossing against the red light at 28th Street. The taxi driver crosses 29th, still riding the brake, clearing a path with his horn. We are in the second lane from the right. Most of the jaywalkers are young, and they hurry to the safety of the corners. But there's a second group beyond the corner, in our lane. A tractor-trailer is illegally parked at a bus stop and these people are waiting for the bus. The driver slows, still making staccato bursts with his horn.

And then directly in front of us, oblivious to everything, looking straight ahead as he walks west against the red light, is an older man. Until this moment, he has been screened by those who have hurried to the corner, and now he is suddenly, vulnerably, alone. The driver blares the horn, hits the brakes, tries to move left, finds that lane blocked by another car, and then there is a hard socking thump, metal smashing into bone, and a blurred image of the man as we go by, the man rolling, brakes screeching, my daughter's scream, and we are stopped.

I look at the older man, who is on his back. Blood pumps from his mouth. He is shoeless. His body doesn't move. And then the crowd, frozen in horror, comes alive. The driver is breathing shallowly, his head on the wheel, holding the wheel with both hands, gripping it. "No," he says. "No. No." He taps his head on the wheel. "Shit." He gazes to his left, away from the fallen man, and then slowly turns, sees the smear of blood. "No," he says. "No."

My daughter is sobbing now, and I try to comfort her, and I hear people shouting, "Don't move him" and "Call the police, you asshole, call the police." And then part of the crowd turns ugly. A suety young man in a zipper jacket comes to the door on the driver's side. "You doin' sebenty miles an hour, man! You murder the guy!" Another shouts: "Fuckin' cab driver, runnin' the yellow light, yeah, that muthafucka!"

I get out of the cab. There are no police on the scene yet and all of this has happened in a couple of minutes. I try to calm down the angrier people, explaining I was in the cab, that the driver wasn't speeding, that the old man simply had not responded, that he was clearly walking across the red light. "Still, he should go *slow!* Look, that's an *old man!*"

That's the way most of us are in New York these days; we have been trained by television and politics to retaliate. An old man is knocked to the ground by a cab, his life spilling onto the dirty tar, and people want to hurt someone back. The driver starts out of the cab. The suety man screams at him. The cab driver explains with some heat about his speed, about his horn, about the red light, but the suety man's eyes are blazing and others are behind him. The passions of a mob are stirring in the cold damp air. "Mothafucka, you drive like a crazy man . . ."

I tell the driver to get back in the cab and keep quiet. Then behind us, pushing through the clotted traffic, comes a police car. The crowd abruptly ends its transformation into a mob. More sirens in the distance. The sense of time slowed is replaced by time become swift. Cops and medics work expertly on the stricken man; his body is covered with rubber sheets for warmth; they press down on his chest. Younger cops move the crowd onto the sidewalk, others try to get the traffic moving. An older cop with a sad, grave face picks up the man's brown loafers.

"I'm through," the driver says. "I can never drive a cab again. I can't even drive this one today." He says he was born in Spain and his family moved to the Dominican Republic when he was six; he has lived in New York since his teens. That night, after months of waiting, he was to see *La Cage aux folles.* "How can I see something like that after this?"

This is how a life can end: The cops take statements. An ambulance arrives from St. Vincent's and the bloody-faced man is placed on a stretcher and into the back; it moves off with siren screaming, slowing behind jammed traffic at 23rd Street. From the lofts of the furriers above the avenue, people gaze down at the scene. Beside the tractor-trailer, there is a two-foot strand of blood, bright red against the dirty tar, and some plastic tubes that had been slipped down the stricken man's throat. His gray plaid hat has rolled under the truck and lies beside the curb. I see a policeman's hand reach down, circle it with chalk, pick it up. A pause. Then he drops it back in place.

"I know this man," a white-haired man whispers. "I saw him 20 minutes ago." I ask him for his name and the name of the man who has been carried away. He is reluctant to give either, and drifts away. The police are also careful; they first want to notify next of kin. The cab driver (still waiting for formal questions) hears this: "Is he — is the man dead?" The cop shrugs sadly. The driver leans on his cab, his body wracked with dry heaves.

This is how a life can end: All the questions have been asked, the forms filled in, names given, witnesses questioned. About an hour has passed. Traffic now moves quickly down the avenue. There is tape where the taxi's wheels had come to a halt, darkening blood and chalk marks and a hat where the old man had come to the end of his life. A woman moves between two parked cars, waits for a break in traffic, hurries across the street. She never sees the blood. A gust of wind lifts the dead man's sporty little hat and rolls it back against the curb.

VILLAGE VOICE,
March 18, 1986

BRIDGE OF DREAMS

In all years and all seasons, the bridge was there. We could see it from the roof of the tenement where we lived, the stone towers rising below us from the foreshortened streets of downtown Brooklyn. We saw it in newspapers and at the movies and on the covers of books, part of the signature of the place where we lived. Sometimes, on summer afternoons during World War II, my mother would gather me and my brother Tom and my sister, Kathleen, and we'd set out on the most glorious of walks. We walked for miles, leaving behind the green of Prospect Park, passing factories and warehouses and strange neighborhoods, crossing a hundred streets and a dozen avenues, seeing the streets turn green again as we entered Brooklyn Heights, pushing on, beaded with sweat, legs rubbery, until, amazingly, looming abruptly in front of us, stone and steel and indifferent, was The Bridge.

It was the first man-made thing that I knew was beautiful. We could walk across it, gazing up at the great arc of the cables. We could hear the sustained eerie musical note they made when combed by the wind (augmented since by the hum of automobile tires), and we envied the gulls that played at the top of those arches. The arches were Gothic, and provided a sense of awe that was quite religious. And awe infused the view of the great harbor, a view my mother embellished by describing to us the ships that had brought her and so many other immigrants to America — the Irish and the Italians and the Jews, the Germans, the Poles, and the Swedes, all of them crowding the decks, straining to see their newfound land. What they saw first was the Statue of Liberty, and the skyline, and The Bridge. The Brooklyn Bridge.

My mother would tell us these things and then lead us down to the Manhattan side and show us Park Row, where the newspapers were, and City Hall, where a wonderful man named Fiorello worked as mayor, and the Woolworth Building, gleaming in the sun. Near dusk we'd take the trolley car back across to Brooklyn. I remember on one of those trips wanting to jump out and climb The Bridge's cables and wrap my arms around those stone towers; nothing that immense could be real. The impulse quickly vanished. I had already walked the promenade and touched the stone and run my hands along the steel; I was from Brooklyn, and to me The Bridge was not a ghost, a painting, a photograph, or a dream. It was a fact. In the years that followed, everything changed, including me, but The Bridge was always there.

It has been there now for a hundred summers. Fiorello is gone, and so are the newspapers of Park Row. The last trolley crossed The Bridge in 1950. The Bridge has been altered, cluttered with the ugly advancements of the twentieth century. But it is as beautiful to me today as it was when I was young and had more innocent eyes. I was a teenager before I realized that all those puny, misshapen other bridges across the river even had names.

There was a long time in my life when I didn't see much of The Bridge, except from the roof or the back window. The reason was simple: Trolleys were replaced by automobiles, and nobody I knew in our neighborhood owned a car. But then when I was sixteen, I got a job in the Brooklyn Navy Yard as a sheet-metal worker, and at lunchtime we would wander out along the cobblestone streets beside the dry docks, and from there we could look up at The Bridge.

"Now the cats that built *that*," a black welder named Fred Thompson said to me one day, "they knew what they were *doin'*."

They certainly did. As I grew older, I came increasingly to see The Bridge as a monument to craft. It was New York's supreme example of the Well-Made Thing. All around us in the sixties, the standards of craft eroded. As aestheticians proclaimed the virtues of the spontaneous, or exalted the bold gesture, or condemned form as an artistic straitjacket, I would cross The Bridge and wonder what they could mean. More than twenty men were killed in the construction of this thing, and others were ruined for life by accidents and disease suffered in its service. To those men, carelessness meant death, not simply for themselves, but for the human beings who would use what they were making. So they had no choice: They had to make it to last. And in doing so, in caring about detail and function and strength, they saw craft triumph into art.

They needed all the craft they possessed, and some that they didn't: Many of the techniques they used were made up along the way. The undertaking was more formidable than any job of engineering ever before attempted in North America. The span over the water is 1,595 feet 6 inches long, and it is 85 feet wide. Each of the four main cables is 3,578 feet 6 inches long and contains 5,434 wires. The cables are capable of supporting 24,621,780 pounds each, and in the years since construction they have carried trolley cars, subway trains, and hundreds of thousands of automobiles with no strain.

Such a structure was not made simply to be looked at; The Bridge was made to be used. Before it could be anything else, it had to fulfill its primary function: the easing of travel for thousands of people across a river. But inevitably that journey became for some people a heavier rite of passage. If you grew up in Brooklyn, The Bridge could be a symbol of escape; sooner or later, the time arrived when some people had to make the crossing in a decisive way. At the other end was the dream of art, or music, or the theater. Many of us were drawn to law schools or the Police Academy or the vast treasures of the university libraries; some simply fled to freedom from the smothering safety of a family. I remember going over The Bridge to Whitehall Street to be sworn into the navy, three of us squandering our last civilian dollars on a cab. I made the fatal mistake of looking back, and carried The Bridge with me all through boot camp. Others enlisted in the armies of business and camped for life in the skyscrapers to the left of The Bridge. A few fled wives or lovers, the church or the Mob.

Few of us knew the history of the building of The Bridge, that saga that began with John Roebling's letter to the New York *Tribune* in 1857 (suggesting "a wire suspension bridge crossing the East River by one single span at such an elevation as will not impede the navigation") and ended with fireworks, giddy editorials, and an opening-day parade of politicians, bankers, civic leaders, and thieves, led by President Chester Alan Arthur.

No moviemaker, novelist, or comic-book artist could have invented John and Washington Roebling, father and son, the dreamer and the engineer. The father came from Germany, where he had been a friend of Hegel's, and attempted various utopian schemes before becoming a manufacturer of steel wire and the man who dreamed the dream of The Bridge. He was dead by 1869, felled by tetanus after his foot was crushed by a ferry while he surveyed the site of the towers. The son took over, and, despite a crippling bout with caisson disease, Washington Roebling soldiered on, commanding his brilliant engineering staff and an army of more than a thousand workers from his house at 110 Columbia Heights, checking the progress of the construction with a telescope.

The story was rife with treachery and cynicism, peopled by rogues like William Marcy Tweed, the blue-eyed, 300-pound "Boss," sitting in the corrupt splendor of Tammany Hall, holding up construction until someone arrived from Brooklyn with $60,000 in a carpetbag, to be spread among the members of the Board of Aldermen. More typical was Abram Hewitt, a dapper little congressman whose act was so slick it conned even Henry Adams. Acting as a spokesman for civic purity, he manipulated a ruling that forbade the Roebling-family firm to manufacture wire for use in the four main cables of The Bridge. Enter a bigamist and thief named J. Lloyd Haig, who got a large part of the wire business, secretly kicking back money to Hewitt. Eventually Haig was caught providing defective wire for The Bridge.

Above all there were the workingmen and their supervisors, of whom E. F. Farrington, the master mechanic, was the most extraordinary. The workers labored in the horrors of the caissons, far beneath the river, chopping away at mud and rock to provide a solid base for each of the towers; former seamen climbed high among the cables, wrapping them by hand, stringing them with great skill. They were paid $2.25 a day, raised, after a four-day strike, to $2.75. Farrington went everywhere they went, and in 1876, when the first steel rope described its lovely arc from one tower to the other, he became the first man to make the crossing. He was almost 60, and showed up for the momentous day in a linen suit and a straw hat, and when he went out over the river on a boatswain's chair, all the tugboats in the harbor began to blow their foghorns, and a crowd of 10,000 spectators cheered in amazement, and Farrington took off his hat and waved. By the time he descended into Brooklyn at the end of his historic trip, church bells were ringing and factory whistles screaming in what the *Times* the next day called "a perfect pandemonium." That was some America. Those were some men.

Growing up with The Bridge, we never knew this history. David McCullough's splendid narrative *The Great Bridge* wasn't published until 1972. But we knew how important the story had been, because there were still some old-timers around who talked about the "1898 Mistake," the decision to join Brooklyn to Manhattan as part of Greater New York. That decision had its origins in politics, of course; the old-timers blamed the upstate Republicans, who hoped that Republican Brooklyn joined to Democratic Manhattan would lead to the permanent submersion of Tammany. But Brooklyn, which was an independent city, with its own mayor and government, was so infuriated at the upstate Republicans that it turned almost immediately Democratic and has stayed that way ever since. There was a quality of the fable to all of this, of course, a tale of a lost Arcadia in Brooklyn. But clearly the decision to join the five boroughs into one city was sealed from the day of the opening of The Bridge.

Since we had no true history of The Bridge (in those days in Brooklyn we were taught more about the Tigris and the Euphrates than we were about the city in which we lived), we were forced to see its utility and art. The use of the structure was obvious; it allowed us to cross the city's most turbulent river, often full of whirlpools and double currents.

But it was also beautiful. That was the thing. And it was beautiful without history, the way a master's painting of some forgotten duke or king is beautiful quite apart from the facts of the subject's fame. It seemed baffling and strange that each succeeding New York bridge was uglier or less human than the first. As a young reporter, running around the city to fires and murders, I crossed all of the bridges, large and small; with the possible exception of the George Washington, they were uniformly ugly and graceless, bridges made not for people but for their cars. Only The Bridge seemed made by humans for humans. It was no accident that one day in the late fifties someone began to notice a lone black man out on The Bridge, playing the most aching blues on a saxophone. The man had been a star and then had gone away to find some new thing to make music about. His name was Sonny Rollins. Today I can't ever cross The Bridge without thinking about him, all alone, accompanied only by the sound of the wind striking the great cabled harp, playing for the gulls and himself. Washington Roebling, who was also an accomplished musician, would have loved that.

Of course, it is the nature of all bridges that they travel in two directions. I know dozens of people who traveled west on The Bridge, wandered the world, and then made the long, wide circle home to Brooklyn. I don't know anybody who ever did that from the Bronx. From the Manhattan shore, The Bridge still seems to whisper: "Come, travel across me. It's only 1,562 feet across the river, and over here, and beyond, lies Oz, or Camelot, or Yoknapatawpha County." And from the Brooklyn side it speaks in plain, bourgeois tones, with a plain, simple message: "Come home."

When I went home to live in Brooklyn, many things had changed, but The Bridge remained. Every day for years, I would drive across it in the morning and feel that combination of intensity and serenity that Manhattan always evoked. It is in the nature of journalism that no day is like any other; your life's work is shaped by events. One result is that you come to cherish those things that do not change. They provide stability of place in a world that insists upon altering its look, its cast, and its rules. The Bridge never changed.

What has changed is the way we see The Bridge. For many, it remains simply a grand fact. But for Hart Crane, John Marin, Joseph Stella, Georgia O'Keeffe, Walker Evans, and hundreds of other writers, painters, and photographers, The Bridge is a symbol, at once permanent and evolving, its image changing with the times. Today it reminds us that there were once men in this country, many of them quite young, who believed that anything was possible. They believed that if you could dream a suspension bridge over the East River, you could build one. And they did. They did it with an eye for beauty, and a love of craft, and the thing they made has endured. In New

York, fads and fashions come and go. Architects inflict novelties upon us that rise, are written about and soon torn down. Politicians make careers, lead millions, and end up as statues in a park. Scoundrels dominate the newspapers, actresses and dancers take their turns in the spotlight, writers and singers bow to acclaim. And soon all of them are gone. A few things remain. And one of them is The Bridge. It stands there, every day of our lives, and it is oddly comforting to think that it will be there long after most of us are gone.

NEW YORK,
May 30, 1983

SPALDEEN SUMMERS

Summer, when I was a boy in Brooklyn, was a string of intimacies, a sum of small knowings, and almost none of them cost money. Nobody ever figured out a way to charge us for morning, and morning then was the beginning of everything. I was an altar boy in the years after the war, up in the morning before most other people for the long walk to the church on the hill. And I would watch the sun rise in Prospect Park — at first a rumor, then a heightened light, something unseen and immense melting the hard early darkness; then suddenly there was a molten ball, screened by the trees, about to climb to a scalding noon. The sun would dry the dew on the grass of the park, soften the tar, bake the rooftops, brown us on the beaches, make us sweat, force us out of the tight, small flats of the tenements.

And if dawn was a tremendous overture, endlessly repeated, the days were always improvisations. How did we decide what to do with our time? We didn't; the day decided. The day had its own rhythms. I don't remember ever drawing up plans, or waiting for some agent of the state to arrive and direct us. Usually, the day would tell us to meet on the corner, with a pink spaldeen and a stickball bat. All through the war, there had been no spaldeens, and the few survivors had been treasured or replaced with those gray furry tennis balls we all despised, because we had never seen tennis played, had no idea what it was about, worshiped no tennis players. When spaldeens returned, stickball entered a golden age. Two blocks away, on 14th Street beside the Minerva Theater, the Tigers played gigantic money games, with pots as large as $300 and audiences jamming the sidewalks. Our games were smaller. We were still amateurs. Literally lovers. Lovers of that simple game with its swift variations on baseball: one strike and you were out, no bases on balls, six men on a team, sewer tops for bases, scoreboards chalked on tar. We made bats from broom handles, and there was an elaborate ritual of transforming broom to bat: clawing away the wire that held the straw by jamming the broom on a picket fence; then burning away the end of the straw; then sanding off splinters and taping the handle. Those brooms made beautiful bats, thin at the handle, thicker at the end. Today, commercially made stickball bats are sold in stores, products of Super Glut; they are terrible bats, as straight and untapered as poles. Playing with them is like playing with a mop handle.

Stickball wasn't always a team game. We played variations called catchaflyerup (or, more literally, catch a fly, you're up), in which a batter kept hitting until someone caught a batted ball on the fly; rolypoly, where you rolled the spaldeen, after it was hit, toward the bat, which lay flat across home plate (if the ball hit the bat, bounced, and the batter missed it, the player who rolled it became the new hitter); and, most simply, tenhitsapiece, in which each batter was allowed to hit ten times. The simpler variations were played early in the morning, before everybody showed up on the court. When there were enough players, we started the full games, with their elaborate, specific ground rules: Off the factory wall was a home run, off the diner was a hindoo (a do-over). Around the city there were dozens of other variations.

We didn't play much baseball because the equipment cost too much money, but we lived and breathed the game. Most of us were Dodger fans, from territorial loyalty, but also because it was one of the greatest of all baseball teams. In all of that neighborhood, I knew one Giant fan and one guy who unaccountably rooted for the Cincinnati Reds. Nobody rooted for the Yankees.

That was before television's triumph, before so many children were turned into passive slugs, before the relentless tides of Super Glut had jammed or pacified so many imaginations. We didn't have those giant $350 radios you see everywhere now (the radio in our house was shaped like a cathedral, and you had to hold the aerial in the back to hear clearly). But somehow we always knew The Score. Red Barber narrated the Dodger games on WHN, and we would shout into the bars — into Rattigan's, Fitzgerald's, Quigley's, Unbeatable Joe's — "Who's winnin' and who's pitchin' and who got the hits?" We knew; we always knew. The Score was like some insistent melody being played in another room, parallel to our own lives and our own scores.

But we also saw a lot of games at Ebbets Field. The Police Athletic League gave away Knothole Club tickets, and so — reluctantly, fearful of the taint of betrayal — we would go into the 72nd Precinct each spring and sign up for the PAL so we could get Dodger tickets. They were almost always in the bleachers, when the worst teams (and poorest draws) were in town against the Dodgers, but we didn't care. There was Dixie Walker, over in right field, and Pete Reiser, playing out the shattered autumn of his career, his brilliant talent broken against the walls of the great ballpark. And on different days in different summers, Reese, Snider, Billy Cox, Stanky, Furillo, Hodges, and the rest. HIT SIGN WIN SUIT, said Abe Stark's sign under the scoreboard in center; the sign was three feet off the ground, and it would have required three simultaneous outfield coronaries for any batter to bounce a baseball off that sign, but it was a crucial part of the furnishings. And there, jittery and wonderful, dancing off third base, ready to steal home, rattling the pitchers, was Jackie Robinson. That was part of being a Dodger fan then: You were forced to take a moral position. To be a Dodger fan in those days was to endorse the idea that a black man had a right to steal home in the major leagues.

Ebbets Field became our second home. We knew how to scale the fence if there were no PAL tickets; we knew where we could rob programs and scorecards. We developed a variety of techniques for getting in; we had one crippled kid in the neighborhood whom we carried out like a prop, telling the guards he had three days to live, or had been hit by a car driven by a Giant fan, or had been caught in Europe during the war and bombed by the Nazis. The guards always let us in. We knew where to wait for the ballplayers when they came out, and which one signed autographs and which didn't. Tell me I'm fourteen and I'll tell you I just saw Cookie Lavagetto.

We collected baseball picture cards, which came with bubble gum, and there was an elaborate system of games and trading that revolved around the cards. We hated the Yankees so much that we despised the entire league that housed them, so there was no value at all to most players from the American League. If a National League player wasn't a Dodger, he had to be good to be valued; if he was good, we feared him, and that meant we saved Stan Musial, Enos Slaughter, Sal Maglie, Johnny Mize, and, later, Willie Mays.

Because there was no television, we came early to newspapers. They would lie under their two-by-four on Pop Sanew's newsstand: the *News, Mirror, Times, Herald Tribune, Journal-American, World-Telegram, Post, PM,* Brooklyn *Eagle,* and Brooklyn *Times-Union.* In that neighborhood, we thought the *Post* was edited by Joe Stalin, just as other neighborhoods thought that the *Daily News* was edited by Francisco Franco. But we didn't care about any of that. Somehow, with deposits from milk and soda bottles, we bought papers: to read Jimmy Cannon in the *Post,* Frank Graham in the *Journal,* Dan Parker in the *Mirror,* and, most important of all, Dick Young in the *News.* Young was the greatest writer in history, we felt, better than Tommy Holmes or Harold C. Burr in the *Eagle* (which I delivered after school, and had other people deliver when I went to ball games), better than anyone we were forced to read at school. He was always going after the bosses, after Branch Rickey and then after the infamous Walter O'Malley. The dream job was to grow up and be Dick Young.

We would read the papers sitting in doorways on the avenues, memorizing statistics, knowing each minor fluctuation in averages, at bats, strikeouts, or walks. In those days, ERA stood for earned-run average; for some of us it still does. And when we had finished with the sports pages, we would turn to the comics: "Dick Tracy," Milton Caniff's "Terry and the Pirates," and, later, "Steve Canyon," and some of us would cut them out, pasting entire runs of the strips into scrapbooks, making our own comic books. I was probably the only reader of *PM* in that neighborhood, because it carried Crockett Johnson's great comic strip "Barnaby," about a young boy with a fairy godfather named O'Malley who smoked cigars and was a Dodger fan.

Reading the papers, before or after a game, was usually accompanied by eating or drinking Yankee Doodles and Devil Dogs, iced Pepsi, Mission Bell grape, Frank's orange. It seems to me I spent hundreds of hours with seven or eight other guys sucking the air out of empty soda bottles and letting them dangle from my lips. Slowly, gravity would pull the bottles away from our lips, air would leak in, the bottles would disconnect and fall. If you were the last man left, you won the deposit money.

You needed money for soda, spaldeens, comics, and newspapers, but you didn't need money for a lot of other things. You knew that sneakers had to last an entire summer, no matter how worn and disgusting they became, so you learned to bandage them with tape. You would have one pair of roller skates for the season, and one skate key. The skates were the kind that clamped on shoes and had metal wheels. When the wheels began to wear out (developing "skellies"), we took the skates apart, nailed them to two-by-fours, nailed milk boxes to the top of the two-by-fours, and scooter season had begun.

Street games were constant: ringolevio, giant steps, buck buck (how many horns are up?), a bizarre wartime game called concentration camp (Nazis were one team, rounding up the rest of us, and torturing us). Off-the-point and single-double-triple-home-run required spaldeens and were played off stoops; boxball was another variation, as restrained as cricket. Clearly, the spaldeen was at the heart of most of the games, and near the end of the day we would prowl the rooftops looking for balls that had been caught in drains, wedged behind pigeon coops, stuck under slats or behind chimneys. We would boil them to make them clean and to give them more bounce. One day, my brother Tommy boiled a half dozen such balls in a big pot, and they came out pink and glistening. Later on, my mother came home from work, and he made her a cup of tea. She gagged. Tommy hadn't changed the water, and the lovely amber-colored tea tasted of pure spaldeens. The rest of us would have loved the brew.

We played touch football with rolled and taped newspapers. Because of the cost, I didn't hold a real football in my hands until I was sixteen, and I never had a bike. I didn't feel at all deprived. Hockey was played with a puck made of crumpled tin cans, and basketball was a Bronx game. We had no backyard because the house was on an avenue, so there were no pools or hoses to cool us off; we opened the fire hydrants with a wrench and made a spray by holding a wooden slat against the cascading water. There was room to run barefoot in the streets then, because there were almost no cars. Later, when the war was over and the cars came, they ended the hydrants and ruined the stickball courts and stained the fresh morning air. But we didn't know that would happen. We lived with nouns: marbles, comics, lots, roofs, factories, balls, newspapers, scores. But we were verbs. Verbs to be, and verbs that were active. We didn't know that the nouns contained their own cemeteries.

Coney Island was the great adventure. We went there by trolley car, on a long clacking journey that took us through the last New York farms, with tomato plants ripening on either side of us; figs and dates growing in yards, farmers scratching at spinach fields. I was there the day Luna Park burned down, the giant plumes of smoke billowing into the sky and women crying. And when that old amusement park was gone, we were left with Steeplechase the Funny Place, 31 rides for half a dollar — that and Nathan's, when hot dogs were a dime and never ever tasted better again anywhere in America. We camped in Bay 12, near Nathan's, and later moved down to the bay in front of Scoville's, a great Irish summer saloon with umbrellas in the back, where the women sat in summer dresses, and the men bought beer by the pitcher, and the bar smelled of pretzels and suntan oil; and we finished at Bay 22, in front of a place called Oceantide, near Sea Gate.

In memory, we never saw the sand. Every inch was covered with blankets and bodies: glistening young bodies, swollen older bodies of women waddling into the surf, the inaccessible bodies of girls. I would plunge into the unruly sea, thinking of white whales, harpoons, Ahab; of my grandfather Devlin, who had seen Rangoon before his death on the Brooklyn docks, far from his Irish home; of strange continents, exotic cities, women with hot, dark eyes. In Coney Island, I drank my first beer, touched my first female breast, received a wounding kiss from my first great love. Alas and farewell. In my mind, there is always a day when I am under the boardwalk, with the beach suddenly clearing, blankets snatched, books swooped up, as the sky darkens and I am alone, leaning against a coarse concrete pillar, in the rumbling fugue of a summer storm. July is gone. August has almost burnt itself out. And September lies ahead, like a prison sentence.

On those days, careening home on the trolley cars, I would go down to the public library on 9th Street and Sixth Avenue and vanish into books. Or I would walk another block to the RKO Prospect, where my mother was a cashier, and go into the chilly darkness with my brother Tommy. Books made us think; the movies let us dream.

One tempered or enriched the other. And both were free. So were the streets. So were we.

That city still exists for me. I live in its ruins. In the mornings of July, I sometimes remember that morning long ago, after a gang member named Giacomo had been killed by a shot from one of the South Brooklyn Boys, and dawn spilled across the park like blood. I remember the rooftops, pigeons circling against the lucid sky, and the blind semaphore of laundry flapping in the breeze. I'm certain that if I turn on the radio, Red Barber will tell me that Reese is on second, with Furillo batting and Snider in the on-deck circle. If I go out and walk to 13th Street, I can ring the bell and Vito will come down and we'll go up to the Parkside and McAlevey and Horan and Timmy and Duke and Billy and the others will be around, and then we can head for Coney. Or we can walk across the park to Ebbets Field and see the Cardinals. Or we can lie on the fresh cut grass and tell lies about women. I can still do such things. Don't tell me the bells no longer ring. Don't tell me those buildings are no longer there. Don't tell me that I have no right to remember. I only remember life. I will have no memory of dying.

NEW YORK,
July 7–14, 1980

CITY OF THE DAMNED

For me, all hope for New York died on the day I read about the arrest of a young man out in the borough of Queens. A special kind of murder. DAD HELD IN KILLING, said the page-three headline in the *Daily News*. Another neat summary of a familiar New York story, reported in the matter-of-fact tone of an aging war correspondent. You know: the cops say this, the neighbors say that, and, uh, pass the jam, will ya, honey?

Familiar. Except for the details . . . those flat details told us that this particular father, who had only recently arrived in New York from the American Midwest, had grown angry when his six-day-old son urinated on him. The man threw the infant to the floor (naturally, the child had to be punished for such effrontery). According to the police, the father then chopped up the infant and threw him to the German shepherd. When the cops arrived, there was nothing left of the boy except the blood on the floor. But even those terrible details weren't sufficient to cause a loss of faith in an entire city. It was the reaction of New Yorkers that settled a swampy chill in my old bones and confirmed a deepening belief that we were doomed. There was no reaction at all. No angry protests. No masses offered in the churches. No memorials planned. Nothing. As the Russian writer Aleksandr Kuprin once wrote, "Do you understand, gentlemen, that all the horror is in just this: that there is no horror!"

In the barbarized city of New York, there is no horror these days. We no longer seem capable of that basic human emotion, which is why so many of us have begun to lose all hope for a more decent future. The cause of this municipal numbness is simple: We have seen too many atrocities. On the day the story broke about the baby who was fed to the dog, exactly two people mentioned it to me. By the following day, this tale of horror had vanished from the newspapers and from our collective consciousness, with an assist from Saddam Hussein. In the next week, various journalistic generals rallied for war in hysterical defense of the noble democrats of Kuwait, while George Bush was sending troops, tanks, helicopters, airplanes, and crates of thirty-screen sun block to Saudi Arabia, at a cost of billions of dollars, to protect Our Way of Life. It was much easier to locate the world's beasts in Baghdad than to mourn the brief life of an American child fed to a dog by an American father, in a city that claimed to be the center of American civilization.

In the month before Bush rose to defend Our Way of Life in the wadis of the Arabian desert, five children were shot dead in the streets of New York, and another six were wounded. All were indirect casualties of the drug wars in this brutalized city, where two million illegal guns are brandished by the citizens as symbols of faith in the creed of the National Rifle Association. Each death was noted in the newspapers, of course, and briefly smothered in the wormy sentimentalities of local television news. Each was then almost instantly superseded by a fresh outrage and instantly forgotten.

And of course, there was no horror.

The desperate truth is that millions of New Yorkers have been as emotionally immobilized as anyone who lives too long in the presence of violence and death: emergency-room doctors, soldiers, Mafia hit men. And at the heart of this grand refusal to feel lies something else: They have come to believe that New York itself is dying.

In many ways, I've begun to agree. Reluctantly. With a sense of grieving sadness; I'm a New Yorker, after all, born and bred. New York made my life possible. As a son of immigrants, I've subscribed to its tough, romantic myths and have spent a half century in thrall to its dazzling and infuriating ways. In the 1970s, when we were afflicted by a great fiscal crisis, there was much talk of doom and collapse; I scoffed then at such drastic predictions. New York, after all, is America's city, the way that Paris is France's city, and Tokyo is Japan's city. It belongs to all Americans. New York couldn't simply collapse into degradation and anarchy; the country wouldn't allow it.

But the fiscal crisis was one big crisis and therefore amenable to one big solution. The current crisis is a death of a thousand cuts. As in virtually every one of America's drug-drowned cities, crime is the most obvious problem; but as residents of the largest city, New Yorkers are overwhelmed by the sheer weight of numbers. The steady grinding force of menace is a texture of daily life here now. When *Time* did its cover story on the collapsing city, some 59 percent of those polled said they would move somewhere else if they could. Nobody in New York was surprised. "I'm sick of looking over my shoulder," one old friend said to me, explaining that he was moving to the Southwest. "I've done it year after year, every year worse than the one before. Just once more, before I get old, I want to walk down a street on a summer night without looking behind me."

That enervating sense of menace isn't mere paranoia. New York is more dangerous now than at any time in its history. Last year, there were a record-breaking 1,905 murders in New York (compared with 305 in 1955); in the first six months of 1990, homicides were running 19 percent ahead of last year, without counting the 87 killed in the Happy Land Social Club fire. We are averaging five murders a day. It is no consolation to be told that, per capita, other American cities are even more dangerous. We live here, where the bullets are killing children. Sometimes the mayhem attracts wide public attention: A family of tourists from Utah is attacked in the subway by a pack of kids looking for disco money; one of the tourists is stabbed to death while defending his mother. "They didn't know the city," one of my friends said. "They just weren't streetwise." But a few days later, in the Bronx, an eighteen-year-old, a son of the city, street-wise and smart, is approached by a panhandler demanding a dollar. The young man refuses. The panhandler jams a knife in his heart and kills him. Headlines, as usual, scream for two days. But there is no horror.

The rich, of course, live well-defended lives. But for millions of others, there is never any relief from the dailiness of menace. Every New Yorker knows one big thing: Nobody is safe. In a recent month, one of my friends was mugged at ten in the morning as he was walking into the building where he works; another was robbed at noon while packing luggage into his car for a summer vacation. Everybody I know has been touched in one way or another. My own mother has been mugged four times; she came out of the last mugging with Parkinson's disease, which has ruined the final years of her life. Nobody is safe. Nobody.

The increasingly casual mayhem of the street has made all New Yorkers adjust. Older people who can't afford retirement in Florida or Arizona have become prisoners of their apartments. It doesn't matter to them that New York is host to such glories as the Metropolitan Museum and the Broadway theater; they can't risk the journey to visit them because predators wait in subways and alleys or the lobbies of their apartment buildings. On Madison Avenue, shopkeepers keep their doors locked through the day, afraid of roaming gangs of teenagers, opening only for customers they feel can be trusted. Larger establishments are patrolled by platoons of private police. The security business is booming, as New Yorkers buy thousands of locks, metal screens, alarms, attack dogs, bulletproof vests. They go to karate classes. They apply for permission (almost always denied) to legally carry guns. And still nobody feels safe.

The leading cause of job-related deaths in New York is now homicide. The victims are usually shopkeepers or taxi drivers (by mid-August this year, twenty-one taxi drivers had been killed, and cabbies were demanding the right to arm themselves). Every day's paper brings fresh news of slaughter. A young Bronx district attorney stops near the courthouse to buy some doughnuts and he's killed in a burst of automatic-weapon fire from a druggie who shot at the wrong group. A guy in Brooklyn is refused entrance to a social club; he comes back with an automatic weapon and shoots ten people. "You don't have to come from Utah to get killed here," a young man says to me in Brooklyn. "You just walk out the door and *Bang!* You're dead."

The ghettos are most dangerous of all, as blacks kill other blacks at a rate that would make the Ku Klux Klan envious. Black youths are killing or being killed over sneakers, jackets, over the choice of songs on boom boxes, over women and attitude and casual quarrels. And, of course, over drugs. The old Mob has lost control of the drug business in New York. But the resulting decentralization has led the hardened young entrepreneurs to slaughter one another over the right to sell crack or heroin outside individual bodegas. Now New York must deal with the babies born to crack addicts. They are a peculiar mutation: children who won't respond in any way to normal human affection. There are tens of thousands of them in the care of the city government now (their mothers dead, in prison, or peddling themselves for more crack on the streets of the city). Thousands of crack babies are born each year; what sort of teenagers will they grow up to be?

Alas, notions of redemption are generally exercises in self-delusion. Most of the druggies are simply incapable of doing anything else; they come out of generations of welfare, from social groupings that can't really be described as families. They've spent more time practicing their walks than they ever did studying, so they are too ignorant to make their way in the real world. They get into the drug business for a few brief years before joining the many thousands who have died or are in jail.

"Crime isn't a job," one wise older cop told me a few years ago, "but it is an occupation. So these guys make it their life for a while and then get slammed into the prison system. They're more or less happy there. It's the way they grew up, the state paying everything. Lock-in welfare. In the joint, they don't have to care for women, raise children, open bank accounts, plead for mortgages, bust their asses to make ends meet. Instead of helping a kid with biology homework, these assholes would rather stand around the yard in Attica and horseshit each other about how they are really victims. . . ."

If some New York cops are especially bitter these days, it's because they are obviously losing the struggle with the bad guys. The army of New York drug addicts spends most of its time roaming the city, in an anarchic pursuit of money for drugs. They have little to fear from the forces of the law. New York has twenty-seven thousand police on the payroll. But when divided into three five-day shifts, and then depleted by vacation and sick time, along with court appearances, there are only 1,500 cops on the street at any given time. In New York, crime pays. And the criminals know it.

In addition, the city has been overrun by endless regiments of the homeless. Again, there are so many that nobody can truly count them. But they are everywhere: rummies and junkies, most of them men, their bodies sour from filth and indifference. They sleep in subways and in parks, in doorways and in bank lobbies. Some chatter away with the line of con that's learned in the yards of prisons. Others mutter in the jangled discourse of the insane.

But these derelicts are not all the sad and harmless losers of sentimental myth. Some are menacing and dangerous, their requests for handouts essentially demands. The squeegee brigades appear at all major intersections, holding rags to clean auto windshields, grabbing windshield wipers to force compliance. Refuse to pay for the unsolicited window cleaning, your wiper might get snapped off. Few New Yorkers are willing to leave their cars to fight with these people, and the cops ignore them. Every night, the homeless rummage through thousands of plastic garbage bags left out for pickup. They are looking for soda cans, which can be exchanged for cash, which then can be used to buy dope (food can be obtained for nothing at the many soup kitchens around the city). Often, they don't seal up the bags when they're finished and the garbage flies away on the city's streets. New York was never a model of cleanliness. But it has seldom been dirtier than it is now.

This enrages those who pay taxes — the price of living here. New Yorkers pay federal, state, and city income taxes, along with an endless array of sales and other taxes, to help meet the city's incredible $28 billion budget. Many of the middle class get virtually none of the services they pay for. The police don't protect them. They have far fewer fires than ghetto areas. They don't often use the public hospitals and seldom send their children to public schools, which are perceived as dangerous and drug-ridden. Since the rich pay very little in taxes (they write the laws), the middle class is supporting the nonworking underclass, which, of course, pays no taxes at all. So it is the middle class that now speaks of leaving New York behind. They want to live in places that are safe. They want to feel normal human feelings, including horror in the face of the horrible.

"I just can't use my kids in a social experiment," one friend said.

"Yeah, I'd like to stay. But I have two children. I don't want them to be killed coming home from school. I don't want them to become drug addicts. Is that unreasonable? If so, then we're completely insane. . . ."

If all of this is by now familiar, there seems to be no way to turn it around with the oratory of optimism. It is certain now that no American city will cash in on the end of the Cold War. After a brief few months of hope, the macho adventure in Iraq, with the humiliating sideshow of the President of the United States panhandling for funds from our "allies," indicates that the U.S. just can't abide peace. It will certainly not begin transforming the military-industrial complex into a social-industrial complex at any point in the foreseeable future. Instead of using our treasure and intelligence to make goods (thus putting the bulk of the underclass back to work), we will keep making this military junk that only employs an engineering elite. And with his gift for syrupy platitude, the President promises us that nothing will change.

Meanwhile, as this dreadful century comes to an end, poor New York will slide deeper into decay, becoming a violent American Calcutta. The middle class will flee in greater numbers, the tax base will shrink, the criminals will rule our days and nights. Drugs, crime, despair, illiteracy, disease: All will increase into the next century. If there are twenty-five bums in the corner park now, make way for another hundred. If there are two thousand murders this year, get ready for four thousand. New York is dying. And if New York dies, so will every other American city. We are feeding our children to the dogs. And nobody in Washington understands — do they, gentlemen? — that the horror is that there is no horror.

ESQUIRE,
December 1990

PART II

THE LAWLESS DECADES

Paul Sann once wrote a book about the Prohibition era and called it *The Lawless Decade*. But the Roaring Twenties have an almost innocent charm when compared with American cities over the past quarter century. In Chicago's famous St. Valentine's Day Massacre in 1929, seven members of the Bugs Moran mob were shot down in a North Clark Street garage. Headlines screamed. Politicians bellowed. The shootings became enshrined in myth and figured in dozens of movies. In New York in the 1980s, we once had 25 murders on a single weekend. They were covered in the newspapers for two days and then forgotten.

The American slide into urban barbarism has yet to find its Gibbon. But someday a great historian must try to answer the most persistent question: What happened to us in the last third of the twentieth century? It's too easy to say that the sixties happened, or Vietnam happened, or Watergate happened. But they are surely part of the story. The apparently endless Cold War — which was their context — insisted on the doctrine of massive retaliation; overwhelming force became essential to our politics and permeated our popular culture. On television news shows, gray-haired statesmen and men from think tanks spoke with icy seriousness about MIRVs and throw weights and the use of force. American governments spent many billions on weapons; our engineers designed amazing new ways for killing people while the Japanese devoted their energies to consumer goods. We killed uncountable Vietnamese. We bombed Cambodia until the Khmer Rouge rose from the ruins to widen the horror. We invaded the Dominican Republic and Grenada, landed troops in Lebanon, armed and paid counterrevolutionaries in Nicaragua, and killed at least 500 human beings in Panama while making the bloodiest drug arrest in history. The leadership of the country obviously believed in the use of violence. Why was anyone surprised that Americans in the worst parts of large cities shared their beliefs? The Crips and the Bloods are Americans. And for more than forty years, Americans were taught that pacifism was a dirty word.

The current violence in American cities has a number of obvious components: poverty, drugs, guns, and race. They can't be easily separated. The poverty caused by the collapse of the urban manufacturing base has been compounded by racism and a failed welfare system. Thousands of young men and women in the ghettos used drugs to obliterate or enhance reality and then some decided to make big scores in the drug trade itself. Why not? Cocaine was fashionable among many people who were not from ghettos: musicians, movie stars, Wall Street brokers. Then some evil genius invented crack, and suddenly this drug of the elite was available to the poor. It was cheap; it could be snorted instead of injected, thus eliminating the fear of AIDS; it was almost instantly addictive. The market boomed.

The shift from heroin to cocaine in the 1970s coincided with the decline of the old American Mob, forged during Prohibition. The crude second-generation hoods couldn't make contact with the Cubans and Colombians who were running the wholesale trade in Medellín, Cali, and Miami. Their own parochialism and racism kept them out of the black and Latino ghettos. The wholesalers built condominiums and office buildings in Miami; the retailers battled over street corners. Decentralization of the drug trade led to endless turf wars and these were made even bloodier by the easy availability of high-powered automatic weapons. This too was endorsed by higher authority; very few politicians would dare to oppose the Great American Gun Cult and its Holy See, the National Rifle Association. They all endorsed the notion, unique in the industrialized world, that every real American had the right to carry a gun and protect himself.

I've included here only a few of the many pieces I wrote on these subjects during this desperate period. There were too many accounts of the deaths of innocent bystanders, of young men shot down for nothing, and widows and mothers and children assembling for funerals. The repetition was numbing. The chosen pieces don't pretend to tell the whole story of what happened to New York, Miami, and other cities; although the use of crack cocaine is declining, the story has not ended. These are situation reports, and though the situation has shifted, its details have altered, its players have been replaced, the basic situation remains. Today, more than a million men are jammed into American prisons (including John Gotti). Thousands of others are in graveyards. The drugs keep coming. So do the guns.

NOTES FROM UNDERGROUND

The slow and tedious processes of justice brought Bernhard Hugo Goetz last week to a fifth-floor courtroom at 111 Centre Street and there, at least, the poor man was safe. Out in the great scary city, the demons of his imagination roamed freely; across the street, many of them were locked away in the cages of The Tombs. But here at the defense table, flanked by his lawyers, protected by a half-dozen armed court officers, the room itself separated by metal detectors from the anarchy of the city, Goetz looked almost serene.

By design or habit, he was dressed as an ordinary citizen: pink cotton shirt and jeans over the frail body, steel-rimmed glasses sliding down the long sharp nose. His hair looked freshly trimmed. You see people like him every day, passing you on the street, riding the subways, neither monstrous nor heroic. From time to time, he whispered to the lawyers. He made a few notes on a yellow pad. His eyes wandered around the courtroom, with its civil service design and the words *In God We Trust* nailed in sans-serif letters above the bench of Judge Stephen G. Crane. Goetz never looked at the spectators or the six rows of reporters. In some curious way, he was himself a kind of spectator.

So when it was time to play the tape-recorded confession that Goetz made to the police in Concord, New Hampshire, on New Year's Eve, 1984, he, too, examined the transcript like a man hoping for revelation. The text itself was extraordinary. Combined with the sound of Goetz's voice — stammering, hyperventilating, querulous, defensive, cold, blurry, calculating — it seemed some terrible invasion of privacy. We have heard this voice before; it belongs to the anonymous narrator of *Notes from Underground,* that enraged brief for the defense.

Goetz furrowed his brow as he listened to this much younger, oddly more innocent version of himself that had ended the long pan-icky flight out of the IRT in the second floor interview room of police headquarters in Concord. He started by telling his inquisitor, a young detective named Chris Domian, the sort of facts demanded by per-sonnel directors: name, birth date, social security number, address (55 West 14th Street, "in New York City, and that's, uh, that's zip code 10011"). But it's clear from the very beginning that he realized these would be his last anonymous hours.

GOETZ: You see, I'll tell you the truth, and they can do anything they want with me, but I just don't want to, I just don't want to be *paraded* around, I don't want a circus. . . . I wish it were a dream. But it's not. But, you know, it's nothing to be proud of. It's just, just, you know, it just *is*.

Exactly. It wasn't a dream, certainly not a movie; it just was. On December 22, 1984, at about 1:30 in the afternoon, Bernie Goetz boarded a southbound number 2 Seventh Avenue IRT train at 14th Street and his life changed forever. So did the lives of Darrell Cabey, Troy Canty, James Ramseur, and Barry Allen. Within seconds after he boarded the train, they were joined together in a few violent min-utes that changed this city. And when you listen to Goetz making his jangled confession, you understand that on that terrible afternoon, there were really five victims.

DOMIAN: Okay, let's start with the person that was, uh, on the right, so to speak, laying down.

GOETZ: Yeah, I think he was the one who talked to me; he was the one who did the talking.

That was Canty. He is now 20, finishing an 18-month drug rehab treatment at Phoenix House. Before he ran into Goetz, he had pleaded guilty to taking $14 from video games in a bar. In his confes-sion, Goetz is trying hard to explain to Domian (and to officer War-ren Foote, who joined Domian) not simply what he did, but its context. The resulting transcript reads like a small, eerie play: the man from the big city explaining a dark world of menacing signs and nuances to the baffled outlanders.

GOETZ: I sat, I sat down and just, he was lying on the side, kind of. He, he just turned his face to me and he said, "How are you?" You know, what do you do? 'Cause people joke around in New York a lot, and this and that, and in certain circumstances that can be, that can be a real threat. You see, there's an implication there . . . I looked up and you're not supposed to look at people a lot because it can be interpreted as being impolite — so I just looked at him and I said "Fine." And I, I looked down. But you kind of keep them in the corner of your eye . . .

DOMIAN: Did he say anything else to you?

GOETZ: Yeah, yeah . . . the train was out of the station for a while and it reached full speed. . . . And he and one of the other fellows got up and they, uh — You see, they were all originally on my right-hand side. But, uh, you know, two stayed on my right-hand side, and he got up and the other guy got up and they came to my left-hand side and. . . . You see, what they said wasn't even so much as important as the look, the *look*. You see the body language. . . . You have to, you know, it's, it's, uh, you know, that's what I call it, *body language.*

That's what started it off: "How are you?" and body language. It just went from there. Goetz remembered: "He [Canty] stood up and the other fellow stood up. And they very casually walked, or sauntered — whatever you want to call it — over to my left side. And the fellow . . . uh, he said, 'Give me five dollars.' "

This is the moment that helps explain the intensity of the public response to the Goetz story. It is one thing to read with detached amusement about Jean Harris or Claus von Bulow; such tabloid soap operas have little to do with our lives. But for millions of New Yorkers, what happened to Goetz is a very real possibility. Being trapped on the subway by four bad guys demanding not a dime or a quarter but *five dollars* is similar to the nocturne about the burglar beside the bed in the dark. A quarter is panhandling; five dollars is robbery. Such scenarios don't often happen, but you wonder what you would do if they did. For Goetz, it happened.

GOETZ: One of the other fellows, he had in his fur coat, he had his hand or something like this and he put a bulge. . . . And even that isn't a threat. Because the people, you see, they, they know the rules of the game, the rules of the game in New York. And you know, they're very serious about the rules. . . . You see you don't know what it's like to be on the other side of violence. It's, it's like a picture. When it happens to you, you see, you *see* it. . . . People have the craziest image; they see, like Captain Kirk or someone like that, getting attacked by several guys and boom, boom, boom, he beats 'em up and — and two minutes later, he's walking arm and arm in, with a beautiful woman or something like that. And that's not what it is. . . .

Goetz was not Captain Kirk. He was a frail bespectacled young man living in New York and he had learned the rules of the game. He knew what was meant when one of four young black men told him he wanted five dollars.

GOETZ: I looked at his face, and, you know, his eyes were *shiny,* you know. He, he, he was, if you can believe that, his eyes were shiny, he was *enjoying* himself. . . . I know in my mind what they wanted to do was *play* with me. . . . You know, it's kind of like a cat plays with a mouse before, you know. . . .

DOMIAN: After you got that impression, what did you wind up doing?

GOETZ: That's not an impression, that's not an impression. . . .

Throughout the confession, Goetz struggles with what he clearly believes is an impossible task: to explain to his rural auditors the terrors of New York.

GOETZ: . . . You have to think in a cold-blooded way in New York. . . . If you don't . . . think in what society's going to brand it, as being you know, *cold-blooded* and murderous and savage and monstrous . . . I feel it's *irresponsible.* . . . How can you understand that here in New Hampshire? How, how, how can you?

He explains to the two New Hampshire cops that he began, in his mind, to lay down "my pattern of fire." He would shoot from left to right. That was the only thing he could do, he insists, because this act wasn't premeditated: "I never knew those guys were on the train, you know, and like I said, I'm, I'm no good guy or anything like that. But if they had acted a little differently, if they hadn't *cornered* me. . . ." Clearly what he feared most from them was humiliation. And so he decided to shoot them with the unregistered nickle-plated featherweight .38 caliber Smith & Wesson Special that he had shoved inside his pants.

DOMIAN: Your, your intention was to shoot these people?

GOETZ: My intention, at that moment, let me explain: when I saw what they intended for me, my intention was, was worse than shooting.

DOMIAN: Okay. Was it your intention to kill these people?

GOETZ: My intention was to do anything I could do to hurt them. My intention — you know, I know this sounds horrible — but my intention was to murder them, to *hurt* them, to make them suffer as much as possible.

No, he explained, he didn't have a pistol permit, because the New

York police department had turned him down. And then, recalling all this to the cops in New Hampshire, the core of his rage began to burn. The reason he wanted a pistol permit was because he had been attacked three years before and was left with permanent damage to his knee. The cops caught the man who did it, Goetz said, and two hours and 35 minutes after his arrest, he was back on the street without bail, charged with malicious mischief; Goetz himself claimed he spent six hours and five minutes filing the charges and talking to the bureaucrats in the victim aid program.

"That incident was an education," he said, his voice beginning to tremble. "It taught me that, that the city doesn't care what happens to you. You see, *you* don't know what it's like to be a victim inside."

And he began to explain what it's like to live in an almost permanent state of fear. This can't be sneered away; thousands, perhaps millions of New Yorkers live with this most corrosive emotion. Most of us have adjusted to the state of siege. We are tense, wary, guarded; but most of us function and do not explode. Goetz was different.

GOETZ: . . . I kind of accept my life, as I know it, is finished. But, but, boy, it would be just — to lead a normal life. If, if you can't, I mean, is it too much to ask? . . . To live being afraid is unbearable, you know? It's too much to ask, goddamn it . . ."

All over the tape, Goetz talks about fear and its denial. "I'm not afraid of dying instantly," he says at one point. "I don't have a family or anything like that. What I'm afraid of is being maimed and of, of these things happening slowly and not knowing what's going to happen from moment to moment. The fear, in this case, the fear is a funny thing. You see, this is really *combat*." He then becomes even more analytical, sounding like a man who had mastered the theory before engaging in practice. "The upper level of your mind, you just turn off. That's, that's the important thing. And you, you *react* . . . your sense of perception changes, your abilities change. Speed is everything, speed is everything."

And so, with speed, he shot Canty, Allen, Cabey, and Manseur. "They had set a trap for me," he tells the cops, "and only they were trapped. It was just so bizarre. It was — I know this is disgusting to say — but it was, it was so easy. I can't believe it. God." He insists that he knew exactly what he was doing when he was doing it. "I don't believe in this insanity stuff. Because you know what you're doing. You cannot do something and not know it. I mean how could I do it and not know it? This is, this is all bullshit. . . . But if you can accept this: I was out of control. . . . Maybe you should always be in control. But if you put people in a situation where they're threatened with mayhem, *several times,* and then if, then if something happens, and if a person acts, turns into a vicious animal — I mean, I mean, you know, how are you supposed, you know, it's, it's, it's, it's, what, *what do you expect,* you know?"

After firing the first shots, dropping Canty, Ramseur, and Allen, he saw Cabey sitting down.

GOETZ: I wasn't sure if I had shot him before, because he just seemed okay. Now, I said I know this sounds, this is gonna sound vicious, and it is. I mean, how else can you describe it? I said, "You seem to be all right. Here's another." Now, you see, what happens is, I was gonna shoot him anyway, I'm sure. I had made up, I mean, in my mind, that I was gonna pull the trigger anyway. But he jerked his right arm. And on reflex, he was shot instantly. You see, that's the whole thing. You're working on reflex. You don't think. . . .

Scattered through the confession there are many other examples of Goetz's fury and rage, which sound as if they too had become reflexes. "If I had more [ammunition] I would have shot them again and again and again." He says that "I wanted to hurt them as much as I possibly could." But even in his rage, he could recognize the fallen men as humans: "I wanted to look at his eyes, I don't even want to say what may have been in my mind. And I looked at his eyes . . . there was such *fear.*" It was as if Cabey's fear was the only sign to Goetz of their common humanity. "You know, the, the, the look had changed. And I started — it was kinda like slowing down. All of a sudden it's like putting on the, screeching of the brakes, and you just start slowing down. . . ."

He talked about the reactions of other passengers, the train slowing down, a conductor coming in and asking what was going on. He talked about jumping out into the tracks after the train stopped in the tunnel, and coming up at Chambers Street and taking a cab home, and then a long drive that night in a rented car to Vermont because "instinctively, somehow I kinda feel like heading north is the way to go if there is a problem."

Goetz stayed in Vermont for a week. And if you can believe the confession, he seems actually to have been happy. What he did in the subway, he thought, would be considered just another New York crime. ". . . When I got back to New York, the stuff was still on the news and people were talking about it. You see, up here people have just forgotten about it. It was one more piece of, excuse me for using the word — one more piece of shit that happened in New York."

Hearing himself say those words, Goetz massaged his temple, and then lifted his glasses and rubbed his eyes. In the end, the eruption that Saturday afternoon on the IRT wasn't just another piece of shit that happened in New York. It was a lot more than that.

VILLAGE VOICE,
May 12, 1987

WHITE LINE FEVER

I. PROLOGUE

Miami is one of those cities with its own peculiar odor and you smell it most distinctly during the hours before dawn. There is salt in the air, of course, a nod to the abiding presence of the southern sea. But on certain nights when a desultory breeze blows east from the Everglades, a more powerful essence soaks the dark air: the ancient memory of the swamp. It's as if all the tar and concrete, all the gleaming hotels and banks and shopping centers, the tract houses, schools, churches, and restaurants are some dull afterthought. In those humid after-midnight hours, the modern city is overwhelmed by a primeval compost of decaying vegetation, rioting flowers, fetid water, the remains of beings that die with thrashing suddenness in the night.

And on almost all such nights, it does not take much imagination to detect something else drifting on the Miami wind: the sweet rotting stench of corruption.

No other American city has melded its natural odor so perfectly with the dailiness of its human activities. If you move around the city, you sense the pervasiveness of the corruption: the cop smoking a cigarette in a doorway, like a supporting player from *Red Harvest;* the chaotic sprawl of weather-stained commercial architecture, evoking deals and variances and the purchased approval of second-rate materials; young men driving Porsches and Mercedes and Caddies as if they owned the nightside streets. Corruption is most tangible, as blunt as an ax, in the bars, discos, marinas, that sleek urban scape so accurately reflected in *Miami Vice*. This world is not fiction; its treacherous glamour is an undeniable element of modern Miami. And the citizens of that world, adorned with Naugahyde-like tans and encrusted Rolexes, rubbing their eroding noses in unwilled salute, are walking symbols of the city's deepest reality. The truth of a time and place is, of course, always illusive; but no historian can tell the story of Miami in the last decade without acknowledging one gigantic fact of municipal life: cocaine.

In the late 1970s, the *Miami Herald* estimated that drugs had become the largest single industry in southern Florida, accounting for a billion dollars a year. Today, in spite of numerous photo opportunities starring George Bush, increases in various antidrug budgets, and some hard dangerous work by the more than 800 state and federal antidrug agents, there is no reason to believe that anything much has changed. Drugs are to Miami what cars are to Detroit. As opium was for some Brits in the 19th century, cocaine has been the essential building block of great Miami fortunes. Narcobucks have erected shopping centers, financed housing developments, built vast mansions, stocked racing stables, paid for boats, cars, and more fleshy trinkets, created and maintained banks (some law enforcement people believe that there isn't a clean bank in the state), and so worked their way into the fabric of life here that nobody will ever be likely to separate the clean money from the soiled.

In almost every way, cocaine dominates the culture of Miami. It is part of the city's power structure, the engine of its economy, the unacknowledged grease of its politics. In Miami, as Christine Evans of the *Miami Herald* has written, "drugs are cheaper, purer and more abundant than anywhere else in the country. Doctors use them. Lawyers use them. Data analysts use them. Rich kids get them from their parents' secret drawers. Poor kids score cheap on the street."

One recent study estimates that the citizens of Dade, Broward, and Palm Beach counties spend $1.69 billion a year on illegal drugs. Employers spend $744 million a year on health care for their druggies or for repairing the messes made by people who go to work loaded. Cocaine — 75 per cent of which enters this country through Florida — is at the heart of a vast capitalist enterprise, a rude democratic industry that follows the most primitive laws of supply and demand while promising great rewards to those willing to take risks. The odds are almost all in favor of the outlaw. Since its inception in

1982, the federal South Florida Crime Task Force has racked up more than 9500 arrests, seized tons of drugs. The result? Drugs are more available than ever before and cheaper by half at $30,000 a kilo. Few street-level dealers are ever touched because the courts and jails are jammed; crack houses operate openly almost everywhere. And the big dealers — the importers and wholesalers — are virtually immune in their Brickell Avenue condos and Coral Gables mansions. The drug business is a very successful American enterprise. Everybody knows this: ordinary citizens, reporters, politicians, school-children.

But the cops know it better than anyone else. And in this world of dirty money and deep cynicism, it is no surprise that some of them have eaten the forbidden fruit. These notes are about some of those cops.

II. DOWN BY THE RIVERSIDE

The Miami River meanders out of the interior, sluggish and dense and hidden from view, crawling to the sea for 5.5 miles under the city's bridges like a huge, flat worm. It passes through a wilderness of boat yards, docks, skiffs, houseboats; it eases past areas full of twisted, anonymous steel, past rusting gas pumps and sun-blasted soda machines, past tiny stores selling shrimp and cigarettes and cold beer, past bars where tattooed whores arrive before noon to service the fishermen. Miami is never thought of as a river town, but its river serves admirably as municipal metaphor: dirty, furtive, lawless.

Sometime after midnight on the river last July 28, six men were unloading 300 to 400 kilograms of cocaine from a beatup old 40-foot scow called the *Mary C.* This was in itself not unusual; the river is sparsely patrolled by police, whose jurisdiction is split between Miami and the larger Metro-Dade police forces, along with 30 other agencies charged with its regulation (Dade County alone has a bewildering 27 separate police departments totaling 4500 police), and the river is frequently used by smugglers of everything from drugs to Pakistanis. The six men worked quickly, moving their precious cargo from boat to waiting van. It seemed like another smooth night's work in Miami.

Then, at the entrance to the boat yard, an unarmed night watchman named Bob Downs was suddenly brought to attention by an urgent banging on his door. He was told to open up. He did, and saw at least six men, two of whom were wearing police uniforms and caps. They said they were police and that this was a raid. Downs let them in.

The new arrivals hurried into the yard with guns drawn. Someone among them yelled, "Kill them!" Panicked, cornered, afraid, the men who were unloading the drugs dove into the filthy river. Downs then was ordered to unlock the padlock on the cyclone fence gates, which he did, and the loaded van was driven away. Three of the men who leaped into the river — Pedro Martinez (described later as one of Dade County's biggest coke dealers, with a fleet of five steel-hulled boats operating from the Bahamas to Florida), Adolfo Lopez-Yanes, and Juan Garcia — never were seen again alive. Their drowned bodies were fished out of the river the next afternoon.

The following December, arrests were finally made: Armando Estrada, Roman Rodriguez, Osvaldo Coello, Arturo de la Vega, Rodolfo Arias, and Armando Garcia. All were young. All were Latin. All were, or had been, Miami cops.

Estrada, Rodriguez, and Garcia were arrested at dawn, each charged with three counts of first-degree murder; under Florida's felony murder law, anyone who kills another in the process of committing a felony can be charged with first-degree murder. The others were picked up later. In addition to the murder charges, all five were charged with cocaine trafficking, racketeering, and aggravated battery; individual charges included armed robbery, conspiracy and solicitation to commit a felony, and possession of marijuana. Two of the surviving civilians who were unloading the boat were also arrested and charged. But the cops got all the attention. When four of them were brought to court, the whole country saw them blowing kisses, giggling, rolling their eyes, sniggering at their pictures in the newspapers. They flexed their muscles as they moved, looking like bags of bowling balls held together with steroids.

Within days, details about these men began to emerge. All were weight lifters, all made the disco scene, both in Little Havana and in the anglo joints out at the beach. They liked to adorn themselves with gold chains, spend money on expensive clothes, women, flashy cars, all the props of *Miami Vice*. And in police jobs paying $10 to $14 an hour, they apparently supported this lifestyle in the only way possible: through crime. They started small, taking drugs from motorists stopped for traffic offenses, and keeping them. A few openly muscled small-time peddlers. And eventually, investigators believe, about 10 cops bonded themselves together into a group the prosecutors call "The Enterprise."

The major target of The Enterprise was the drug dealer. As cops, they would learn on the street (or from straight cops) who was dealing, when big buys were taking place, and then they would go in with shields and guns and take the goods for themselves. Some simply invaded the homes of suspected dealers at gunpoint, a variation of the old crap game stickup. Obviously, if you're not supposed to be doing something, it is very hard to call the cops when you're robbed. It's even harder if the cops are doing the robbing.

When they weren't robbing drug dealers, the rogue cops were working for them. The key man was a short dapper 42-year-old Mariel refugee named Luis Rodriguez, who had gone from two 1982 arrests for possession of burglary tools and firearms, and four arrests in two years for possession of narcotics (for which he did no time) to the obligatory Mercedes, beeper, and cabin cruiser of the successful drug dealer. Like many drug dealers, he moved around a lot, seldom staying at his Coral Gables apartment, spending nights in various hotels, traveling on occasion to New York.

But Rodriguez was not exactly a master criminal, some Cuban wedding of Professor Moriarty and Meyer Lansky. In fact, he was pretty damned dumb. An example: on March 1, 1984, while driving south on the Jersey Turnpike, Rodriguez and another man were stopped by a trooper for driving 70 miles an hour. The trooper searched the 1981 Chevy and found two bags of cocaine, $14,000 in cash in the trunk, $5000 in the glove compartment, and $44,000 under the dashboard. Rodriguez pleaded guilty to cocaine possession then changed his mind, decided to fight the case, and went back to Miami to wait for trial. He obviously preferred the warm embrace of the Miami legal system to the chill vastness of the North. After his last period of probation in Florida, for example, Rodriguez asked the judge to give him back his 9 mm. Browning. I mean, what is a drug dealer without his piece? And Miami being Miami, Circuit Judge Ted Mastos agreed.

Rodriguez ran a joint called the Molino Rojo Bar, on 3084 NW 7th Street, where drug deals were often made (according to court documents) and where Rodriguez himself was once nabbed with two bags of cocaine. The bar was usually packed (even a brutal double homicide one night in December 1984 didn't keep the customers away) and among those who came around were the young cops.

Luis Rodriguez had a 49-year-old assistant, a hustler off SW 8th Street known as Armando Un. In the bar, Un got to know the cops and apparently he was a good judge of character; in 1984 he suggested they work for Rodriguez. And they were willing. In an affidavit, Un said that the drug thefts began in September 1984, the period cited by prosecutors as the beginning of The Enterprise. Soon the young weight lifters were moving drugs around the city for Rodriguez, often in patrol cars, sometimes peddling on duty. They didn't always work in combination. Officer Estrada, Un said, once gave him a kilo of cocaine in mid-1985 and took a $2000 down payment; that sounded like a private deal. Some other jobs were small; The Enterprise even helped collect gambling debts, the public servant functioning as private muscle. But according to Un, in mid-1985 he helped plan a successful 300-to-400 kilo ripoff at the Tamiami Marina, with six cops doing the heavy lifting. And then they started going after even bigger deals. In the anarchic world of Miami drugs, business was good, although Metro-Dade homicide detective Alex Alvarez later told reporters that business wasn't always very smooth; there were, for example, too many men involved — at least 10 — and they began to squabble. Said Alvarez: "Everyone wanted to kill everyone else."

Immediately after the Miami River arrests, there were expressions of surprise and rage. But the Miami establishment should have known. The police brass. The politicians. The prosecutors. They should have smelled the rotting odor, drifting in the Miami night. Way back in February 1985, a banker whose own activities were under investigation said that three masked men broke into his Coral Gables home, robbed him of $100,000 in cash and jewelry, and threatened him with death. The thieves were "built like body builders," and that April, after his own investigation, he told the cops that one of the three was a Miami police officer who worked out in a gymnasium near Bird Road. Coello and Garcia owned a gym on Bird Road. The cops investigated but did nothing. They were busy elsewhere.

On July 9 last year, a group of men invaded the home of a Miami weapons manufacturer, shot him to death, stole jewelry and a safe; neighbors said men who looked like "off-duty cops" had been seen casing the home. On the day of the Miami River deaths three men in a blue Cadillac flashed a police badge, kidnaped a woman, took her to her home and robbed her husband of $50,000; a car matching the description of the Cadillac was stopped two weeks later. Officer Osvaldo Coello was driving. He had borrowed the car, he said. Nothing happened. On August 17, two days after he resigned from the police department (after an investigation into allegations that he was using cocaine), Coello was stopped doing 120 miles an hour in a $59,000 red Lotus. He was carrying $4500. As a cop, he earned $10.40 an hour. He was not locked up. The police brass saw no evil. On August 26, two cops were arrested while trying to sell police badges, radio scanners, and automatic weapons to a drug dealer. On October 7, Miami police admitted that $150,000 had been stolen from a safe in the office of the Special Investigations Unit (the real name for the Miami vice squad) right in police headquarters. On October 10, a Metro-Dade officer was arrested for being part of a home-invasion gang; he specialized in posing as a mailman. A week later, two cops were arrested for possession of cocaine. The following month, two former Miami cops were charged with stealing (while still on the force) 150 pounds of cocaine from a 1000-pound seizure also made on the Miami River. In February, a cop was arrested while driving a stolen $40,000 Porsche. The next month, a cop was arrested for using a police car in the ripoff of a drug dealer and then planning the man's murder. The cops in the Miami area were rapidly acquiring a substantial collective yellow sheet of their own.

The most obvious questions were asked first: Who *are* these people? What kind of cops *are* they? The answers were sketchy.

All became cops in the aftermath of the bloody 1980 riots, when the Miami force was expanded from 630 officers to 1050 over three years. To reflect the changed ethnic composition of the city (42.3 per cent of Dade County's 1,771,000 inhabitants are now Latin) about 80 per cent of the new officers were black or Latin. Some veteran cops insist that to attract the new officers, standards were lowered. And one result was that some bad apples ended up with badges and legitimate guns. Former Police Chief Kenneth Harms says, "Instead of taking the cream off the top of the barrel, we took the whole damn barrel."

There are some indications that the contents of that barrel were drawn from a Miami generation to whom money was holy, its acquisition sacramental. This is, of course, in the grand American tradition. These, after all, are the children of immigrants, the same kind of people who — in the old days in a dozen American cities — made up the soldiers of the police and the Mob. Many came from the same neighborhoods. Two members of The Enterprise went to Miami High together. Three were in the class of '81 at the Police Academy; all were known as "aggressive" cops, muscular machos who volunteered for tough assignments, actually preferring the high-action midnight shift. They also moved around with a certain swagger, letting everyone know they were hard guys — as hard as anyone else on the street. They worked at this, wearing muscles as if they too were a kind of uniform. Bodymasters, the gym owned by Coello and Garcia, attracted a lot of police officers; investigators now believe that while pumping iron at Bodymasters, members of The Enterprise also planned some of the drug ripoffs. But it's not clear when these young men went bad.

Some Miami cops told me they believed the baddies became cops *in order* to enrich themselves, knowing that access to police intelligence and the gossip of informers would help them locate potential victims. Since the victims were also criminals there were few ethical problems. There might never have been ethical problems.

"Look, there have always been bad cops," one cop told me. "They're usually cops for years and all they see is the scum of the earth and a court system that doesn't give a rat's ass and after a while they might say, 'Hey, why don't I get a piece for myself?' In Miami, a cop can make a few grand by looking to the left instead of the right. But these young guys weren't cops long enough to have that happen. I think they were bad from the day they went to the academy."

If Rodriguez (through Un) was the corrupter, the relationship with the young cops didn't last very long. At 5:30 p.m. on July 30, 1985, the day after the murders on the Miami River, in a field about a mile from the Dolphin Expressway, someone dumped a pine box that was three feet high and three feet wide. Inside the box was the body of Luis Rodriguez. He had been shot quite a few times. When the cops found the crate and opened the lid, Luis's body popped out, and for a brief time his death was happily known to cops and reporters as the "Jack in the Box" murder.

Investigating the murder of Rodriguez, the cops heard that Officer Estrada had been around the night before the drug dealer disappeared, saying he would have to kill him. In a taped conversation after the killing, Un said to Officer Estrada: "I could care less if they killed Luis 40 times over. He had to be killed. If they had not killed him. . . ." On the tape, Estrada finished the sentence for him: "We would have killed him."

Officers Arias, Garcia, and Estrada have been charged with conspiracy to murder Rodriguez, but nobody has yet been charged with the actual murder. The larger story of the Miami River murders (or, as defense attorneys call them, "suicides by drowning") seems to have eclipsed the death of Luis Rodriguez.

III. RUNNING AT HIALEAH

At some point, crime and politics always seem to intersect. This can be seen most clearly in the town of Hialeah. A stranger could cross from Miami into Hialeah without knowing that he has crossed any boundary; it's like traversing the frontier between Brooklyn and Queens. But to those who know the place, Hialeah has its own special character these days. It is the second largest city in Dade County, with 180,000 residents (more than Fort Lauderdale). The city's centerpiece is the once-lovely, now rather shabby racetrack that bears its name. In the old days, famous hoodlums came each winter to the track, carting along their fancy women, each northern don protected by a flying wedge of pistoleros.

In those days, there were almost no Latins in the town; those Latins who did live in Hialeah were third-rate jockeys, exercise boys, vendors, and petty hustlers who made a living off the track. Hialeah in the '50s was a redneck town, full of hard-drinking shit-kickers who loved to batter each other on a Saturday night while Webb Pierce or Lefty Frizzell sang counterpoint on the jukebox. Then, after Castro took power, at first gradually and soon in a great rush, Hialeah began to change; vowels replaced consonants; Joe Cuba and the La Playa Sextet shoved Hank Williams and Merle Haggard off the juke. Today, Latins make up 80 per cent of the population and in 1983 finally took control of the city council. They have come to dominate an ugly, sprawling town, predominantly working class, whose main artery is 49th Street with its fast food joints and used car lots and grungy shopping centers. They have also inherited a ripe tradition of corruption.

"Politicians steal," a Miami cop said to me. "That's their business. But in Hialeah, they think they're supposed to steal everything."

For years, the press and the prosecutors were after a Hialeah mayor named Henry Milander, citing various cases of alleged malfeasance. Milander brushed them away as if they were visiting fruit flies, until at last in 1970 he was convicted of grand larceny. Even that didn't change Hialeah very much. The following year he was again elected mayor. Other pols, a visitor is told, made fortunes on developing the town, ridding the land of farms and open spaces, planting fields with warehouses and factories, jerry-building housing so unrelentingly ugly that it might even have offended Joe Stalin.

Into this fast-buck heaven have arrived many of the new-breed hustlers, and among them was a man named Alberto San Pedro. Born in Havana in 1950, Alberto was four years old when his parents brought him to Miami. In recent years, he called himself a developer, and hosted extravagant parties each December 17 in honor of his favorite saint, the wonderful San Lazarus, who is not recognized by the Catholic Church anymore but remains big among Cubans. The last two of these $50,000 parties were held at the posh Doral Hotel in Miami Beach, and among the guests were Hialeah mayor Raul Martinez, Representative Claude Pepper, Miami Beach mayor Alex Daoud, WSVN-Channel 7 weekend anchor and reporter Rick Sanchez, Miami police major Jack Sullivan, ordinary cops, political fundraisers, lawyers, various right-wing bravos, and a load of judges. San Pedro brought along a nine-foot statue of the saint, dressed himself in a tuxedo, was flanked by bodyguards, and posed with the assembled celebrities.

San Pedro's father was a delegate to the 1984 Republican National Convention, and Alberto San Pedro was cleared for an audience with Ronald Reagan in Tampa in 1985. The son told all inquisitors that in addition to his activities as a developer, he was also a bookkeeper and salesman for his father's business, the San Lazaro Racing Stables at Calder Race Track. These occupations obviously rewarded him handsomely: according to Jeff Leen of the *Miami Herald,* Alberto San Pedro's six-bedroom mansion in Hialeah has eight and a half bathrooms and bulletproof windows.

The windows should have been the tipoff that there was more to Alberto San Pedro than his own résumé might indicate. He was, in fact, leading a far more interesting life than the one he presented to the public and seems to have studied for it with the same respect for basic texts that a seminarian would reserve for Thomas à Kempis. Leen, whose wonderfully detailed profile of Alberto for the *Herald* is the basis of many of these notes, also learned that Alberto kept a hardcover copy of *The Godfather* in the bathroom closest to his bedroom and a biography of Al Capone behind the desk in his office. It was in that same office that police set up a hidden microphone and learned many things about Alberto's other, perhaps more characteristic, life. As we learned from listening to the Watergate tapes, the bulk of a hoodlum's day is consumed by bullshitting with other hoodlums, and the San Pedro tapes — recorded in thousands of pages of transcripts — are a fascinating journey into the true underbelly of life in a corrupt town.

For these tapes, the police say, show that Alberto San Pedro was a major corrupter, a fixer, the classic cacique who works behind the scenes to secure power and wealth and enforces his presumed right to both with fear and violence. Among the institutions he is accused of corrupting is the Hialeah police department. It was a task he had trained for all of his life.

We don't know if Alberto San Pedro's reading of Mario Puzo moved him to see his life as a novel, but if so, the early chapters followed the traditional pattern. In junior high school he learned that force can be rewarded. According to a Florida Parole and Probation Commission case analysis quoted by Leen, "Subject began extortion in the 9th and 10th grades, making the other students do his homework or work projects."

By age 20, San Pedro, like so many other characters in this squalid story, was into weight lifting. And he began to take karate lessons from a Hialeah cop named Leo Thalassites. On the tapes, San Pedro says that he spent much of his youth beating up people for 50 or a hundred bucks ("that's how I made my money"). By the time he was 21, his yellow sheet was lengthening: three arrests for aggravated assault, one for resisting a police officer, two for assault and battery, another for buying and possessing stolen property. In 1970, police reports said, after being flattened by a hard block in a sandlot football game, an enraged San Pedro stabbed the blocker, then went to his car, took out a machine gun, and sprayed the field. In all of these cases, he was either acquitted or had the charges dismissed. He wasn't properly nailed by the law until 1971, when he took part in a drug rip-off and discovered that the subjects of his attention were undercover cops. He was convicted of conspiracy to commit murder and given three years probation.

Even this didn't convince San Pedro to go into a quieter line of work. In 1972, he was in trouble again, charged with armed robbery and assault with the intent to commit murder. His victim this time was a hooker's john. There are clearly marked roads to heaven. But the customer wouldn't testify and San Pedro got off. Three years later, he almost got off the earth when a hit man shot him five times. San Pedro survived. The hit man disappeared. And San Pedro began to give his annual thanks to Saint Lazarus. He also began to think more about the style of his life and the reach of his ambitions. On a July 26, 1985, tape, he says:

"I'm not a doper. I dedicate myself to my business. I was fucking broke when I was a kid and I got the shit beat out of me by the cops and by . . . the whole group. That's what made me think there's only one way to get around in life here. That's politics and money."

San Pedro was correct; the grand old American combination of politics and money is certainly not unique to south Florida. But there was something else going on in Hialeah. By last year, the police chief was a man named Cecil ("Whitey") Seay, whose earlier career didn't seem to shape him for extraordinary moral leadership. In 1970 he was accused by a drug dealer of trying to cut himself into a $150,000 marijuana smuggling plot (no charges were filed); he was indicted in 1971 after a Dade County grand jury investigation demanded by 70 Hialeah officers who said that nine officers, including Seay, didn't meet ethical standards (he was accused of thwarting a burglary investigation, but when the chief witness against him changed his story the charges were dropped); in 1973, a teenage girl appeared before the city's personnel board and claimed that Seay had forced his attentions upon her (no investigation was made). At the hearings that led to his choice as chief, Seay said: "Those guys who have a clean record have never done anything."

One of Seay's most important officers was San Pedro's old karate instructor and still his good friend, Leo Thalassites. He was now a sergeant. Leo suddenly found himself in the newspapers on January 30 when he threatened to kill two detectives named Eddie Preston and Tom Nevins. He made this threat in the lobby of the Hialeah City Hall in front of three other officers. Preston and Nevins were in the intelligence section of Hialeah's police department, and Thalassites accused them of sending anonymous letters to various police organizations and the media accusing Leo and some other Hialeah veterans of corruption. Although the two cops denied this, Chief Seay and Mayor Martinez backed Thalassites. One fine morning, the two detectives found the locks on their office changed, with their personal possessions and pending cases still inside. They were then shifted to other jobs, one washing police cars, the other pounding a beat. Hialeah's intelligence section was disbanded.

But the story didn't end there.

The Metro-Dade police were already looking hard at Alberto San Pedro. An undercover agent, posing as a corrupt cop, had ingratiated himself with San Pedro and had a series of meetings and telephone conversations with the man. All were recorded. More than anything else, San Pedro told detective Nelson Perry, he wanted to get rid of the rest of the records of his youth so that he could obtain a full pardon for his youthful crimes and become a U.S. citizen. He planned to do this, he said, with money.

"Everybody's got a friend and everybody needs friends," he said on an August 30, 1985, tape. "Everybody likes to be loved and everybody wants to be loved. Money, everybody loves money. Everybody likes to spend it. . . . And unfortunately, politicians are the worst motherfuckers in the world. . . . They only look at one thing, how much can I steal as long as I'm there."

Among the records that San Pedro wanted destroyed were accounts of his dealing with a middle-level Gambino family hoodlum named Joseph Paterno. Police recorded conversations in April 1985 indicating that Paterno tried to buy from San Pedro two silencer-equipped guns for use in the killing of two of his own cousins in New Jersey. San Pedro didn't refuse; his price — $4000 for each piece — was simply too high for Paterno's budget, according to Arthur Nehrbass, commander of Dade's Organized Crime Bureau. Almost immediately after this conversation, Paterno was arrested.

The cops took a closer look at San Pedro. In June, he offered $5000 to a police informant to get the Paterno transcripts and tapes. The cops then sent their undercover man to San Pedro (setting up the meeting through San Pedro's bodyguard) and listened to his various offers, and accepted sums ranging from $2000 to $11,000. Over a period of time, the cops fed San Pedro a combination of real and fictitious police material, and listened to his bragging, his philosophy, and his schemes. Those schemes were not empty; San Pedro was the real thing. They knew, for example, from the Hialeah records chief, Lieutenant Thomas Bardon, that San Pedro's file had disappeared three times from that city's police department. A narcotics intelligence file on San Pedro also disappeared. And his records were missing from the Dade Circuit Court clerk's office and the State Attorney's office. San Pedro was clearly attempting to create a new personal history through elimination.

Nelson Perry, who was president of the Police Benevolent Association (which began representing Hialeah cops in September 1985), says he started smelling the rot in Hialeah when he was approached by a 350-pound political press agent and community newspaperman named Don Dugan (later indicted in a separate case for being the bagman in a bribery case in Opa Locka). Dugan told Perry that he could earn "a personal profit" if he stayed out of Hialeah police affairs. This shocked Perry, who told his superiors of this; they assigned him to pose as a corrupt cop. He soon met San Pedro for the first time at the Treetop Restaurant in the Miami Springs Holiday Inn. They continued to meet for weeks. At two of Perry's meetings with San Pedro, a Hialeah cop was also present. It was Sergeant Thalassites.

When police overheard San Pedro in February talking about killing two men who owed him a total of $4000, and conspiring to sell a kilo of cocaine, they decided to move. On February 13, San Pedro was arrested on bribery charges, and rearrested March 2 for murder, conspiracy, and cocaine trafficking. Hialeah erupted. Within weeks, Chief Seay resigned. Thalassites went on paid leave. Some of the tapes were released, littered with the names of various politicians who were claimed by San Pedro as friends or property. TV reporter Rick Sanchez was heard discussing an exchange of favors with San Pedro; good old Alberto had found a job in Panama for Sanchez's uncle; Sanchez, who served as a non-voting adviser to the board of the First American Bank & Trust, got a share of San Pedro's business for the bank. (What a reporter was doing serving on the board of a bank — and sucking after customers on behalf of that bank — nobody could answer; Sanchez also was granted a paid leave but his superiors at the TV station said they saw nothing wrong with his connection to the bank. The ethics of Miami strike again.) It was then remembered that Sanchez had emceed the 1984 San Lazarus party and had led the group in prayer. Someone else noticed that Hialeah had a 29.6 per cent increase in crime during 1985 and the joke was that this was "not including cops."

Then in mid-March, the *Herald* tossed a few more bombs into the discussion.

Reporters Leen and Sydney P. Freedberg discovered that in 1979, Florida's former attorney general, Robert Shevin, and the state's esteemed Congressman Claude Pepper had written letters to the Florida parole board extolling San Pedro's character. They now claimed that they didn't really know San Pedro, couldn't remember him; since their letters claimed that they did in fact know San Pedro either the letters or the statements were lies. The former attorney general certainly should have known something about San Pedro. His law partner, a Democratic fund-raiser and adviser to Governor Bob Graham named Ronald Book, represented San Pedro during his 1983 application for a full pardon. Pepper and Shevin spluttered, suffered from amnesia, hung up the phones.

Even more bizarre was the story of San Pedro's access to Governor Graham himself. Last December, when there were cops all over Hialeah investigating San Pedro, a woman named Marcia Ludwig emerged to support San Pedro's application for a full pardon. Marcia Ludwig was once Marcia Valibus and in 1957 she was queen of the Orange Bowl; in Miami there is always an element of the surreal. Later Marcia Valibus was a runner-up in the Miss Universe contest and had a screen test at Paramount Studios. She was also a classmate of Adele Graham, the governor's wife, and over the years they had remained friends. For more than a decade, the *Herald* said, Marcia Ludwig has been an intimate friend of one Robert (Bobby) Erra, son of the late Pasquale (Patsy) Erra, who once worked for Vito Genovese. Marcia and Erra are often seen together, friends told the *Herald,* at the La Gorce Country Club. More important, there are pages of conversations between Erra and San Pedro on the various tapes. On December 11, Ludwig sent a hand-written note to her friend, the governor's wife:

"Dear Adele, This is a note for Bob's mirror. A good friend of mine — Alberto San Pedro — has a case coming before Bob and his Cabinet on Dec. 18 . . . I appreciate you calling my words to Bob's attention."

On December 19, Adele wrote back to Marcia: "I placed the note on Bob's mirror — so he's aware." This was the day after Graham presided over the hearing. During that session, he said: "Unfortunately, there continues to be this lingering question as to what might be in his background. I'm concerned that Mister San Pedro is sort of being cast under a shadow that he seems to be unable to extricate himself from and which shadow hasn't yet, or after four or five years, moved to the substance of some action. It has been a long time since the criminal offense for which he's requesting pardon was committed and he has an impressive statement of his community record." Graham "reluctantly" moved to continue the case, stating that the next time San Pedro's pardon was discussed, he would come to a decision. There is no indication that he checked with any of the cops; he certainly didn't give San Pedro a flat rejection. What the hell: when you're a kid in Hialeah it's only natural to fool around with machine guns. Still, Graham didn't say yes either. And his need to decide was made academic by San Pedro's February 13 arrest.

The honest cops in Hialeah had long despised San Pedro and to some extent feared him. He was the shadowy man, the fixer, called upon for help by arsonist, hoodlum, dealer. On the day he was arrested, someone placed a note on the police department's bulletin board. It said very simply: "The untouchable has been touched."

IV. OUT OF THE SWAMP

Obviously, every cop in southern Florida is not a crook. Most of the arrests have been made as a result of good tough police investigations along with continuing pressure from the *Miami Herald*. But it's unlikely that corruption will soon vanish, the drug dealers joining the dinosaurs in the rot of the swamp. They won't go away, and cops will continue to be corrupted because there is simply too much dirty money lying around. Cocaine will not soon be legalized: Americans won't soon surrender their national lust for some form of chemical nirvana.

But if you wonder what happens to some of these men who briefly and luridly occupy page-one headlines, consider recent events in North Bay Village, another suburb of Miami. In 1971, a cop named George Staphylaris was fired from the Miami force for allegedly encouraging a police informant to rob a department store. He appealed the firing, was reinstated with a six-month suspension, then resigned. Six years ago he joined the North Bay Village force. He was soon known to many kids as Officer George, ran the drug education program at Treasure Island Elementary School, often took kids on trips to the Everglades, and had prepared a children's seminar called "Just Say No To Drugs."

On the North Bay force, he met another former Miami cop named William David Risk. He too was once fired, for battering a prisoner with a nightstick. He too fought his firing, was reinstated, and resigned in 1979. Last year, he was North Bay Village's officer of the year, cited for his "superlative performance and dedication." He was also a weight lifter.

A third former Miami cop was on the North Bay force. This was Sergeant Fernando Gandon. He quit the Miami force in 1977 after being charged with aggravated battery. While interrogating a man on the street, the charges against him said, he shoved his pistol in the man's mouth, rattled it around and broke some teeth. Five years ago, he arrived at North Bay and was again given a badge and gun.

On February 27, all three men were arrested by the FBI for selling protection to men they believed to be drug dealers. A Mob guy named Stephen Nahay told FBI agents (posing as drug dealers) in a recorded conversation that if they were moving drugs they should see the three North Bay cops. "They'll help you out," Nahay said. "In other words, if you want to kill a guy there . . . you just tell them the guy and they'll kick him on to the coroner. . . ."

Clearly, redemption does not flourish under the southern sun. There are no second chances for such people, only the main chance. A good number of Miami cops have the integrity to resist the lure of narcodollars. But just as surely, others will plunge into the swamp and rise covered with the kind of slime that will never wash off. They are there now, driving Chevvies and longing for Porsches, dressed in baggy suits and lusting for Giorgio Armani, hearing preachments of denial, while drug dealers leave with the women, and the country at large throws roses to the greedy. They are men of the law but nobody in Miami would ever be surprised to see them leaving the sunshine in handcuffs. Their sweet decaying odor will not go away.

VILLAGE VOICE,
August 26, 1986

THE LAST MOB GUY

Late one night a few months ago, a man named John Gotti walked into a jammed Manhattan restaurant called Columbus. This is a New York hangout favored by actors, models, ballplayers, agents, reporters, and second-string hoodlums. On this night, the big corner table was filled by Steve van Zandt, most of the E Street Band, and some beautiful women. As usual, nobody paid any attention. Then Gotti walked in with two very large associates. The room hushed.

Impeccably dressed, his body thick and powerful, a diamond ring glittering on the pinkie of his left hand, his small eyes searching the room for friends or danger while a thin smile played on his face, Gotti was pure Mob. Not just a soldier. Not just some strong-arm boy who muscles people tardy with payments to the loan sharks. John Gotti was bigger than all of that. In fact, at this moment in the long, dark history of American organized crime, he was the Boss.

There was only one empty table, and Gotti and his friends were led there by the maître d'. As the gangsters sat down, the hum of conversation resumed. Gotti's eyes drifted to the corner table. The musicians were dressed with the calculated raffishness of rock 'n' rollers: headbands, bandannas, leather vests over bare skin, earrings, beards. Gotti called the maître d' over.

"Tell me something," he said, looking down at the corner table. "Who are these guys dressed like fuckin' *pirates?*" He was told about the E Street Band and how they were the musicians for the great Bruce Springsteen.

Gotti smiled.

"You see," he growled, "*everybody* wants to work for the Boss."

That was pure John Gotti: hip enough to know that Springsteen is called the Boss, sardonic enough to suggest that he considered the show-business title an act of hubris. Gotti, at forty-eight, was the first major Mob leader to have grown up with rock 'n' roll. But in the world he inhabited there was only one boss at a time, and on that evening in the big city, the time belonged to John Gotti. He was certainly making the most of it. Nobody since Al Capone had taken such sheer pleasure in the role and been embraced so ecstatically by the media and the public.

One night last spring, I came out of a restaurant in New York's Little Italy and saw a crowd gathered down the block. I went to see what was happening and found myself among a group of tourists, late-night diners, and neighborhood regulars. They started to cheer John Gotti, who had just left the Ravenite Social Club, as if he were a hero. In a demented way, he was. Gotti smiled, climbed into a Lincoln, and was driven away. It is impossible to imagine Meyer Lansky, Frank Costello, or Carlo Gambino having that effect on people or appearing to welcome it so grandly.

Gotti clearly cherished the myth of the Mob, even in the years of its precipitous decline, and seemed to have shaped his public image to fit that myth. This is not surprising. John Gotti, after all, is an American — profoundly shaped by movies and television over the past thirty-five years. To his generation of hoodlums, *The Godfather* was a training film. In the way that Ronald Reagan drew on our nostalgia for the simple patriotic myths of old movies, Gotti had begun to draw upon a similar nostalgia for the clarity and romanticism of the gangster film. Even in the 1980s, nothing excites Americans more than the glamour of the outlaw, his existential drama, his willingness to risk all, even his life, to obtain power and riches. Image is everything these days, and when it can be reduced to a ten-second bite, the media embrace it and so does the public. Reagan derived much of his personal power from the fact that he looked the way Americans wanted a President to look. When Gotti appeared on the public stage, he looked like the Boss.

Here, at last, was a gangster who dressed like a gangster, down to the pinkie ring; the clothes were cut a little too sharply, the shoes almost too highly polished. His hands were carefully manicured, and when he was seen in public, his skin was so closely shaved it seemed glossy. The perfectly waved gray hair added a touch of Old World dignity. And more important, he had mastered the Walk. All stars have a great walk; think of the way John Wayne walked, or Cary Grant. I saw Gotti stroll into a courthouse one morning, dressed in a white raincoat, engulfed by lawyers, while the cameras recorded every detail. Still photos caught the amused, almost ironic smile, and the chilly foreboding in his eyes, acknowledging that Gotti might lose a Mob primary some bloody evening while reaching for the pepper. But only the video cameras captured the Walk: the back straight, the hips rolling, the feet moving in a rhythm that was at once swaggering and delicate, defying the dark knowledge that lived in his eyes. When other kids in Franklin K. Lane High School in Brooklyn were trying to master algebra, Gotti must have been working on the Walk.

"I don't know what he did bad," a black woman said of Gotti in another courthouse last year, "but he sure looks good to me."

Until December 16, 1985, not many Americans had ever heard of John Joseph Gotti. At 5:26 that evening, a neatly dressed seventy-year-old man named Paul Castellano arrived with a friend for an early dinner at Sparks Steak House on East Forty-sixth Street. Castellano looked like a businessman; he was in fact the boss of the Gambino family, and his companion, Thomas Bilotti, was an underboss. Neither man made it to the bar. Three gunmen suddenly appeared and blasted them into eternity. By midnight, those police scholars who major in the Mob were predicting that an obscure younger hoodlum from Howard Beach, Queens, would emerge as the new boss. A "good fella" named John Gotti. They were right.

The next day, Gotti's name and face were all over the newspapers and local television news shows. The rough sketch of his personal story was burnished into the thrilling shape of tabloid legend. For Gotti was a throwback, as elemental as an ax.

The most frequently related tale was about the death of Gotti's son Frank and what happened later. One day in March 1980, twelve-year-old Frank was riding a minibike on the quiet bourgeois streets of Howard Beach. He was the middle child of two girls and three boys born to John and Victoria Gotti. As Frank darted out from behind a Dumpster, he was struck and killed by a car driven by a man named John Favara. On July 28, while John and Victoria Gotti vacationed in Florida, Favara walked out of the Castro Convertible plant where he worked and went to his car, parked in front of the Capitol Diner. Suddenly, a heavyset man walked over and clubbed him. Favara was thrown into a blue van and driven away, never to be seen again. His car also vanished. When Gotti returned from Florida and was visited by police, he said, "I don't know what happened. I am not sorry if something did happen. He killed my kid."

That story became central to the Gotti myth, because it was so direct, personal, dramatic, unforgiving; that is, it resembled a scene in a movie. In the years since then, witnesses against Gotti in other cases forgot what they once saw; others disappeared; prospective jurors declined the privilege of judging him; he has developed an *aura*. He did what gangsters were supposed to do: he inspired *fear* — simple, runny fear. Nobody wanted him as an enemy. The Feds and the police watched his movements; they developed stool pigeons to report on his activities; they placed bugs in and around the Bergin Hunt & Fish Club in Ozone Park, a storefront private club that Gotti used as his personal Sierra Maestra. They could not nail him.

And a peculiar thing seemed to be happening. When Gotti took power, the Mob was in terrible shape, as bad off as Chrysler was before the advent of Lee Iacocca. Cubans and Colombians totally dominated the multibillion-dollar cocaine business. The old days, when such as Lansky and Costello owned county leaders, judges, and politicians, were long gone.

By the early '70s it was becoming clear that the Mob had no bench. The hoodlums who remained in the rackets were generally dim-brained *gavones,* reduced to hijacking, loan-sharking, stealing cars, or peddling heroin. Some were even *using* the drugs they were supposed to be peddling, something the older generation never permitted, because a junkie would rat on his own mother. At the same time, the federal government was attacking the Mob with a variety of sophisticated electronic techniques, and with the RICO statutes.

Then along came Gotti, with a message of inspiration and hope. It was morning in Mob America. In private, Gotti was apparently a shrewd and persuasive politician. In the first months after accepting what Adlai Stevenson called the "bitter cup," he moved among the various Mob families, offering conciliation, peace, and revival. The tattered legions of the Mob knew he was willing and able to use lethal force to exert discipline; he wanted to show them that he could also think (he claimed to have scored 140 on an IQ test in prison) and that he had a vision of the future.

At one point, the Feds managed to place a bug in the doorway of the Nice 'n' EZ Auto School, down the block from the Bergin Hunt & Fish Club. And in January 1986, while Gotti was consolidating his power, they heard him tell another wise guy:

"The law's gonna be tough with us, okay, if they don't put us away. If they don't put us away, for one year or two — that's all we need. But if I can get a year run without being interrupted: get a year — gonna put this thing together where they could never break it, never destroy it. Even if we die, be a good thing."

The other wise guy said: "It's a hell of a legacy to leave."

"Well, you know why it would be," Gotti answered. "Ah — because it would be *right*. Maybe after thirty years it would deteriorate, but it would take that long to fuckin' succumb, you know...." Then, like De Gaulle or Mao, he quoted a third party in reference to himself. One of the men he'd asked to join the grand new coalition of the Mob, its version of the Popular Front, had said to Gotti: "You were our last hope...."

The last hope was soon part of the texture of the popular imagination. The tabloids labeled him the Dapper Don. He was followed by TV crews. He starred in the gossip columns. But mobologists were also talking about his troubles. Like most Americans, the major problems he had were within his own family. His brother, Gene, was convicted of peddling heroin at a time when the Boss was telling his infantry to get out of the smack racket. Then his son Little John got in trouble. Last winter, the young man and some friends beat up a man in a diner in the neighborhood where Gotti lives. The guy turned out to be a cop. Gotti apparently ordered the kid to do his drinking out of the neighborhood. So Little John, who dresses like his father right down to the pinkie ring, went to the next county. There he and his friends got into a fight in a club and punched out a woman.

"The old wise guys don't like this stuff," one mobologist told me. "There's two laws: one for everybody, one for John's relatives. And who could imagine Frank Costello punching out a woman?"

The grumblings about the Boss were not, however, in evidence at the twentieth annual Fourth of July block party thrown by Gotti's Bergin Hunt & Fish Club this year. Like any decent American politician, Gotti had long ago learned the importance of securing a local base; every year since 1969 his club had donated hamburgers, sausages, and fireworks to celebrate the birth of the country that has allowed the club's members such affluent and leisurely lives. In return, the locals spoke of Gotti with a certain affection. "If he does bad things," one said, "he doesn't do them around here." But great fame, alas, also brings great scrutiny. Under pressure from editorial writers, the cops told Gotti he could cook sausage but he couldn't blow up firecrackers. Ah, fame: the two-edged sword.

Gotti threw the party anyway. As reporters, cops, and kids looked on, homemade barbecues were set up in the street (they were made from split fifty-five-gallon drums, of the sort sometimes used for disposing of stool pigeons). A Mister Softee truck arrived early and stayed late; an inflated rubber Kiddie Kastle filled 101st Avenue, and one corner was occupied by a ride called Ernie's King Kong. Gotti himself slipped quietly into the club in the afternoon; on the street, orders were barked by Little John, dressed in a sleeveless undershirt, trim Guido haircut, Bermuda shorts.

As daylight faded, the crowd grew to about four thousand. And the assembled jackals of the press wondered about only one matter: Would the Boss defy the law and set off fireworks? Some of Gotti's neighbors complained about the injustice of life under the embattled American flag. "It ain't fair," said one. "They're blowing up firecrackers all over the city and we can't do it here, because the newspapers say all those rotten things about John."

After a while, as the TV lights brightened the street, a group of young men started chanting, "We want the Boss!" But members of the wise-guy directorate whispered to them, and the chant became "We want John!" and then was transformed once more into "We want the works!" And then suddenly, from the rooftop of the building housing the Our Friends Social Club (a branch of the Bergin), the sky exploded with fireworks. The cops moved to seal off the building, and from another direction, a gigantic volley went off on the rooftop of Ozone Electric Inc. The crowd roared. The rockets now seemed to come from everywhere: rooftops and backyards and a railroad trestle down the block, spiraling through the summer night. The crowd was delirious with triumph and defiance. The cops looked timid in the face of . . . the *aura*.

Then the door of the Bergin Hunt & Fish Club opened. Inside, where the Italian flag was hung on the wall and another door led to the inner sanctum where his dead son's picture is on the wall, John Gotti could be seen laughing. He came to the door, engulfed by ten sides of Mob beef, and stood on the doorstep. The Boss then nodded at the cheers of the exultant populace, but he did not smile. He just stood there, solemn and dignified, staring up at the rockets' red glare. John Gotti, American.

ESQUIRE,
October 1989

ON THE RUN

t was almost midnight. The girl on the beach had a thick, chunky body encased in denim shorts and a dark blue T-shirt. There was a man in front of her, kissing her violently, and another man behind her, running his hands over her body. Above them, the people on the pier at the foot of Main Street were watching, some of them smiling, as the girl struggled. She pushed one of the men back and then darted away among the parked cars on the beach.

"Come back here, girl," one of the men shouted. He was wearing a pair of dirty white jeans, his hair tied back in a ponytail. The thick little girl looked to her left and saw the signs of Big Daddy's Lounge, the Saxony Motel and The Seahorse; she saw the lights of the Skylift and the Skyneedle. She dashed between the parked cars to her right, then in front of the slow-moving cars that are allowed to drive on the beach here, then she ran into the surf. The two men were behind her, running hard. The people on the pier just watched.

The two men caught her in the surf. One of them pulled her hair back while the other fondled her. The traffic moved along slowly.

At one end of the pier was a place called The Pit Stop, a dark little saloon, with pinball machines, aging hippies nursing drinks, the Rolling Stones singing "Miss You" on the jukebox. I went down there to find a cop. I saw a fat special standing on the steps to the right of the saloon.

"Hey," I said, "you got a little girl in trouble down on that beach."

"There's lots of little girls in trouble down on that beach," he said, walking away.

When I got back to the pier, the girl was running under the dance hall that was halfway to the end of the pier. I leaned out over the edge of the Solarcaine sign and saw the two men tumble her into the surf.

The chunky little girl squealed and laughed as one of the men yanked at her T-shirt. Then she got up, soaking, and walked slowly away with them, like a prisoner.

Late the next afternoon, I saw her sitting alone at a yellow table in front of McDonald's, a block behind the boardwalk. Her dark brown hair was dirty and matted and there were grease stains on her bare feet. She was wearing the same clothes she had on the night before. Her skin looked coarse in the late afternoon sun. She was tearing greedily at a Big Mac, and I went over and sat down across from her. She was about 16.

"How'd you make out last night?" I said.

Her eyes were suddenly jittery and scared and she stopped chewing.

"I'm not a cop," I said. "I just wondered how you got through the night alive."

"I'm here, ain't I?" she said. She had a hoarse, small, girl's voice.

"How'd you get here?" I said.

Her eyes became icy nuggets. "I don't know you, Mister. I don't have to say nuthin' to you."

"You're right," I said, and went into the main room of the Mc-Donald's and ordered a milk shake. I paid for it and went outside and sat at another table. Pick-up trucks lumbered down the street, waiting at the light to turn on Main Street and go out to the beach.

Two 45-year-old hippies with scoured eyes walked into McDonald's, shirtless and shoeless, and looked blankly at the chunky girl. She had finished eating, and was sipping a soda. One of them went inside and the other stared at her. She got up and came over to sit across from me.

"You got a dollar?" she said.

"Sure," I said, and gave her a dollar. The second hippie went inside. "What's your name?"

"Kathy."

"Where you from, Kathy?"

"Up North. Albany, N.Y. You're not a cop?"

"Do I look like a cop?" I said, laughing. She smiled then, and said, "Yeah."

"Well, I'm not. I'm a reporter." I showed her a press card. She looked at the picture on the card and then at me, and handed it back. It was starting to get dark now and I asked her how she'd come to Daytona Beach.

"I ran away last May," she said. "I couldn't take them no more. I couldn't take my mother, always naggin', always on me, you know?

So I just took off one night, me and a girlfriend. She quit on me in New York City and went home, but I kept goin'."

Somewhere in New Jersey, she was picked up by a truck driver. They went all the way to Virginia together.

"I thought he was a nice guy," she said. "He was doin' a lot of pills, reds and stuff, and he'd sing the songs right along with the radio, and he knew every word. We come to some place, a truck stop they call it. They had a separate restaurant, just for truck drivers. He gave me some pills and I took them. I didn't care, and we drank some beer."

They stayed there all night, and the driver passed her around to five other drivers.

"I didn't mind," she said flatly. "It was better than Albany. But when I woke up in the morning in the woods beside that place, they were all gone, every last one of them. I left my shoes in one of the trucks, and I only had $4. So I had to hitchhike. Some old farmer picked me up. He wanted to take me someplace, but he was so old, man. I said no, and he got mad and left me out on the road in the middle of the night."

It took her six days to reach Jacksonville. She stayed there for a while, living on the beach. There were a lot of sailors in town, she said, and they liked her. "Nobody liked me in Albany," she said. "They used to laugh, I was too fat." One of the sailors took her to Daytona on the Fourth of July weekend, then left without her. She had been here ever since.

"It's nice here," she said. "The dudes here are nice."

A few more beach rats arrived, and she seemed nervous.

"I gotta go," she said. "There's a guy over there I don't wanna talk to."

Her eyes were bright with panic. She got up quickly, and we walked together back to the boardwalk. An enormous fat man in green shorts lay on a bench, his hair cut short, his eyes pinwheeling, fanning himself with a pocket mirror.

It was dark now. Two scrawny men with junkie eyes stood in front of Lacey's Beachware, watching the evening's arrivals from the small towns of Florida and Georgia.

"Why don't you go home, Kathy?" I said.

"I don't ever want to go home," she said, her voice rising. "I don't want to go home ever again."

She ran across the boardwalk, down the steps to the powdery

sand, rushing toward the lights of the passing cars, and the dark Atlantic beyond. I stayed two more days, but I didn't see her again.

NEW YORK TIMES SYNDICATED SALES CORP.,
September 8, 1978

CRACK AND THE BOX

One sad rainy morning last winter, I talked to a woman who was addicted to crack cocaine. She was twenty-two, stiletto-thin, with eyes as old as tombs. She was living in two rooms in a welfare hotel with her children, who were two, three, and five years of age. Her story was the usual tangle of human woe: early pregnancy, dropping out of school, vanished men, smack and then crack, tricks with johns in parked cars to pay for the dope. I asked her why she did drugs. She shrugged in an empty way and couldn't really answer beyond "makes me feel good." While we talked and she told her tale of squalor, the children ignored us. They were watching television.

Walking back to my office in the rain, I brooded about the woman, her zombielike children, and my own callous indifference. I'd heard so many versions of the same story that I almost never wrote them anymore; the sons of similar women, glimpsed a dozen years ago, are now in Dannemora or Soledad or Joliet; in a hundred cities, their daughters are moving into the same loveless rooms. As I walked, a series of homeless men approached me for change, most of them junkies. Others sat in doorways, staring at nothing. They were additional casualties of our time of plague, demoralized reminders that although this country holds only 2 percent of the world's population, it consumes 65 percent of the world's supply of hard drugs.

Why, for God's sake? Why do so many millions of Americans of all ages, races, and classes choose to spend all or part of their lives stupefied? I've talked to hundreds of addicts over the years; some were my friends. But none could give sensible answers. They stutter about the pain of the world, about despair or boredom, the urgent need for magic or pleasure in a society empty of both. But then they just shrug. Americans have the money to buy drugs; the supply is plentiful. But almost nobody in power asks, *Why?* Least of all, George Bush and his drug warriors.

William Bennett talks vaguely about the heritage of '60s permissiveness, the collapse of Traditional Values, and all that. But he and Bush offer the traditional American excuse: It Is Somebody Else's Fault. This posture set the stage for the self-righteous invasion of Panama; Bush even accused Manuel Noriega of "poisoning our children." But he never asked *why* so many Americans demand the poison.

And then, on that rainy morning in New York, I saw another one of those ragged men staring out at the rain from a doorway. I suddenly remembered the inert postures of the children in that welfare hotel, and I thought: *television.*

Ah, no, I muttered to myself: too simple. Something as complicated as drug addiction can't be blamed on television. Come on. . . . But I remembered all those desperate places I'd visited as a reporter, where there were no books and a TV set was always playing and the older kids had gone off somewhere to shoot smack, except for the kid who was at the mortuary in a coffin. I also remembered when I was a boy in the '40s and early '50s, and drugs were a minor sideshow, a kind of dark little rumor. And there was one major difference between that time and this: television.

We had unemployment then; illiteracy, poor living conditions, racism, governmental stupidity, a gap between rich and poor. We didn't have the all-consuming presence of television in our lives. Now two generations of Americans have grown up with television from their earliest moments of consciousness. Those same American generations are afflicted by the pox of drug addiction.

Only thirty-five years ago, drug addiction was not a major problem in this country. Yes: There were drug addicts. We had some at the end of the nineteenth century, too, hooked on the cocaine in patent medicines. During the placid '50s, Commissioner Harry Anslinger pumped up the budget of the old Bureau of Narcotics with fantasies of reefer madness. Heroin was sold and used in most major American cities, while the bebop generation of jazz musicians got jammed up with horse.

But until the early '60s, narcotics were still marginal to American life; they weren't the $120-billion market they make up today. If anything, those years have an eerie innocence. In 1955 there were 31,700,000 TV sets in use in the country (the number is now past 184 million). But the majority of the audience had grown up without the dazzling new medium. They embraced it, were diverted by it, perhaps even loved it, but they weren't *formed* by it. That year, the New York police made a mere 1,234 felony drug arrests; in 1988 it was 43,901. They confiscated ninety-seven *ounces* of cocaine for the entire year; last year it was hundreds of pounds. During each year of the '50s in New York, there were only about a hundred narcotics-related deaths. But by the end of the '60s, when the first generation of children *formed* by television had come to maturity (and thus to the marketplace), the number of such deaths had risen to 1,200. The same phenomenon was true in every major American city.

In the last Nielsen survey of American viewers, the average family was watching television seven hours a day. This has never happened before in history. No people has ever been entertained for seven hours a *day*. The Elizabethans didn't go to the theater seven hours a day. The pre-TV generation did not go to the movies seven hours a day. Common sense tells us that this all-pervasive diet of instant imagery, sustained now for forty years, must have changed us in profound ways.

Television, like drugs, dominates the lives of its addicts. And though some lonely Americans leave their sets on without watching them, using them as electronic companions, television usually absorbs its viewers the way drugs absorb their users. Viewers can't work or play while watching television; they can't read; they can't be out on the streets, falling in love with the wrong people, learning how to quarrel and compromise with other human beings. In short, they are asocial. So are drug addicts.

One Michigan State University study in the early '80s offered a group of four- and five-year-olds the choice of giving up television or giving up their fathers. Fully one third said they would give up Daddy. Given a similar choice (between cocaine or heroin and father, mother, brother, sister, wife, husband, children, job), almost every stone junkie would do the same.

There are other disturbing similarities. Television itself is a consciousness-altering instrument. With the touch of a button, it takes you out of the "real" world in which you reside and can place you at a basketball game, the back alleys of Miami, the streets of Bucharest, or the cartoony living rooms of Sitcom Land. Each move from channel to channel alters mood, usually with music or a laugh track. On any given evening, you can laugh, be frightened, feel tension, thump with excitement. You can even tune in *MacNeil/Lehrer* and feel sober.

But none of these abrupt shifts in mood is *earned*. They are attained as easily as popping a pill. Getting news from television, for example, is simply not the same experience as reading it in a newspaper. Reading is *active*. The reader must decode little symbols called words, then create images or ideas and make them connect; at its most basic level, reading is an act of the imagination. But the television viewer doesn't go through that process. The words are spoken to him by Dan Rather or Tom Brokaw or Peter Jennings. There isn't much decoding to do when watching television, no time to think or ponder before the next set of images and spoken words appears to displace the present one. The reader, being active, works at his or her own pace; the viewer, being passive, proceeds at a pace determined by the show. Except at the highest levels, television never demands that its audience take part in an act of imagination. Reading always does.

In short, television works on the same imaginative and intellectual level as psychoactive drugs. If prolonged television viewing makes the young passive (dozens of studies indicate that it does), then moving to drugs has a certain coherence. Drugs provide an unearned high (in contrast to the earned rush that comes from a feat accomplished, a human breakthrough earned by sweat or thought or love).

And because the television addict and the drug addict are alienated from the hard and scary world, they also feel they make no difference in its complicated events. For the junkie, the world is reduced to him and the needle, pipe, or vial; the self is absolutely isolated, with no desire for choice. The television addict lives the same way. Many Americans who fail to vote in presidential elections must believe they have no more control over such a choice than they do over the casting of *L.A. Law*.

The drug plague also coincides with the unspoken assumption of most television shows: Life should be *easy*. The most complicated events are summarized on TV news in a minute or less. Cops confront murder, chase the criminals, and bring them to justice (usually violently) within an hour. In commercials, you drink the right beer and you get the girl. *Easy!* So why should real life be a grind? Why should any American have to spend years mastering a skill or a craft, or work eight hours a day at an unpleasant job, or endure the compromises and crises of marriage? Nobody *works* on television (except cops, doctors, and lawyers). Love stories on television are about falling in love or breaking up; the long, steady growth of a marriage — its essential *dailiness* — is seldom explored, except as comedy. Life on television is almost always simple: good guys and bad, nice girls and whores, smart guys and dumb. And if life in the real world isn't that simple, well, hey, man, have some dope, man, be happy, feel good.

The doper always whines about how he *feels;* drugs are used to enhance his feelings or obliterate them, and in this the doper is very American. No other people on earth spend so much time talking about their feelings; hundreds of thousands go to shrinks, they buy self-help books by the millions, they pour out intimate confessions to virtual strangers in bars or discos. Our political campaigns are about emotional issues now, stated in the simplicities of adolescence. Even alleged statesmen can start a sentence, "I feel that the Sandinistas should . . ." when they once might have said, "I *think*. . . ." I'm convinced that this exaltation of cheap emotions over logic and reason is one by-product of hundreds of thousands of hours of television.

Most Americans under the age of fifty have now spent their lives absorbing television; that is, they've had the structures of drama pounded into them. Drama is always about conflict. So news shows, politics, and advertising are now all shaped by those structures. Nobody will pay attention to anything as complicated as the part played by Third World debt in the expanding production of cocaine; it's much easier to focus on Manuel Noriega, a character right out of *Miami Vice,* and believe that even in real life there's a Mister Big.

What is to be done? Television is certainly not going away, but its addictive qualities can be controlled. It's a lot easier to "just say no" to television than to heroin or crack. As a beginning, parents must take immediate control of the sets, teaching children to watch specific television *programs,* not "television," to get out of the house and play with other kids. Elementary and high schools must begin teaching television as a subject, the way literature is taught, showing children how shows are made, how to distinguish between the true and the false, how to recognize cheap emotional manipulation. All Americans should spend more time reading. And thinking.

For years, the defenders of television have argued that the networks are only giving the people what they want. That might be true. But so is the Medellín cartel.

ESQUIRE,
May 1990

FACING UP TO DRUGS

Hard drugs are now the scariest fact of New York life. They have spread genuine fear among ordinary citizens. They have stained every neighborhood in every borough, respecting no boundaries of class or color or geography. They have destroyed marriages, corrupted cops and banks, diminished productivity, fed the wild spiral of rents and condominium prices, overwhelmed the public hospitals, and filled the prisons to bursting.

The price of the drug scourge increases by the day. Hard drugs have injured thousands of families, some named Zaccaro and Kennedy, many others less well known. They have ruined uncountable numbers of careers and distorted others. Last year, when Dwight Gooden was sent off to the Smithers clinic, hard drugs almost certainly cost the Mets a championship. Gooden's friend, the brilliant pitcher Floyd Youmans of the Montreal Expos, learned no lesson from this; he was recently suspended indefinitely after once more failing a drug test. But Gooden and Youmans are not isolated cases, young men ensnared by the life-style of the poor neighborhoods of Tampa. Hard drugs have damaged the lives of pitcher Steve Howe, prizefighter Aaron Pryor, and football players Mercury Morris, Hollywood Henderson, and Don Reese, to mention only a few. Many other talented Americans, with no excuses to make about poverty or environment, have been hurt by hard drugs. And they cost Len Bias, Janis Joplin, Jimi Hendrix, Jim Morrison, and John Belushi their lives.

These terrible examples seem to make no difference; for the druggies, there are no cautionary tales. All over New York today, thousands of people are playing with drugs as if nothing will happen to *them.* And in this dense and dangerous city, such a taste for folly usually results in corpses.

New York, of course, is not unique. With the drug plague spreading all over the United States, the Feds now estimate that the country's cocaine-user population is at 5.8 million. These new druggies include prep-school students, bankers, policemen, railroad workers, pilots, factory hands, stockbrokers, journalists, and — with the arrival of crack — vast numbers of the urban poor. According to the National Institute on Drug Abuse, the average age of first-time drug-users in the United States is now thirteen.

The drug trade is one of the most successful of all multinational capitalist enterprises, brilliantly functioning on the ancient rules of supply and demand. The demand is insatiable, the supply apparently limitless. In a business estimated by the president's South Florida Task Force to gross more than $100 billion a year, there are fortunes, large and small, to be made. And the art of the drug deal always contains the gun. As the authority of the old mob faded in the seventies (with the breakup of the Istanbul-Marseilles-New York pipeline), new bad guys moved in: Cubans and Colombians first; then, as the cocaine business flourished, Bolivians and Dominicans. Israeli hoodlums out of Brighton Beach took a big hunk of the heroin trade. And 30 to 40 Jamaican "posses" began operating in the United States, starting with marijuana and hashish, then moving hard into the cocaine trade. The Shower Posse works out of the Bronx, the Spangler Posse in Brooklyn, the Dunkirk Boys in Harlem. Experts say the posses killed about 350 people last year, and the number could be much higher (more than 200 homicides here last year involved Jamaicans). Now the word on the street is that the Pakistanis are moving into town, with an endless supply of heroin from home.

But the advent of crack has led to the true decentralization of the drug trade. The old days of iron control by the Gambino or Bonanno families are clearly over. Small groups of violent entrepreneurs now run the trade in individual housing projects, on specific streets, in the vicinity of valued high schools. Men have been killed in disputes over control of a single street corner. Such drug gangs as the Vigilantes in Harlem, the Wild Bunch in Bed-Stuy, and the Valley Boys in the northeast Bronx are young and deadly. And unless something is done, they are here to stay.

They all have guns, including automatic weapons, and they have a gift for slaughter that makes some people nostalgic for the old Mafia. Nearly every morning, the newspapers carry fresh bulletins from the drug wars, full of multiple homicides and the killing of women and children. The old hoodlums were sinister bums who often killed one another, but they had some respect for the innocence of children. Not this set. The first indication that the rules of the game had changed dawned on us in 1982. In February of that year, on the Grand Central Parkway, the eighteen-month-old daughter and the four-month-old son of a Colombian drug-dealer were destroyed by shotgun blasts and automatic weapons, after their parents had been blown away. One Dominican dealer was forced to watch the disembowelment of his wife before being shotgunned to death. In Jackson Heights, according to New York *Newsday,* the favored method of execution is now the "Colombian necktie": The throat is cut and the tongue pulled through the slit to hang down upon the chest. The drug gangs are not misunderstood little boys. Their violence is at once specific and general: When they get rid of a suspected informer, they send chilling lessons to many others. Yet most of us read about their mayhem as if it were taking place in some barbarous and distant country and not the city that also contains the Metropolitan Museum.

It isn't as if these people are simply breaking the law; in some places, the law doesn't even exist. Whole neighborhoods in Brooklyn and Queens have been abandoned to the rule of the men with the Uzis, the MAC-10s, and the 9-mm. pistols. When police officer Edward Byrne was stationed outside the South Jamaica home of a witness in a drug case, the bad guys just walked up and killed him. When police officer George Scheu started crusading last year against drug-dealers in his Flushing neighborhood, he was shot down and killed outside his home. These actions remind us of the criminal anarchy in Colombia, where scores of police officers, judges, and public officials (including the minister of justice) have been assassinated by the drug caudillos. The new drug gangs enforce their power with violence, demonstrating that they can successfully murder witnesses and cops who might get in the way. When the first prosecutor is killed, there may be outrage in New York, but there will be no surprise.

Officers of the law are not the only casualties. Every weekend, discos erupt in gunfire as drug gangs fight over money or women or the ambiguous intentions of a smile. Every other week, innocent bystanders are shot down, provided a day of tabloid mourning, swiftly forgotten.

These killers are servicing a huge number of New Yorkers. The population of the stupefied can no longer be accurately counted. It is estimated that New York heroin addicts number about 200,000, or ten full-strength army divisions. But nobody knows how many people are using cocaine or crack. Some cops say it is more than a million. This might be hyperbole, the result of what some perceive to be anti-drug hysteria. But nobody who lives in New York can deny the daily evidence of the drug plague.

You see blurred-out young men panhandling for crack money from Columbus Avenue to Wall Street. Every night, wide-eyed, gold-bedecked teenage crackheads do 75 miles an hour on the Henry Hudson Parkway, racing one another in BMWs. In the age of AIDS, schoolgirls are hooking on street corners. Thousands of other young New Yorkers, whacked on drugs, are now incapable of holding jobs or acquiring the basic skills that might make a decent life possible. They amble around the ghettos. They fill the welfare hotels. They mill about the Port Authority bus terminal. They careen through subway cars, sometimes whipping out knives or pistols. The eyes of the heroin-users are glazed, their bodies filthy. The shooters among them often share "works," knowing that dirty needles can give them AIDS; they choose to risk an agonizing death in order to get high. The crackheads are wilder — eyes pinwheeling, speed-rapping away, or practicing various menacing styles. Smack or crack: They'd rather do either than go to a ball game, love someone, raise a child, listen to music, read a book, or master a difficult craft.

All of us are paying for this sick and disastrous binge. Crime in New York, after tailing off for a few years, has risen drastically. The reason is simple: Most junkies don't work. To feed their habits, addicts must either deal or steal. A Justice Department study released last winter showed that 79 percent of men arrested in New York for serious crimes tested positive for recent use of illegal drugs, 63 percent for cocaine. In 1977, there were 505 cops in this city's Narcotics Division; today, there are nearly 1,200. They made 35,774 drug-related arrests last year and estimate that 40 percent of the city's murders (there were 1,672 in 1987) were drug-related. In the first three months of this year, murder was up 10 percent in the city; car theft, 18.2 percent; assault, 9.4 percent; larceny, 5 percent; robbery,

4 percent. New Yorkers must come up with billions of tax dollars to pay for the police work involved, along with the cost of the druggies' hospital treatment, the operation of various clinics, and welfare payments to those who are so blitzed they can't support themselves.

With the pervasive use of hard drugs, and the enormous profits involved, it is no surprise that policemen all over the country have been dirtied, most sickeningly in Miami. But there is evidence that the corruption goes beyond cases of underpaid street cops looking the other way for their kids' tuition. A few years ago, a veteran agent became the first FBI man to plead guilty to cocaine-trafficking. Assistant U.S. Attorney Daniel N. Perlmutter, a rising star in Rudolph Giuliani's office, went to jail for stealing cocaine and heroin from a safe where evidence was stored.

No wonder Jesse Jackson was able to make drugs a major part of this year's presidential campaign. No wonder a New York *Times*/CBS News poll in March showed that Americans were far more concerned with drug-trafficking than with Central America, arms control, terrorism, or the West Bank. Americans have learned one big thing in the past few years: There has been a war on drugs, all right, and we have lost. Nobody knows this better than New Yorkers.

The ancient question is posed: What is to be done? The drug culture is now so pervasive, the drug trade so huge, powerful, and complex, that there are no simple answers. But the attack on the problem must deal with the leading actors in this squalid drama: dealers and users. That is, any true war on drugs must grapple with the problems of supply and demand.

SUPPLY

It is one of the more delicious ironies of the Cold War era that the bulk of the cocaine and heroin supply comes from countries that used to be called part of the free world. While trillions have been spent on national security, the security of ordinary citizens has been destroyed by countries that are on our side. The cocaine cartel is headquartered in Colombia. Most coca leaves are produced in Bolivia and Peru, where they are turned into coca paste for processing in Colombia. Most heroin is coming from Pakistan, Thailand, Turkey, and Mexico. The Colombians and Mexicans also produce much of the marijuana crop that is grown outside the United States.

The big supply-side coke-dealers control processing and distribution, leaving the grungy details of retailing to thousands of Americans. Many Caribbean islands are crucial to distribution, as was Panama until the indictment of Noriega. Mexico also is used as a transshipment point for huge supplies of cocaine and heroin that it does not produce. In all these countries, the governments themselves have been corrupted by the trade. The government of Colombia has virtually surrendered to the violence of the drug barons, while the governments of Panama and Bolivia are flat-out drug rings. Some Caribbean nations — the Bahamas in particular — have been accused of the same partnership with traffickers. The civilian government of Haiti was recently overthrown by the military in a dispute over the drug trade. In Mexico, the corruption is low-level in many places but is said to involve higher-ups in various state governments. In Thailand and Pakistan, drug-traffickers ply their trade with little interference from their governments; Thailand is more worried about Vietnam than about 110th Street, and Pakistan is making too much money off the war in Afghanistan to care about junkies in the United States.

Frustrated Americans have demanded that something drastic be done about the drug traffic. And over the past few years, the following measures have been advocated:

1. *War.* This is one of the most frequently voiced demands, what Maxwell Smart would have called the old let's-go-in-and-bomb-the-bejesus-out-of-them plan. Massachusetts senator John Kerry and Los Angeles police chief Daryl Gates are among those who have suggested military action. After all, if the United States is truly the most powerful nation on earth, why can't it *go to the source?*

From 1839 to 1842, the British actually did fight a war in China over drugs. But in the case of the Opium War, the British were the drug-pushers. They went ashore in China and killed a lot of Chinese in the name of their holy cause (opium was produced in British India, sold in China), the equivalent of Colombia's attacking the United States for the right to sell cocaine.

But a United States war against the drug-producing countries would be a forbiddingly expensive enterprise. You can't do it with one or two Grenada-style public-relations spectacles. And a war against one country — say, Colombia — would have no effect; the bad guys would just move next door. To use military force effectively to stop the production of poppies and coca leaves, the United

States would have to attack all of the offending countries *at the same time.*

But it is hard to imagine a simultaneous declaration of war against Panama, Colombia, Peru, Bolivia, Mexico, Turkey, Thailand, and Pakistan, with a smaller expedition against the Bahamas. We have had some comical adventurers in the National Security Council lately, but none *that* comical. There are 80 million people in Mexico alone, with rugged, mountainous terrain through the center of the country and dense jungles in the southern regions. Bolivia is twice the size of France and also mountainous. In Pakistan, American troops would face all the guns the CIA has been supplying to the anti-Communist Afghans. Another war in Southeast Asia (to cut off the Thai supply) would be no fun, but it would carry its own ironies, since much of the current mass stupefaction in America can be traced to the Vietnam era.

The logistics of Drug War One would be staggering; planes, ships, and rockets would be sent on their way to three continents. In every country from Turkey to Thailand, an American invasion would unite most of the local population on nationalist grounds. (We had a mild sample of that recently in the wholly owned CIA subsidiary of Honduras when the arrest of a drug-dealer by U.S. agents led to the burning down of one of the embassy buildings, along with several nights of anti-U.S. rioting.) Various international agreements would get in the way (the Organization of American States is unlikely to authorize a mass invasion of its own most important member states). U.S. casualties in such a worldwide operation would be very heavy as local armies and nationalist guerrilla bands descended upon the invaders, prepared to die, as they say, for their country. In the event that the Americans won all of these simultaneous wars, they would then have to occupy those countries for a generation if they truly hoped to wipe out the sources of drugs. The cost of a dozen huge garrisons would finish off the already precarious U.S. economy.

2. *Economic pressure.* On paper, this sounds like a more rational means of eradicating drugs. The United States (and the other leading industrial countries) would cut off credits, foreign aid, and all legitimate trade with the drug-producing countries. Presumably, the governments of those countries would then realize swiftly that they must get rid of the drug barons and would dispatch their own soldiers to wipe them out. While wielding the economic Big Stick, the United States would hold out the carrots of crop replacement, expanded

foreign aid, guaranteed purchase of legitimate crops. (Bolivia, for example, went heavily into coca-leaf production in the seventies after
its cotton industry collapsed with the fall of worldwide cotton prices.
This followed the sharp decline of its tin industry.) The idea would
be to create as much domestic pain as possible, so the local governments would get out of the drug racket — or crush it.

Unfortunately, the recent fiasco in Panama showed us on a small
scale that this probably wouldn't work. Again, nationalism would be
a major factor (in Panama, most people blamed the U.S. for their
plight, not Noriega). And in using economic sanctions, the U.S. could
not make distinctions among drug-dealers; Washington would have
to be as tough on NATO ally Turkey as it is on Bolivia, as ferocious
against Thailand and Pakistan as against Colombia and Mexico.

But U.S. companies also need most of these countries as markets.
Economic sanctions work both ways; all American goods would be
stopped at other nations' borders, thus closing plants all over our
own country. Mexico would stop paying its multi-billion-dollar debt
to U.S. banks, which would then collapse — perhaps pulling the entire country into a major depression.

3. *Moral persuasion.* Don't even bother.

4. *The sealing of the borders.* Again, this would cost uncountable
billions. We have a 5,426-mile undefended border with Canada. It
was crossed without problem by Prohibition rumrunners, vaulted for
decades by Mafia drug-peddlers, and is easily traversed these days by
the cocaine-runners. The 1,942-mile border with Mexico is a sieve.
In spite of tough immigration laws, several million illegal aliens are
expected to cross it this year; well-financed drug-runners with their
fleets of small aircraft and trucks are unlikely to be stopped.

Enlisting the Armed Forces as border guards almost certainly
would only complicate matters — as the Israelis have learned on the
West Bank, soldiers are not policemen. Chasing druggies back home
to Mexico or Canada (in "hot pursuit") could lead to an international incident every other day. The first time a private plane flown
by some orthodontist with a defective radio was shot down over
Toronto, the plan would be abandoned.

America's miles of coastline are guarded by an underfinanced, un-
dermanned Coast Guard. Florida alone has 580 miles of coast, and
there are more than 120,000 pleasure boats registered in southern
Florida. Smugglers have become very sophisticated about penetrating
our feeble defenses. The South Florida Task Force — headed by Vice-

President George Bush and supported by the Drug Enforcement Administration, the FBI, the Customs Service, the U.S. Army (which supplied Cobra helicopters), the Bureau of Alcohol, Tobacco & Firearms, the Internal Revenue Service, the Coast Guard, the U.S. Navy (whose warships gave the Coast Guard support), the U.S. Border Patrol, the U.S. Marshals, and the Treasury Department — has been a colossal flop. After more than six years of this effort, there are more drugs on the streets than ever before, and their lower prices (down from $47,000 a kilo for cocaine six years ago to about $12,000 now) indicate that all those well-photographed record-setting busts haven't stopped the flow.

The reason is simple. The demand and the profits are enormous. So it's no surprise that when the government concentrates its efforts in one spot (as it did in southern Florida), the druggies simply go elsewhere: to the Florida panhandle, the bayous of Louisiana, the shores of Mississippi. Many even follow the old rumrunner trails, dropping anchor off Montauk and using small boats to make runs against the unguarded shores of Long Island. One unexpected consequence of the patchwork War on Drugs has been the spread of the trade to places that once were free of it. Brilliant.

6. *Draconian measures, including the death penalty.* Mayor Koch and others have called for the death penalty for big-time drug-dealers. The problem is that most of them don't live here. For every Carlos Lehder, convicted recently after a long trial in Florida, there are thousands of others whose immunity is guaranteed by use of violence.

But if the death penalty is to be employed to solve the drug problem, why should it be limited to the few foreign wholesalers who are extradited and tried here? To be fair, you would have to attack every participant in the production and distribution systems. That is, you would have to do more than fry a few thousand pushers; you would have to execute every crooked cop, every corrupt banker who launders drug money, every politician who is on the take. You would also have to lock up all members of the CIA involved in the *contra* drug-running scheme (persuasively described in Leslie Cockburn's *Out of Control*) and strap them into the electric chair, along with their bosses and whoever in the White House collaborated in these operations. The death penalty for drug-dealing is a slogan, not a solution. Even if exceptions were made for ideological zealots, the state would have to kill several hundred thousand people. And the drugs would continue to flow.

DEMAND

One night a year ago, I had dinner with a Mexican diplomat and asked him about the drug problem in Mexico. He said, "You have to understand something: If thousands of North American yuppies suddenly decided tomorrow to get high by shoving bananas up their noses — and they were willing to pay $10 a banana — Mexico would bloom in bananas."

His point was a simple one: The drug problem in the United States is one of demand, not of production. Poor countries are like poor people — in order to survive, they will sell whatever the market demands. In our time, in this country and this city, the market demands hard drugs.

There have been a variety of suggestions about dealing with the insatiable appetite that Americans have developed for cocaine and heroin.

1. *Willpower.* This is the Nancy Reagan plan, beautifully described by a recent beauty contestant as "Just Say Don't." It is primarily directed at teenagers, imploring them to resist the peer pressure that could lead to using drugs. A few weeks ago, I asked some New York street kids about this program. They just laughed and laughed.

2. *Education.* This is getting better. In the past, the country paid a heavy price for lies told in the name of education (marijuana will lead to heroin, etc.). Television has been playing a more responsible role lately, with a variety of series and programs about the cost and consequences of drugs (*48 Hours on Crack Street;* the two Peter Jennings specials on ABC). If this effort is sustained, we may begin to see a slow, steady decline in drug use (the way cigarette-smoking began to wane after the truth was told about its connection to lung cancer and heart disease). The great risk is that education about drugs will merely provoke curiosity and lead to wider use. Kids always think they are immortal.

3. *Treatment.* I visited a drug-treatment center in Suffern a few weeks ago. The facilities were secure, the 28-day program tough, the

staff dedicated. There were exactly 28 beds for junkies. There are 250,000 smack addicts in New York State alone. Around the state, there are about 5,000 beds available to treat heroin addicts. Obviously, not everyone who wants treatment can get it. Those who have summoned all the desiccated vestiges of their pride and hope in order to enter a treatment program should be able to do so. But this, too, will cost many billions if all the country's addicts are to be handled by such programs.

4. *More Draconian measures.* This would follow examples set in China, Singapore, and a few other places. It would attack both dealer and user, supply and demand. All would be subject to heavy prison sentences (or the electric chair, if the death-penalty advocates had their way). The user would be considered as guilty as the seller.

Again, those good old Draconian measures make better rhetoric than reality. In New York, the Rockefeller drug law was one such measure. Put into effect in 1973, this was the "nation's toughest" drug legislation: For possession of two ounces of heroin, the minimum sentence was 15 to 25 years in prison; the maximum was life. A repeat conviction for possessing any stimulant or hallucinogen "with intent to sell" sent a felon to jail for one to eight and a half, again with a maximum of life. Probation, alternate sentences, and plea bargaining were forbidden. Yes, a lot of bad guys did go to jail, and by 1975, 91 percent of convicted drug felons were serving maximum prison sentences.

But these measures also helped cause the current crisis. The courts were soon jammed with accused drug felons demanding jury trials. The spending of many additional millions on judges and new courtrooms didn't ease the problem. And it was also now worth killing cops to avoid doing life in Attica. The old mob *did* respond to the new laws. Many of them got out of the smack racket (with the usual exceptions), but that only opened the way for the Cubans and Colombians. Judges began releasing first offenders and low-level dealers for the simple reason that there was no room in our prisons: They were already packed with druggies. And as cops became more cynical about the justice system, corruption became more possible.

New Yorkers are already the most heavily taxed Americans. It's unlikely that they would agree to billions of dollars in additional taxes to pay for another 30 prisons or an additional 500 judges to deal with all the users and pushers in the state. Nor would anybody be happy paying even more for welfare to handle the women and children left behind by the imprisoned druggies.

WHAT IS TO BE DONE?

After watching the results of the plague since heroin first came to Brooklyn in the early fifties, after visiting the courtrooms and the morgues, after wandering New York's neighborhoods to see for myself, and after consuming much of the literature on drugs, I've reluctantly come to a terrible conclusion: The only solution is the complete legalization of these drugs.

I did not originate this idea, of course. In the past year, the mayors of Baltimore, Washington, and Minneapolis have urged that legalization be looked into. Various shapers of public opinion, including such conservatives as William F. Buckley Jr. and Milton Friedman, have done the same. Many have cited articles in such publications as *The Economist, Foreign Policy,* and the British medical journal *The Lancet,* all suggesting that the only solution is legalization.

Legalization doesn't mean endorsement. Cigarettes, liquor, and prescription drugs such as Valium are now legal, though neither government nor society endorses their use. Any citizen can now endanger his health with cigarettes (and 300,000 people die each year from smoking-related illnesses). Or make a mess of his life with whiskey (alcohol abuse costs us more than $100 billion a year). Or take too many Valiums and die. These drugs, however, have become respectable over the years. State banquets are often marked by the drinking of toasts, in which the drug called liquor is offered in honor of the distinguished visitor. Business, politics, and love affairs are often conducted with the lubricant of alcohol. I have no patience anymore for drunks, and I can't abide the company of cokeheads and junkies. But every sensible citizen must recognize that the current system under which some drugs are legal and others are not is hypocritical.

I think a ten-year experiment with legalization is worth the risk. If it doesn't accomplish its goals, legislators could always go back to the present disastrous system. And we might learn that we can live without hypocrisy.

The strongest argument for legalization is economic. We simply don't have the money to deal with eliminating supply or demand. Too many Americans want this stuff, and we are again falling into the trap created by Prohibition: We try to keep people from buying things they want, we cite moral reasons as our motives, and we create a criminal organization that will poison all of our lives for decades. The old mob was the child of Prohibition. A new mob, infinitely more ruthless, is certain to come out of the present crisis. That can be prevented by eliminating the illegal profits that fund and expand the power of the drug gangs.

How would legalization work? A few possibilities:

1. Marijuana — not a hard drug, of course, but described as one in the debate — could be the first to be legalized. About 20 million Americans smoke grass on a regular basis and about 400,000 are arrested every year for possession. Mark Kleiman, former director of policy analysis for the Criminal Division of the Justice Department, estimates that legalizing the sale of marijuana would save about $500 million in law-enforcement costs and produce about $7 billion in revenues. Those numbers alone should settle this part of the argument.

Pot could be sold openly in licensed liquor stores all over the country (legalization must be national; if it were limited to New York, every pothead, cokehead, and junkie in the country would soon arrive here). All laws now applicable to selling liquor (used legally by 100 million Americans) would apply to marijuana. Citizens would be arrested for driving under the influence. The weed could not be sold to minors. Advertising would be restricted. All taxes — including those on domestic farmers and importers — would be applied to drug treatment, education, and research for the duration of the ten-year experiment.

2. Heroin could be legalized a year later, dispensed through a network of neighborhood health stations and drugstores. While the old British system of registering addicts was in effect, the number of those receiving daily maintenance doses was low (about 500 in London). In the late sixties, the system was changed. The number of dispensing doctors was reduced nationwide to a few hundred (from thousands), and new registered addicts were required to enter methadone programs. The number of addicts soared. Obviously, the old system was better.

After legalization, this vile drug would be banned from commercial sale. The price would be very low (25 cents a dose), perhaps even free. All current addicts would have to register within six months of the passage of the enabling legislation. They would be supplied with identity cards resembling driver's licenses, showing their faces. They would also be given the opportunity to go drug-free through a greatly expanded system of treatment centers (funded by the marijuana tax and import fees). Their records would be kept confidential, but they would have to register.

Presumably, this would accomplish two things: (1) take the profits out of heroin sales and (2) contain the present addict population. Most junkies support their habits by dealing; they create new addicts to have more customers. There would be no economic point to creating new junkies. The street junkie also would gain relief from the degrading process of making his day's connection. He would stop stealing from old ladies, his family, and strangers. He would no longer have to risk AIDS infection by sharing works.

The mechanics would be difficult; some junkies need five or six doses a day, and if you hand them the supply all at once, they are likely to sell some of it to others. The cost of six separate needles a day for 200,000 junkies would be very high. New junkies would be a different problem. Certainly, there would be a continuing, if diminished, supply of young addicts, for a variety of reasons. Some would get heroin from family members who are junkies, the way young alcoholics have been known to raid the family liquor cabinet. There will always be sick old junkies ready to corrupt the young and others who may want to spread their personal misery to as many as possible. But new junkies would be able to enter the system only by telling the authorities how they got turned on. And this would be a point where one of those good old Draconian measures would be useful. Part of the law could mandate life sentences for anyone who created a new junkie.

3. Cocaine could be legalized soon after heroin and sold in its conventional forms through liquor stores. The same regulations that govern the sale and use of liquor and marijuana would apply. The drug barons of the world could then go legitimate. The drug-user would have a regulated supply of cocaine that was not cut with Ajax or speed. He would pay a variety of prices depending on quality, as the drinker does for various wines, liquors, and champagnes. Even the crack-users, at the bottom of the social scale of coke-users, would be able to buy cocaine legally, thus putting the hoodlums out of business. If the customers wanted to go home, then, and cook up some crack in a microwave (all they would need is cocaine, hydrochloride,

baking soda, and water or ammonia), they could do so. If they then sold it to kids, they would end up doing life.

I say all of this with enormous reluctance. I hate the idea of living in a country that is drowning in drugs. I know that if drugs were freely available, some of the most damaged people in society could fall into degradation, as many of the poor have across the years in countries where alcohol is legal. There would be casualties everywhere, and the big-city ghettos might suffer terribly (although the assumption that blacks and Hispanics automatically would fall into addiction faster than others is a kind of racism). I know that it would be strange to travel around the world and be an automatic drug suspect, my luggage searched, my body frisked, a citizen of a drug country. Alas, while researching this article, I realized that I live in that country now.

There are good and decent arguments against legalization that go beyond the minor problems of embarrassment and humiliation. The most obvious is that the number of addicts might increase dramatically as legalization and easy access tempted millions of citizens to experiment. History suggests that this is likely to happen, at least for a while. One study shows that the number of drinkers in this country increased by more than 60 percent after the end of Prohibition, returning to the level reached before the noble experiment. Forty years after the British drug-dealers won the Opium War, the number of opium addicts in China had risen to 90 million. In laboratory experiments with cocaine, animals keep taking larger and larger amounts of the drug, until they die. Dr. Frank H. Gawin, director of stimulant abuse, treatment, and research at Yale University, said recently, "I would be terrified to live in a cocaine-legalized society."

Another objection is that nobody knows whether legalization would work — and if it drastically increased the number of addicts over a ten-year period, reversing the process might be impossible. So I'm not suggesting that legalization would transform this violent city into Pericles' Athens. But all of us know that the present system doesn't work. And if the tax revenues from sales of legal drugs could fund real treatment programs, if we treated drug addiction the way we treat alcoholism (as a health problem instead of a crime problem), if education more powerfully stressed that all drug abuse is the pastime of idiots, an experiment with legalization might be worth the attendant risks.

Some of those risks could be covered by specific proposals in the new laws. Congress could insist, for example, that all law-enforcement money freed by legalization be used to attack the deeper problems of poverty, housing, family disintegration, and illiteracy, which make life in the ghettos so hopeless and drugs so tempting. With any luck, we then might see the number of drug-users decline as more citizens realized drugs' heavy costs and as the young realized that it isn't very hip to make yourself stupid. Certainly, as the huge illicit profits vanished, the level of urban violence would be swiftly reduced.

The police who have been diverted to the drug wars could be employed against more terrible crimes. The strain on the courts and prisons would ease, leading to a criminal-justice system that guarantees more thoughtful prosecutions, fairer trials, and certain punishment for malefactors.

Legalization wouldn't be a license to go wild. Drug use would continue to be regulated, perhaps in a tougher way, with heavy penalties for doctors, nurses, pilots, train engineers, and others who have heavy social responsibilities. The Armed Forces could continue to forbid the use of drugs. Employers could insist that they don't want drug-users working for them any more than they want drunks. There would be sad and tragic examples of people fallen into the gutter, as there have always been with alcohol. A few hustlers would work the margins of the legal-drug business, trying to avoid taxes and duties. But we would rid ourselves of a lot of hypocrisy. We would be forced to face some truths about ourselves, deprived at last of the comforting figures of those foreign ogres who are supposed to be corrupting all these poor innocent Americans.

Perhaps, along the way, we might even discover why so many millions of Americans insist on spending their days and nights in a state of self-induced mental impairment. Perhaps. For now, we just have to discover a way to get home alive.

NEW YORK,
August 15, 1988

PART III

MEXICO

―――――

For almost forty years, I've been going to Mexico. I've lived, gone to school, and worked there. It's the country I know better than any other except my own. As a gringo in Mexico, I've learned much about the feelings of all immigrants: the initial strangeness of language, food, music, culture, the uncertainty of legal rights, the unfair legacy of historical stereotype. I've tried hard to understand the history of Mexico; I've made friends with Mexicans of varied trades and backgrounds; I've come to comprehend some basic Mexican myths. But whenever I return to Mexico, I remain a foreigner, a man standing on the margin of Mexican life.

Even as an outsider, I know that Mexico is part of me. Without the experience of Mexico, I wouldn't be the same man. Mexicans have taught me much about work, honor, and pride, about courage, about the need to keep on going after common sense tells you to give up. In my attitude to the world, Mexican fatalism has been grafted onto the Irish fatalism inherited from my father; that *mestizo* fatalism tempers the American optimism that was so powerfully encouraged by my mother. As a writer, I've been enriched by the work of Carlos Fuentes, Octavio Paz, Juan Rulfo, and Carlos Monsivais. I get great pleasure from the poetry of Homero Aridjis. I have been entertained and enlightened by the crime fiction of Paco Ignacio Taibo II. Where I live, Mexican folk art is everywhere, masks and surrealist altars and mirrors made from tin. My library contains almost 500 volumes on Mexican history, art, music, and culture. On the wall above my desk, there are showcards featuring the stars of the Golden Age of Mexican cinema from the mid-1930s to the late 1950s: Pedro Infante, Jorge Negrete, Pedro Armendariz, and Arturo de Cordova. If they'd been French instead of Mexican, every critic in New York would know their work. *Ni modo,* as the Mexicans say. It doesn't matter. Life goes on, and I'm still looking for posters of Maria Felix and Dolores del Rio.

On other walls, there are framed photographs by Agustin Casasola, the great photographer of the Mexican Revolution, and posters by such artists as Rufino Tamayo, Diego Rivera, Frida Kahlo, Jose Luis Cuevas, and Alejandro Colunga. My friends think this is all very strange. Other people's passions always are. But in my small part of New York, and in my consciousness, Mexico lives.

Obviously, these pieces can't express my complicated feelings about Mexico and Mexicans; that would require a book. But I hope they make clear that at least one old gringo is thankful to the Mexicans for their grace and tenacity. As I write, ten years after the terrible earthquake, Mexico is deep into another crisis. This one seems worse than any other, because so many hopes and expectations were raised during the presidency of Carlos Salinas de Gortari. Mexico, everyone said, was about to move from the Third World to the First World. Not in some distant future, but now. That didn't happen. Once more, there are grave predictions that Mexico will plunge into bloody revolution.

Perhaps.

But I wouldn't bet a centavo on it.

CITY OF PALACES

We opened the drapes in the hotel room and there before us in the brilliant winter sunshine lay the Zócalo. Everything was in its familiar place: the great wheezing pile of the cathedral to the left with the smaller chapel called the Sagrario beside it, starlings and sparrows darting gaily around their somber rooftop crosses. On the far side of the vast square was the low, scalloped outline of the National Palace, a building begun by Hernán Cortés in the 1520s beside the ruins of Montezuma's palace. To the right: the City Hall, from which the largest city in the Western Hemisphere is governed.

And directly below us was a panorama from the continuing history of Mexican surrealism. More than a thousand high school students in leotards were dancing to the sounds of "La Bamba." The steel framework of a portable stage was climbing four stories above the ground, to be filled, in a few days, by hundreds of performers celebrating the Day of the Revolution. Over on the side, workmen were hammering together the numbered sections of a plywood pyramid. Three teenage boys, balanced precariously on an upper rung of the framework, perfectly mimicked the movements of the dancing schoolgirls. And at their feet, appearing from behind a work shed, there was a man gazing up at me and my wife. He was Mexican. He was holding a blanket. I backed away from the window and gazed at the blue roof of cloudless sky.

For more than thirty years of traveling in Mexico, I've been seeing the Man with the Blanket. I came here first in 1956, twenty-one years old and wanting to be a painter. I enrolled at Mexico City College on the GI Bill, and every month the Veterans Administration sent me $110 to pay for tuition, housing, food, and supplies. I was never happier. I just never could afford the wares of the Man with the Blanket. Still, in one guise or another, sometimes young and other times old, he has pursued me. When I came back to Mexico in the early sixties, my easel abandoned for a Smith Corona, he signaled to me from the darkness outside the Hotel Maria Cristina on Río Lerma. I saw him at the 1968 Olympics, appearing suddenly from behind the last ahuehuete tree on Insurgentes Sur. He trailed me for a week during the first giddy year of the seventies oil boom. He never says anything. Not a word. Just holds up the blanket, his eyes full of insatiable hope. A few years ago, after surviving a terrible car accident on the Toluca Highway, I retreated to my room in a fancy Zona Rosa hotel, soaked with rain, my ribs and back bruised and aching. I opened the blinds. And there he was. Eight stories below me on the rain-lashed street. Staring up at my silhouette in the small yellow rectangle of my room. The Man with the Blanket.

"Why does he look so sad?" my wife asked, gazing down at his lonely presence.

"Because he is," I said.

And I lay down to rest, knowing I was back in the city I loved more than any other except my own.

It is difficult to explain an affection for any city, least of all for this great, noisy, dangerous, and polluted megalopolis that the Mexican writer Carlos Fuentes calls "Makesicko City" in his latest novel. Here, in the largest landlocked city in the world, at an altitude of 7,350 feet above sea level, in a long, broad valley rimmed by mountains that climb more than 3,000 additional feet into the sky, some people are certain they have seen the shape of hell.

"Not one of us will spend a day in purgatory," said my friend and driver, Ricardo Hernandez, who has been a resident for forty-seven years. "We have paid for our sins just by living here."

A few years ago I spent two months in Mexico City without ever glimpsing the sky. Every day its more than thirty thousand factories and 3 million buses, trucks, and automobiles pump fifteen thousand tons of microcarbons, metal, dust, chemicals, and bacteria into the thin air. That winter (temperature inversions are most common from November to the end of February) more than two hundred birds fell dead one morning upon the manicured lawns of the Lomas de Chapultepec, killed by the poisoned air. Last April the environmentalist Homero Aridjis, president of the Group of 100, did laboratory tests on twelve dead sparrows found in the Alameda Park. Six birds had high levels of lead, mercury, cadmium, and chromium, along with pesticides, in their lungs, livers, and hearts. The immune system of one bird had been damaged by the high chromium levels. Employees of the American embassy are entitled to a hardship allowance simply because they have the unfortunate habit of breathing. Some Mexican ecologists estimate that thirty thousand people die every year of respiratory diseases caused by *la contaminación*. It is sickening to see, worse to breathe, particularly if you were here in the fifties when the population was about 3.5 million and each morning you could gaze from a high window and see the volcanoes, Popocatépetl and Ixtaccíhuatl, framed against the blank sky. In those years, this was a great big wonderful city.

When I'm here now, I still carry that beautiful lost city around in my head, and that helps explain my irrational affection for a place that I know doesn't love me back. It also underlines my sense of horror. I know that the city now contains thousands of beggars; I know that some twenty thousand human beings make their living by picking through its seven immense garbage dumps, to which are added fifteen thousand tons of garbage every day; I know that, in spite of pollution and poverty and the ravages of the September 19, 1985, earthquake, hundreds of people still arrive from the hungry provinces every day, and that by the year 2000 the population could reach 30 million. The city now is simply immense, its more than one thousand *colonias* (neighborhoods) spreading thirty-five to forty miles in all directions from the Zócalo. It has spilled into the Valley of Mexico, where it has eaten what was once the richest farmland in the country. Mexico City is so large now that it actually contains a 535th Street.

And yet I still feel a small tremble of a lover's excitement when I get off the airplane, still love that first moment among Mexicans, feeling drowned in vowels, can still detect in odd drafts the old aroma of the city, that intangible compound of charcoal fires, tortillas, flowers, herbs. In some way, here I am always twenty-one: walking down the Paseo de la Reforma at dusk, when the paths were still made of hard-packed earth instead of tiles; listening to Cuco Sanchez sing "La Cama de Piedra" from the jukebox of that cantina on Melchor Ocampo; waiting for a girl named Yolanda in the Alameda Park with my hair freshly cut and my shoes shined and wondering why she is late.

So I come here now and see the horror, and I can also see the city that has survived, the city that was here when I was young, the city that existed long before I ever walked the earth. The Zócalo remains the heart of that city and the very heart of the country of Mexico. All roads in the republic are marked in kilometers leading to this immense place — the largest public square in the Western Hemisphere. As it did in the fifties, the Zócalo still gives off the aura of a tremendous, inarticulate sadness. Once there was a park here, palm trees, a depot for trolley cars; today, when not occupied with the circuses of the state, it is a bald, paved plain, devoid of green, with a Mexican flag standing in the center of the emptiness. The reason for its denuding is unclear; the most plausible explanation involves the need for a clear field of fire for the palace guards in the event of revolutionary unpleasantness. One tenet in the military version of urban design is that you cannot hide a regiment behind a flagpole.

But the bleak emptiness doesn't fully explain the sadness. Wandering under the arcades along the side of the square, I remembered a passage in the brilliant 1957 travel book on Mexico by the Brazilian novelist Erico Verissimo. Looking at the Zócalo, he spoke of the city's "dark, ominous tone that gives us the sensation that something tragic is always about to occur — a murder, an earthquake, a revolution."

That tone infuses the National Palace, where soldiers spend their days directing tourists to the Diego Rivera murals and guarding that tiny fraction of the city's 2.5 million civil servants who labor in the upstairs offices. The ominous quality exists primarily in the imaginations of those who read history. For centuries this building was the seat of secular power in Mexico. The sixty-three colonial viceroys ruled from here; poor Maximilian, the handsome and doomed Austrian, arrived here in 1863 with his Belgian wife, Carlota, to claim the throne of Mexico; Benito Juárez, the Zapotec Indian lawyer who fought and then executed Maximilian, issued his reforms from its balcony; the dictator Porfirio Díaz entertained British and American oilmen in its salons and sold them huge portions of his country; Zapata and Villa walked its halls; most of the revolutionary presidents of the modern era worked here. But Carlos Salinas de Gortari, the newest Mexican president, labors in Los Pinos on the edge of Chapultepec Park; except on days of patriotic ceremony, the palace is another empty symbol. In the midst of the worst Mexican economic crisis in sixty years, the ominous tone has receded and the tragic has increased.

The Metropolitan Cathedral on the north side of the plaza is another matter. Begun in 1573, consecrated in 1667, and finished in 1813, it is built upon part of the old Aztec ceremonial grounds. For hundreds of years its bishops worked with the inhabitants of the palace to control and exploit Mexico for the profit of God and the distant Spanish throne. But for most native Mexicans in those days, Christianity was a calamity. There were, of course, kind friars and priests who fought for the rights of Indians and tried to preserve the pre-Columbian heritage; but they were exceptions. This cathedral was intended from the beginning to be a symbol of the utter triumph of the Christian god over the gods of the Aztecs. Its gloomy power can best be sensed in the interior, which is high, smoky, and dim. Indian slave labor carved and hand-fitted these slabs of *tezontle, cantera,* and marble. It is said that there are no nails in the cathedral, except in the hands and feet of the dying Jesus, no iron except on the doors. The place has five naves, fourteen chapels, and a jumble of styles.

Beggars appear from the gloom, their glazed eyes a reproach; they are called *pordioseros* after the imploring Spanish phrase meaning "for the love of God." You turn from them to examine the famous Altar of the Kings, and the mind teems with images of what has happened in this injured country for the love of God. Designed in 1737 by Jerónimo de Balbas, the altar is an operatic extravaganza, at once a celebration of death and a vision of heaven, clearly designed by an agnostic who must have hoped somehow to cure his doubts. Everything is gold. The baroque swirl of twisted gold columns, gold angels, gold flowers, gold sculptures, the golden visions of pain and ecstasy, the two dark, gold-framed paintings incorporated into the design, the polychrome statues, the opulent golden glaze applied over the Christian images of suffering and death: All combine to demand submission.

The modern man flees.

And in the bright, hazy sunshine, among Pepsi stands and trinket shops, he wanders down a street on the right called Seminario into the remains of the world the Spanish destroyed.

There is the splendid new museum of the Templo Mayor. Part of it is an excavation of the Great Temple of the city the Aztecs called

Tenochtitlán, part of it an exhibit that reconstructs life and culture here before Cortés. Tenochtitlán was founded in 1325 on some islands in the midst of Lake Texcoco. By the time Cortés arrived almost two hundred years later, it had grown into a city of 300,000 inhabitants; fifty thousand white buildings, palaces, and pyramids; exquisite gardens; even a zoo — and a dense, complex civilization that encompassed both astronomy and blood sacrifice. From this city, the Aztecs ruled over an empire of almost 6 million subjects.

The Spaniards were astounded: This city of heathens and barbarians was the size of Seville. Years later the tough old conquistador Bernal Díaz del Castillo would write: "And some of our soldiers even asked whether the things that we saw were not a dream." No wonder that Cortés, after conquering the Aztecs with guile, courage, gunpowder, and luck, was capable of describing Tenochtitlán in his report to Carlos I of Spain as "the most beautiful city in the world" while determining to wipe it from the face of the earth.

We stayed at the Hotel Majestic, whose entrance is on the street named Madero, after the martyred leader of the 1910 revolution; it was once called Calle Plateros — "Street of the Silversmiths" — and is still crowded with jewelry shops. All over this city of intense bargaining, shops selling similar goods are clustered together; there is a street of bookdealers, a street of goldsmiths, a street of musical instruments, another of bridal gowns, one of religious articles, a street that specializes in bathroom fixtures, streets devoted to boilers, TV sets, sexy underwear, old radios — even stolen car parts.

A few blocks north of the Zócalo is one of my favorite places in the city, under the arcades facing the Plaza de Santo Domingo. This is the street of the *escribanos,* the public writers who help illiterate people fill out government forms and tax returns, send notices to family members in distant parts of the republic, and write love letters. Most of them are old men now, clattering away at wonderfully preserved old Royals or working at antique hand-operated printing presses. Illiteracy in Mexico has been cut to 6 percent, but there are still many customers. I am always cheered on this block, knowing that no matter what might happen in my life, I can always retreat here to write for strangers.

"I like most of all writing the love letters," one old *escribano* told me one afternoon. "That is the most creative work. The government documents are the worst."

Not far away, the first printing shop was established in the New World in 1539 — twenty-five years before the birth of Shakespeare, eighty-one years before the Pilgrims glimpsed Plymouth Rock, eighty-seven years before the first Dutch settlers established what was to become New York City. Mexico also established the first university in the Americas (1553), and the first hospital, Jesus the Nazarene, where the bones of Cortés came to a final resting place after his death in Spain in 1547. People of the United States ethnocentrically call themselves Americans, but even the most superficial reading of Mexican history teaches us that "America" was a Spanish creation, an imposed mixture with the great civilizations that existed here before any European ever raised a lance in triumph.

The modern American city called Mexico is also an extraordinary accomplishment. It is brighter, more French, more given to wide boulevards than most of those in what Mexicans still call the Colossus of the North. The masterpiece is the Paseo de la Reforma, one of the great avenues of the world. Maximilian built it in 1864, supposedly at the urging of the adoring Carlota, who wanted to see him ride from Chapultepec Castle to work at the National Palace. He modeled it on the Champs-Elysées, lined it with the bronze busts of various now-forgotten men, and called it the Paseo de los Hombres Ilustres ("Boulevard of Illustrious Men"). After the illustrious Maximilian was himself placed against a wall in Querétaro and shot, the name was changed to honor the reforms of Juárez, who had ordered the emperor's execution. Today there are still some blasted office buildings standing on the Reforma as reminders of the 1985 earthquake, but it remains a wonderful street for walking, on days when the air is breathable.

At the far end of the Reforma (past the hotels, the fortress of the American embassy, the various branches of Sanborn's) is Chapultepec Park. This urban glade covers about a thousand acres and has been called the lung of Mexico City (the singular is well-advised). On a Sunday afternoon, when Mexicans of all classes gambol on its lawns and kids watch in awe as the last *charros* move by on horseback, the park is a delight. The great Museum of Anthropology is here, as is the Rufino Tamayo Museum (not so great) and the erratic, sometimes surprising Museum of Modern Art, which owns collections of the splendid photography of the Mexican master, Manuel Alvarez Bravo, and superb nineteenth-century landscapes by José María Velasco, whose gifts, in the opinion of some critics, were in a class with Lorrain or Constable.

Again, strolling through Chapultepec, we are in a place that is at once used in the present and suffused with the past. The Aztec emperors repaired here during the rainy summer months (Chapultepec means "hill of the grasshoppers" in the old language), and Cortés lived for a while here with his Indian mistress, Doña Marina. In the clumsily designed castle you can still see the rooms where Maximilian and Carlota lived, the brocaded walls, the Sevres vases, petit point chairs, and crystal chandeliers; guides tell you that late at night you can still hear ghostly laughter, tinkly music playing a waltz, the murmur of foreign tongues. Carlota is said to have designed the lovely gardens, with their thousand-year-old ahuehuetes, bougainvillea, creeping myrtle, Spanish moss, and violets, and to have played here with her lovers while Maximilian was off trying in vain to convince the Mexicans of his decent intentions. The garden features a monument to Don Quixote, a perfectly apt symbol of the folly of their brief and bogus empire.

And it was from the ramparts of this castle that a group of young Mexican cadets chose to leap to their deaths rather than surrender to the conquering troops of General Winfield Scott at the end of the U.S. war against Mexico in 1847. At the park's entrance, a monument to the boy heroes honors their sacrifice while reminding all Mexicans that long ago the United States took one-half of Mexico's territory at gunpoint. I remember gazing at this monument one afternoon, wondering what sort of twentieth century both Mexico and the United States might have had if Mexico had retained the oil of Texas, California, and Oklahoma. Brooding on these cosmic matters, I turned and saw the Man with the Blanket. He stared at me as if the purchase of a blanket from Saltillo would be the only sensible act of reparation. I shook my head and walked away.

When the Reforma moves through the park it climbs into the Lomas of Chapultepec, where many rich Mexicans and foreign diplomats live in superb modern houses. There is a belief that the Lomas is above the smog line; on most days its air is as vile as that of El Centro. Many of the older trees are brown around the edges, withering in the pollution. And the automobile traffic is horrendous. Among other things, the traffic of Mexico City has virtually ended that most intelligent of ancient rituals, the siesta. In the old days (just twenty years ago), men would leave their shops or offices and lunch at home, or in the *casa chica* occupied by a mistress. Then they would nap and return, replenished, to their labors. Today this is impossible: Enduring two traffic jams a day is punishment enough; four a day would be to reside in the dark night of the soul.

In the 1985 earthquake there was almost no damage in the Lomas; the same could not be said for the other end of the Reforma, the area called Tlatelolco. In the heady days of the 1960s, a vast development of state-financed high rises was built here. But even the most modern architecture could not hold back the ancient Mexican gift for the tragic. In 1968 in the Plaza de las Tres Culturas, where a small Aztec pyramid, a colonial church, and a modern building symbolically shared a space, the government chose to save the Olympics by killing more than five hundred protesting students. I remember interviewing some of the survivors; they were in flight, hiding in safe houses, trying to leave the country. Many of their friends were dead, others in prison. Suddenly they had grown up. But if the massacre was bad, nobody in Tlatelolco was prepared for the utter destruction caused by the 1985 earthquake. This is where that fourteen-story building fell over on its side. When I arrived two days later, an army of human beings was digging in the dust of broken plaster and twisted beams. One of them, without announcement, was Placido Domingo. Members of his family lived in the building. Today there are blank spaces where the buildings were.

"Life goes on," an old Mexican woman shrugged, when I went by the project. "You can do nothing about some things."

That fatalism is one of the most attractive qualities of the Mexican character. You see it on the faces of prizefighters at the Arena Coliseo when, bleeding and beaten, they refuse to quit. It is general among those trapped in the coiled traffic. There is a hopeless patience among those on line at the Correo Mayor, the central post office on San Juan de Letran (a broad street that nobody calls by its new name of Avenida Lázaro Cárdenas). This is another amazing building designed by the Italian architect Adamo Boari, who began, but did not finish, the Palacio de las Bellas Artes, the grand old museum across the street. Neither suffered any damage in the earthquake while their more modern neighbors were crumpling into broken piles. And the fatalism is most apparent in the way so many Mexicans have reacted to the appalling economic crisis that has afflicted the country since

1982. Income, purchasing power, and the value of savings have been cut by at least 50 percent; Mexico remains peaceful.

My wife and I were in Mexico once when the government allowed a 32 percent devaluation of the peso against the dollar. We arrived on a Sunday, with the peso fixed at 1,700 to the dollar; by Wednesday it was 2,300 to the dollar, and the afternoon papers were screaming that it might go to 6,000. We sat down to breakfast in Sanborn's knowing that our meal would cost less when we finished than it did when we ordered. Our hotel was $35 a night when we checked in; when we checked out it was $22. Everywhere else on earth the U.S. dollar was weak; in Mexico it retained its old swaggering power. And although there were scare headlines, much talk on TV shows, great muttering and complaining among ordinary citizens we talked to in the street, nobody *did* anything.

"What can be done?" a mechanic named Esteban Torres said. "The government people knew it was coming, so they all bought dollars ahead of time. The rich keep their money in Texas. The middle class, they keep it in dollars, under their mattresses. The poor don't have any money anyway. So what can be done?"

Fatalism is combined in this city with a deepening cynicism. In the 1988 presidential elections, thirty-seven of the city's forty election districts were won by the opposition candidate, Cuauhtémoc Cárdenas, who headed a coalition of leftist parties. They voted against mismanagement of the economy that had eroded the value of their work, against the pollution of the air, and most of all, against the endemic corruption.

Most Mexicans can recite personal examples of bureaucrats holding up business licenses for small (and sometimes large) *mordidas;* traffic cops extorting money for real or imaginary infractions; telephones magically installed after months, even years, of waiting, by the simple expedient of passing money across a desk. Much of the corruption involves low-level bureaucratic members of the ruling Party of Revolutionary Institutions (PRI), and even some of its most ardent acolytes admit that their candidate, Salinas de Gortari, probably lost the election to Cárdenas. But after days of counting and recounting, of unexplained computer breakdowns, of charges and countercharges, Salinas was declared the winner by the smallest margin in modern Mexican history.

Even then there wasn't much talk of revolution. There were protest marches, angry rhetoric, insults cast back and forth, but no guns fired in anger. After taking office the Harvard-educated Salinas moved quickly to repair his soiled image: He arrested the boss of the corrupt petroleum workers' union; he jailed one of the hottest players in Mexico's corrupt stock market; he moved against some of the drug kingpins in northern Mexico, arresting several hundred corrupt cops in the process. Most important, he arrested and indicted the killers of Manuel Buendía, who was Mexico's most influential newspaper columnist when he was shot in the back and killed five years earlier. The "intellectual author" of the crime turned out to be the man placed in charge of its investigation by Salinas's predecessor. These moves were at once practical and symbolic; Salinas was proving he had the right to govern by actually governing. And in Mexico City the fatalists began to suspend their disbelief.

"He has some set of *timbales,*" said my friend Ricardo Hernandez. "Everybody is surprised. But still . . . we'll see, we'll see."

(By early 1995, only weeks after completing his six-year term as president, Carlos Salinas found his reputation in ruins. The economy had collapsed. There was an unresolved armed rebellion in the southern state of Chiapas. Salinas's older brother, Raul, was in prison, charged with being the "intellectual author" of the murder of a high-ranking official of the PRI. The man Carlos Salinas had appointed to investigate that murder was in an American jail awaiting extradition to Mexico. The victim was his own brother and the Mexican government wanted to try him for covering up the truth about the crime. At the same time, American investigators had discovered more than $10 million in his Texas bank accounts. Carlos Salinas went on one of the shortest hunger strikes in history, about four hours, to demand the restoration of his own reputation; the entire country mocked him, and he soon was forced into exile. In Mexico City, one of my friends shrugged, smiled bitterly, and said: "They're all the same. Poor Mexico.")

Most "Chilangos" (as Mexico City residents are called) have long felt that they have little control over the management of the city. The mayor (or regent, as he is called) is appointed by the president and doesn't have to submit his performance to the approval of the voters. The last mayor is now in charge of the National Lottery. The new mayor, Manuel Camacho Solis, is a forty-three-year-old economist with an M.A. from Princeton. He is very good on television, speaking with a merciful minimum of nationalistic oratory. In several minor disasters (the explosion of a fireworks factory, a subway crash), he took personal charge on the scene, giving orders with a bullhorn like a Mexican Fiorello La Guardia.

His job has been made easier lately as a result of Salinas's ardent courting of Japan (the president's children attend a Japanese school in Mexico City). A few months ago the Japanese government promised to send teams of antipollution technical experts to Mexico City *and* pledged one billion dollars in credits over three years to help clean up the city's most critical problem. That amount is only one-third of what Camacho Solis and Mexican environmentalists believe they need; they hope to get the rest from the World Bank and the International Development Bank. But for the first time in twenty years, there is some hope. Meanwhile, of course, children still die and birds fall from the sky.

In spite of the enormous problems, the city remains a vibrant and surprising metropolis. Whenever I go back I return to the same places. I walk the Reforma. I have my shoes shined in the Alameda Park and tip my hat to the splendid memory of Don Tomás Treviño de Sobremonte, who, while being burned here by the Inquisition in 1649, shouted: "Throw on more wood! I paid for it with my own money!" I have lunch at the San Angel Inn, where the food is adequate but the setting, in an old colonial hacienda, is simply beautiful. Then I stroll through the cobblestoned streets to the Plaza San Jacinto and lay a rose before the memorial to the Batallón de San Patricio — the St. Patrick's Battalion — a group of Irishmen in the U.S. Army who swiftly decided that the American war against Mexico was unjust and switched sides. They fought alongside the Mexicans all the way to Mexico City, and after the defeat Winfield Scott ordered sixty of them executed for desertion. Mexico, of course, honors them as heroes.

On the last trip I drove out to the neighborhood called Coyoacán. The first stop was the house of Frida Kahlo, the powerful and disturbing Mexican painter who was married (twice) to Diego Rivera and whose brave and painful life was the subject of a 1986 film starring Ofelia Medina, Mexico's finest actress. This was the famous "blue house" on Londres Street, where Kahlo grew up and where she lived off and on with Rivera from 1929 until her death in 1954. The excellent biography of Kahlo by Hayden Herrera tells most of the story. In this house, while Rivera worked at his studio in San Angel, Kahlo had an affair with the sculptor Isamu Noguchi; he once had to escape by way of an orange tree, missing a sock, when Rivera came marching on the house with a gun. Here, too, she and Rivera gave shelter to Trotsky when he arrived in Mexico in 1937. And here she painted her fierce, unsettling pictures.

Wandering through the first floor gallery (Kahlo's best paintings are elsewhere), you can sense the crippled woman's naive and desperate need for faith. Her spinal column, collarbone, and right leg and foot were broken in a bus accident when she was eighteen; a steel bar pierced her body at the pelvis. For the rest of her life she was in pain. She found no solace in religion; she sought it in Marx. One of her paintings here is called *Marxism Will Give Health to the Sick*. It shows Kahlo still wearing the corset that held her broken body together, but she is throwing away the crutches, holding a red book.

In Frida's bedroom, her four-poster bed faces a wall adorned with portraits of Marx, Lenin, Stalin, and Mao, surely a grim and solemn quartet to ponder before sleep. But Herrera's biography contains one final mention of Isamu Noguchi. In 1946, Frida traveled to New York for still another operation on her ruined spine. Among her visitors was Noguchi, who brought her a gift: a glass-cased box of butterflies. On my visit to the Blue House, I glanced at those pictures of old Communist icons and then squatted to see how Frida might have seen them from her pillow. Attached to the canopy above her bed was the box of butterflies.

Not far from the Kahlo residence is the house where Trotsky was murdered in 1940. He had come here the year before, after his break with Rivera (some say it was because of Trotsky's own brief affair with Kahlo; others blame politics). Behind the high walls Trotsky is buried in the garden, and the house remains as it was when he was killed by a Stalinist agent named Ramón Mercader. The small doors are still covered with sheet iron; there are guard towers in the corners of the garden. This security was added after the painter David Alfaro Siqueiros and a group of other mad Stalinists tried to kill Trotsky with rifles and machine guns on May 24, 1940. Those bullet holes are still ugly gouges in the wall of Trotsky's bedroom, where he and his wife, Natalya, escaped death by rolling onto the floor. And the study is just as it was three months later when Mercader stepped behind Trotsky's desk and split his skull with an ice ax. There are books everywhere: Dos Passos's *The Big Money*, D. H. Lawrence's Mexican novel, *The Plumed Serpent*, many Russian books, Trotsky's own works, books on Stalin and Hitler in French and English, a copy of *Dreiser Looks at Russia,* stacks of yellowing ideological magazines, newspaper clippings, letters, a Dictaphone, a Russian typewriter. The air seems stale with old quarrels, made only more intense by the presence of murder.

But Mexico City is not a museum; it is a vibrant, pulsing organism, like any great city, and is always shifting. What is astonishing to me is how much of the city I knew still remains. So whenever I go back, I visit the two government-run handicraft shops on Avenida Juárez and buy masks, Michoacán altars, ceramic sculptures, or handmade toys. The prices are low and clearly marked; no bargaining is necessary, and the workmanship and imagination are extraordinary. On any given afternoon I might stop for coffee at the Opera Bar on Cinco de Mayo Street, where you can still view the bullet hole made in the ceiling by Pancho Villa to bring calm to an unruly meeting of his comrades in the Division of the North. I usually go at least once to the vast market at Lagunilla, behind the Plaza Garibaldi, where you can buy everything from VCRs to used toothbrushes and where years ago I actually saw a guy selling snake oil. "It's the only thing for your nerves!" the man shouted to a small crowd. "Did you ever see a nervous snake?"

In the evenings I might dine on the roof of the Majestic, at the Fonda del Refugio in the Zona Rosa, or at the Café de Tacuba, where musicians, artists, and ordinary citizens feast together on the posol or the enchiladas in *pipián* sauce, in a long, bright room decorated with Puebla tiles. There are dozens of other good restaurants: Bellinghausen, Prendes, Suntory for Japanese food, the Rivoli, La Gondola, Delmónico's — hell, I even like the *huevos rancheros* at Sanborn's. I always go at least once to the Tenampa on Plaza Garibaldi to hear the mariachis sing and to look at the murals and watch people submit to *toques* ("electric shocks") from a wizened old man who has been there, I think, since about the time of the sack of Tenochtitlán. Or I might go out to the Salon Margo, where some of the most beautiful women in Mexico show up on Saturday nights to dance to such visiting salsa bands as those of Ray Barretto, Celia Cruz, and Tito Puente.

And as a newspaper freak, I load up on the city's papers. There are twenty-one dailies published in the capital, along with more than two hundred magazines, ranging from *Vuelta* (edited by Octavio Paz and Enrique Krauze) to a wide variety of porno rags. My favorite paper remains *Esto,* an all-sports tabloid that led its earthquake coverage with the headline: WORLD CUP SAFE! The best of the city's morning broadsheets is *El Universal;* it's well written, carefully edited, and allows some diversity of opinions. *Excelsior* waddles around like an aging clubman, calling itself the *New York Times* of Mexico; but it is atrociously edited, with some stories jumping through six or seven pages in the back, so that only the archaeological mind can track them to their finish.

Many Mexican newspapermen still take money *(embutes)* from the people they cover and are expected to solicit advertising from the various government agencies, for which service they are paid a commission. The best newspaper of all is a left-wing morning tabloid called *La Jornada;* it resists the Mexican penchant for running oratory as news, draws on the best international news services, does the most sustained reporting on the horrors of life in the Mexican countryside, and has the hippest cartoonists. The staff is known as the least corrupt in the city. There is an English-language newspaper called the *Mexico City News;* I can't be objective about it, because I once spent some months unhappily trying to make it into a good newspaper. It does carry *Doonesbury.*

The city contains some enduring mysteries. Over the past few years I've visited the bookshop of the Palacio de las Bellas Artes seven times. It has been closed each time "for inventory." I think I have personally counted the books at least three times through the locked glass doors. Over the past thirty years I've gone to the San Carlos Academy a dozen times. It is said to contain a superb El Greco and some fine paintings by Cranach, Titian, Tintoretto, and Zurbarán. It has never been open. Not once. The last person I know to have ever been inside was Diego Rivera, who was thrown out of the art school in 1902.

I did solve one mystery for myself. For years the circular *glorieta* at the intersection of Bucareli and the Reforma featured a huge bronze statue of a man on a horse. The man was Carlos IV of Spain, and the massive statue was affectionately called El Caballito, "the little horse." The piece had a history of peregrination: It was originally planted in the Zócalo in 1802, was hidden away during the first revolutionary era, then emerged on the grounds of the old university beyond the Zócalo and finally came to rest on the Reforma. In post-revolutionary twentieth-century Mexico nobody cared much about the dead Spanish king. Nor did anyone claim it was great art. But the statue was a familiar reference point; people would meet in its shadow as they once did in New York beneath the Biltmore clock. Then a few years ago it disappeared.

"Where is El Caballito?" I would ask a cabdriver.

"It moved."

"Where?"

"*Quién sabe?*"

Who knew? The statue was hardly worth a search, but sometimes I would drive through the intersection and its memory would become another part of the Mexico that was lost. I imagined it being crated and shipped north, to help pay off the foreign debt. Or saw it coming to rest in some squalid and forgotten warehouse. And then one afternoon, coming out of the main post office, I looked to my right. And there was El Caballito. It was standing before the Palace of Mining in a small, gloomy square. I spoke to a young guard with a flat Indian face; he had no knowledge of how the statue had arrived in its final neighborhood.

"I'm from Oaxaca," he said and shrugged.

Later I learned that the mining building was designed by Manuel Tolsá, who was also the sculptor of El Caballito. So the man's major works are joined at last. But I no longer see girls standing beside the great beast, wearing starchy dresses, eating ice-cream cones, and waiting for their boyfriends.

Every morning during our most recent stay in Mexico, the bells of the Metropolitan Cathedral would begin to ring. The two towers of the cathedral house a great variety of bells, ranging in size from the 27,000-pound giant in the west tower to a variety of smaller ones that sound almost like jingle bells. On the first morning the sound had a certain charm. But every morning after that, the bells played without any relationship to the time. One morning they rang at 6:42, on another at 7:20. Sometimes a bell was struck nine times, the following morning three times, the next eleven times. On the one morning when I decided to get up early and defeat the bells, they didn't ring at all. Here mysteries abide.

One final mystery also eluded solution. At about six one morning a few years ago, I awoke to the sound of a band playing the brass parts of that traditional Mexican tune "I Left My Heart in San Francisco." I gazed out the window, but my view was blocked by the great stage. The band stopped. Then started again, played two-thirds of the tune, stopped, then began again. They were going to play this thing until they got it right. My mind teemed with explanations. The parade marking the Day of the Revolution was to have a sports theme; the baseball players Fernando Valenzuela and Teddy Higuera were honored guests. But neither played for San Francisco. Was Roger Craig a Mexican? Or was Tony Bennett staying in our hotel? I asked at the front desk. Nobody had an answer.

Days later my wife and I went to the parade, hoping to solve the riddle. At least thirty-five bands played "La Bamba," that year's unofficial anthem of Mexico. We watched drum majorettes twirling batons to "La Bamba." We watched five motorcycle cops do amazing stunts to the strains of "La Bamba." We saw *charros* do roping tricks to the rhythms of "La Bamba." We watched great armies of bureaucrats trudge by, properly devoid of music, sending only one blunt message to the thinning crowds: Look How Many Jobs We Have Invented. We saw guys in Villista costumes waving from wooden railroad trains and singing "Yo no soy marinero. . . ." We watched the entire parade. Nobody played "I Left My Heart in San Francisco."

At the end, as fathers took their sons by the hand and headed to the Metro, and traffic began to appear again on the blocked streets, and the many cops smoked in doorways, I glanced across the Reforma and my eye stopped on the sign of the Kentucky Fried Chicken store. Suddenly he whirled: the Man with the Blanket. I was sure he could answer the question about the San Francisco song. But I'd avoided talking to him now, in all of his guises, for more than thirty years. I took my wife's hand and we started walking back to the hotel. In the distance, we could hear the bells tolling in the cathedral.

CONDÉ NAST TRAVELER,
November 1989

CITY OF CALAMITY

For days, the sirens never stopped. The ambulances came screaming down the Paseo de la Reforma, the sound preceded by cars packed with young men waving red flags, honking horns, demanding passage. The ambulances went by in a rush. And then more came from the other direction, cutting across town on Insurgentes, grinding gears at the intersection. In the ambulances you could see doctors, nurses, tubes, bottles, a dusty face with an open mouth and urgent eyes. And then they were gone, heading for one of the hospitals in the great injured city of Mexico.

"Somos los chingados," a man named Victor Presa said to me, standing in the crowd in the Plaza of the Three Cultures in the district called Tlatelolco. We are the fucked. Presa, 41, a tinsmith, didn't know if his wife and three children were alive or dead. He lived with them in the 13-story Nuevo Leon building of the Nonoalco-Tlatelolco housing complex (one of 96 buildings erected in the '60s to make up the largest public housing development in the country). When the *terremoto* hit at 7:19 on the morning of September 19, Victor Presa was coming home with friends. "We were up all of the night. Yes. I don't have work, you understand? Still, no excuse. I was out, yes, we were drinking, yes . . ."

The residents of Nuevo Leon had been complaining for eight months to the project's officials about the dampness of the concrete, seepage of water, unrepaired fractures, the feeling of instability. The housing bureaucrats ignored them. And at 7:19 a.m., when Victor Presa was still almost a mile from home and thick with *pulque,* the building seemed to rise up, swayed left, then right, then left again, and all 13 stories went over, reeling down, slab upon slab, concrete powdering upon impact, pipes and drains crumpling, steel rods twisting like chicken wire. Within the gigantic mass, smashed among beds and stoves, sinks and bathtubs, among couches and cribs, bookcases and tables and lamps, ground into fibrous pulp with the morning's freshly purchased bread, boxes of breakfast cereal, pots of coffee, platters of eggs, bacon, tortillas, there were more than a thousand men, women, and children.

*   *   *

"*Somos los chingados,*" said Victor Presa, sore-eyed, his hands bloody, voice cracked, smoking a cigarette, staring at the ruins, as a small army of firemen, soldiers, and residents clawed at the rubble. A woman kept calling for a lost child: *Ro-baiiiiiir-to, Ro-baaaaaiiiii-irrrr-to.* The scene seemed almost unreal; surely some director would now yell "cut" and everyone would relax, the calls to the dead and dying would cease, the special effects men would examine their masterpiece. But this was real all right, and Victor Presa stared at the building, summoning whatever strength he had left to join the others who had been smashed by what was being called *El Gran Chingon.* The Big Fucker.

"This was all we needed," said an exhausted, hawk-nosed 24-year-old doctor named Raul Tirado. "Things were bad enough. Now this, the *catástrofe. Pobre Mexico . . .* poor Mexico."

Before the catastrophe was the Crisis, always discussed here with a capital C, a combination of factors that were at once political, economic, social. The $96 billion foreign debt. The incredible $30 million a day that leaves Mexico just to pay the vigorish to the banks, never denting the debt itself. The accelerating slide of the peso (for years, 12.5 pesos were pegged to the dollar; last week you could get 405). The collapse of the price of petroleum. All these were intertwined with a wide-ranging cynicism; a loss of faith in the Institutional Revolutionary Party (PRI) that has ruled Mexico without interruption since 1929; contempt for the obesity of the state, where almost four million Mexicans are employed by federal, state, and local governments out of a total work force of about 20 million; despair at the monstrous growth of Mexico City and its transformation into a smog-choked, soul-killing crime-ridden purgatory; fatalism about the daily, hourly arrival of more and more and more children; and above and below everything, touching every level of the national life, persisting in the face of exposure in the press and President Miguel de la Madrid's oratory about "moral renovation": the rotting stench of corruption.

"There will be a Mexico when this is finished," said Dr. Tirado. "But if they only clean up the physical mess, then we are doomed."

So the cranes will soon arrive to remove the top four floors of Continental Hotel on the corner of Reforma and Insurgentes, but neither the building nor Mexico will be easily healed. In 1957, when an earthquake measuring 7.3 on the Richter scale rolled through the city, killing 51 people, the Continental was a year old, a proud new member of the Hilton chain, with a blue-green mosaic mural rising from street level to the roof. That quake split the mural and fractured the building, but repairs were made and business went on. There were only 3.5 million people in Mexico City that year, and the city brimmed with optimism. But Hilton's name was long ago removed from the building, and the mural torn away, and when I walked around the corner to Calle Roma to look at the aging weather-stained edifice from the rear, the top floors seemed to have been mashed by some gigantic fist. Business there will not go on. Not after *El Gran Chingon.* Across the street from the Continental there's a statue of Cuauhtehmoc, the valiant Aztec prince who fought Cortez after Montezuma had failed; Cuauhtehmoc survived 1957 and survived September 19. But his pollution-blackened face now seemed sadder than ever.

"There'll be nothing there next year," said a 31-year-old insurance executive named Maria Delgado, staring at the Continental. "Who would build there again? Who would grant insurance? Who would build in many other parts of the city?"

Walking the city in the days after the quake, much of the damage did seem permanent. On the corner of Hamburgo and Dinamarca, a gallery called the Central Cultural de Jose Guadalupe Posada had been compacted from five floors into two; the art work had been removed, the building cordoned off behind a string of sad dusty pennants, but it didn't matter now: there was nothing left to steal. Across the street, rescue workers combed the rubble of an apartment building: cops, soldiers, doctors in Red Cross vests, university students, men with flat brown Indian faces, all lifting broken concrete, smashed furniture, calling for sounds of life, hearing nothing. Such groups would soon be familiar all over the ruined parts of the city, and they helped compile the statistics of disaster: nearly 5000 dead, another 150,000 hurt, an estimated 2000 trapped in the rubble, dead or alive. Some bureaucrats, afraid of permanently losing tourist business, rushed to minimize the effects of *El Gran Chingon;* Mexico is a large city, they said (it sprawls over 890 square miles); only 0.1 per cent of its buildings were destroyed. And that was true.

But you couldn't minimize what happened to the people who'd been directly affected. On Calle Liverpool, a blue moving van from Romero's Mudanzas was parked in front of Shakey's Pizza y Pollo, loading furniture from a damaged apartment house; in middle-class areas, moving vans were part of the scenery, like salvage boats after a shipwreck. A few doors down, the tan cement skin had peeled off the facade of another apartment house, revealing cheap porous concrete blocks underneath. On Calle Londres, two buildings to the right of the Benjamin Franklin Library tilted to the side like drunks in a doorway; cops warned pedestrians not to smoke because there was gas in the air. At the corner of Londres and Berlin, tinted windows had been blown out of a building, its walls sagged, the street was piled with broken glass and rubble; but in one window you could see the back of a spice rack, its jars neat, orderly, domestic, suggesting life in a place where nobody would ever live again.

The contrasts from one block to another, one building to the next, seemed baffling. Why did this house survive and that one collapse? Of the more than 450 colonial-era buildings listed with the Mexican equivalent of the landmarks commission, not one had been destroyed. But more than 100 new government-owned buildings had fallen, including three major hospitals and many ministries; hundreds of others (including many schools) were mortally wounded. Fate had never seemed more capricious. But every Mexican I spoke to offered the same basic explanation and it had nothing to do with God, faith, subsoil erosion, fault lines, the Cocos Plate, or the superiority of the 19th century to the 20th. Their answer was simple: corruption.

"Today, more than ever, it has been shown that corruption is a very bad builder," said the Committee of 100, a group formed last March to combat the environmental disasters of Mexico (its members include writers Gabriel Garcia Marquez and Octavio Paz, artists Rufino Tamayo and Jose Luis Cuevas). "It is no casual thing that the historic center of the city, made to last, has survived the two tremors . . ."

Senator Antonio Martinez Baez, a professor emeritus of the National Autonomous University, said that corruption was widespread in the building industry, particularly in the 1970s, when Mexico was booming with oil money. Martinez Baez said the corruption involved more than government bureaucrats, who looked the other way when shoddy materials were used; it included contractors, engineers, building owners and their intermediaries, usually hustling lawyers.

"They should not be allowed to clear these areas until a thorough examination has taken place," said an engineer named Rafael Avellanor. "Concrete, steel, everything must be tested, measured against the original specifications. And then the guilty should be jailed for murder."

Corruption is, of course, one of the oldest, saddest Mexican stories; didn't Montezuma first offer Cortez a bribe to go away? But corruption doesn't explain everything. If the earthquake toppled many modern buildings, if it seemed a horrible act of architectural criticism to enrubble the Stalinoid fortresses of the permanent bureaucracy, well, *El Gran Chingon* also rolled into Tepito.

And while the camera crews faithfully assembled each day at the Children's Hospital, at the Medical Center, at the Juarez housing project, where dramas of rescue and redemption were played out with touching regularity; while cameras for three hours followed Nancy Reagan in her yellow jacket and professionally concerned mask; while journalists sought out Placido Domingo, bearded and dusty in the ruins of Tlatelolco, working alongside ordinary citizens, searching for four of his lost relatives "until the last stone is lifted"; while cameras at the airport recorded the arrival of volunteers and aid from 43 countries; while all of that was happening, almost nobody went to Tepito.

There seems always to have been a Tepito in Mexico City; it's perhaps the city's oldest slum, maker of thieves and prizefighters and entertainers. For most of this century, the Tepito poor have crowded into tiny dollar-a-month, one-room flats in *vecindades* (apartment houses assembled around damp central courtyards, described in detail by Oscar Lewis in *The Children of Sanchez*). They built houses for themselves too, of scraps of wood, homemade brick, parts of cars, discarded advertising signs. Boys from Tepito became *toreros* and football players; they went to the great gym called Baños de Jordan and fought their way onto page one of *Esto* or *Ovaciones,* the city's daily sports papers; at least one, Raton Macias, became a champion of the world. Some became musicians and worked in Plaza Garibaldi, not far away, singing, playing horn or guitar for lovers, tourists, and each other in the Tenampa Club or the Guadalajara del Noche; some became cops; a few went on to become lawyers, doctors, teachers; many ended up a dozen blocks away in the notorious Black Palace of Lecumberri, the city's major prison, until it was torn down a few years ago.

The women of Tepito had harder lives. They married young, bore children young, suffered young, died young. Most were faithful to the code of machismo, imposed upon them by the men; those who violated the code often ended up in the pages of *Alarma,* a weekly crime journal that specializes in the mutilated bodies of the dead. Too many became prostitutes, working in the three famous *callejones,* or alleys behind the Merced marketplace, alleys so narrow that men stood with their backs against the rough walls while the women sat on stools and performed for a dollar. They started there when young, *las putas de Tepito,* and many ended up back in the *callejones* when old. Along the way, perhaps, there were stops in the houses and cribs of Calle de Esperanza (now lost to reform), or if they were pretty enough, smart enough, tough enough, they'd move up to the dance halls on San Juan de Letran, or the more expensive whore houses beyond the Zona Rosa, where the politicians and generals arrived each night with their sleazy *cuadrillas.* They might hook up with a married man and be installed in a *casa chica.* Some went off to the border towns. But they were always men and women "de Tepito," a phrase said with the tough pride of someone from Red Hook or the Lower East Side.

And now, a few days after the earthquake, Tepito was gone. In the *cerrada* of Gonzales Ortega, all of the houses were destroyed. *Vecindades* were in rubble along Brasil Street, on Rayon, Jesus Carranza, Tenochtitlan, Fray Bernadino de Las Casas, Florida, and Las Cardidad, all the way to the Avenida del Trabajo. This had always been a barrio whose true god was noise. A mixture of blasting radios, shouts, laughter, rumors, deals, quarrels, jokes, screaming children, imploring mothers, furious husbands. You could hear young men playing trumpet in the afternoons. You could hear lovers careening into melodrama, while dealers hawked contraband radios, hot jewelry, used clothes, drugs.

Now Tepito was silent except for one lone radio somewhere, playing a tinny mariachi tune. A drunk of uncertain age, grizzled and dirty, sat on a pile of broken brick, talking intensely to himself. A tinsmith poked at the ruins of his shop, a small boy beside him looking grave. An old man who had run a small antique record store trembled as he looked at his smashed collection. "I have great treasures here. Jorge Negrete. Carlos Gardel. Lara. Infante. Treasures. Of the old style. *Ahora . . .*"

Ahora. Now. Now the men, women, children, and dogs of Tepito had moved by the thousands to the open spaces around the Avenida del Trabajo. They had improvised tents. They'd formed teams to search for water. Old women had set up charcoal mounds to boil water and cook. Together, they consoled each other, fed each other, cursed at politicians, cops, fate, God. They passed along news: the

Bahia movie house was wrecked ("Ay, *chico,* where will we go now to get fleas?") and on San Juan de Letran all six stories above the Super Leche cafeteria had collapsed, killing many people having breakfast ("*Cuate,* the coffee killed more . . .") and more than one hundred government buildings had been wrecked, including the Superior Court, with all the city's criminal records ("There is a God . . ."). They joked, as most jokesters do, because they are serious men.

"We want to go home," said a white-haired wood finisher named Jesus Torres. "But we have nowhere to go. . . ."

He was standing with a crowd of men among the tents. Someone said that the government estimated the homeless at 35,000. Torres said, "That means there must be one hundred thousand on the street."

A young man named Eloy Mercado arrived with a copy of *Esto.* A story in one of the back pages said that Kid Azteca was among the missing. When I first came to Mexico in 1956, to go to school on the GI Bill, Kid Azteca had been fighting since the 1920s. He had been the Mexican welterweight champion for 17 years, an elegant boxer, good puncher, and in his forties he kept having one six-round fight a year to extend his record as the longest-lasting Mexican fighter in history. Now he and his two sisters were missing in Tepito, perhaps dead. Jesus Torres shook his head: "He's not dead." An old man leaned in, his face dusty, teeth stained with tobacco, smelling like vinegar. "You know how to find Kid A'tec'? Go in the street and start to count to 10. Then he'll get up . . ." He and Torres laughed, two men as old as the lost Kid Azteca who had managed to remain true to their origins. *Somos de Tepito, hombre . . .*

So to experience Mexico after the earthquake, you had to go to Tepito too. You had to go to the corner of Orizaba and Coahuila, where seven bodies were spread across the sidewalk, packed in plastic bags of ice, waiting for hours for ambulances too busy with the living. You had to smell the sweet corrupt odor that began to drift from collapsed buildings. You had to hear the sirens: always the sirens.

You could also see Mexico after the earthquake in the baseball park of the Social Security administration, where more bodies lay under blue plastic tents, waiting for identification. In other times, a team called the Red Devils played here. Now a somber line of men and women waited patiently for admission, searching for their dead, while bureaucrats in the third base dugout compiled their mournful lists. The corpses were photographed and fingerprinted and those that were not identified were wrapped in plastic bags and taken away.

Some were taken to the Cemetery of San Lorenzo Tezanco, and this too was Mexico in the autumn of 1985. Those who had lost their names along with their lives were given numbers: *Cuerpo 127, Cuerpo 128.* About 20 gravediggers chopped at the weed-tangled earth. More people came to look at the bodies, and many brought flowers. The unidentified were buried in a common grave. Presiding over this rude democracy was a white-haired, white-bearded priest named Ignacio Ortega Aguilar, who gave the blessings and offered the prayers. On the fifth day after the earthquake he told a reporter: "With this tragedy God has placed all of us in the same condition. In only a few minutes, while the earth shook, God permitted us to understand who he is and who we are. Today we know that we are owners of nothing."

And to know Mexico after the earthquake, you had to listen to the sound of rage. There was rage in Colonia Roma, because some cops were demanding a 500 peso *mordida* to allow residents past barriers with cars or moving vans; rage at unconfirmed stories of cops who had looted wrecked apartments or pried wedding bands off the fingers of the dead; rage at flower sellers who tripled their prices outside cemeteries; rage at *tienda* owners who doubled and tripled the price of food, and at men who sold water among the almost two million who had none at all; rage at the makers of coffins, who jacked up their prices (some donated free coffins, too). In Colonia Roma I saw a man who had rescued hundreds of books from the ruins of his apartment sitting among them on the sidewalk.

"The rest has no value," he said, his voice trembling, angry. "Only these. These I love." He touched the books, some of them in expensive leather bindings. "But when my brother-in-law came to help me take them away, the police said he would have to pay 1000 pesos. I insisted no! I asked for a supervisor. Nothing! So I will stay here. I hope it doesn't rain. But I'm prepared to die here before paying them anything."

One morning I walked to Calle Versalles, where I'd lived in a friend's apartment with my wife and daughters one winter in the '60s. The street was blocked at both ends by rifle-toting soldiers, while rescue workers chopped at the ruins of the old Hotel Versalles. Mattresses jutted from the rubble at odd angles. Men used plastic buckets to pass along the broken brick, plaster, concrete to waiting trucks. The house where we had lived was intact, with a lone broken window on the third floor. But the Versalles, across the street, was gone, along with the building beside it and another one at the corner. I showed a New York press card to a soldier who shrugged and passed me through the lines. The smell was then richer, loamier, the sweet sickening smell of putrefaction.

Suddenly everything stopped. Workers, soldiers, firemen called for silence. A body had been found. A middle-aged woman. Her jaw was hanging loose, hair and face bone-white from broken plaster, tongue swollen, eyes like stone. Her pale blue nightgown had fallen open. A man in a yellow hardhat reached down and covered her naked breasts. Mexico.

Nothing had prepared me for Avenida Juarez. In the old days, this was one of the city's great streets, a busy hustling thoroughfare. Turning into it from the Reforma, the Hotel Regis was on the left, along with a movie house, a pharmacy, the huge Salinas y Rocha department store. On the right was the Del Prado hotel, with one of Diego Rivera's finest murals inside. Past the Del Prado was a mixture of shops, both elegant and tacky, silver stalls, handicraft shops, book stores, restaurants. In the distance, there was the great green space of the Alameda park, with its baroque red shoeshine stands, and the Palacio of the Bellas Artes beyond. In the 1950s, I went out with a woman named Lourdes who worked on this street, and for years afterwards I thought that one form of heaven would consist of the Avenida Juarez on a Saturday afternoon, with a new book or a newspaper in hand and a shine on my shoes and a nap in the grass of the Alameda park.

On this day, the old avenue was a shambles. It was as if some brutal general, bored with the tedium of a firefight, had called in an airstrike. The Salinas y Rocha store was now a giant shell, blackened by fire. Across the street, the Del Prado was closed (a Mexican reporter told me the Rivera mural was intact) and so were all the shops and restaurants. Three huge buildings leaned at a precarious angle.

The street was packed with soldiers, sailors, doctors, nurses, reporters, and all attention was on the Regis.

The old hotel lay in a huge jagged mound; all 367 rooms had been destroyed. And I thought about the novel of Mexico City written by Carlos Fuentes in the 1950s, called (in English) *Where the Air Is Clear*. This was another city when he wrote his book, but Fuentes had premonitions of its ferocious future. One of his major characters was a revolutionary gone bad, an industrialist named Federico Robles.

> *But not he, he moved straight toward*
> *what he saw coming: business.*
>   *the spot which will remain the center of style and wealth*
>   *in the capital: the 'Don Quixote' cabaret of the Hotel Regis . . .*

They were still at the Hotel Regis when I was there in the '50s, the models for Federico Robles eating with Fuentes's other great character, Artemio Cruz, laughing and drinking with all the other "robolutionaries" who came to power with President Miguel Alemán in '46. They sat in booths or at small dark tables, heavy-lidded men dressed in silk suits and English shoes, graduated at last from tequila and *mezcal* and *pulque* to good Scotch whiskey, while their chauffeurs parked outside and the blond girls waited in the *casas chicas* on Rio Tiber. They were the men who made the present horror: the choked decaying capital, the failing banks, the greedy cement companies, the porous hotels. They invented Acapulco (with Alemán their leader), added Zihuatenejo, Cancun, Ixtapa, providing oil and shelter for the pampered bodies of the north. They were men who were all appetite. They ate the forests, they swallowed the rivers, they sucked up water from beneath the surface of the city and the regurgitated cement. In the end, under presidents Echeverría and Lopez Portillo, they ate Mexico.

But even in the '50s, when they still could be seen at the Hotel Regis, there were some who sensed what was coming. In Fuentes's novel, a journalist named Ixca Cienfuegos says:

"There's nothing indispensable in Mexico, Rodrigo. Sooner or later, a secret, anonymous force inundates it and transforms it all. It's a force that's older than all memory, as reduced and concentrated as a grain of powder; it's the origin. All the rest is a masquerade. . . ."

In a way, that secret anonymous force arrived at 7:19 on the morning of September 19, fierce and primeval. And now the Regis, along with so much else, was destroyed. Most of the men from the Don Quixote bar are gone too, dead and buried, the profits of old crimes passed on to their children; they stand now only as examples to the hard new hustlers of Mexico. There will never be statues of these men on the Paseo de la Reforma, but there are monuments to them all over the city: mounds of broken concrete and plaster, common graves in Tezonco.

And while many of the dead remained unburied in the week after the earthquakes, jammed among the slabs of the fallen buildings, everyone talked about the future. *Mexico will never be the same again:* the phrase was repeated over and over again in the newspapers. There were calls from the left and right for investigation of the corruption that led to the faulty construction of so many new buildings; there were demands that Mexico decentralize the government, sending many ministries to other cities; there were suggestions that the ruined sites be converted into parks, to allow some green open spaces for Mexico City to cleanse its lungs. Some insisted that Mexico would have to postpone its payments on foreign debt until after reconstruction.

And there were a few published reminders of another earthquake, far to the south, that had led to the eventual overthrow of the Somoza regime in Nicaragua. That 1972 earthquake killed thousands too. And when the generosity of the world sent money, supplies, medicine, clothes to Managua, Somoza and his gang stole it. The great fear of some Mexicans is that the same massive robbery will happen here, that the endemic, systemic corruption will absorb most, if not all, of the money that should be spent on the people of Tepito and Colonia Roma, on the survivors of Tlatelolco and the Juarez housing project and all the other ruined places of the city. If that happens, Mexico will not require agents of the Evil Empire to provoke the long-feared all-consuming revolution.

VILLAGE VOICE,
October 8, 1985

UNDER LOWRY'S VOLCANO

The novel can be read simply as a story which you can skip if you want. It can be read as a story you will get more out of if you don't skip. It can be regarded as a kind of symphony, or in another way as a kind of opera — or even a horse opera. It is hot music, a poem, a song, a tragedy, a comedy, a farce, and so forth. It is superficial, profound, entertaining, and boring, according to taste. It is a prophecy, a political warning, a cryptogram, a preposterous movie.

— Malcolm Lowry to Jonathan Cape
January 2, 1946

The novel was, of course, *Under the Volcano*. Lowry began writing it in December 1936, when he was twenty-seven, and finished the final draft on Christmas Eve 1944. He finished almost nothing else in his life, certainly no other major novel, as he lurched through the United States, Mexico, Tahiti, Italy, and the emptiness of British Columbia, forever a long way from home. He was by his own account an alcoholic, often falling into delirium tremens, sometimes collapsing into Mexican jails or charity wards; he was a terrible husband to both of his wives; he was by most accounts the sort of drunk who would pass a certain point and become a disgusting bore. But about one thing he was certain, and so are we: With *Under the Volcano*, he made a masterpiece.

When the book at last was published in 1947, critical praise was virtually unanimous (one notable exception was Jacques Barzun, who felt Lowry's novel was "derivative and pretentious"). The critics marveled at its classical structure, its dense, layered texture, its feeling for history, its use of myth and symbols, and its powerful examination of an alcoholic's descent into damnation. Lowry's language was baroque, intense, difficult — a style in direct contrast to the many neo-Hemingways who flourished at the time.

But there was more to the novel's reception than Lowry's literary accomplishment. There was also the legend of Lowry, the man. In many ways, he was a throwback to the romantic tradition of the artist consumed by his art to the point of self-destruction. Tales of his drunken escapades were common knowledge in literary circles;

such a man was no isolated inhabitant in an academic ivory tower; he was down there carousing with the bandits and groveling with the cockroaches on the floor of the cantina, passing through paradise on the way to the inferno. The novel was not a huge popular success, selling only thirty thousand copies in its first ten years of existence, but that, of course, helped feed the legend; nothing enhances the romantic agony better than neglect. And later the legend was made complete by the squalid facts of Lowry's death.

Eight years after *Volcano*'s publication, Lowry and his wife, Margerie, were finally home in England, living in a cottage in Sussex. But home didn't provide peace; in 1955 and 1956, Lowry was committed to two different London hospitals for psychiatric treatment, in an attempt to combat his alcoholism. By this time, Lowry had failed three times to kill himself, twice to kill his wife. At one point, a lobotomy was even considered. The psychiatrists and the hospitals eventually gave up. After these failures, Lowry returned to the cottage in Sussex, where he wrote sporadically. On June 26, 1957, he had one final row with Margerie and threatened to kill her. She ran to a neighbor's house for refuge and spent the night. Lowry was found the next morning in his bedroom, a plate of dinner scattered on the floor, along with an almost empty gin bottle and a broken bottle of orange squash. He'd swallowed more than twenty tablets of sodium amytal. It was a dingy way to die. He was forty-seven and was buried in the appropriately named town of Ripe.

The scene is Mexico, the meeting place, according to some, of mankind itself, pyre of Bierce and springboard of Hart Crane, the age-old arena of racial and political conflicts of every nature, and where a colorful native people of genius have a religion that we can roughly describe as one of death, so that it is a good place, at least as good as Lancashire, or Yorkshire, to set our drama of a man's struggle between the powers of darkness and light. Its geographical remoteness from us, as well as the closeness of its problems to our own, will assist the tragedy each in its own way. We can see it as the world itself, or the Garden of Eden, or both at once. Or we can see it as a kind of timeless symbol of the world on which we can place the Garden of Eden, the Tower of Babel, and indeed anything else we please. It is paradisal: It is unquestionably infernal. It is, in fact, Mexico.

— Malcolm Lowry to Jonathan Cape
January 2, 1946

Almost from the beginning, there was talk of a movie. This was itself surprising. The best movies generally come from pulp material, where action, narrative, character exist on the surface of the work; literary masterpieces, with their refinements of prose style and their deep interior lives, tend to resist adaptation to film. But *Under the Volcano* had two major attractions.

One was its principal character: the Consul. His name was Geoffrey Firmin, the despairing, alcoholic British envoy in the Mexican city of Quahnahuac (Lowry's name for Cuernavaca). Eleven of the novel's twelve chapters take place on the Day of the Dead, 1938, when the Consul goes on one final drunken odyssey that ends, as all tragedies do, in death. There are other characters: the film director Jacques Laruelle; Yvonne, the Consul's estranged wife and a former film actress, who has returned to Mexico in one final attempt to rescue the Consul from damnation; Hugh, the Consul's half brother, who shares his belief in the values of Western civilization, but actually does something about them, going off to the Spanish Civil War. Yvonne has betrayed the Consul by sleeping with Laruelle and Hugh, and is a critical character in the drama. But the novel belongs to the Consul, and his intense, brooding, ironic, sometimes comic, and ultimately tragic self-absorption. He is a character, like Lear, that actors would kill for the chance to portray.

The second protagonist is Mexico itself. Lowry's volcanoes rise to heaven; the barranca lies behind the villas and cantinas, winding through Quahnahuac, choked with the rotting garbage of history. On the Day of the Dead, the Consul is faced with a fearful choice: escape to heaven or descent into hell, and he lives his last hours in a private purgatory. Mexico is a perfect setting for such a drama. And almost no foreigners have evoked that country with such chilling accuracy as Lowry. He and the Consul traverse the cruel landscape together, and then abruptly face the abyss.

All of this is told in a way that has always attracted movie people. In fact, Lowry himself longed to write the screen version of his own novel. Frank Taylor, a friend who went to work for MGM in 1949, told Lowry he was working on a film of F. Scott Fitzgerald's *Tender Is the Night*. Lowry, perhaps thinking a successful production of Fitzgerald's novel would lead to an MGM commission for *Under the Volcano*, bestowed on Taylor an unsolicited script of *Tender Is the Night*. It was about five hundred pages long, and Taylor described it in 1964 as "a total filmic evocation — complete with critical remarks, attached film theory, directions to actors, fashions, automobiles: The only things like it are the James Agee scripts." Neither project happened.

In 1962, the actor Zachary Scott optioned *Under the Volcano*, but couldn't get it made, and after his death in 1965, his widow sold the rights to the Hakim brothers (Robert, Raymond, and André), who wanted Luis Buñuel to direct. This began a long, tangled story of hirings and firings, scripts and revisions and announcements of productions that never materialized. Buñuel gave way to Jules Dassin, who, in turn, was replaced by Joseph Losey. The Hakims' option lapsed; they sued the Lowry estate and lost. Then one Luis Barranco acquired the rights. More scripts. Even Gabriel Garcia Marquez took a crack at a treatment, as did Carlos Fuentes; directors Ken Russell and Jerzy Skolimowski were involved at other points. When the professionals failed, amateurs tried: Students read the novel and wrote adaptations: cultists, kabalists, professors, actors, all tried to transform their totemic novel into a workable movie script. And many of these versions arrived eventually in the hands of director John Huston.

"When I think back," Huston says, "there seem to've been dozens of them. Hundreds of them."

At first glance, such casting seems odd. Huston's special talent has always been for the spare and the laconic, as if either Hemingway or Marcus Aurelius were forever present behind his shoulder. There is very little self-pity in Huston or his work; compared with him, Lowry is a babbling whiner. But there are several strains in Huston's work that do display an affinity with those in Lowry's. Starting with *High Sierra* (for which he co-wrote the screenplay from a novel by W. R. Burnett), through *The Treasure of the Sierra Madre, The Red Badge of Courage, Moby Dick, The Night of the Iguana, The Misfits, Fat City, The Man Who Would Be King*, and others, Huston has been fascinated with doomed heroes. These men (they are almost never women) accept fate stoically, knowing that for them it is too late to change or compromise; in an odd way, the Consul is one of them.

Huston has also been intricately involved with Mexico. As a young man, or so the story goes, he rode as a cavalry officer with one of the Mexican revolutionary armies. One of his first notable screenplays (written with Wolfgang Reinhardt and Aeneas Mackenzie) was for *Juarez* (1939), when Huston was a contract writer at Warners. *The Treasure of the Sierra Madre* and *The Night of the Iguana* were filmed in Mexico, and since 1974, Huston has lived in a rambling house in Puerto Vallarta. It is easy to imagine Huston and Lowry wandering the streets of Cuernavaca together, visiting its cantinas and brothels, speaking of prizefighters and Mexican gods and the tragic end of the Spanish Republic. But the two men never met. The scripts for *Under the Volcano* continued to be written, following Huston to his estate in Ireland through the fifties and sixties, to locations around the world, and finally to Puerto Vallarta. None of them were any good.

Then a script arrived by a young man named Guy Gallo.

Although I have had a certain amount of youthful success as a writer of slow and slippery blues it is as much as my life is worth to play anything in the house.

— Malcolm Lowry to Conrad Aiken
March 13, 1929

Guy Gallo is twenty-eight years old, soft voiced, black haired, and handsome. He is also a good whiskey drinker. On this day, he is sitting on a crude wooden box on a path cut into the side of a hill in the village of Metepec, a dozen miles from Cuernavaca. Across the path, perched on the edge of a steep barranca, is a reconstruction of the Farolito, Lowry's mythical cantina-whorehouse, where the Consul comes to his squalid end. The infantry of a movie location — technicians, grips, actors, drivers — seems to be everywhere; trailers jam a side road; horses whinny in an improvised corral. Behind Gallo, standing on a hill, their flat Indian faces as impassive as masks, a family of Mexicans watches.

Gallo started writing plays at Harvard, and had two produced. "I went on to the Yale School of Drama, to get a doctorate. At some point during that year, I began to think about *Under the Volcano*. I'd heard of the book before, of course, but it wasn't in any course work I'd had, and I hadn't read it. Then I saw this survey of maybe twenty-five or thirty writers, in the *New York Times Book Review*, asking them for their favorite books and why, and Lowry's book was on a lot of the lists. So I went out and bought the book and read it. About three months later, I had this meeting with Paul Bluhdorn, an independent producer who was a friend of a friend, and started talking about *Under the Volcano* as a possible project. And he said,

'Well, yeah . . .' It wasn't as if it were preproduction — there was no money — it was more a friendly challenge than anything else. But it became a kind of carrot that was dangled in front of me. That's before we knew how complicated the rights situation was."

Gallo then went to work. He read Lowry's novel closely, wrote several critical papers on it, made a bony structural outline. Bluhdorn then told him about a possible producer from Mexico. Could Gallo fill in the skeletal outline, for presentation to this Mexican producer? "It sort of seemed silly to write a prose treatment of a novel," Gallo says, "so I wrote the screenplay very, very quickly, trying to give Bluhdorn something to sell."

But then it turned out that the rights were not available, and Bluhdorn lost interest. Gallo put the script away, continued with his schoolwork at Yale, and wrote two original screenplays. Then his name was given to Michael Fitzgerald, the son of poet and translator Robert Fitzgerald, and the producer of Flannery O'Connor's *Wise Blood,* which Huston had directed. Fitzgerald was looking for a writer on another Huston film, and wanted to see some samples of Gallo's work. Gallo told him he had the original screenplays and his version of *Under the Volcano;* he'd be glad to send them to Fitzgerald.

"Fitzgerald said no, don't send *Under the Volcano,*" Gallo says. "Just send me the original work. So I thought *Volcano* was dead again." Then a couple of weeks later, Gallo got a phone call from Fitzgerald. "He had mentioned *Volcano* to John Huston. Michael had never, ever read it, but just mentioned it to John, something on the order of, 'Still another version of *Under the Volcano.*' And John wanted to see it. I sent along a copy and that's when things started happening."

Gallo's screenplay was a stripped-down and simplified version of Lowry's novel. The novel begins on the Day of the Dead in 1939, with Laruelle remembering the events of the Day of the Dead the year before, when both the Consul and his wife were killed. In his screenplay, Gallo removes Laruelle as a character, merging some of him with Hugh, making a more cleanly structured triangle of the Consul, Yvonne, and Hugh. He gets rid of the 1939 chapter, and has all the action take place in present time, 1938.

"Basically, it was a structural decision," Gallo says. "If you can do it in one day, how do you do it? In one of his letters, Lowry talks about his version of *Tender Is the Night,* and says, when he delivers it, that 'we left out enough for a Puccini opera, but here it is!' That gave me some confidence. As a writer reading his work, and thinking of it as a film, already the premise was: Something had to go. I mean, you couldn't do everything. So it became a matter of my reading of the novel, and what could go without a loss. Lowry understood the difference between the two forms, and if he could do a different Scott Fitzgerald, perhaps I could do it to Lowry."

For Gallo, the task wasn't simply a matter of chopping away at the book; first it had to be understood. "You see, you gotta distinguish between what appeals to you about *Under the Volcano* as a *writer,* which is the lyricism and the complexities of the pattern, and what appeals to you thematically, which is actually the story. It's difficult to imagine this story without the narrative strategy that he employs to tell it. There is a strong, central thematic line in this book that is not impervious to dramatization: the character of the Consul, and that very central, dramatic issue of betrayal and the times, the historical inevitability. . . . In the novel you get to the kernel of the story through many different avenues, and the task you have to figure out, early on, is that you can't duplicate those avenues."

Gallo remembers working with Huston as if it were an intense seminar with an old master, which, in a way, it was. "There are a lot of things in the book — images, good images, startling images — but whenever I would have anything like that in the script, the question would always boil down to: 'It's very good, but *what does it mean?*' And the answer isn't: 'Well, this is a reference to Faustus, and that's an adumbration of this particular fall and it's prepared and it has to be. . . .' What does it mean in terms of *present tense?* What does it mean for our *character?* And our *situation?* And if it didn't do *both* something for the present tense and something for the overall structure, then it wasn't doing enough."

Inside the Farolito, someone yells, "Silencio, por favor!" The Mexican family on the hill behind Gallo has yet to say a word.

And now at last, though the feeling had perhaps been growing on him all morning, he knew what it felt like, the intolerable impact of this knowledge that might have come at twenty-two, but had not, that ought to at least have come at twenty-five, but still somehow had not, this knowledge, hitherto associated only with people tottering on the

brink of the grave and A. E. Housman, that one could not be young
forever — that, indeed, in the twinkling of an eye, one was not young
any longer.

— Malcolm Lowry
Under the Volcano

Here is John Huston, seventy-seven years old, five times married, director of thirty-eight motion pictures, actor in dozens more, winner of awards, storyteller, poker player, horseman, long-ago prizefighter, legend. He is in the Farolito, his squinting eyes taking in everything. He sees an ancient Mexican man playing with a four-piece band, a man so old he remembers seeing Halley's comet flash through the skies in the first year of the Mexican Revolution. He sees nine whores, a transvestite, a dwarf. Along one wall is a bar, and behind the bar is Indio Fernandez, one of the greatest Mexican directors, now almost eighty, a survivor of prisons and gunfights, acting in this movie as a favor to the man everybody calls John. Behind the camera is Gabriel Figueroa, the fine Mexican cinematographer, another old comrade. Huston looks at them all, suggests a change in a whore's costume, adjusts the angle of the camera.

There is, of course, a judgmental line on John Huston these days: He doesn't work at directing any more; he has the job done for him, looks on, and cynically picks up his fee. In the five days that I watched him direct *Under the Volcano,* the line turned out to be as false as most lines, political or artistic. He was involved in every shot; he cared about the details of setting and performance and the placement of the camera.

On this day of shooting, he seems to be everywhere, tall, slightly hunched, oddly frail, so bony now that his hands seem immense, like drawings by Egon Schiele. He has had a heart bypass and he wheezes from emphysema. But John Huston is not yet old.

During a break, he talks about what finally brought him to this movie in this place: "People had been sending me scripts since, oh, not long after the war. For some reason, people connected me to this book, and most of the scripts were, not surprisingly, pretty bad. The book attracted an esoteric element, the astrologists, the numerologists, the occultists and kabalists; each one found something of themselves in this material. Of course, almost anyone can find something of themselves in this one; the mirror is very clear and clean.

But one after the other, these opaque scripts kept arriving. I admired the book very much, not for the same reasons that all readers do. I objected to — how shall I say this? — Lowry's taking *every* experience and writing it into his own use. Yes, just acquiring anything that has happened and putting it into the context of the book. And some of it was nonsense, absurd. For instance, there's a poster about boxing; it's about a boxing match. And in one biography, he's asked about this, and said it symbolized the Consul's conflict with Yvonne. Well, that's bullshit."

He pauses, and whispers something to Tommy Shaw, his production manager and assistant director; they go back to *The Night of the Iguana* together, and are friends. Shaw nods; Huston returns to the conversation. "Across the years, there *were* some fairly good scripts," Huston says, covering his mouth to smother a cough. "But none of them had the *solution* to the picture. None offered the hope for a motion picture." Pause. "Until Gallo's came along." Pause. "He had simplified it."

Huston smiles. "I had a conversation a few months ago with Garcia Marquez, whom I'd met for the first time, and *he* had done a script — of which he *thoroughly* disapproved — and we were talking about some of the possible solutions to the novel, which he admired very much. We discovered we were in complete agreement. And by this time I was well into it with Guy Gallo. In his script, all those literary curtains had been pulled aside, Lowry's mists had been blown away. He got through to the central idea, without all the literary persiflage."

A number of Huston's movies, beginning with *The Maltese Falcon,* have been adapted from novels. How did this project differ? "Well, each one was different, of course. In the case of the *Falcon,* I didn't have to cut through anything. There it all was. It was practically a film script in novel form. *Under the Volcano* is quite the opposite. I have great admiration for the novel, and there are those who put it on the same plane as *Ulysses* and *Waste Land* and *The Magic Mountain* and so on. I don't think of it in those terms. But I think it's very fine. One of the best novels of our generation, surely. Even though there is a cult, yes, that maybe endows it with mystic qualities that I don't appreciate, or fail to appreciate."

He enjoyed working with Gallo on the script, a process that took place almost entirely during six weeks last summer in Huston's home in Puerto Vallarta. "In this picture particularly, I wanted it to be an immediate experience, rather than telling a narrative with a beginning, a middle, and an end, with frozen climaxes. I wanted something that was happening *constantly,* that gives you a feeling that you are present, as though it were an actual experience, rather than a *remembered* experience." He pauses, watches a whore go by. "To me, one of the great things of American writing is when you feel you are directly *witnessing* something. One has that feeling in O'Neill, that you are directly witnessing a *happening.* And are you familiar with W. R. Burnett? This is one of the least appreciated American writers, and you get that thing of direct experience in reading Burnett."

Huston watches Tommy Shaw whip the extras into their assigned roles and smiles. "That man is the true hero of this production," he says of the white-haired Shaw. "I don't know what I'd do without him."

He turns and sees Albert Finney, dressed in the soiled white suit of the Consul, smoking a cigar in the corner, mumbling to himself, as if rehearsing one final time before the cameras turn. "This fellow Finney is giving one of the finest performances I've ever seen. I thought he would be good; but I never dreamed that he would be as good as he is. Or that *anybody* would be as good as he is."

> *It was one of those pictures that, even though you have arrived in the middle, grip you with the instant conviction that it is the best film you have ever seen in your life; so extraordinarily complete in its realism that what the story is all about, who the protagonist may be, seems of small account beside the explosion of the particular moment, beside the immediate threat, the identification with the one hunted, the one haunted.*
>
> — Malcolm Lowry
> *Under the Volcano*

It is impossible, on these days at the Farolito, to imagine anyone other than Albert Finney in the part of the Consul. When he is supposed to be drunk, he is drunk; not the comic drunk, not the grotesque, exaggerated drunk of so many bad performers. Finney as the Consul plays an intelligent man, a man of language and smothered passions, who has moved past the point where the world is clear, yet remains capable of sudden explosions of clarity. It's in the way he stands, in the looseness of his features that suddenly snap into tension. It's in his great angers, breaking out of the emotional ice jam that the Consul has made of his life. This performance displays one possible solution to the old problem of making a movie out of a literary masterpiece: Strip away the literary style, get down to the bones of the narrative, and then fill the bony structure with performance.

"Where the book has helped me is to fill in the internal life, the subtext, the thoughts that go through my mind above and beyond what one says," Finney says one afternoon in his room at the Racquet Club in Cuernavaca. "Because often in life, you don't think of those things, or about what you say; you say what you say. A phrase may come out, a line may come out; but the general feeling behind it is often, in life, a sort of nonspecific area that you're preoccupied with, from which lines come out. So I thought the novel was important to me to fill in that sort of interior thought pattern. One does this anyway as an actor; that's one of the things that you're *supposed* to do. I mean, that's what one *does:* invest the undercurrent with all kinds of thoughts that may be applicable to the situation the character is in at any time. But it helped to have the novel."

In Mexico, when not before the cameras, Finney is living to some extent the way Geoffrey Firmin might have lived in 1938. He drinks only tequila, usually taking a taste before shooting; he makes a ritual of eating breakfast each morning with a Mexican family living near the location that has begun to make special meals for the crew. Such activities are not simply a device to find the character of the Consul.

"It's all to me part of the total *experience,* of trying to live the moment — the present tense of the matter — when you work," Finney says. "The whole Mexican experience of doing this film is not repeatable in my lifetime. I'm not saying I won't do another film in Mexico, but this subject, this experience, these circumstances at this time are not repeatable. One wants to relish all that, as well as the work. And, of course, it all feeds the work. So in this part, I find myself having a tequila; I had never really drunk tequila before. I'd been to Mexico before, but I never drink tequila in London or Spain. So suddenly I tried one or two kinds of tequila and mescal, just for the flavor. So that one is mildly — *mildly* — sort of savoring what the Consul *seriously* put himself through. It's not that they, or it, help; but they might help. One of the jobs is that [as an actor] you're going somewhere that's unfamiliar to you. You're trying to get yourself into unfamiliar territory in your imagination. So you help prepare the ground so you *might* get an idea you never had before. There's no guarantee. It's not to be relied upon. But it might help."

Finney was first asked about playing the Consul in 1981, while he was portraying Daddy Warbucks in *Annie,* also directed by Huston. He was approached by a bearded, New York–based German intellectual named Wieland Schulz-Keil, who with his partner, Moritz Borman, was determined to bring *Under the Volcano* to the screen (at that point, they were almost finished with the enervating task of clearing the rights).

Huston loved the way Schulz-Keil looked, and drafted him for the part of a bomb-throwing anarchist in *Annie.* But Lowry's novel was the German's primary concern. He'd read it as a boy; now he wanted to see it on the screen. Huston was the ideal director, Finney the perfect Consul. Finney hadn't read the book before Schulz-Keil's first approach. "He told me they had an outline for this script, and could he send it to me," Finney remembers. "I said, 'Of course.' " A friend coincidentally gave him a copy of *Under the Volcano;* there had been some industry talk about the possibility of the movie being made, and she thought he should read the novel. At the same time, Schulz-Keil sent over his outline.

"It was the thickest document I'd ever seen," Finney remembers, "so I thought, Well, I might as well read the novel. Like most people, I found the novel very difficult to get into. To plug into somebody else's stream of consciousness is always hard. But then I thought what an interesting story it was, what an interesting situation it was. The pain of it, the anguish of it kind of struck me. Then periodically I would get new outlines, and then scripts."

Meanwhile, thirty-two-year-old Michael Fitzgerald had been brought into the production end of the movie. Huston invited him to come to The American Film Institute's Life Achievement Award dinner honoring Huston last year in Los Angeles, where a deal was worked out with Schulz-Keil and Borman. The two Germans had exhausted their bankroll in the process of clearing the rights, and had been turned down by four studios. At the Huston dinner was Alberto Isaac, a director general of the Mexican Cinematographic Institute, who expressed interest in helping with the financing. Fitzgerald sent Tommy Shaw to Mexico to work with Isaac, and three weeks later Fitzgerald arrived to make a deal.

"For twenty years," Fitzgerald says, "Mexicans have gotten screwed by virtually every outsider that has come in here. I wasn't prepared to do that. In our picture, they are full participants, from every source of income, all over the world. They recoup in the same position, they have the same proportionate profit participation that everybody has. On top of that, they were given all profits in Mexico itself, as a gift from John." Fitzgerald sold American rights to Universal Classics, while Twentieth Century-Fox took the rest of the world.

At the same time, casting was proceeding. Finney agreed to do the picture. Huston wanted Jacqueline Bisset for Yvonne; he'd directed her early in her career in *The Life and Times of Judge Roy Bean*. Fitzgerald had been impressed by Anthony Andrews in *Brideshead Revisited* and showed his work to Huston, who approved him for the part of Hugh. And the work with Gallo continued at Puerto Vallarta.

"All of a sudden," Fitzgerald says, "we were . . . I mean this all started at the AFI dinner in March for Chrissakes, and by mid-June we were in feverish preproduction in Mexico." He remembers Huston's original interest. "He said, 'Well, *Volcano* is there, and it will never get done otherwise; what about taking it over and doing it in the same vein that we did *Wise Blood?*' Which was basically: small, tight, putting every fucking dime on the screen, rather than on bullshit. And that's what we've done."

Jacqueline Bisset was approached indirectly, through John Foreman, who was Huston's friend and had produced *The Man Who Would Be King*. "He told me about the project and asked me would I read it," Bisset says. "And I thought, Well, it's an interesting idea, an interesting combination of people." A first-draft screenplay was sent to her. "My part was not particularly fascinating, but I felt it had to go one way or another: more enigmatic, or much more 'directioned.' Both of which seemed fine, if they could move it in one direction or another. John, Wieland, and Guy were all down in Puerto Vallarta working together when I got the second script. So I went to Puerto Vallarta to see them. I read the book in between. In the book Yvonne is not that clear. She's there very much, if you go through the book looking for her. But I needed to start from some concrete point. There are a lot of abstractions in the book, a lot of symbolism, and things difficult for me to understand: just in terms of story line, from A to B to C, to the end. In the second script, a lot of my queries were answered. I was very touched by the atmosphere of the piece; it haunted me completely; it's still with me very much. I think it'll stay with me."

Bisset had some apprehensions about working again with Huston, and thus found the novel a comfort; it, too, answered some of her questions. "I didn't imagine John Huston would be someone with whom I could be having a million detailed conversations. I felt one would go to him during the course of shooting for major decisions, rather than quibbling-quabbling. I heard he liked actors to prepare — I'd worked with him before, and didn't have a particularly close contact with him. I was in that film [she played Paul Newman's girlfriend in *Judge Roy Bean*], but didn't have the benefit of scene preparation or anything like that; I did my bit and it was fine. I think it's important to know the style of the director and what he expects. Some people like to change everything. And on *Judge Roy Bean,* they were rewriting the script before every scene, and actors were left with quite large speeches to learn, fifteen minutes before. And I thought, That's something I would not like to be in [again], because I'm a slow study."

Bisset laughs when asked about the macho atmosphere of the *Volcano* set ("It has its moments; it has its nonmoments, too"), but seems quite happy with the experience of making the film. "I quite like things to be run in a fairly businesslike fashion, because there's a tendency on location for people to start thinking they're on holiday."

By the time the film finished shooting last November, it was under its $4 million budget, and five days under its eight-week shooting schedule. "What matters," Fitzgerald says, "is that we've made a film of *Under the Volcano,* one that some people said could never be made."

Certainly, a major share of the credit, if the film works, must go to Finney. On one of the last days of shooting, the actor talked about the process that goes into the making of such a performance. "In the beginning, I'm obsessed," he said. "Getting up at three in the morning, lines buzzing in my head, I'd sit with the script, just think about it. *Now,* of course, I'm not so obsessed. No, I don't make notes, don't write anything down. I just try to remember, to understand what's going through the character's mind. Of course, sometimes those thoughts are *not* going through your mind while you shoot, but I believe that they're *there,* that they're part of the hoped-for density, or the life effect. I don't make a claim that there *is* one; but if there is any, they're there."

Does he draw on the experiences of his own life to fill out a charac-

ter like the Consul? "Well, yes. But I've never gone this far, as far as
the Consul goes, and I don't think I ever will. There are times in
one's life where one is scratched or kicked, or maybe there was a
strange accident of responsibility, because you're supposed to be
good at something and, therefore, you have to deliver. And you want
to say, 'Ah, fuck it, *I'll* decide whether I'll deliver; that's up to *me*,
not to some sense of responsibility.' As the Consul does. Therefore,
we *use* those occasions when one's felt that. But what one needs here
is a much deeper, a much more painful extension of that. The Consul
goes all the way. So far, I've not. I'm still walking about. I've not
actually thrown the reins away."

To illustrate what he meant, he talked about acting in *Shoot the
Moon*. "If you are doing a part which is about the breakup of a
marriage, about the pain of a relationship coming to an end, a good
relationship, a love coming to an end, then constantly you are tinkering subconsciously with your own past. And the memory's a remarkable thing. I mean you do actually, if you concentrate hard enough,
you *do* remember, you *do* go back. You don't only remember the
locations, you don't just remember the apartment you stormed out
of with your few belongings. But a capsule opens, and I'm flooded
with the *emotions* I felt at that time. The memory stores those emotions; not just pictures of it; not just facts or figures; it actually does
store the emotions. Therefore, doing a picture like *Shoot the Moon*
is very depressing, because you're constantly in that area that you
can't help but be."

Finney said it isn't simply a matter of using one's life; certainly
for younger actors, there isn't enough life to draw on, not enough
memories. "Imagination *does* come into play. And possibility. 'If
only I *had*. . . .' 'And what *if* . . . ?' There's more in the vault than
one thinks, isn't there? The big problem as you get older is to retain
the lack of self-consciousness, to retain a kind of child in your work,
to be open. One of the things I love about John is that it's your own
total responsibility. John just says, 'Well, show me.' John thinks if
he's cast it right, if the actor's got some degree of talent, he doesn't
need to direct him. He doesn't direct. He won't direct. In other
words, he doesn't direct *a lot* — seemingly. If you say to John before
a scene, 'Would it be a good idea if . . . ,' he'll say, 'Show me.' He
doesn't say, 'That's quite interesting, *but,* on the *other* hand . . .'; he
says, 'Show me.' And then you show him, and he says, 'Well, maybe.'
So John likes to see you offer something. And then he will cajole it,

nudge it, bully it, or just say, 'A little less oil and vinegar — a little more lemon.' Or he may say nothing. If you don't know John, you may say, 'Well, he isn't giving me any direction.' But when you get to know him a bit, you know that when he doesn't say anything, he's happy."

Finney, of course, has had extensive theater experience and is clear about the differences between the two forms. "The most elusive thing about film acting is that when they say go, or when they say action, you've got to be in the state of mind to do it. You've been sitting around for two hours, while they are tinkering around with this, that, and the other thing, and then someone will say, 'OK, we're ready; we don't want to lose the light.' And I think you must be ready. I suppose that's theater training: when the curtain goes up at seven-thirty, it's no good saying you'll be ready at ten . . . I prefer that we do it on take one; we don't have to keep flogging ourselves. But I also think the operator, the film puller, the sound man, the camera man should be ready, too. That doesn't always happen.

"Therefore, in movies, an actor has to spend most of the day sort of being on *simmer*. Obviously, when it's lunchtime, you get away from it; but sometimes I like to think about it, just brood over it, sit in a chair and look down into the barranca and fret. If I think it's going to be useful . . . On some days it might be useful to just go and play catch ball with the boys. Sometimes you wake up in the morning, and you think you've got a feeling, a little *feeling*, you're ready for the day's work, and you want to nurse this feeling and use it. And then about twelve-thirty or something, you look for it, and say, 'Where's that feeling? Where did it go? It's gone. Gone.' That's the intangible thing about film. You can stay so long on simmer that you evaporate."

At the end of *Under the Volcano,* Finney utters the Consul's dying words: "Christ, what a dingy way to die." And yet the scene is not dingy; it is genuinely tragic. Through the power of Finney's performance, we've seen the Consul revealed as a remarkable man, which transforms his stupid, dingy death into something of enormous artistic value. One reason is that Finney has infused the part with so many complicated feelings.

"I suppose what I might do better than anything else is somehow record feeling," Finney said one Sunday afternoon. "If I was a painter, I'd record light and shade and color. But I record *feeling,* and so I think about feeling a lot. And then channel it into a role where I think it might be useful. That's part of what acting's all about, I think. One uses *anything*. And, yes, one *is* ruthless. Because there is no one way of going down the road, is there? There can't be. There're too many things, too much of a variety, too many possibilities for there to be one correct way. And if that's how one does it, well, that's what one does. I've not caused anyone's death. I've not pressed any buttons or triggers in my life. Do you know what I mean? I might have been ruthless in my later use of emotions, and people's pain. But no lives have been lost."

Finney paused. Through the windows of his suite, we could see tennis players and old men cleaning lawns and a bus taking tourists on the mandatory ride to the pyramids or the volcanoes. "At its best, acting hopefully does help to ameliorate human behavior," he said. "At its simplest, it's often just maudlin. Some jobs you think — Well, it's a bit like *that*. But at its best, when you get something that is really demanding and you have a go, it's very honorable work. It's also telling a story. But at its best, I think that somehow a recognition of ourselves might come about. In this film, we might know the Consul. We might know ourselves." Finney smiled. "At least one likes to think so."

AMERICAN FILM,
July–August 1984

IN ZAPATA COUNTRY

Each day after lunch, we walked under the hot, scoured Mexican sky to the center of the town of Tepoztlán. Off to the left were the sour remains of old cane fields where shirtless kids played soccer in the dust. Down the broad valley behind us, we could see men riding horses and the sudden glint of sun on a machete. In the town's graveyard, tiny cones of dust whirled among the headstones. On both sides of the valley were the mountains of Morelos.

Those mountains, surrounding this town about 60 miles south of Mexico City, are a spectacular sight: sheer cliffs, sudden crags, rocky formations that seem split by some cosmic ax. Behind them, other mountains rise, big and broad-shouldered, with the dark purple silhouettes of still more beyond — all part of the Sierra Madre, the primordial spine of Mexico. Each day, as my wife and I walked to town, they became as familiar as the road itself.

A half mile from the house where we were staying, the modern two-lane blacktop abruptly gave way to 18th-century cobblestones and rose steeply into the town. Here, visiting automobiles slowed to a crawl in a tenuous and losing negotiation with the colonial past. At the top of that steeply terraced hill, sitting in doorways, wearing the familiar white pajamas of the *campesino* — the countryman — their eyes cloudy with the past, their faces gullied by time, were the last old soldiers of the man who once was the revolutionary master of these mountains: Emiliano Zapata.

"*Si, fue un Zapatista,*" an old man told me one afternoon. Yes, I was a *Zapatista*. Then he paused, in modest clarification: "We all fought. In Tepoztlán, we were all *Zapatistas*."

The sight of these old men moved me in complicated ways. I've been going to Mexico since the mid-1950s, when I was a student there on the GI Bill. In 1956, on the Transportes del Norte bus heading south from Laredo, I carried Zapata in my psychic baggage, or at least the version of the great revolutionary leader that Marlon Brando played in *Viva Zapata!* In that fine, tragic 1952 movie, directed by Elia Kazan, Brando gave Zapata a muted and melancholy grandeur. For once, the movies got it right; over the years, as I studied the history of this great, tormented country, it became clear that *Viva Zapata!* might be of limited use as literal history, but was absolutely true as legend.

Here in the village of Tepoztlán, among the mountains of Morelos, was the proof. The legend lived. But for these old men, Emiliano Zapata wasn't simply a character in a movie, a figure in a mural, or a name in the history of the 1910–1920 Mexican Revolution. He had lived, he'd fought, he'd died here. Or in places within a day's horseback ride or three days' walk. These men saw him, heard him speak. "All of Morelos followed him," one man said. "Right to the end."

Even today, many decades after his death, the spirit of the *Zapatista* struggle seems to permeate Morelos, while haunting Mexico. "He is one of our legendary heroes," wrote the great Mexican writer

Octavio Paz. "Realism and myth are joined in this ardent, melancholy, and hopeful figure who died as he had lived: embracing the earth."

That earth was, above all, the earth of Morelos, where Zapata was born in 1879 in Anenecuilco, a village whose name in Aztec means "place where the water moves like a worm." And though as a young man Emiliano was a master horseman, not a tiller of the soil, his ancestors had lived and worked the land for generations. Much of that land was communal — the grazing fields, the rivers — and was theirs according to land grants that went back to the earliest days of the Spaniards. But over the centuries, and increasingly under the dictator Porfirio Díaz, who took power in 1876, the common lands were taken from the men of Morelos by the owners of the expanding haciendas. Stolen village cornfields were planted in sugar, rivers diverted to irrigate the lands of the rich. Guns proved more powerful than paper. Those who protested were humiliated, jailed, sometimes killed; after the turn of the century, when the Díaz regime was in full power, those who protested were often sent off to penal slavery in the henequen plantations of distant Yucatan. More and more, the men of Morelos whispered about revolt; someday, they said, they would have to fight for the land with guns.

In Anenecuilco in 1909, the 400 citizens turned for help to 30-year-old Emiliano Zapata, electing him their leader. He was a proud, tough man who did not toady to the rich. He spoke Spanish *and* Náhuatl — the language of south-central Mexico — and had traveled beyond the valleys, beyond even Cuernavaca, the capital of Morelos; he had even lived in Mexico City, *la capital,* where he had handled horses for a rich family. And he had demonstrated his love for Morelos by coming home. "Uneasy and depressed," wrote John Womack Jr. in his classic 1968 biography, *Zapata and the Mexican Revolution,* "he was soon back in Anenecuilco, remarking bitterly how in the capital horses lived in stalls that would put to shame the house of any workingman in the whole state of Morelos. . . ."

For more than a year, Zapata and the men of Morelos tried to use the law to settle their grievances. Basically, they wanted the return of the *ejidos,* the communal lands that had been theirs since before the Conquest. They pleaded with the owners of the haciendas; they sent letters to the governor. They were ignored. Finally, in 1910, initially over the narrow issue of reelection of the dictator, Mexico exploded into full-scale revolution. And with Zapata as its leader, Morelos was the most revolutionary state of all.

Although he never learned to read (in 1910, 77 percent of all Mexicans were illiterate), Zapata soon proved to be a more daring and intelligent commander than the well-read graduates of the military schools. He was quick when they were slow; he was patient when they were not; above all, he had the respect and support of his people (who supplied food, information, and troops), while they had only the heavy artillery.

"Seek justice from tyrannical governments," he said, "not with your hat in your hands but with a rifle in your fist." For the next decade, with a rifle in his fist, Zapata made clear that he wanted nothing for himself. He was offered haciendas, land, power. He turned them all down, remaining true to the basic *Zapatista* demand: *"Tierra y Libertad"* — land and liberty — for the people who worked the land.

This was, of course, a conservative vision; Zapata offered no blurry Utopian future. He asked only that stolen land be returned to its owners, the *campesinos,* and that they be allowed to work that land in peace. *Now,* before the planting. That, plus the freedom to speak what they felt and elect whom they wanted. The troops of his army marched under the banner of the Virgin of Guadalupe, not Karl Marx.

There was fighting all over Mexico, of course, but Morelos suffered more than any other state. Hundreds of villages were damaged; Cuernavaca, the state capital, was reduced to rubble; the state's economy was destroyed, as was the sugar industry. The people suffered horrendous losses; almost half the population was killed or driven away by the war. That's why here, of all the regions of Mexico, the hope and pain of the revolution remain so vivid.

You drive down a side road near Cuautla, where there is a monument to Zapata, and off to the right is the chimney of a destroyed house, the smashed bricks and beams of a church, and more often the oddly splendid ruins of a once more splendid hacienda. The last always evoke images of Mexico's *ancien régime,* when men in tight chamois pants and silver spurs built grand mansions they thought would last forever. In 1910, 30 haciendas owned 62 percent of the total surface area of Morelos and almost all of the arable land. Their ruins are also monuments to Zapata. "The land free, the land free for all," he said. "Land without overseers and without masters, is the war cry of the revolution."

From that, Zapata never deviated, even in 1918, the worst year of the long struggle, when the ruthlessness of the Carranza government combined with an influenza epidemic to devastate his Army of the South. Morelos was the grinder; Carranza's troops burned crops, drove off cattle, raped and murdered women and children. The widespread hunger and misery, combined with sheer human exhaustion, probably led Zapata into the trap that would cost him his life.

In March 1919, a colonel in the government army named Jesús M. Guajardo agreed to join forces with Zapata, defecting with guns, ammunition, and more than 500 men. The colonel was stationed in the hacienda of San Juan Chinameca. From his mountain hideout, Zapata was suspicious but intrigued — and possibly desperate. He asked for proof of Guajardo's sincerity. The colonel appeared to supply it, attacking a Carranza garrison (blanks were supposed to be used, but 19 men were killed anyway), and executing 59 soldiers of a *Zapatista* officer who had defected. Zapata was convinced; no plotter could be *that* ruthless. He met with Guajardo, made arrangements for the delivery of the arms and men, and told the young colonel that he soon would be a general in the *Zapatista* army. Guajardo then invited Zapata to a fiesta at the hacienda in Chinameca, where they could celebrate the new alliance. Ignoring rumors of a trap, Zapata came down from the mountains on April 10.

Leaving most of his troops standing guard down the road, Zapata entered the hacienda with 10 of his officers. As historian William Weber Johnson described the scene: "Guajardo's men were standing at attention in the patio, their weapons in the present-arms position. A bugle sounded three times just as Zapata passed through the gate into the patio, and on the third note Guajardo's men raised their rifles and fired at Zapata and his followers. Zapata turned his horse, his pearl-handled pistol still in its holster. He stood in the stirrups with his arms outthrust and then crashed to the ground. His companions fell with him. . . ."

The bullet-riddled body of Zapata was then draped over a horse and taken to Cuautla, where it was unceremoniously dumped on the floor of the Municipal Palace for all to see. But almost from the beginning there was skepticism among the people. It was not his body. No: Zapata was taller. Or shorter. He had a crescent-shaped scar on his face that was not on *this* face. And where was the mole above the mustache? No, they said: Zapata was alive. He was said to have gone to Arabia — or to Nicaragua in the 1920s — where, they said, he fought with the guerrilla Augusto Sandino. Most placed him closer to home. As Johnson wrote in his book, *Heroic Mexico:* "For years afterward, they insisted that on dark nights 'Miliano could be seen back in the hills, dressed in white peasant clothes and riding — not the sorrel on which he had been killed — but a fine, white horse of the earlier, happier days."

That was the image used at the end of *Viva Zapata!* — the white horse riding in the mountains. And it is the image employed by Diego Rivera in his portrayal of Zapata in the great mural on the balcony of the Palace of Cortés in Cuernavaca. The town was rebuilt after the revolution, its sumptuous homes serving throughout the 1940s and '50s as refuge for the Mexican and foreign rich. Today it's a gritty city of about a half-million people, with some good language schools, a few wonderful restaurants, and what appears at first sight to be 200,000 auto parts shops, staffed by the great-grandchildren of the *Zapatistas.* Zapata and his wonderful white horse live on in music, too. You hear the legend in the *corridos* sung in a thousand towns about the years of the revolution. And you sense the presence of Zapata in the towns of Morelos, where he and his followers fought and prayed and died.

"I saw him the year of the comet," another old man told me one day (Halley's Comet streaked through the skies in 1910). "I was a boy and I knew he was a great man. He came here with his soldiers and they stayed right over here. In the convent." He was pointing at the 16th-century Dominican convent that is the largest building in the center of Tepoztlán (a smaller building houses a lovely collection of pre-Columbian art donated by the Mexican poet Carlos Pellicer).

History tells us that during several periods, the convent did serve as Zapata's temporary headquarters, with guards posted on its rooftops, the horses tethered in the great walled yard. Today, the convent is the property of the state. It remains an imposing structure, with walls two feet thick, its stone hallways and dim cells recalling an era of chilly asceticism in spite of the lustier graffiti of the present. Some fine frescoes made by Indian artists have been scraped, defaced, or whitewashed over many years; their old visions, expressed in black and gray and terracotta, are slowly being retrieved through the tedious craft of the restorers. The artists and their models are long gone, but their faces live on in the halls of the convent.

From the second floor of this old structure, Zapata surely must have looked out over this same valley. Like so much of Morelos, it was part of the original 25,000-square-mile land grant that was awarded to Hernán Cortés after the conquest of Mexico in 1521. After Cortés died, the land fell to others, speculators and adventurers, most of them iron-willed exploiters, some actually men of decency and taste. The conqueror's son, Martín, lived in Tepoztlán for years after his father died and is said to have had a private chapel built so that he would not have to leave home to hear Mass. Other families stayed for many generations. During the long, peaceful centuries of New Spain, in a place of fine climate and great natural beauty, they had no reason to leave.

At its lower altitudes the valley was planted with sugar cane imported from Cuba. In the early years of New Spain, many Indians died of European diseases to which they were not immune. The Spaniards then imported black slaves, whose number in all of Mexico eventually rose in the mid-17th century to 150,000. But the Spaniards were always afraid of slave revolts because they would have been much more difficult to suppress on the mainland than in their island colonies in the Caribbean. Eventually they stopped importing Africans, and sent away the troublemakers. Those who remained were absorbed in the Mexican *mestizaje*. But they did leave traces of the old African religions in places like Tepoztlán.

The town is known today as one of the major centers in Mexico for *brujos* (witches) and *curanderos* (crudely, a kind of witch doctor). They are said to be capable of casting and removing spells, causing and curing illness, and helping with all the infinite complexities of love. Much of the witches' lore remains secret, but is apparently a mixture of pre-Columbian belief, transformed Christianity, and aspects of Afro-Cuban religions. I asked several times if I could meet with one of the *curanderos*; as a foreigner I was refused with a polite blank look. But when I asked if the *curanderos* do, in fact, exist, one man laughed out loud. "Oh yes," he said, "they exist. Yes. Yes."

So, in spite of television, radio, newspapers; in spite of daily bus service to Cuernavaca and Mexico City and the arrival of city dwellers on weekends, the pre-Christian past remains powerful. Time is simply not measured here the way it is measured in, say, Miami. The town of Tepoztlán (like many of its neighbors in Morelos) has existed since about the time of Jesus, and was dominated by the Aztecs for a century before the arrival of Cortés. The *zócalo,* or main plaza, through which both Cortés and Zapata strolled is located on exactly the same spot as the pre-Conquest Aztec market, and today is still laid out on the same basic design. The great mounds of chiles, corn, beans, tomatoes, and chocolate; the great slabs of beef being cured by sun and flies; the ceramics and masks: All were sold in virtually the same way in Aztec times, under the same colorful arrangements of tents and poles.

Also surviving from the pre-Conquest days is the monument to Tepozteco on top of the mountain of the same name, rising a thousand abrupt feet above the village. This was built by the Aztecs on a familiar pyramid base to honor the god of drunkenness, the inventor of *pulque,* a white, slightly sweet brew made from the maguey plant. The old tales insist that when the Spaniards arrived, they hurled the idol off its pedestal into the valley below. But to the delight of the inhabitants, it did not break. The conquerors were forced to attack it with hammers and saws, breaking it into chips and dust. Today, the base of the old pyramid remains on top of the mountain, badly eroded, but with some of the ancient decorations still visible; you can reach it on a hiking trail. The view of the valley from the peak is glorious. But Tepozteco is more than a view. In September of each year, a fiesta honors the old idol, and much *pulque* is drunk by nominal Catholics, and many dances danced. Here, human beings hold on to sensible gods.

In the slow afternoons in Tepoztlán, moving through the amber torpor of the sun, you can still see those small powerful women, built like tree trunks, pounding fresh tortillas on three-legged *metates* as their ancestors did for centuries. You can buy chickens killed that morning. You can see boys negotiating the cobblestones of Avenida de la Revolución on burros, comic books jutting from their back pockets. There are a few good restaurants, but most people here eat at home, as they always did. They seem entirely indifferent to the groups of city people who own second homes here as refuges from the horrors of modern Mexico City: writers and painters, businessmen and intellectuals, and a few American expatriates. This is a proud town in a state of proud people. They don't kowtow to strangers but they almost never descend to rudeness either. At the same time, you witness none of the fawning theatrics of those who live in tourist towns. And you see no beggars.

What you do sense, if you read the history and allow the town's layered past to seep into you slowly, is the eventual triumph of Zapata. The agrarian reform for which he lived and died came slowly. In the early years, the *campesinos* were given the worst land: on untillable mountain slopes, in places devoid of water or topsoil. The new politicians, the thick-fingered hustlers of the revolution, grabbed the best land for themselves.

Irony was without limit. In Anenecuilco, where Zapata was born, the worst abuser of the *campesinos* in the 1940s was a man named Nicolás Zapata. He was 13 when his father, Emiliano, was killed. Everywhere, human beings have a gift for outrage. But during the presidency of Lázaro Cárdenas (1934–1940), the worst abuses were ended. Schools and hospitals were opened, transportation made easier, farmers helped with credit and supplies. Eventually, Nicolás Zapata was hustled out of Morelos.

The people of Zapata country soon had to face a harder task than the fighting of a revolution. As Mexico's population soared in the 1940s, a new generation soon learned the obvious: There simply wasn't enough arable land to be divided up, generation after generation; even the holy Mexican *tierra* was finite. Many young people from Morelos began to emigrate, to Cuernavaca, to Mexico City, to the United States. Some never came back. Obviously, agrarian reform wasn't the answer to all of the problems of Morelos or Mexico; in this world, nothing is *the* answer.

And yet, for all of the disappointments, there is something about the people of Morelos that is healthy and enduring: They bow their heads to no man. That is surely the most valuable inheritance passed down by the generation of Emiliano Zapata. That is Zapata's triumph. He wanted humble people to be proud. Not vain. Not haughty. Proud. And you sense that pride here in the way ordinary citizens move, in the confident (if reserved) way in which they deal with strangers. You see it in the way they take care of their children and their homes. You see it in the poorest barrios, where flowers are planted in tin cans on doorsteps and windowsills.

The pride is not merely in self, but in place. The anthropologist Oscar Lewis believed that the name Tepoztlán means "place of the broken rocks," after the spectacular peaks and buttes that rise above the town. If so, the name is no longer completely accurate. The name doesn't truly describe the abundant beauty of bougainvillea and avocado trees, the citrus green in the sun, the mango and papaya trees, the fields of coffee and bananas appearing around a sudden bend. Nor does it portray the handsome homes of the city people who have moved here in the past few decades, adding the bright shimmer of swimming pools to the town, behind walls of volcanic rock. Nor does the name explain why so many of those who went away have begun to return, as dismayed as Zapata by what they encountered in the cement streets of big cities, explaining that at least here they had *"petates y parientes"* — a place to sleep, and parents, too.

In short, the name of Tepoztlán doesn't explain the beauty of the place, or its mood, or its ghosts. Sometimes they all appear after the sun has vanished. You walk here at night with no sense of the menace that stains the night in almost all the cities of *el Norte*. On the dirt roads of the lower town, faceless strangers pass in the dark and murmur hello. A few drunks sing the old *canciones*. Somewhere, but never seen, dogs are always barking, and the odor of jasmine thickens the air. On such a night not long ago, as I sat behind the house, gazing up at the black silhouette of the mountains, the wind shifted subtly and a cloud acquired the gleaming texture of mother-of-pearl: still, beautiful, perfect. The moon was hidden. A lone dog howled. And I swear that up on the ridge, high above this dark valley in Morelos, I saw a white horse.

TRAVEL HOLIDAY,
October 1990

EL NOBEL

Out on Fifth Avenue, the crowd is unusual for an urban evening in the last decade of the American century. Nobody fires a gun. Nobody plays a giant radio. Nobody speaks at full moronic bellow or offers dope for sale or screams in utter loneliness for help. But the people here are as excited as any group in thrall to the usual New York distractions of noise or violence. They are gathered outside the Metropolitan Museum of Art to hear a talk by Octavio Paz.

Paz is seventy-six, Mexican, a poet, an essayist, a critic, and an editor. Naturally, most Americans have never heard of him. Not even on this evening, a few days after Paz has been awarded the 1990 Nobel Prize for literature.

"What's the line for?" a young American asks me, outside the museum. "Who they waitin' to see?"

"Octavio Paz."

"Who?"

In Mexico, of course, Paz is a gigantic, luminous star. So it was no surprise that the Mexican newspapers carried the story of the Nobel award in type sizes usually reserved for declarations of war or victories in the World Cup. Paz is not the first Latin American to win, but he *is* the first Mexican. And though he has directed the energies of a long lifetime against dumb nationalism, Paz did not defuse the surge of Mexican national pride by turning down the award or the $700,000 that goes with it. And why should he have? In a time of slick frauds, Octavio Paz is an authentic world-class writer; nobody can say of *him* that he did not deserve the Nobel Prize. And nobody knows this better than Paz.

A great writer belongs to people everywhere. I remember seeing Paz on Avenida Juárez in Mexico City in the early 1970s, after he'd returned from a few years of exile. He came out of a bookstore looking exactly the way a poet should look: handsome, distracted, his hair in need of tending, the collar of his shirt curling, a small bundle of books in his hand. He was alone. A young man recognized him, perhaps for the same reason I did: an appearance on television two nights earlier.

"Don Octavio," he called, using the aristocratic *don* to address Paz.

"Please," Paz said in Spanish, "don't call me 'don.' "

The man looked embarrassed. "I'm sorry, I —"

"And don't *apologize*," Paz said.

Then generosity took over. Paz fell into an animated discussion with the young man, who said that he, too, was a poet. They discussed poetry with the seriousness of theologians, mentioning such vanished deities as Rubén Darío and Wallace Stevens. Abruptly, Paz shook the young man's hand in a gesture that was really an act of polite dismissal. The young man passed into the bookstore while Paz glanced at his watch.

And then an astonishingly beautiful young woman came down the crowded avenue. She had clove-colored mestizo skin, high cheek-bones, sleek black hair pulled tight against her skull and tied in a bun. Every man, and some women, turned to look at her.

So did Paz. He froze. His jaw went slack. He gazed at her as she approached, and his eyes followed her as she went by. And then, the moment of erotic transport over, the aesthetic impulse satisfied, he exhaled, shook his head sadly, and hurried across the street.

I thought: Yes, he is one of us.

Standing along the wall in the Grace Rainey Rogers Auditorium all these years later, I remember that small encounter with its perfect mixture of the cerebral and the sensual, thinking: This is the essence of Paz's writing. That sinuous style (plus the sudden fame of the prize) surely brought most of the crowd to this place, a long way from the Avenida Juárez. All seven hundred seats are filled, with additional spectators sitting on chairs in the aisles and flanking the lectern. This is exhilarating; there are never enough places on earth where poets have sellouts. But to those who know the great poet and his work, there is the usual uncertainty about *which* Octavio Paz will appear. Like Walt Whitman, or David Bowie, he contains multitudes.

Transcending all other identities is the modernist poet of the senses, shaped in his youth by Paris, admirer of the work of Mallarmé and Baudelaire, and later, in Paris and Mexico City, a close friend of the poet and chief theoretician of Surrealism, André Breton. After Paz the poet, there is Paz the philosophical essayist, whose 1950 classic, *The Labyrinth of Solitude,* explained the Mexican character and identity both to the world and to other Mexicans.

But there are even other versions of Octavio Paz. There is the practical public servant who spent decades in his country's foreign service, living in Tokyo, New York, San Francisco, Paris, and New Delhi; it is hard to imagine such assignments being granted to Robert Lowell or even Robert Penn Warren. There is the public philosopher, the courageous man who has worked so long and hard to create a language for political discourse that would break the century's ideological ice jams. I was in Mexico once in the 1980s when *that* Paz was hanged in effigy by a few self-righteous relics of Stalinist romanticism. They objected to paragraphs such as this:

Ideological militance of whatever kind inherently disdains liberty and free will. Its vision of the *otherness* of each human being, of his unlike likeness to us, is simplistic. When the *other* is a unique being, irreducible to any category, the possibilities of winning or netting him vanish; the most we can do is enlighten him, awaken him; he, then, not we, will decide. But the *other* of the militant is a cipher, an abstraction, always reducible to an *us* or a *they*. Thus the proselytizer's concept of his fellow man is totally lacking in imagination. Imagination is the faculty of discovering the uniqueness of our fellow man.

Anybody who has ever heard a Klansman discuss blacks, a Black Panther speak about whites, an ACT UP militant describe Catholics, or Jesse Helms bellow about homosexuals knows the truth of what Paz is saying. He added: "The fusion of belief and system produces the militant, a warrior fighting for an idea. In the militant, two figures are conjoined: the cleric and the soldier."

Paz has long been a witness to the calamitous results of that fatal union. As a young man in Europe in the 1930s, he rallied to the cause of the Spanish republic, traveled to Madrid, and saw the cynical maneuvers of the Stalinists. Their ruthless assaults on anarchists and socialists cooled his youthful embrace of the Marxist poem, but not his intellectual respect for Marx himself. "Each generation has two or three great conversational partners," Paz says. "For my generation, Marx is one of them."

The mature Paz evolved his own clear-eyed view of the world, rooted in a healthy skepticism about all utopias, all the iron geometries of the state, all social systems imposed by force. "Every system," he says, "by virtue as much of its abstract nature as of its pretension to totality, is the enemy of life."

Finally Paz appears in this New York auditorium, clutching his speech. The crowd roars, standing and applauding, shouting "bravo." He seems at once embarrassed and pleased; in Mexico, those who know him well say that he is not without his small vanities.

"On August 13, 1790 . . ." he begins. And we know that we shall hear the Paz who is a brooding student of his country's history, myths, ironies, and contradictions. He speaks about the discovery, reinterment, and rediscovery of a colossal statue of the Aztec goddess Coatlicue, and how her passage from temple to museum reveals the changes in our societies over the past four hundred years. The lecture is brilliant, learned, dense, and to some, incomprehensible. "I don't know what I expected," one woman says to me later, "but it wasn't *that.*"

But still, this is Octavio Paz. A winner of the Nobel Prize. When he is finished, the audience applauds, long and warmly, as much for the prize as for the talk.

Paz remains behind to talk to a few reporters. He's asked what the end of the Cold War will do to poetry and to Octavio Paz.

"There are two possibilities," he says. "Countries will organize themselves in regional terms. The model could be the European community of states. . . . Or we could go back to the old nationalist fanaticism — *that* would be a very devious and bloody solution. But poetry has to face this authority, whatever it is. . . . Poetry is not identical with history, but poets who are leading the struggle know that there are no special answers. The answers are always instantaneous, spontaneous. That is one of the most important things about this great debacle, this great collapse of the communist system. It was based on a great theoretical scheme, and now we know it *doesn't work.* . . ."

He seems uneasy with a question about the role of writers and artists in Latin American politics. "Writers and artists should take part in the public life of their countries, as *citizens.* That's all. But I don't think poets or artists have special duties, or a special role. Of course, many of our greatest poets have been very interested in politics, but the best part of their work is not about politics."

He says the exhibition of Mexican art then showing at the Metropolitan will help Americans understand Mexicans better. He is equally insistent that Mexicans also make a greater effort to understand their neighbor to the north. "We are going to be neighbors until this planet ceases to exist. Perhaps it's time to understand each other. The Americans must understand that Mexico is not a picturesque, half-savage country, but a country with a vast past, a long history, a great identity. And Mexicans must stop worrying about losing their identity to the Americans. We Mexicans are not in danger of losing our identity; we have, sometimes, too *much* identity."

Everybody laughs. There are handshakes, a few autographs to sign, and *abrazos* for friends just arrived from Mexico and Paris. Slowly, Paz and his people walk out to Fifth Avenue. There, a car is waiting for the great poet. There is a final joke, a few small goodbyes, and then Octavio Paz, with all of his sheer vitality and appetite for being, gets into the backseat, closes the door, and waves farewell. A derelict in a filthy camouflage jacket stares at the car as it pulls away.

"Who the hell is that?" the derelict says.

"A poet," someone explains. "From Mexico."

The man snorts. "All we need is more fuckin' Mexicans," he says, and shambles into the New York night.

ESQUIRE,
March 1991

IN PUERTO VALLARTA

It was dusk in Puerto Vallarta, and we were in a restaurant called El Panorama, dining with a Mexican woman we'd met that afternoon. The restaurant was on the top floor of the Hotel La Siesta, rising seven precarious stories above the ground on a hill overlooking the town. For once the name of a restaurant was accurate. From our table, while the mariachis played the aching old songs of love and betrayal, we could see a panorama of cobblestoned streets glistening after a frail afternoon rain. We saw the terra-cotta patterns of a thousand tiled rooftops, along with church steeples and flagpoles, palm trees and small green yards, and little girls eating ice-cream cones. The aroma of the Mexican evening rose around us: charcoal fires, frying beans, fish baking in stone ovens. Over to the left in the distance was the dense green thicket where the Rio Cuale tumbled down from the fierce mountains of the interior. And beyond all of this, stretching away to the hard blue line of the horizon, there was the sea, the vast and placid Pacific.

"It's so beautiful," the Mexican woman said, gesturing toward the sea. My wife followed her gesture to gaze at the rioting sky, which was all purple and carmine and tinged with orange from the dying sun. The woman's face trembled as she talked about her husband and her son. They had died within six months of each other, the husband of a heart attack after many years in the Uruguayan foreign service, the son in a senseless shooting at a party in Mexico City.

"When those things happened," the Mexican woman said, "I couldn't live anymore. I didn't want to. I sat at home in the dark." She sipped her drink. "My daughter was the one who told me to come to Vallarta. She said I had to heal myself. I had to go away and get well. And she was right. Beauty heals. Don't ever forget that. Beauty heals. I hurt still. But I am healed."

Not all the stories we heard in Puerto Vallarta contained such elements of melodrama and redemption. But there were other tales of healing — the woman from Minnesota, broken by a difficult divorce, who wandered south with a vague hope for escape. Now the gray years were erased by the sun and sea and the sound of children laughing in the still hours of the siesta; she worked in a clothing store and was catching up on two decades of lost laughter. There was a man broken by the culture of greed during the American eighties; back in Boston he had left a bankrupt company, a ruined marriage, a defaulted mortgage; now in the mornings he took a boat out on the blue water to fish for shark. Another man had lost a much loved son to drugs; another had lost a career to whiskey; a third had postponed an old dream of becoming a painter. All had come to Puerto Vallarta to live a little longer or, perhaps, for the first time.

For centuries it was a fishing village, a few huts thatched with palm dozing along the shore of the great natural harbor called the Bahía de Banderas, which is 25 miles wide. The town was built around the Rio Cuale, one of the four streams that now traverse the city. It never became a major port, because the merchants of Mexico preferred to greet their Manila galleons in Acapulco, 800 miles to the south and a much shorter journey to the capital, Mexico City. For years no roads connected the tiny village to the large cities of the interior; mule trains labored for weeks to travel the 220 miles due east to Guadalajara. And Mexico City, 550 mountainous miles to the southeast, was beyond reach.

In 1851 a man named Guadalupe Sanchez settled his family on the edge of the Rio Cuale, which divides the present Vallarta into north and south, and he is usually credited with transforming the cluster of fishing shacks into a town. But it did not prosper, and the locals apparently preferred it that way. They lived out their lives in its quiet cobblestoned streets to the familiar rhythms of day and night, rainy summers and balmy winters. Even the great upheaval of the Mexican revolution had little effect on the fishermen and small farmers who lived on the adjoining coastal plains. Occasionally cruise ships or tramp steamers would drop anchor in the empty bay, and locals went out in dugout canoes to sell chili and beans. The ships would vanish and leave Vallarta in its solitude. After World War II some of the Guadalajara upper classes discovered the town. A rough road was built, followed by a small airstrip. By the end of the 1950s the population was about 5,000.

Then, in 1963, everything changed. That year John Huston arrived with a crew of 130 to direct the movie version of Tennessee Williams's *The Night of the Iguana*. This produced one of the most amusing scenes in movie history and the true beginning of modern Puerto Vallarta. The star of the movie was Richard Burton, out of Wales and Shakespeare. His female costars were Ava Gardner, Deborah Kerr, and Sue Lyon. Miss Gardner had abandoned Hollywood for Europe after disastrous marriages to Mickey Rooney, Artie Shaw, and Frank Sinatra. She arrived with a personal entourage and her Ferrari and soon became interested in a beachboy named Tony. Miss Kerr was married to Peter Viertel, who had written a scathing novel about Huston and was once involved with Ava. The 17-year-old Miss Lyon, who had become a star as the nymphet in *Lolita,* was there with her boyfriend, while the boyfriend's wife shared quarters with Miss Lyon's mother. The cinematographer was the splendid Gabriel Figueroa, who burst into operatic song while drinking, and Huston was supported in his work by the Mexican director Indio Fernandez, who had shot his last producer. For good measure, Tennessee Williams was there with his lover and his dog.

The movie set leaped into fantasy with the early arrival of Elizabeth Taylor, who was not in the movie. She and Burton had begun their great love affair on the set of *Cleopatra* the year before, and when she showed up, presumably to protect Burton from his female costars, a media riot broke out. Taylor was a gigantic star in the Hollywood galaxy, and her presence was a monument to the old style. She brought with her dozens of trunks and suitcases, an ex-fighter to serve as bodyguard, her own secretary and one for Burton, a British cook, a chauffeur, and three children by two ex-husbands. One of these ex-husbands, Michael Wilding, was also on hand, reduced to working as an assistant to Burton's agent. And back in the States her current husband, the singer Eddie Fisher, was pouting and working on a divorce. The film's producer, Ray Stark, loved it (a few years ago he told me, "It was the greatest single movie location in the history of movies"). And Huston had grand fun. At one point he gave each of the players — Burton, Taylor, Gardner, Kerr, Lyon, plus Stark — a gold-plated derringer, laid in a velvet-lined box. Each box contained five golden bullets, engraved with the names of each of the others. He left his own name off the bullets.

Within weeks reporters and photographers from all over the world were making their way to the obscure little town of Puerto Vallarta. This was not easy; only one small plane a day flew in. Until then, few people had ever heard of the place. "They're giving us ten million dollars' worth of free publicity," the exultant Stark said. "We've got more reporters up here than iguanas." The Mexican tourist board was equally excited.

Although Williams had set his play in Acapulco, Huston thought that the port city had become too modernized, too sleek; he chose Vallarta. Huston knew the country; he'd been coming to Mexico since the 1920s and set one of his greatest films there, *The Treasure of the Sierra Madre.* The set for *Iguana* — a run-down hotel — was built by a team of almost 300 Mexican workers in the jungle above Mismaloya Beach, seven miles south of town, and some of the ruins can be seen today. But much of the action was around the bar of the Oceano Hotel, still at the corner of Paseo Díaz Ordaz and Calle Galeana. The bar is gone now, but the ghosts of Burton and Taylor remain.

"Burton was the greatest single drinker I ever saw," said a man named Jeffrey Smith, who claimed to have been here during the shooting. "He could drink anything and never get drunk."

Among the potions that Burton downed was *raicilla,* a Mexican form of moonshine, made from cactus, as mind-bending as absinthe and still available at the older bars outside of town. Burton told one interviewer, "If you drink it straight down, you can feel it going into each individual intestine." Taylor was tolerant. She told one reporter, "Richard *lives* each of his roles. In this film he's an alcoholic and an unshaven bum, which goes a long way toward explaining his appearance and liquid intake."

Burton and Taylor took a house called the Casa Kimberley, up the side of the hill beside the Rio Cuale, and by all accounts they fell in love with Puerto Vallarta with only slightly less passion than they felt for each other. The movie company eventually finished its work and moved on, with no casualties from Huston's derringers. But Taylor and Burton bought the Casa Kimberley and added a house across the narrow street and built a bridge to connect them. It would be nice to say that they lived happily ever after. Almost nobody does, least of all movie stars.

Still, they had good years in Puerto Vallarta. They came down with great crowds of children and staff, spent holidays there, too often recuperated there from the bruising life of celebrity. The Mexicans loved them. The Burtons created scholarships for local children. They were an attraction that validated the town, and its population exploded (it is now about 250,000). By 1970, even Richard Nixon had come to Puerto Vallarta, for a state visit with the Mexican president. The Burtons had various celebrities as guests, but often they were alone. From the testimony of Burton's diaries (quoted by his biographer Melvyn Bragg), Puerto Vallarta also helped him heal. Sometimes Burton hid out in the top floor of one of the houses, reading and writing. He read eclectically, Octavio Paz, W. H. Auden, Ian Fleming, Philip Roth; he came back again and again to the work of his Welsh compatriot Dylan Thomas. Burton was an excellent writer, a self-punishing diarist, and a good, sly, open-eyed observer.

"Elizabeth is now looking ravishingly sun-tanned," he wrote in 1969, "though the lazy little bugger ought to lose a few pounds or so to look her absolute best."

In the late 1970s John Huston was to come back to Puerto Vallarta too, hauling his aging bones from the drizzly disappointments of a long sojourn in Ireland. He built a house in the jungle near Las Caletas, 30 miles from the town's center. It could be reached only from the sea. He didn't see much of Burton and Taylor. When the Burtons divorced, Taylor got the houses. For a while Burton lived in another Vallarta house with a new wife. Her name was Susan. The house was called, after half of each, Casa Bursus. Today nobody can tell you its location.

But the old Burton-Taylor houses, with their connecting bridge, are still there. They've been sold and converted into a bed-and-breakfast. One afternoon my wife and I went to visit. A long flight of stone steps begins at a now dry fountain, where we saw a Domino's Pizza carton darkening in the sun. At the top of the steps you can see in the distance the fabled bridge, painted the color of strawberry ice cream. We rang the bell of a wooden door at 445 Calle Zaragoza, and a lean, tanned man named Jacques gave us a tour. He said he had worked in many places, from St. Bart's to Polynesia, but was entranced with Puerto Vallarta.

"The people are very pure," he said, "and the town is very romantic. It has everything you don't find in the United States now. Puerto Vallarta is 1938. You can regenerate yourself here. It's very charming and not damaged."

Stairs led us to an open, white-tiled floor with a bar and couches and a cool breeze off the ocean. There were photographs of Taylor and Burton, posters for *Butterfield 8* and *Becket,* other reminders of lives once lived here. Off to the side (and in the house across the little bridge, beside the small swimming pool) we saw rooms named for various Burton-Taylor movies: the VIPS Room and the Comedians Room, the Sandpiper Room and the Night of the Iguana Room, the Taming of the Shrew Room and the Who's Afraid of Virginia Woolf? Room. Some were excellent movies; others were among the worst ever made. I found a bookcase against a wall, and among the weathered books was a copy of *Sanctuary V,* by my friend Budd Schulberg, dedicated to Burton and Taylor and dated December 17, 1969 — a remnant of some lost Christmas. The place is clean and bright and pleasant. It also made me melancholy.

A vagrant feeling of waste and loss followed me to the top floor, where a bedroom is now called the Cleopatra Room. According to the Bragg biography, this is where Burton came to do his writing, where he tried to make sense of his life, to find some center among the swirling currents of celebrity and alcohol. He never found it. He knew that once he had been a serious actor but had been transformed into a cartoon figure, part of a team called Dick 'n' Liz. Here, where there are now tasteful wicker chairs and fresh-cut flowers, he could walk onto the balcony and look out over the town to the sea. Too often he saw only the waste of his own talent and his life. We looked around, feeling oddly like intruders at the scene of some private tragedy, and then we fled.

The town that Huston, Burton, and Taylor saw in 1963 has been enveloped by the much larger Puerto Vallarta that is here now. It has the usual transcultural clutter that you see in places designed to give pleasure to strangers from El Norte: Denny's and McDonald's and a lot of boutiques. But it's still a good town for walking. In the mornings we strolled along the beaches, often pausing on the one called Los Muertos (The Dead), named for a group of silver miners who were murdered here by pirates long ago. The sea is clear and translucent; the city fathers have worked hard to avoid the calamity that ruined Acapulco. On most days the leaves of the palm trees drooped in the heat. We saw a lean brown horse tethered to a lone palm tree on a spit of shore, waiting for riders. Mexican men contentedly sold blankets and hats.

"I have the best job in the world," said a brown-skinned man named Marcos Villasenor, who was 44. "I come on my horse in the morning from there, up by Nayarit. I give people rides. They pay me. Then I go home." He smiled broadly. "And all day while I am working I am in a beautiful place."

His feelings were clearly shared by others. On each day of our stay the beach was crowded with a mixture of tourists and Mexican families. The Americans looked pink and awkward and lonely. The Mexicans were friendly, even sweet, but they were more concerned with children than with visitors. Here, as everywhere in Puerto Vallarta, a visitor sensed a relaxed manner among the Mexicans. Among workers and visitors, no one felt the seething hostility that poisons so many resorts, particularly in the Caribbean.

But there were irritations. In our hotel the prices of newspapers, aspirin, and candies were extortionate. At night the bands sometimes played at poolside; the acoustical setup was arranged as if our room were part of the walls of Jericho. The music in the hotel bars was the usual international soft-rock pap: watered-down Beatles, creaky Barry Manilow. Instead of the glorious, vibrant music of Mexico, we were greeted each evening by the dead products of Area Code 800.

"That is what the Americans want," a waiter said to me one night. "It's terrible, no? But they *want* this. They want to feel at *home*."

Far and away the worst irritation in Puerto Vallarta was the insistent, driven, obsessive selling of time shares. In the lobby of our hotel, on the beaches, in the streets, the time-share sellers came upon us like piranhas. Many of them were displaced Americans or Canadians, trying to look respectable; others were young Mexicans; in either language, their song was an infuriating hustle.

In the hotel, the Buganvilias Sheraton, staff members steered us to restaurants. We suspected that this was probably a racket, with the restaurant owners kicking back money to the steerers (you were supposed to hand over a printed "discount" card when you arrived). But on our first, innocent day in town, we tried one of the recommended places anyway, a seafood joint called the Andariego. The sound system insisted that we listen to banal versions of "My Way" and the theme from *A Man and a Woman* and, God help us, "Feelings." The combination was so deadly that all additional appetite completely disappeared.

Among the ordinary Mexicans life was sweeter. We saw flowers growing everywhere: on the streets, on balconies, in small private gardens; a fragrant profusion of blue jacaranda, bougainvillea, jasmine, roses. There were wild orchids here, too, and in December, we were told, you can see African tulips. Scattered through the town we saw banana trees, mangos, papayas. The stalls of markets displayed a Tamayo-like profusion of all these and more: watermelon, guava, cantaloupe, avocado. Street vendors sold shaved ice, sugarcane, and coconut milk.

Not much of the Mexican past remained here. The cathedral dates only from the turn of the century, and in a land where brilliant artisans once worked with brick or stone it is made of concrete. No pyramids rise here, no ruins of the cultures that existed in Mexico before the arrival of the Europeans. There's a small, badly lit museum on the island in the center of the Rio Cuale. We visited one afternoon and saw some fine pre-Columbian pieces and a few folk paintings by a man named Gilberto Grimaldi. But the place had an empty, forlorn feeling to it; nails in the wall marked where paintings had been removed, and I wondered if somehow the museum's collection had been sacked while nobody was looking.

But Puerto Vallarta does have a vibrant gallery scene. The sculptor Sergio Bustamente has his own gallery. There are a number of other galleries, several antiques shops, and stores selling Mexican folk art. We spent some time at the superb Galería Uno, on Calle Morelos, run by an American woman named Jan Lavender, who has been in Vallarta for more than 20 years. She features many of the best new Mexican painters, but for many American residents her gallery also served as hangout and communications center, a place for hearing gossip, making business contacts, and buying gifts for friends in the States. While we were there Lavender was excited about a new discovery, a young Mexican artist named Rogelio Díaz, whose brilliantly colored paintings combined power and draftsmanship in a style that could be called Mexpressionist. "This is the finest artist I've seen in years," she said. "He is something else." She produced cold drinks, smoked a cigarette, and talked awhile about Puerto Vallarta.

"First of all, it's a street town," she said. "Everybody is out in the streets. You see your friends there. You meet new people in the streets. The town is not social; it's certainly not formal. It doesn't have all those *obligations*. You can wear whatever you want to wear here, go as you want to go. It's not like Acapulco. My friends come down from New York or Los Angeles and say, 'Where are the parties?' And I say, 'There aren't any.' And there aren't. God knows, they have a good time, but it isn't a *scene*."

Running an art gallery has made her even more aware of the uniqueness of Vallarta and of Mexico. "You can't really capture Mexico in photographs or paintings, because they leave out two essentials, smell and sound. Here we're used to *air moving*. We live open. In the States the windows are always closed and the air is imported and smells like cement." She laughed. "Here the weather is always great. I go to New York, and it's cold outside and sweltering inside. I go to Phoenix, and it's blistering outside and freezing inside. But here the windows are always open."

There were no real problems with crime. "Oh, you can get in trouble if you ask for it, like any place," she said. "You know, going to the beach at four in the morning. But this is a street town. There are too many people around for there to be any danger."

We never felt menaced while in Puerto Vallarta. There were no obvious hoodlums, no street gangs, no dope peddlers. We never saw the kind of homeless people who now collect on the streets of American cities like piles of human wreckage. Even after great expansion this remains a Mexican town built upon the hard foundation of the Mexican family. We did see poor people across the river in the area named after the Mexican revolutionary hero Emiliano Zapata. They live in dark, crudely built single-wall housing. You walk by and smell the rank odor of poverty. On the street called Francisco Madero we also passed a deep, wide, evil-looking high-ceilinged poolroom, the sort of place in which young men always find trouble in Mexican movies.

But the poor are not typical of the town. In the evenings you can walk along the seawall called the Malecón and see young men flirting with young women as they do in the evening in a thousand Mexican towns. The ritual is all eyes, glances, whispers; the private codes of the young. You can hear the growl of the sea. You can dine in the many restaurants, annoyed only by the garrulous flatulence of the public buses, throwing the fumes of burnt gasoline upon all who come near. One evening we sat at a window table in the second-floor Japanese restaurant called Tsunami. The food was good, but strolling Mexicans kept stopping on the Malecón and staring up at us: groups of men, fathers with children, old women with disapproving faces. Or so we thought. When dinner was over we crossed the street and finally saw the true objects of their scrutiny. On the floor above the restaurant was an aquarium, the tank filled with the gaily colored denizens of the deep; above that a disco; and in the window we could see dark-skinned girls in tight bright dresses, the gaily colored denizens of the Mexican night.

That is Puerto Vallarta to me. You can wander down to Le Bistro, on the island in the river, and hear good recorded jazz. You can pause in the restaurant's garden beside the statue of Huston, which quotes from the director's eulogy to his friend Humphrey Bogart: "We have no reason to feel any sorrow for him — only for ourselves for having lost him. He is irreplaceable." Or you can have a good laugh at the restaurant called La Fuente de la Puente (The Fountain on the Bridge), where a statue of Burton, Taylor, and an iguana stands, carved from what seems to be Ivory soap but which turns out to be some kind of plastic. I wish Burton could have cast his caustic eye upon this masterpiece.

You can see these things or just watch a carpenter laboring with an artist's intensity in a small crowded shop or kids pedaling tricycles down the steep hills or country people in sandals and straw hats gazing at the wonders of the metropolis. I carried all of them home from Puerto Vallarta, along with the sound of the rooster at dawn and the healing benevolence of the sun and the salt of the sea.

TRAVEL HOLIDAY,
December 1992–January 1993

THE TORTILLA CURTAIN

You move through the hot, polluted Tijuana morning, past shops and gas stations and cantinas, past the tourist traps of the Avenida Revolución, past the egg-shaped Cultural Center and the new shopping malls and the government housing with bright patches of laundry hanging on balconies; then it's through streets of painted adobe peeling in the sun, ball fields where kids play without gloves, and you see ahead and above you ten-thousand-odd shacks perched uneasily upon the Tijuana hills, and you glimpse the green road signs for the beaches as the immense luminous light of the Pacific brightens the sky. You turn, and alongside the road there's a chain link fence. It's ten feet high.

On the other side of the fence is the United States.

There are immense gashes in the fence, which was once called the Tortilla Curtain. You could drive three wide loads, side by side, through the tears in this pathetic curtain. On this morning, on both sides of the fence (more often called *la línea* by the locals), there are small groups of young Mexican men dressed in polyester shirts and worn shoes and faded jeans, and holding small bags. These are a few of the people who are changing the United States, members of a huge army of irregulars engaged in the largest, most successful invasion ever made of North America.

On this day, they smoke cigarettes. They make small jokes. They munch on tacos prepared by a flat-faced, pig-tailed Indian woman whose stand is parked by the roadside. They sip soda. And some of them gaze across the arid scrub and sandy chaparral at the blurred white buildings of the U.S. town of San Ysidro. They wait patiently and do not hide. And if you pull over, and buy a soda from the woman, and speak some Spanish, they will talk.

"I tried last night," says the young man named Jeronimo Vasquez, who wears a Chicago Bears T-shirt under a denim jacket. "But it was too dangerous, too many helicopters last night, too much light. . . ." He looks out at the open stretch of gnarled land, past the light towers, at the distant white buildings. "Maybe tonight we will go to Zapata Canyon. . . ." He is from Oaxaca, he says, deep in the hungry Mexican south. He has been to the United States three times, working in the fields; it is now Tuesday, and he starts a job near Stockton on the following Monday, picker's work arranged by his cousin. "I have much time. . . ."

Abruptly, he turns away to watch some action. Two young men are running across the dried scrub on the U.S. side, kicking up little clouds of white dust, while a Border Patrol car goes after them. The young men dodge, circle, running the broken field, and suddenly stand very still as the car draws close. They are immediately added to the cold statistics of border apprehensions. But they are really mere sacrifices; over on the left, three other men run low and hunched, like infantrymen in a fire fight. "*Corre, corre,*" Jeronimo Vasquez whispers. "Run, run. . . ." They do. And when they vanish into some distant scrub, he clenches a fist like a triumphant sports fan. He is not alone. All the others cheer, as does the woman selling tacos, and on the steep hill above the road, a man stands before a tar-paper shack, waves a Mexican flag, and shouts: "*Gol!*" And everyone laughs.

We've all read articles about the 1,950-mile-long border between the United States and Mexico, seen documentaries, heard the bellowing rhetoric of the C-Span politicians enraged at the border's weakness; but until you stand beside it, the border is an abstraction. Up close, you see immediately that the border is at once a concrete place with holes in the fence, and a game, a joke, an affront, a wish, a mere line etched by a draftsman on a map. No wonder George Bush gave up on interdiction as a tactic in the War on Drugs; there are literally hundreds of Ho Chi Minh trails leading into the United States from the south (and others from Canada, of course, and the sea). On some parts of the Mexican border there is one border patrolman for every twenty-six miles; it doesn't require a smuggling genius to figure out how to get twenty tons of cocaine to a Los Angeles warehouse. To fill in the gaps, to guard all the other U.S. borders, would require millions of armed guards, many billions of dollars. And somehow, Jeronimo Vasquez would still appear on a Monday morning in Stockton.

Those young men beside the ruined fence — not the *narcotraficantes* — are the most typical members of the peaceful invasion. Nobody knows how many come across each year, although in 1988 920,000 were stopped, arrested, and sent back to Mexico by the border wardens. Thousands more make it. Some are described by the outnumbered and overwhelmed immigration police as OTMs (Other

Than Mexican, which is to say, Salvadorans, Guatemalans, Nicaraguans, Costa Ricans fleeing the war zones, and South Americans and
Asians fleeing poverty). Some, like Jeronimo Vasquez, are seasonal
migrants; they come for a few months, earn money, and return to
families in Mexico; others come to stay.

"When you see a woman crossing," says Jeronimo Vasquez, "you
know she's going to stay. It means she has a husband on the other
side, maybe even children. She's not going back. Most of the women
are from Salvador, not so many Mexicans. . . ."

Tijuana is one of their major staging grounds. In 1940 it was a town
of seventeen thousand citizens, many of whom were employed in
providing pleasure for visiting Americans. The clenched, bluenosed
forces of American puritanism gave the town its function. In 1915
California banned horse racing; dance halls and prostitution were
made illegal in 1917; and in 1920 Prohibition became the law of the
land. So thousands of Americans began crossing the border to do
what they could not do at home: shoot crap, bet on horses, get drunk,
and get laid.

Movie stars came down from Hollywood with people to whom
they weren't married. Gangsters traveled from as far away as Chicago and New York. Women with money had abortions at the Paris
Clinic. Sailors arrived from San Diego to lose their virgin status, get
their first doses of the clap, and too often to spend nights in the
Tijuana jail. The Casino of Agua Caliente was erected in 1928, a
glorious architectural mixture of the Alhambra and a Florentine villa,
complete with gambling, drinking, a nightclub, big bands, tennis,
golf, a swimming pool, and fancy restaurants. Babe Ruth and Jack
Dempsey were among the clients, and a Mexican teenager named
Margarita Cansino did a dance act with her father in its nightclub
before changing her name to Rita Hayworth. The casino was closed
in 1935 by the Mexican president, and only one of its old towers
still remains. But sin did not depart with the gamblers or the end of
Prohibition. The town boomed during the war, and thousands of
Americans still remember the bizarre sex shows and rampant prostitution of the era and the availability of something called marijuana.
Today the run-down cantinas and whorehouses of the Zona Norte
are like a living museum of Tijuana's gaudy past.

"It's very dangerous here for women," Jeronimo Vasquez said.

"The coyotes tell them they will take them across, for money. If they don't have enough money, they talk them into becoming *putas* for a week or a month. And they never get out. . . ."

Although commercial sex and good marijuana are still available in Tijuana, sin, alas, is no longer the city's major industry. Today the population is more than one million. City and suburbs are crowded with *maquiladora* plants, assembling foreign goods for export to the United States. These factories pay the highest wages in Mexico (although still quite low by U.S. standards) and attract workers from all over the republic. Among permanent residents, unemployment is very low.

But it's said that at any given time, one third of the people in Tijuana are transients, waiting to cross to *el otro lado*. A whole subculture that feeds off this traffic can be seen around the Tijuana bus station: coyotes (guides) who for a fee will bring them across; *enganchadores* (labor contractors) who promise jobs; roominghouse operators; hustlers; crooked cops prepared to extort money from the non-Mexicans. The prospective migrants are not simply field hands, making the hazardous passage to the valleys of California to do work that even the most poverty-ravaged Americans will not do. Mexico is also experiencing a "skill drain." As soon as a young Mexican acquires a skill or craft — carpentry, wood finishing, auto repair — he has the option of departing for the north. The bags held by some of the young men with Jeronimo Vasquez contained tools. And since the economic collapse of 1982 hammered every citizen of Mexico, millions have exercised the option. The destinations of these young skilled Mexicans aren't limited to the sweatshops of Los Angeles or the broiling fields of the Imperial Valley; increasingly the migrants settle in the cities of the North and East. In New York, I've met Mexicans from as far away as Chiapas, the impoverished state that borders Guatemala.

Such men are more likely to stay permanently in the United States than are the migrant agricultural laborers like Jeronimo Vasquez. The skilled workers and craftsmen buy documents that make them seem legal. They establish families. They learn English. They pay taxes and use services. Many of them applied for amnesty under the terms of the Simpson-Rodino Act; the new arrivals are not eligible, but they are still coming.

I'm one of those who believe this is a good thing. The energy of the Mexican immigrant, his capacity for work, has become essential to this country. While Mexicans, legal and illegal, work in fields, wash dishes, grind away in sweatshops, clean bedpans, and mow lawns (and fix transmissions, polish wood, build bookcases), millions of American citizens would rather sit on stoops and wait for welfare checks. If every Mexican in this country went home next week, Americans would starve. The lettuce on your plate in that restaurant got there because a Mexican bent low in the sun and pulled it from the earth. Nothing, in fact, is more bizarre than the stereotype of the "lazy" Mexican, leaning against the wall with his sombrero pulled over his face. I've been traveling to Mexico for more than thirty years; the only such Mexicans I've ever seen turned out to be suffering from malnutrition.

But the great migration from Mexico is certainly altering the United States, just as the migration of Eastern European Jews and southern Italians changed the nation at the beginning of the century and the arrival of Irish Catholics changed it a half century earlier. Every immigrant brings with him an entire culture, a dense mixture of beliefs, assumptions, and nostalgias about family, manhood, sex, laughter, music, food, religion. His myths are not American myths. In this respect, the Mexican immigrant is no different from the Irish, Germans, Italians, and Jews. The ideological descendants of the Know-Nothings and other "nativist" types are, of course, alarmed. They worry about the Browning of America. They talk about the high birthrate of the Latino arrivals, their supposed refusal to learn English, their divided loyalties.

Much of this is racist nonsense, based on the assumption that Mexicans are inherently "inferior" to people who look like Michael J. Fox. But it also ignores the wider context. The Mexican migration to the United States is another part of the vast demographic tide that has swept most of the world in this century: the journey from the countryside to the city, from field to factory, from south to north — and from illiteracy to the book. But there is one huge irony attached to the Mexican migration. These people are moving in the largest numbers into precisely those states that the United States took at gunpoint in the Mexican War of 1846–48: California, Arizona, New Mexico, Texas, Nevada, and Utah, along with parts of Wyoming, Colorado, and Oklahoma. In a way, those young men crossing into San Ysidro and Chula Vista each night are entering the lost provinces of Old Mexico, and some Mexican intellectuals even refer sardonically to this great movement as *La Reconquista* — the Reconquest.

It certainly is a wonderful turn on the old doctrine of manifest destiny, which John L. O'Sullivan, the New York journalist who coined the phrase in 1845, said was our right "to overspread the continent allotted by Providence for the free development of our yearly multiplying millions."

The yearly multiplying millions of Mexico will continue moving north unless one of two things happens: the U.S. economy totally collapses, or the Mexican economy expands dramatically. Since neither is likely to happen, the United States of the twenty-first century is certain to be browner, and speak more Spanish, and continue to see its own culture transformed. The Know-Nothings are, of course, enraged at this great demographic shift and are demanding that Washington seal the borders. As always with fanatics and paranoids, they have no sense of irony. They were probably among those flag-waving patriots who were filled with a sense of triumph when free men danced on the moral ruins of the Berlin Wall last November; they see no inconsistency in the demand for a new Great Wall, between us and Mexico.

The addled talk goes on, and in the hills of Tijuana, young men like Jeronimo Vasquez continue to wait for the chance to sprint across the midnight scrub in pursuit of the golden promise of the other side. *Corre, hombre, corre. . . .*

ESQUIRE,
February 1990

PART IV

OUT THERE

The work, and my own curiosity, carried me to many places. I've paid rent in Rome and Barcelona and Dublin. I've written pieces from hotel rooms in Paris and Belfast, Brussels and Managua, Helsinki and Havana and East Berlin. I've been to Saigon and Panama, to Vienna and Tangier. Over the years, pages of my passports grew lacy with the rubber-stamped graffiti of visas and departures. I wanted it that way; the world was out there and I wanted to see it. In 1967, on a long, comical diplomatic journey with Lyndon Baines Johnson to Asia, we stopped for fuel in the middle of the Pacific and I wrote a story in twenty minutes just to get the dateline into my resume: Pago Pago. It was a long way from Brooklyn.

For almost ten years, Vietnam was the foreign place above all others for most Americans. I spent very little time there, but the presence of the war informed almost everything I wrote. After 1973 — the ominous year of Watergate and OPEC and the beginning of the steady decline of the American economy — the war was lost. It should have been the task of statesmen to arrange its conclusion with some dignity. They could not bring it off.

There were other wars too: a long, grieving drizzle of a war in

Northern Ireland; a dirty little war in Nicaragua; the horrendous civil war in Lebanon. In Belfast and Beirut, the killing was entangled with the dark certainties of religion. In Nicaragua, a similar impulse was in play: adepts of the Marxist faith fought against the hired acolytes of the anti-Communist faith, Sandinista against Contra, sometimes brother against brother. The warring creeds were everywhere in those places, each driven by visions of utopia, each prepared to kill or die to bring them into existence. In all three parts of the world, the common result was more human misery. On my visits, I tried to understand the aims of the various players, but most often I found myself in agreement with E. M. Forster's famous remark: "I do not believe in belief."

In 1989, the Cold War finally ended in a kind of mutual exhaustion. Mikhail Gorbachev still claimed to believe in the socialist ideal; but he was also a man of sanity, lucidity, and common sense. More than any other public figure on the planet, he acknowledged, at last, that something had to change. In a major way. He knew that the Soviet Union was a gigantic, bankrupt lie, sick with poverty, corruption, and the memory of terror. Only terror could keep it going. The Americans had suffered, too, in the long ideological struggle with the Communists. More than a hundred thousand Americans had been killed in Korea and Vietnam. American cities were a shambles. The United States had been transformed from the largest creditor nation in the world to the world's largest debtor. Ideologues on both sides resisted change, but after Vietnam, most Americans wanted nothing to do with dying over abstractions. Gorbachev made it possible for everybody to surrender the chilly certitudes of belief. Of all the public men of my time, only he changed the world.

I saw some of the great change in the streets and squares of Prague in 1989. Those defiant days and boisterous nights made up the most thrilling story I'd ever covered. In a matter of days, the brave men and women of Civic Action, led by a writer named Vaclav Havel, brought down the Communist regime. They did it by speaking truth to power. They did it with cartoons and jokes and music. They did it by placing their bodies in the line of fire and daring their opponents to shoot. The Communists did not shoot. They did not shoot because Mikhail Gorbachev had made clear that he would not maintain Czech communism with Russian tanks. At the end, the Czech Communists looked like archbishops who had ceased to believe in God.

The world soon learned that the end of the Cold War did not

bring an end to man's invincible capacity for folly. From Bosnia to the Persian Gulf, human beings still killed each other over belief. But nations no longer wave hydrogen bombs at each other. Missiles are no longer aimed at the homes of distant strangers. In a lot of places, from South Africa to South America, human beings are free at last. No small thing. And I'm glad I had a ticket to the show.

VIETNAM, VIETNAM

Sometimes, in odd places, it all comes back. You are walking a summer beach, stepping around oiled bodies, hearing only the steady growl of the sea. Suddenly, from over the horizon, you hear the *phwuk-phwuk-phwuk* of rotor blades and for a frozen instant you prepare to fall to the sand. Then the Coast Guard chopper moves by, its pilot peering down at the swimmers, but your mind is stained with old images. Or you are strolling the sidewalks of a northern city, heading toward the theater or a parking lot or some dismal appointment, eyes glazed by the anonymous motion of the street. A door opens, an odor drifts from a restaurant; it's ngoc nam sauce, surely, and yes, the sign tells you this is a Vietnamese restaurant, and you hurry on, pursued by a ghost. Don't come back, the ghost whispers: I'll be crouched against the wall, grinning, my teeth stained black from betel root.

Vietnam.

Ten years have passed since the North Vietnamese T-54 tanks rolled down Thong Nhut Boulevard in Saigon to breach the gates of the presidential palace. Ten years since the last eleven marines climbed into a CH-53 helicopter on the roof of the United States Embassy and flew away from the ruined country, while thousands of compromised Vietnamese pleaded in vain for evacuation and thousands of others took to the sea. Ten years since the end of the war.

Across those ten years, a sort of institutionalized amnesia became the order of the day, as if by tribal consent we had decided as Americans to deal with Vietnam by forgetting it. Vietnam belonged to the parents, lovers, wives, and children of the 58,022 dead, to the maimed men hidden away in veterans' hospitals, to the bearded young man you would see from time to time in any American town, with a leg gone as permanently as his youth. Vietnam? That was in another country, man, and besides, the wench was dead.

There was no large-scale congressional inquiry into the war, no major attempt to divine its bitter lessons. We had the assorted felonies of Watergate to entertain us, the injured economy to distract us, the Iranian hostage crisis to infuriate us. The war had shaken American society to its core, eroding authority, splitting families, setting generation against generation, forcing citizens to define basic beliefs.

During the war, thousands of draft-age Americans refused to serve in the armed forces, and left in unprecedented numbers for exile in Canada or Sweden, some never to return. Demonstrations grew in sound and fury, at first exuberant, then bitter, as protests increasingly ended with tear gas, mass arrests, violence, even death. Four were killed at Kent State in 1970 as Nixon expanded the war into Cambodia. Two died at Jackson State. There were others, their brains scrambled on acid, ruined with speed. Kids toppled over in crowded fields as the chants rose: *Hey, hey, L.B.J., how many kids did you kill today?* Some walked off rooftops in the Haight or on the Lower East Side, while others chanted, *Ho, ho, Ho Chi Minh, the N.L.F. is gonna win.* The roads of America in those years seemed crowded with the young — guitar armies in advance and retreat, all of them hating the war, some of them hating America. And when they paused, stopped, turned down the volume on the Stones or the Dead, and looked at the news, they could see veterans home from 'Nam, bearded and wild, unlike the neat, proud, dusty members of the American Legion, and they were hurling their medals over the White House fence. They could see body bags arriving at military airports. They could see the war going on and on and on.

But when it was over at last, it seemed like some peculiar television series that had been canceled. Some of us had hoped that defeat would create a healthy national skepticism, a communal refusal ever again to take innocently the sermons of our leaders. We would be a nation of adults, at last, having learned what Europeans had learned long ago: that defeat is the great teacher, that there are limits to power, that slogans are no substitute for thinking.

Ten years later, the anti-Communist sermon is again the dominant factor in our foreign policy. Those little men with the quartz eyes and pink hands who sit in safe Washington buildings are again signing papers that allow young men to go off and kill and die, in Beirut or Grenada or the hills of Nicaragua. The conquest of Grenada, which proved definitively that a nation of 235 million could overwhelm a country of 110,000, was greeted as a famous victory. The president was hailed as a firm leader, and medals dropped from the Pentagon like snow. Less than ten years after the end of the longest, most disastrous war in American history, we seemed to have learned nothing. Nothing at all.

Yet Vietnam will not go away. On the evening news, ten years later, we see General Westmoreland trying in a courtroom to win from CBS the victory that he could never wrest from General Giap. We see tearful ceremonies in the rain beside a generation's wailing wall in Washington as those who lived through Vietnam come together to mourn those who did not. Occasionally we hear politicians, from President Reagan down, speaking of the war in the oratory of a Fourth of July picnic, attempting with porous language to transform disaster into victory, stupidity into wisdom, folly into glory.

But more than 2.6 million Americans passed through Vietnam, and they will carry with them until they die the psychic shrapnel of their time in that place. The names of the places are like beads in a bitter rosary: Khe Sanh, Pleiku, Ap Bac, Cam Ne, Qui Nhon, Tuy Hoa, Da Nang, Hue, Bien Hoa, Tan Son Nhut, the Iron Triangle, the Mekong, and a thousand others that evoke rain, helicopters, blasted trees, snake-colored rivers, the green watery light of forests, and the death of friends. They spoke a language that is now forgotten: incoming, L.Z., capping, medevac, Chinook, tree line, punji stick, spider hole, jolly green giant, trip wire, claymore, Huey, klick, body bag, pogue, Charlie, fragging, COSVN, in country, payback, slick, hootch, doo-mommie, gooks and dinks and slopes. These were the nouns of the war; the verbs didn't matter, or the tenses; war is always present tense for the men who fight it, and combat is illiterate.

There were other nouns, of course, common and proper, all now abandoned and rusting like old weapons. Does anyone remember the face of Ngo Dinh Diem, plucked from a Maryknoll retreat in New Jersey in 1954 to become president of the South Vietnam he had not seen in years? Diem was a Catholic in a Buddhist country, a conservative mandarin in a region seething with revolution. Yet the Americans thought he would do just fine. After all, he had been promoted and recommended by Cardinal Spellman, hustled from office to office in Washington to meet the few men in America who knew anything at all about Vietnam. For a while he served Washington's interests well, refusing to honor the Geneva agreements by taking part in the 1956 elections, which would have unified Vietnam. The reason was simple: in a free election, Ho Chi Minh would have won. And in an American election year, neither John Foster Dulles nor Dwight Eisenhower was prepared to let a Communist come to power in a free election. So Diem built his army, expanded his corps of American advisers, took his American millions. The Communists went back to the hills.

But Diem was remote and mystical. The regime was soon controlled by Diem's sinister brother, Nhu, a corrupt drug addict, and Diem's snarling sister-in-law, Madame Nhu. Non-Communist opponents were killed or jailed; puritanical laws were clamped on the population; the South Vietnamese Army — the ARVN — was wormy with thievery and paranoia. And in the early sixties the Vietcong began to fight, and to win. By the time Diem and Nhu were assassinated in a coup on November 1, 1963, and Madame Nhu had departed for exile, the war was almost lost. The Americans came piling in like the cavalry riding to the rescue. Right into the quagmire.

Diem and Nhu and the Dragon Lady are forgotten now, their faces blurred by time. Forgotten too is all the optimistic gush that rolled out of the typewriters of Saigon flacks, the nonsense about strategic hamlets, electronic fences, Special Forces A-Teams, the C.I.D.G., the winning of hearts and minds — all those lights at the end of all those tunnels. A billion words must have issued from the collective mouths of official spokesmen; the men in the black pajamas, however, kept coming down those trails to fight. Who now remembers the hundreds of thousands of words that dropped from the lips of Sir Robert Thompson, who periodically retailed his wisdom to the gullible Americans? He had had a part in the British victory over the Malayan insurgents; that made him an expert. So the Americans listened, while Thompson declared himself a clear-and-hold man rather than a search-and-destroy man, and none of it mattered, because neither strategy worked. In offices in Washington and Saigon, the slick charts looked persuasive; on the field of battle, the Communists were absorbing the most horrendous punishment, and winning.

Only a handful of Americans can remember when M.A.A.G. changed its name to M.A.C.V., or when Chase Manhattan opened its Saigon office, or how many tons of Coca-Cola were unloaded at Cam Ranh Bay. Such details exist in the dusty files of the outfits that managed the war, but they don't, of course, matter anymore. Other details should. How many remember that the first American killed in Vietnam was Specialist Fourth Class James T. Davis, of Livingston, Tennessee? He died in an ambush on December 22, 1961, just outside Duc Hoa, twelve miles from Saigon. The last to die were Marine Corporals Charles McMahon, Jr., twenty-two, of Woburn, Massachusetts, and Darwin Judge, nineteen, of Marshalltown, Iowa. They perished under a North Vietnamese artillery barrage that was laid upon Tan Son Nhut airport on April 29, 1975, the day before the war ended. Their bodies, forgotten in the panic of evacuation, were not brought home until the following March. Their families remember, but almost nobody else in America knows their names. They are as forgotten as the almost 2.5 million Vietnamese, Laotians, and Cambodians who died between 1961 and 1975.

Everybody who went to Vietnam carries his or her own version of the war. Only 10 percent engaged in combat; the American elephant, pursuing the Vietnamese grasshopper, was extraordinarily heavy with logistical support. Tours were for a single year, so a man who fought through the 1968 Tet offensive would remember one war, a man who was there in 1971 another. Some cooked eggs in mess halls; others waded through muck in the swamps.

All the reporters remember the Five O'Clock Follies, held downtown in the old Rex Theater under the auspices of JUSPAO (Joint United States Public Affairs Office). These daily briefings, held by the men who clerked the war, were usually a bizarre amalgam of kill ratios, body counts, incident counts, weapons recovered. The flacks were neat, clean, invariably crew-cut, and optimism was the order of the day. Occasionally a visiting politician or labor leader would be introduced, after seventy-two hours in the country, to serve up the official line. The message was understood: surely the richest country on earth, the world's most powerful military machine, would eventually triumph over these badly equipped, badly fed little Orientals. We had technology. We had B-52s and patrol boats and electronic sensors and fighter planes and aircraft carriers and money, endless billions of dollars. Of course we would win. Above all, we would win because we were right. We would roll back the Communist tide.

Out in the field, the grunts who were fighting one of the best-motivated armies in history knew better. The grunts always knew better.

In Saigon, you didn't see the infantry of either side. The great early cliché of the war was the irony of sitting in the bar on the roof of the Caravelle Hotel, sipping a vodka and tonic, watching artillery light up the night sky only a dozen miles away. Saigon calls up other memories as well, among those who paid rent there long ago: the zigzagging geometries of traffic, the pedicabs, motorbikes, bicycles, and battered cars coughing up filthy blue exhaust fumes; the damp smell of much handled piasters; the bars of Tu Do Street, not much different from those frequented by the French when the street was the rue Catinat (so carefully described by Graham Greene in *The Quiet American,* that chillingly prophetic novel, which was ignored by the men who made policy). The whores and bar girls were everywhere, citizens of the country of money; *you numbah one, he numbah ten, you like Saigon tea?* The old whorehouses of the French epoch were almost all gone by the time the Americans arrived, banished by the puritanical Diem; the old-timers talked with fondness of mirrored walls and ceilings, silky thighs, elegant meals, opium in ivory pipes, mauve dawns.

That was not the American epoch. There were men who loved women in that country, and many who learned to love the country itself, but you could never love Tu Do Street, the lithe whispering whores in Mimi's Bar, the women with the enameled faces whose eyes said nothing. They too were casualties of the war, stunned out of feeling, and their sisters could be found all over the country, wherever young Americans were stationed in large numbers. They lived in the half-dark of the bars, where the music of Aretha Franklin and the Doors and the Stones pounded from the jukeboxes, where phrases were dropped, money was exchanged, and men were led upstairs, or into ambushes. The young Vietnamese men, eyes glittery with hatred, watched the Americans parade their purchased ladies along the avenues, where tamarind trees were dying from the exhaust fumes, and sometimes they reached out and slashed an American belly before vanishing into the crowds. Packs of small children roamed too, forcing collisions, slicing at pockets for wallets, flipping watches off the wrists of drunks. In Saigon, the Americans were far from the war, but living in its very heart.

There were some who came to love the very pain of Vietnam, the way lovers surrender to the fierce ache that makes them feel most truly alive. Reporters, spooks, bureaucrats, officers, A.I.D. officials, missionaries — they kept returning, as if convinced that if they made one final desperate attempt Vietnam would love them back. Vietnam never did. Those Americans wanted an affair; most had to settle for a heartless fuck.

There is a widely held theory that television and a free press lost the war. Americans at home, the theory goes, could not bear the sight of all those wounded boys, crying for medics on the far side of the earth, and eventually the people rebelled and told the statesmen to bring the boys home. The truth is that, even in this living-room war, Americans saw a false, sanitized version of the struggle. There were no cameras around to see the soldiers who, after 1970, began shooting up with *bach-bien,* which is what the Vietnamese called heroin; no cameras to show ARVN officers collecting their profits from the filthy trade. Cameras couldn't transmit the smells of Vietnam: the coppery smell of fresh blood, the farting and gurgling of a mortally wounded boy, the sweet odor of decaying bodies, a week after a firefight, putrefying under the punishing sky. There were sluggish streams in country that gave off the stinking odor of a brown, fetid scum produced by upstream blood. The smells were never to be forgotten. Nor were the sights. In field hospitals you could see young men, only months away from ball fields and Saturday-night dates, their bodies ruptured, full of morphine, skin blistered, legs or arms or eyes gone; they seldom made the seven o'clock news. And the cameras couldn't capture the terror of a man cut off from his unit, unavoidably left on the field of fire, in the night that belonged to the Vietcong, his body no longer obeying his mind, his words dropping like obscene prayers: *oh mama, oh fucking jesus mama, oh jesus fucking christ, oh mama, oh.* The cameramen were extraordinarily brave; they saw more combat than any general, more in a day than any of the best and the brightest back in Washington would ever see; but the true televised history of Vietnam was in the outtakes, those moments, that footage, deemed too obscene to be shown to Americans or the rest of the world.

Such details are forgotten now in what passes for public discourse on the war. That is understandable, of course; no nation can dwell forever on pain and defeat. But it remains an astonishing fact that so little was learned from the long, heartbreaking experience.

There were many valuable lessons to be learned. For instance, that technology alone cannot beat motivated infantry, a lesson that Iraq is now learning in its war with Iran. Perhaps more important, statesmen should have learned that if there is a chance to end a conflict with a deal, take the deal, no matter how imperfect (Diem turned down a 1962 offer from the Vietcong to lay down arms and join a coalition government; the Americans turned down a similar deal the following year). Our leaders should have learned to avoid, if possible, taking sides in a civil war; any city cop will tell you that he would rather face a professional murderer than intervene in a domestic dispute. We should have learned that a great nation must never enter a war unless the goals are absolutely clear, and agreed upon by a majority of citizens; then you formally declare war, instead of sliding into it a foot at a time.

Vietnam should have taught us that mindless anti-Communism is not a cause worth killing or dying for, in a world in which Communism is hardly a monolithic force. Vietnam should have taught us that nationalism, with its engines of independence and self-determination, is a more powerful force by far than Marxism, and must be understood and respected. We should have learned that in a democracy such as ours, lying is fatal, whether to the press or to the people or to ourselves. We should have learned that we can't ever talk in the flowery pieties of democracy and freedom while supporting a right-wing military dictatorship. As citizens, we should have learned never again to place our trust in princes, *or* in abstraction, and never to entrust the war-making decisions to men who have not directly experienced combat.

Above all, Americans should have learned that before they go barging into some remote place in the world they must study its history. In Vietnam, the Americans were deep into the swamp before they started reading Joseph Buttinger, Bernard Fall, the accounts of the French defeat at Dien Bien Phu, the thousand-year story of the tenacious Vietnamese struggle for independence from China. Discovering these things after the commitment was made led to folly, pain, death, and tragedy. Yet in Lebanon and Central America, less than ten years after Vietnam, the old mistakes are general once more; ignorance is apparently invincible, the American capacity for human folly without limit.

There is no excuse for this anymore, of course. The literature on Vietnam grows daily, filling the shelves of libraries and bookstores. The complete story of the war remains elusive, to be sure, because historians and journalists still have little access to the other side, to the men and women of Vietnam, North and South, who endured so much misery and pain for so many years. Until the Vietnamese war in Cambodia ends, until the United States, with the good grace of a defeated prizefighter, at last offers the hand of friendship to the people who won, we won't know it all. We don't even know all of the American part of the tragic tale. We'll be learning about Vietnam for the rest of our lives.

But the interim texts of the war are there for this generation of politicians, military men, and ordinary citizens to examine, brood upon, and absorb. In the Pentagon Papers, we can see the instinct for bureaucratic self-deception, the presentation of false options, the insistence on illusion in the face of the facts. We can understand the difference between genuine national pride and a self-centered national vanity when we read the memoirs of Lyndon Johnson, Richard Nixon, and Henry Kissinger. We can experience the fury, pain, and craziness of combat in Michael Herr's *Dispatches,* in Mark Baker's *Nam,* in Wallace Terry's *Bloods.* The works of Frances FitzGerald and Jonathan Schell show with agonizing clarity what the war did to the ordinary Vietnamese, living in those poor villages that got in the way of the juggernaut. From Gloria Emerson's *Winners and Losers* to Joe Klein's *Payback,* we've had books that explored the shattering effect of the war on the generation that fought it. And there is a huge shelf of books about the way the war changed America itself, all those books about the sixties. All are connected: the multipart PBS series, the Stanley Karnow history, the Time-Life volumes. And the novels: Tim O'Brien's *Going After Cacciato,* Stephen Wright's *Meditations in Green,* John M. Del Vecchio's *The 13th Valley.* The war hangs over all the novels of Ward Just, and it is the offstage presence in Jayne Anne Phillips's *Machine Dreams.* The movies have been less successful — *Apocalypse Now, Coming Home, The Deer Hunter,* and all those films about daring missions to rescue M.I.A.'s still held by the Dirty Commies. Film is almost too literal to capture Vietnam; the truth of the war was internalized, mythic, surrealistic, allusive; its darkest furies, deepest grief, and most brutal injuries could not be photographed. This war belongs to the printed page.

The extraordinary thing is that the men who make the hard decisions in government don't seem to have read a sentence of the literature, or to have applied the lessons to the present world. The tangled, hurting history of Nicaragua is there to be discovered, its culture and myths can be examined; but policy is still determined on the basis of the old 1950s East-West quarrel. If the hard men in the Kremlin had read carefully the story of the American adventure in Vietnam, they might have paused before blundering murderously into Afghanistan. Those statesmen who refuse to allow the rebels into a coalition government in El Salvador should examine the lost diplomatic opportunities in Vietnam.

Last year, in Nicaragua, I thought a lot about Vietnam. There were no exact analogies, of course, but in the Intercontinental Hotel in Managua, I remembered walking through the same kind of lobby in Saigon, talking to correspondents fresh from the fields of battle, exchanging the small talk of war. Late at night, I recalled the faces of soldiers I'd met long ago, marines in the hills and jungles of I Corps, grunts traveling through the treacherous passes around Bong Son.

Talk about Vietnam to old soldiers, meet an old reporter, and they'll remember another thing: the beauty of the place. One afternoon, in the lovely hills of Nicaragua, where the contras now roam, I remembered an afternoon near Dalat when a group of us saw a flock of birds, white against the bottle-green hills, move slowly to the north. They looked like doves, and we laughed at the obvious symbolism and moved on. It's difficult to explain to people how beautiful napalm can look, scudding in orange flames across a dark hillside. Seen from a helicopter, the natural green feminine beauty of Vietnam was forever underlined by man-made damage; those blue and brown rain-filled pools had been made by B-52s; those ghastly dead forests, as skeletal as Giacometti figures, were created by Agent Orange. In the night, you could hear hot wind blowing through the trees, as sibilant as Asia, a wind with its own language, its own sound, atonal; that was Vietnam too.

I'm never surprised when I meet once-young men who want to go back. For a day, a month, an hour. They want to see Vietnam when its beauty does not hold the potential of death. They want to know if the con men and hustlers still deal on Lam Son Square. And what about the whore named Ly, whose husband died fighting for the VC, the woman who lived in the blue room and never smiled? Are all those women now graduates of re-education camps? What do they remember about all those clumsy young Americans who arrived to throw seed into flesh before rising to hurl metal at hills and hootches and people? How many Vietnamese listen now to Aretha and the

Doors and the Stones? Who lives in Soul Alley, out by Tan Son Nhut, where black soldiers danced to Marvin Gaye, where deserters lived with their Vietnamese women? Have the Communists sealed the tunnels of Cholon? Does anyone live on Hamburger Hill? Who sits by the pool of the Cercle Sportif, or drowses on the veranda of the Continental Hotel, drinking "33" beer? What has become of the old French cemetery in Da Nang, where in 1966 you could see the gravestones sinking into the dark earth? Do children laugh in My Lai 4? The ghosts whisper.

Vietnam, they say.

Vietnam, Vietnam.

VANITY FAIR,
April 1985

IRELAND

I.

BELFAST

We spent the first night high up on Finaghy Road North in streets completely devoid of light. IRA guerrillas waited in the darkness behind barricades made of sheet-iron and paving stones. The Falls Road, the main street of the Catholic district, was sealed off. There was heavy fighting in the White Rock Road. Finaghy was deadly quiet. There was no moon and occasionally the stillness would be punctuated by a distant burst from an automatic rifle.

The lads want the Army, an old friend said, they want to have a go.

Now, finally, everyone seems to want to have a go. The men of the IRA are fighting a civil war against 12,000 heavily armed British troops. In addition to the British troops there is the Ulster Volunteer Force (UVF) built on the remnants of the old discredited B-Special militia. Since Saturday at least 25 people have died in the fighting, hundreds have been injured. Almost 4000 refugees have traveled across the border into the Irish Republic. Factories have been demolished, homes put to the torch. More than 300 men have been arrested and held without arraignment under provisions of the Special Powers Act, a law that the Greek or South African government would love to have for themselves. The city is in a shambles and still the fighting goes on.

Yesterday the fighting was sporadic. A light drizzle fell through the day. There was shooting from the Divis Street flats, a brief battle made more complicated by the presence of UVF snipers. Most of all it was a day in which all sides caught their breath. The English Prime Minister Edward Heath had finally finished the yacht race he had been on while his subjects died and was back in London. There had been a call from Dublin for a three-party conference and some wanted to see what would develop. But nobody had any real hope.

In the light of day the signs of the bitterness and blood were everywhere on the Whiterock Road which leads to the largely pro-IRA housing estate of Ballymurphy. The walls of the city cemetery had been torn out in big gaping piles for use as barricades. Along the wall of the cemetery one of the "lads" (frequently a euphemism for the IRA) had painted in two-foot-high letters the ultimate question of an oppressed people: "Is There A Life Before Death?" It stood there in the gray morning light at once very Catholic and very revolutionary while children played in the rubble which had been pushed aside by the British bulldozers. Is there a life before death?

The night before, sitting in someone's parlor on Finaghy Road talking to the women, who were fearful for their men, one middle-aged woman burst out, "If I was a man I'd get a gun myself. I was never bitter before. I thought you could take this life here and hope for the best. Well, there's a lot of us here now just won't wait. The men on this street are all unemployed, every last one of them and they've got nothing to lose. They feel disgraced in front of their women and children. Now they're fighting. They're goin' after something and even if it's all bloody hopeless, at least they'll go like men."

The women have been extraordinary. In the afternoon on the Falls Road at the corner of Broadway about 300 women and a few dozen children gathered around a Saracen tank and battered away on it with the metal tops of garbage cans until it left. Across the street a knot of men gathered in front of the Beehive, an ornate saloon full of brass and wood. They wore the sullen masks of men who had been too long unemployed. But the women were firebrands, led by a red-haired, tight-lipped young woman who gripped a stick in her hand.

"If the nationalists was all together, see, they'd be able to do it," she said tossing her hair in the drizzle. "Too many of the men are Jilly-Janes. They wear the skirts. But the women, we're not afraid to die for the country."

She talked about the First Presbyterian Church, a great orange-brick pile that stood in silence a few doors away. "We haven't done anything to the Protestants. We haven't touched that church of theirs. They've burned our churches. They've driven our people out of their area. But we know it's not the Protestants. It's the politicians."

"I don't know where it's goin'," the red-haired woman said, "but they can't put the best of our men in prison. They can't keep doing this without a fight. It's a war now and I don't care because I'm not afraid to die."

The clouds moved slowly through the sky. The rain fell. An empty hearse from O'Kane's Funeral Parlor came down the Falls Road. Someone else had been buried at the cemetery up on the hill and standing in the strange chill you were certain that before it was over Mr. O'Kane would have a lot more customers.

II.

BELFAST

From 8000 feet it looked like the same old Ireland; the green, placid rectangles running off to the Atlantic, as if the earth were celebrating its own sweet order; farm houses and hedgerows and cattle decorating its face; mists lacing the low hills. But as we descended into this hard northern city, that old Ireland began to fade, as the cold smoke of revolution twisted up from the red-brick streets, and the faces of the other passengers tightened into masks. The Belfast face is an anthology of masks.

"Too long a sacrifice," wrote W. B. Yeats, "can make a stone of the heart." And moving into Belfast in this desperate week, you saw that too long a sacrifice had already taken place: too many years of bigotry, too many years of being offered humiliation or exile as the sole choices of a life, and finally too much blood.

Instead you saw the skeletons of transmitting towers rusting in the countryside; suburban houses reduced to rubble; great gaping holes in the once tight-packed walls of the downtown avenues; plywood and tin covering a thousand shattered windows. Belfast was a town at war, its heart turning to stone.

And as we walked into customs, at Aldergrove Airport, for a long and tedious search, everyone there knew that the crunch had come. The day before, 13 Irishmen had been returned to the Irish earth, while 20,000 people stood in lashing rain and sleet outside St. Mary's Church in Derry. Inside the church, the bishops and lord mayors and aldermen sat in silken mourning beside the families of the dead. But Ireland flowed up the hills of the Catholic ghetto called the Creggan, made up of men with cloth caps, women with worn faces, the working people of Derry, scattered under umbrellas holding off the rain. Bernadette Devlin stood outside in the rain, with Ireland.

That ceremony was at the heart of the crunch. Those 13 had been shot down on Sunday Bloody Sunday, and the Irish tragedy hurtled forward in a series of jump cuts: Bernadette Devlin slamming Reginald Maudling in the House of Commons; the British Home Stores in Belfast being blown apart at dawn; the Republic withdrawing its ambassador from London and sending Foreign Secretary Hillery to New York; and then 30,000 people in Dublin burning out the British Embassy. After Sunday there was more happening in Ireland than the IRA.

In the afternoon we went to the Lombard Room of the Royal Avenue Hotel, where officers of the Northern Ireland Civil Rights Assn. announced to a packed smokey press conference that Sunday's march in the border town of Newry would go on as scheduled. The British reporters practically interrogated the civil rights people as if simply showing up in a public place in Northern Ireland was a guarantee of violence. But in Derry last Sunday the only dead were Irishmen, none of whom were armed. If this Sunday's march turned violent it would be the British Army that turned it violent, not Irishmen asking for civil rights.

At nightfall, a dense brown fog mixed with the smoke of burning buildings seeped through the city. We started to move towards the Catholic ghetto in the Lower Falls Road. British soldiers edged their way through the fog, their blackened faces looking as blank as the nose of a machine gun. In the distance, we heard a burst of automatic

weapons fire, muffled shouts, and men running in the fog. There was
no edge to the buildings, no conventional geography in those darkened streets.

We were put up against a wall and searched. There was the tap-
tap-tap of a rifle again. Up ahead, a mangled pile of vehicles burned
an orange hole in the brown fog. The British were trying to clear the
barricades, which had been built to prevent them from having easy
access to the area, and from the Divis Street flats, Irishmen with guns
were shooting back. A knot of young people, grim and almost in-
sanely courageous, heaved rocks and curses at the Saracen light
tanks.

"Bastards, murderin' bastards," someone shouted from the darkness. There were more voices in the dark, running feet, smashing
glass, isolated shots, and still the fog moved down the Falls Road.
The British laid down a barrage of 4-inch-long rubber bullets from
grenade launchers and the young people scattered. More shots came
from the Divis Street flats. Two rounds slammed into the plywood
covering of the shuttered bar where I was standing. And then suddenly it was quiet. The fog covered everything, and the British soldiers started to withdraw.

It was Friday morning and the night belonged to the IRA.

III.

BELFAST

You see them shopping along the Shankill Road in the dull grainy
Northern afternoons: tidy women pushing baby carriages, men in
wool suits, children playing with plastic guns. The side streets are
bristling with Union Jacks and red, white and blue bunting, and you
can see the gray iron wall of the "peace line" at the end of some of
the streets, and the spray-can graffiti of the Protestant ghetto: "IRA
Beware" and "No Pope Here" and "Home Rule Is Rome Rule" and
"No Surrender."

These are the Protestants of Northern Ireland, and seldom has a
majority ever acted more like a minority; these are people who inhabit a fortress, their minds in a state of siege.

"We're British," a man told me one afternoon, standing angrily
on a corner of Sandy Row, with the stunted slum houses of the Prot-

estant working class ghetto spread out behind him. "We'll remain British, even if Heath sells us out, even if Faulkner sells us out."

The man was a welder in the Harland and Woolf shipyards (in which there are only 100 Catholics in a 9000-man work force). He spoke in the hard, heavy accents of the Belfast working class; his tone, with all its cargo of intractable resentment and suspicion of betrayal, was unmistakably Irish. In London, he would be labeled "Paddy" along with the rest of the Irish. But here in Belfast, this city strangling on the stale meal of history, he was insisting that he was British; it was as if a can of tomato soup, through some act of pop alchemy, could describe itself as a ham sandwich.

"The basic confusion here," a British reporter said to me one night, "is that they've got their notions of lunatic patriotism mixed up with their notions of lunatic religion. They're sick with religion."

The phrase was apt. If Belfast is not precisely sick with organized religion, it is certainly sick with churches (the buildings, not the faiths). The churches are everywhere: 55 for the Church of Ireland (Anglican), 65 for the Presbyterians, 35 for the Methodists, 4 for the Reformed Presbyterians, 17 for the Baptists, 9 for the Congregationalists, 6 for the Evangelical Presbyterians, 24 for the Roman Catholics, 4 for the Non-Subscribing Presbyterians, 8 for the Elem Pentecostals, 1 for the Christian Scientists, 13 for the Salvation Army, 2 for the Society of Friends, 2 for the Moravians, 5 for the Apostolics, 1 for the Plymouth Brethren, 2 for the Emanual Mission, 5 for the Free Presbyterians, 3 for the Church of Latter Day Saints, 1 for the Seventh Day Adventists, plus 1 Railway Mission, 1 Coalmen's Mission, and a number of smaller gospel halls. There is one church for every 1000 adults. And in the 1961 census, only 64 people in all of Northern Ireland (pop: 1,500,000) described themselves as atheists.

The result of this overdose of organized Christianity has been destruction, bigotry, fear, hatred, paranoia and death. Walking the streets of this town, where the smoke from the bombed-out buildings hangs in the air for days while church spires stab at the skies like the spears of pagan armies, it is difficult to understand what Christianity thinks it is doing here.

There are, of course, thousands of Protestants who are neither bigots nor Bible-thumping fundamentalist lunatics, and a number of them have finally begun to talk about the inevitability of a 32-county

Ireland. But down in those Shankill churches, many of the less educated are continuing to lock themselves into the prison of dogma.

The phrases have the high keening tenor of apocalypse about them: "Roman Catholicism is the Anti-Christ, Greatest of all Harlots, and Cause of all Our Present Discontents. Bernadette Devlin is the Pope's Whore."

The mixture of lurid sexual metaphor with statements of moral purity laces the language of the Protestant ghettoes; the language is accompanied by an almost touchingly naive belief in the now-forgotten slogans of the past. Consider the words of one Protestant battle hymn ("Ye Loyalists of Ireland"):

> Ye Loyalists of Ireland
> Come, Rally round the Throne!
> Thro' weal or woe prepare to go,
> Make England's Cause your own;
> Remember your allegiance,
> Be this your Battle Cry,
> "For Protestant Ascendancy
> In Church and State we'll Die!"

It's a measure of how removed some sections of this city are from the rest of the world that grown men can still sing that song and mean it, in the last third of the 20th century. They can still march in the great Protestant parades on the 12th of July, festooned with orange sashes, crowned with bowler hats, in some pathetic imitation of their old rulers, talking as if the Battle of Boyne, when the Protestants smashed the Catholics, had taken place the week before and not in 1690.

"Rem. 1690," of all things, is still scrawled on the crumbling walls of the Protestant ghettos, and wonderfully decorative paintings of William of Orange appear everywhere.

The terrible thing, of course, is that when all the festive marching has finished, and the dread invasion of the Papists has been repulsed, and all the defiant songs have been sung, the men of the Orange Order retreat back to Sandy Row and the streets off the Shankill Road, and they are poor again and wondering whether their sons will have to quit school and go to work, and whether their daughters will go off to England, and whether this week they might actually have a piece of steak.

There is much talk now in the North about the possibility of a violent Protestant backlash. In effect, there has been no fighting here between Protestants and Catholics since 1969; the fighting has really been between the IRA and the British Army. All arms searches have been in Catholic areas; no members of the Protestant militant groups — the Ulster Volunteer Force, the Tartans and others — were interned last Aug. 9th.

One reason for the ferocity of the Catholic and Republican resistance here is that the British Army's task appears to be to disarm the Catholics, thereby leaving them at the mercy of a heavily armed Protestant majority. There are 100,000 *licensed* guns in the hands of Protestants, and one Belfast reporter told me that the number of unlicensed ones might be double that.

"This is what the backlash is supposed to be about," the reporter told me. "It won't actually happen, of course. You won't get 100,000 Protestants fighting the Catholics any more than you ever see 50,000,000 Arabs assembling to fight Israel. But it serves the political ends of the people in power to keep talking about a backlash. They might, though I doubt it, actually talk it into happening."

IV.

On the last day, the Saracens still moved through the city with their guns bristling and the eyes of the soldiers alert for sudden movement, while people stood on the streets in sullen hostility. The prisoners were still behind the wire at Long Kesh and Magilligan; there were still Irishmen stuffed in the hold of the prison ship Maidstone, standing in the Belfast harbor, within sight of the country they loved so much they were willing to die or be jailed for it.

A department store had been blown up, a bank raided, soldiers fired on in some country town." Once again, it became devastatingly clear that reporters are essentially tourists at other people's tragedies.

And yet when you prepare to leave this tragic country, there is always a sense that the story has not been fully told, that there is neither language nor sufficient compassion to properly spin the tale. The country hurt Yeats into poetry. It has not changed. Not in 50 years. Not in 300.

I wish I had been able to tell it all better, to explain that what is happening in the northeast corner of this island off the shores of Western Europe has something important to say to those of us who live in America. All the big abstractions are in it: the need for justice, the oppression that can lead men to violence, the destruction that always follows when decency and human goodness are set aside with contempt and bitterness.

But this is also about men who cannot feed their children and have seen them go off to Australia and America and Liverpool for five generations, and have decided at last that no more children will have to abandon the country in which they are born.

If that takes the Thompson gun, if it takes gelignite in the night, if it takes membership in the IRA, no matter; in Andersonstown, the Belfast stronghold of the Provisional IRA, there is 41 per cent unemployment among heads of families; but they are not leaving. They are prepared to die on their feet in their own land.

The story is also about women: easily the most extraordinary group of women I've ever met. Their men are in the concentration camps, or on the run. But go down into the Bogside in Derry, move through Ballymurphy and Andersonstown and Ballymacarat in Belfast, and you will see women holding it together; they paint the walls white in the afternoons to make the British soldiers better targets at night; they bang the garbage can lids when the soldiers approach, to warn the IRA men that the soldiers are coming and the arms must be stashed or used. They manage families, and have time for tea and gossip; but they are the iron of the Irish rebellion. In Edward R. Murrow's phrase (used about the British in 1940), they are people who have decided to live a life, and not an apology.

Northern Ireland means something to Americans because much of what is happening here is happening in other forms in the United States. "We're the blacks of Northern Ireland," one young Irishman said to me. And there are of course parallels to the black experience in America. In Northern Ireland, Catholics are the last to be hired and the first to be fired. The artificial barrier of religion is used in the same way that the artificial matter of skin color is used in the

United States, to separate working men from each other, to the advantage of a few.

In fact, since 1969 there have been no direct clashes between Catholics and Protestants in Belfast. There has been an urban guerrilla war between the IRA and the British Army; there has been much destruction of property. But there have been no true religious riots, no more than there were actual race riots in America during the late 1960s.

A number of blacks employed violence against property and against authority, an authority they believed was corrupt and oppressive; but there were never any large confrontations between blacks and whites. The IRA men are now essentially doing the same thing, with the large differences being that they are fighting in a much smaller country and they are a much larger minority in Northern Ireland than the blacks are in the United States. But their basic motivations, like those of the blacks, are economic. They are poor; they are the men of no property, and they want to live decent lives.

At present, the IRA are winning their guerrilla war. Even with internment, even with the presence of 15,000 British troops, the men and women of the Provisional wing of the IRA are continuing to fight. It is not just the killing of British soldiers by which you measure their effectiveness; they are also destroying the economy of the country.

They are winning because they are not losing. When a band of urban guerrillas can hold off the British Army and provide protection for their own people while causing extensive damage to the opposition, they are winning.

When I first went to Northern Ireland in 1963, the IRA were considered a tiny band of dreamy fanatics. That is no longer the case.

The two most recent events that insured their continued existence were the start of internment on Aug. 9 last year, and the killing of 13 civilians in Derry on Bloody Sunday. Those killings ended any possibility that the general Catholic population could ever accept the authority of the Northern Ireland government at Stormont, and destroyed any vestigial belief that the British Army was there in a spirit of fair-minded good will.

After Bloody Sunday, it was up to the IRA to fight on forever, if necessary, because there seemed no other choice.

They will not have to fight on forever, of course, because the British government will not be able to sustain the Northern Ireland situation much longer. Public opinion polls show that a majority of British people want the troops out of Northern Ireland.

The Heath government is floundering around in multiple crises: Rhodesia, the miners' strike, the great power shortage, and unemployment that has passed 1,000,000 and is climbing. Before this year is out, and probably sooner than later, the war in Northern Ireland will go to a conference table.

At that conference table, everyone who might upset a settlement must be represented. The IRA will be there, because, like the Viet Cong, they have bled for the right to be there. The militant Protestants will be there, so that their suspicions about the motives of the Catholic South can be eased; in talks with literally hundreds of Catholics in Northern Ireland, not one ever said that he or she would like to do to the Protestants what the Protestants have been doing to the Catholics for so many years. Not one argued for union with the Catholic South on terms dictated from Dublin.

Such a peace conference must lead to the final end of the British presence in Ireland and the creation of a new state. The tough, hard people of Northern Ireland have fought for too long to see their fight usurped by the comfortable middle-class bureaucrats of Dublin.

They want a new Ireland, not simply an Ireland in which the six counties in the North are tacked onto the South. A peace conference would almost certainly lead to an all-Ireland constitutional convention, with full representation for every possible point of view, from right-wing fascist to the Maoists and the great majority in between. And from that convention will come the new Ireland, shaped and led by the Irish.

All of this assumes that there is reason and compassion in London, which might be a false assumption. But if Heath and the British government keep on this way, there is no prospect for anything except more killing and more destruction. Until the day when reason prevails, the fighting will go on.

v.

There are no Saint Patrick's Day parades in the Ireland of Gerry Adams. There are no leprechauns. There is no green beer. There are few toora-loora-loora sentimentalities, no room for sure-and-begorrah stage-Irishmen. Gerry Adams lives in the real Ireland, and it's a very dangerous place.

"I suppose there's a 90 per cent chance I'll be assassinated," Adams said in early 1984, "and that upsets me on a human level."

On March 14, 1984, some of the people who would like to permanently upset Adams on a human level made their move. In broad daylight in the shadow of the Victorian city hall in Belfast, three members of the Ulster Freedom Fighters, a Protestant paramilitary group, came roaring from a side street in a gray Cortina and fired nine shots at a car carrying Adams and three friends. Adams was shot in the neck, right shoulder and upper arm. But this time, to the dismay of his enemies, Adams would live.

At 38, lean, bearded, tweedy, he is the head of Sinn Fein, the legal political party that supports the outlawed Irish Republican Party (IRA) in its fight for a unified Ireland. He is the elected member of the British Parliament from West Belfast, although he refuses to swear an oath of loyalty to the British Crown and formally take the seat. Adams is a republican, with a small "r," and a socialist. And though he is capable of self-mocking laughter, dark ironies, private humors, Gerry Adams is a very serious man.

Some of that seriousness is evident in the major facts of his life. Consider just one: from 1970 to 1980, Gerry Adams, the son of a day-laborer, spent 4½ years in British prison camps without ever coming before a jury. During that same decade, he was on the run for 14 months, always moving, wary of informers, hunted by British Army agents and the Royal Ulster Constabulary (RUC), which is the British-financed police force in the six counties of the North.

It was a heartbreaking decade in modern Irish history, and Adams was an intricate part of its numerous tragedies. He was a close friend of Bobby Sands, who died in a hunger strike, and he knew most of the others who followed Sands to the martyr's grave. Many of Adams' other republican friends have been killed, maimed or imprisoned in the grueling war that started in August 1969. Some have given up, left the field of battle, stepped away from the movement, emigrated. Adams struggles on. Dismiss him as a romantic revolutionary, say that the dream of a united Ireland is hopeless, that Irish nationalism is an anachronism, but you must give Gerry Adams this: he has not chosen to live an easy life.

"Adams speaks with the authority of his experience," a Dublin newspaperman told me. "That's his advantage over all other politicians in this country, north or south. He has paid a stiff personal price for his beliefs, and that can't be taken away from him."

In the years since the 1981 hunger strikes, Adams has led Sinn Fein ("Ourselves Alone" in Irish) to a prominent place in Irish politics. Sinn Fein has broadened its base, rolled up large votes, and begun to build a Tammany-style service organization, with six advice centers in West Belfast alone. It now seems possible that Adams might supplant John Hume, of the Social Democratic and Labor Party (SDLP), as principal representative of the Catholic nationalist side of the northern political equation. At the same time, Sinn Fein has become more active in the 26-county Republic to the south, battering heroin peddlers in the slums of Dublin, trying to channel the anger and disillusion of unemployed Irish youth into politics, presenting an alternative to what Adams calls "the tweedledum and tweedledee" of the Republic's two major political parties.

"I think we'll do all right in the next elections," Adams says. "We've got a few things going for us."

There are a number of people who believe that Adams is a mere front man for the IRA, if not its actual leader. Since membership in the IRA would send him to jail, the truth might not be known until the war is over. But to some extent, the question is academic; Adams frankly, warmly, openly supports the IRA.

"If a section of the Irish people chose to resist by use of arms the British presence in Ireland, as needless to say they have chosen to do, generation after generation, then politically I will, of course, defend their right to do so."

He is obviously aware of the terrible excesses of the war, the often murderous stupidity and carelessness, the outrages of the bombing campaigns. "I would certainly not attempt to justify any action in which civilians are killed," he has said. "I naturally regret very much all such deaths. But since it's not the policy of the IRA to kill civilians, I could not condemn them for accidental killings. In any war situation, civilians unfortunately suffer and die."

And he adds: "The presence of the gun in Irish politics is not the sole responsibility of the Irish. The British were responsible for putting it there in the first place. And they continue to use it to stay in Ireland. No amount of voting will get them out."

When Pope John Paul came to Ireland and delivered a homily on the need to end the violence, Adams said:

"I believe the Pope left a bigger, greater challenge to the Catholic

Church than he did to the republicans. In principle, most republicans would agree with what the Pope said, but republicans don't see themselves involved in violence. They see themselves involved in a perfectly legitimate struggle. I'm sure that if the Pope was asked for an opinion on an armed Communist takeover of some country, he would say it was quite legitimate to use force to resist it, and our opinion is that it is quite legitimate to resist the armed takeover of our country."

Adams has spent most of his life in resistance to the British presence in Ireland. He lived as a child in Leeson Street in one of the worst Belfast slums, went to St. Finian's primary school, St. Mary's Christian Brothers School, and first saw action in 1964, when he was involved in the Divis Street riots. These were triggered by the display of a forbidden Irish tricolor in a window, an act that provoked a brutal attack by the RUC in which many civilians were injured. Soon he was deeply involved in republican politics, reading the literature of Irish revolution while working as a bartender at the Duke of York pub on Donegal Street. In those same years, he joined committees trying to alleviate housing and employment problems in Belfast and became a founding member of the Northern Ireland Civil Rights Association. At the time, there were almost no IRA members in the North; the organization had virtually ceased to exist. Then in August 1969, Belfast exploded, and Adams joined the self-defense teams in the Catholic ghettos. In March 1972, he was interned without charges, along with hundreds of other young Irishmen, and sent to the prison camp at Long Kesh. He soon found himself in the notorious Cage 11, from which many IRA leaders were to emerge. Adams does not, however, agree with the widely held theory that Long Kesh was the university of Irish republicanism.

"Maybe I'm wrong," he said one recent morning. "But I think that aspect was very much exaggerated. They've got to explain this so they say, 'Well, they were all stupid, they all got arrested, they all went to jail, and in jail they all got very clever, and then they got out and caused all this trouble.' I don't agree with that."

But for Adams and his friends, much of the time in Cage 11 was well spent. "It was really a matter of putting in order what people already knew. That was my experience. Cage 11 was actually a wee bit different from all the other cages, because it was a wee bit crazy. It was sort of a M*A*S*H camp. The rest of the camp was militaristic, regimented, like a British Army thing, with officers of the day and so on." Adams smiled. "Cage 11 didn't have any of that."

Today, Adams works most days in Connolly House, the headquarters of Sinn Fein in the Andersonstown section of Belfast. In a large room on the ground floor, local people wait to see Sinn Fein volunteers for help with problems. Sometimes the problems involve domestic disputes, erring husbands, disturbed children, other casualties of the war. Some visitors might have problems with government agencies or conditions in government-owned housing.

"We always did some of this work," Adams says. "But now, with electoral legitimacy, we can call up on behalf of a constituent and do the same work with some clout."

Connolly House is located in a small area of shops and two-story houses, and it was here that Martin Galvin of Queens came to speak last year in defiance of a British ban on his presence in the northern democracy. As soon as Galvin appeared at the side of Adams, the RUC charged, smashing into Irish and American members of the crowd. One RUC man fired a plastic bullet at a 20-year-old Irishman named John Downe and killed him. The American visitors, most of whom were members of Irish Northern Aid, which supports Sinn Fein and the IRA, were shocked by the viciousness of the assault. Adams was not.

"That's the way they are," Adams says. He likes to point out that the British have "a political code disguised as a moral code; they can use force and nobody else can." Noting the current discussion of "widespread alienation" in the North, Adams says, "Thatcher's way of dealing with alienation is to shoot the alienated."

Adams clearly wants the support of Irish-Americans, but doesn't believe Sinn Fein or the IRA should alter their goals to please potential supporters. He is, for example, frank about being a socialist, and doesn't accept the conventional analysis that the Northern Ireland struggle is just a tribal conflict between Catholics and Protestants. He certainly doesn't want a "Catholic Ireland" and has clashed on a number of occasions with the Catholic hierarchy. The Sinn Fein vision of a united Ireland is decidedly nonsectarian.

"Historically, the church was always in the position of being fairly divorced from the people and not being involved with them in any social issues," Adams says. "There are all sorts of examples of absolute stupidity here. Ballymurphy, here in Belfast, has a fantastically high rate of unemployment and poverty, and it had visited upon it a multi-thousand-pound church that the people had to pay for, which didn't even have dwellings for a priest. So now they have this big mausoleum in the middle of Ballymurphy, but the priest is still two miles up the road."

As it did in 1916, the church has repeatedly come down hard on the IRA. "It's a conservative church, there's no doubt about it," Adams says. But there have been some changes — in Irish terms, very big changes. The fact that so many priests could come out against the Reagan visit, so many nuns and sisters oppose the Central American policies — that's a change, a big one. And there are a sprinkling of radical priests about the place. But you have to distinguish between the church and the hierarchy. I mean, I'm a member of the church, as is every other Catholic in Sinn Fein; the hierarchy is only part of the church, too."

Religion is not, however, the critical problem. Adams says the first order of business is independence, and from that would flow an independent Irish foreign policy, built on "positive neutrality," unaligned either with NATO or the Warsaw Pact: A socialist economy would include nationalization of natural resources, banks and major industries; limits on the ownership of large tracts of land; most of all, a planned economy.

"The present economy," he says, "which is called a free-enterprise economy, is actually a planned economy, but it's planned in favor of the small minority who control the wealth."

He says charges that Sinn Fein and the IRA plan to create "another Cuba" in Ireland at the point of a gun, or institute some sort of totalitarian government on the Eastern European model, are absurd. The IRA gunmen are here for the moment, Adams says, "but once independence is secured, armed struggle is finito. Sinn Fein would then figure in an Irish democracy — which is denied us at present — for the things we want. But it would be up to the Irish people to say yea or nay. If the people accept it, fair enough. If they accept part of it, fair enough. If they reject it, fair enough."

Adams doesn't believe that such independence will come easily. The British, in his analysis, will not leave the North of Ireland quietly because "many of the reasons why Britain colonized in the first place still stand."

One major reason, in Adams' view, was national security. "She was always concerned that her opponents like France and Spain

would form an alliance with the Irish and come in through the back
door. That still comes up with NATO, still comes up with some of
the right-wing Tories." Adams believes there was also an ideological
reason for the initial British conquest; Britain at the time was a feudal
society, while Ireland was decentralized, somewhat radical, with
communal ownership of lands and sharing of labor.

"That's what they fear now," Adams says. "A victory for Irish
freedom, if it led to the radicalization of Ireland, would have an effect
on Britain itself. You can see what the Tories are afraid of in the
way they're treating their miners. They would just have nightmares
if people like me had something to say about the way this country is
governed."

In addition, there is British jingoism and racism. "We are the first
and the last colony of Britain. And there is almost a racist attitude
about Ireland. It probably would be simpler if we were black. We're
only 20 miles from their shores at some points. If we were in Cyprus,
or Rhodesia, or Hong Kong, it would be much easier. And finally,
although everybody doubts it, I believe there's an economic factor,
too. We are a market for their goods. Whatever industry is here is
still majority-owned by the British. All the clothes I wear, the wallpa-
per on the walls, the tea I drink, everything comes from Britain."

But what about the Protestants in the North? They represent at
least 60 per cent of the population of the six counties, and their
leaders have vowed to fight if they are forced into a union with the
South. If the British pulled out tomorrow, as the Belgians once pulled
out of the Congo, wouldn't there be a bloodbath?

"I think there'd be a violent reaction, for understandable reasons,
from some of the loyalists," Adams says. "The reaction from loyalist
paramilitaries, or what we call unofficial paramilitaries, would be
fairly minimal, because they are small forces. The hard reaction
would come from the official paramilitaries: the RUC and the Ulster
Defense Regiment, which is kind of militia. We maintain that they
are actually British forces, and it would be the British responsibility
to disarm and disband them."

Adams says it is crucial for Irish nationalists to assure the loyalists
that they want them as part of the united Ireland, with full civil and
religious liberties. But a separate Northern Ireland state, or statelet,
independent of both Britain and Ireland, is "no go."

"I think, at the end of the day, that people only fight, and only use physical force, when they think they are going to win, and when they have something very meaningful to fight for," Adams says. "That's what sustains the republicans. The Unionists, too, think they are going to win, and they think *they* have something very worthwhile to fight for. But they'd be fighting to persuade a power [the British] that's withdrawing, not to withdraw. And what would they be fighting for? A 2½-county statelet?"

In June 1983, Adams said: "The ordinary Protestant needs reassurances and full guarantees of civil and religious liberties. But they cannot be expected to move away from their position of marginal privilege while there is no reason to do so. The British prop is what maintains this privileged position. It is the prop which created and maintains the sectarian division. Only when that prop is removed will Protestant, Catholic and dissenter be able to sit down and work out their own destiny."

Adams obviously believes that the old dream of a united Ireland will come to pass, perhaps not soon, certainly not easily. But eventually. On this winter afternoon, he lights a small cigar, glances about the cramped cold room in Connolly House, and smiles.

"It'll come," he says. "I might not see it. You might not see it. But a united Ireland will come." He pauses. "Would you like some tea?"

NEW YORK POST,
August 12, 1971, and February 4, 16, and 17, 1972 (parts I–IV);
NEW YORK DAILY NEWS,
March 17, 1985 (part V)

LEBANON

I.

BEIRUT, LEBANON

The apartment house was on the Avenue du Gen. Charles de Gaulle, on a cliff at the edge of the sea and its whitewashed facade was stained by the cold steady rain. I asked the cabdriver to come in with me, but he glanced out at the sea, and puffed on a cigarette and said he would wait in the cab. He turned off the lights of the 1971 Impala and kept the motor running. It was very dark.

The entrance to the 10-story building was around to the side, and more apartment houses climbed away behind it, each positioned for a clear view of the sea. There were lights showing in some of the windows, with wooden screens pulled down to the floor of the balconies. A few blocks away was the ruin of the St. George's Hotel, destroyed two years ago in the civil war.

In the old days, this was one of the wealthiest sections of the city, with apartments renting for as much as $2,000 a month. But then the civil war happened and, when it ended, not many people wanted apartments in Beirut. So the owners kept them off the market rather than rent for less than the accustomed price. Then Israel invaded southern Lebanon and almost 265,000 refugees began making their way to Beirut. Some of them had guns.

One of them was standing right inside the door as I walked into the lobby. He was about 19, with a dark face gullied by acne. He was wearing a dirty dark-green uniform, and he was holding a submachine gun.

He said something in Arabic, barking out the words, and looking menacing. I smiled and slowly put my hands up.

"Press," I said. "Reporter. I'm an American reporter." He was very nervous and so was I. Then he shouted something over his shoulder, and another young man came out of the shadows from where the elevators must have been. His boots made a clacking sound on the marble floors. The first kid put the nose of his machine gun against my belly.

"What do you want?" the second one said, in faulty English.

"I am a reporter," I said, as quietly as possible. "I want to talk to some refugees."

"Reporter?" he said.

The first one took the tip of the gun away and started searching me. He found my wallet. There was a press card inside.

"For a newspaper," I said to the second one. "In New York. Here's my press card."

"In New York?" he said. "Are you Jew?"

"Irish," I said. He blinked.

Then the first one found my money clip. It contained some Lebanese pounds, some Italian lire, some dollars: a perfect roll for a spy. He showed it to the second one. They spoke quickly in Arabic.

"If you want to see migrants, you need to help them," the second one said.

"With money?" I said. My hands were at my side now.

"Yes. Money," the second one said. A huge truck groaned along the boulevard and the first man stepped to the front of the lobby and looked out. He kept moving the machine gun from one hand to the other.

"Of course," I said, nodding at the money. "Take all of it."

The second one had slung his gun over his shoulder, with the barrel pointing at the floor. He seemed relieved that he wouldn't have to take a shot to get the money. He jerked his head, indicating I should follow. He said something to the first young man, who went back into the shadows. The elevators weren't working, so we walked up two flights. He produced a flashlight from some where.

"You're Palestinian?" I said.

"Yes."

"Were you in the south during the fighting?"

"Yes."

"What was it like?"

He shrugged. "Soon we go back."

We stopped on the second floor and he led the way down the hall. He knocked on a door: bop-bop, bop-bop, bop. Something heavy scraped on the tile floor behind the door and then it opened. I could smell dampness and human beings and babies. The door frame was shredded where it had been smashed open. A chain hung from a sprung lock.

I couldn't see anything in the apartment, but the young man said something in Arabic and a small oil lamp was lit.

"No electric," he said to me. "They stopped all electric."

My eyes adjusted to the dim light, and then there seemed to be people everywhere. An old man, with a beaked nose, a dirty white shirt, and a dark vest came forward. Behind him was a girl about 18, a woman in her 60s, and others: two boys about 10, a boy about 14. Somewhere in another room a baby was crying.

"Ask them how long they've been here," I said.

"Three days," the young man said, without asking. He said something in Arabic, apparently explaining who I was. They all started talking at once. I could see now that we were in a living room area, and people were asleep on two couches and on the floor.

"They want you to write about them," the young man said. "They have been in a bad time for a week. They come from Burj al Shemali. They were bombed by airplanes. The Jews destroyed all their homes."

Yes, there were some PLO commandos in the village, but they had all left for the south the night before the bombing. The Israelis bombed them a second time and four people were killed, including the husband of the teenage girl. That was when they decided to leave. No, they were not all related. They had joined the other refugees on the main highway for the north, and crossed the Litani River. It took them two days to walk to Beirut. They had left everything behind, cows, clothes, food. On the way north, they lived on oranges taken from plantations.

The old man said something, a long and complicated complaint, and the young man with the machine gun nodded.

"He said that when they came here there is no house to stay in. Too many people everywhere. He said that it was so cold here and they were all afraid because there was shooting in the street. He said that is why he came to this building."

The young man looked around the dimly lit apartment.

"We took this place for them," he said proudly. "Why is it empty when people are cold? So we come here and took it. The rich don't care if people die."

I asked if the people here would be going back to Burj al Shemali. The teenager started shouting, getting nearly hysterical, then suddenly kicked at a glass-topped table. It tipped over and glasses fell to the floor and smashed.

"She says that there is no more Burj al Shemali."

Then he turned to me. "Are you finished?" The girl was crying now and the young machine gunner seemed embarrassed. I offered him a cigarette.

"No, you go now," he said. "Not safe. You go."

I said goodnight to the people in the room and followed the young man to the door with the baby still crying behind me. In the lobby, the first kid came over, more jittery than ever. His hands were on the gun and he pointed it at me, saying something in high-pitched, rapid Arabic, the barrel of the gun bobbing as he emphasized his points. The second one made a disparaging expression and casually touched the barrel, pushing me aside slightly, and tapping me on the back in the same motion. He was saying goodnight, and telling me to go while the going was good.

The cabdriver was still there and seemed surprised to see me. The rain fell steadily. I got in the back and lit a cigaret and tried to control the shaking of my hands.

II.

TYRE, LEBANON

We left in the morning, heading south along the coast. Men climbed telephone poles near the refugee camp of Ouzai, repairing lines wrecked in the Israeli bombing. A woman picked through the ruins of a house. The road was an inch deep in mud from two days of steady rain and the skies were a sullen gray.

But yesterday, as the first United Nations troops moved south to create a buffer zone between Israel and those Palestinians who live in Lebanon, the first signs of peace appeared. A man with his face wrapped in a faded blue kaffiyeh herding sheep along the edge of the road; farmers with dark sun-scorched faces selling lettuce and lemons; a young girl smiling and waving plastic sacks of oranges at the passing cars. The Syrian soldiers at the first roadblock were relaxed and pleasant, waving us on without a check.

But the aftermath of the brief week of war was everywhere. Trucks loaded with furniture, bedding and human beings still moved north, the contents piled impossibly high, held together with ropes and wires. In Doha, refugees squatted listlessly along the sides of the road, or moved into old abandoned luxury hotels with names such as Hawaii Beach Club, Milio's and Kangaroo Beach. On the hotel balconies, I could see uniformed young soldiers of the Palestine Liberation Organization, watching the roads, cradling their Kalashnikov assault rifles.

"Everybody here from before went away in the civil war," the cabdriver said. "Nobody came back. Now it is for the refugees. They just take it."

A PLO armed personnel carrier went by in the other lane, a mustached young man in a blue sports shirt standing up as if posing for a poster, his hands on the grips of mounted twin .50-caliber machine guns. He was followed by two truckloads of bananas, being hurried north to market in the interval of peace. Another truckload of refugees, another checkpoint, and then we were in Damour.

Some of the most ferocious fighting of the civil war took place here. Every building in sight had been demolished or hit. There were mounds of broken bricks everywhere, twisted steel girders, caved-in rooftops. A small grove of olive trees withered in the spaces between two damaged buildings. After all the previous destruction, the Israelis had bombed it again last week. Damour made the South Bronx look like 57th St. And still people were living there: Two men in a makeshift grocery store, listening to a syrupy ballad on the radio and arguing in Arabic; a man alone in an improvised liquor store set up in a shed; six Arab women in brightly dyed gowns pounding laundry in flat pans, living in a garage.

"Most of them are from Tal al Zaatar," the driver said, shaking his head. "Now they have to live in these places."

He was referring to the Palestinian refugee camp in northern Beirut that was under siege for 17 months before falling to the Phalangists in August 1976. Between 1,400 and 2,000 of the refugees were massacred then.

"That was terrible," the driver said. "I was not involved in the war. I am Muslim. I want people to live together, Christian, Jew, whatever. But Tal al Zaatar, that was criminal."

There was a traffic jam outside Sidon, as eight huge diesel trucks unloaded supplies that had been driven from Iraq. In the main street, kids played pinball in a place called the Morison Club, and others lined up at a small moviehouse to see "MacKenna's Gold," with Gregory Peck. Spray-canned political graffiti covered all the walls. For the first time we saw refugees heading south, instead of north.

"We want to go home before the Christians steal everything from our homes," said a man driving a tractor, upon which were piled his family and seven black plastic bags full of clothing and food. "We left when the fighting started. Now the radio says the fighting is over. So we are going home."

We passed the last Syrian checkpoint into PLO territory. Cypress trees lined the road. PLO fedayeen were everywhere, all of them carrying guns, a number of them young women. Some were hidden in trees, others walked in twos and threes along the road. They had their own checkpoints, announced in advance by rows of truck tires in the center of the two-lane road.

"The Israelis are over there," one young PLO officer said, pointing to the rocky hills about three kilometers away. "They have not come any closer. The UN is supposed to go up there today and get them out."

Outside Aadlun, we saw the shot-up hulk of a maroon Mercedes taxicab, one of two ancient cabs into which 16 members of two Lebanese families had piled to escape the Israeli shelling of Tyre. They left in the early hours of March 17, heading for Beirut. But they were stopped by a group of Israeli commandos who had come ashore looking for a Palestinian leader. The commandos opened fire on the cabs. Fourteen people, including four children under age 5, were killed. At dawn, when reporters reached the site, the two cars were still jammed with corpses. Now the cabs lay like the shells of strange giant beetles, picked clean by ants.

The driver moved along more slowly now. We went through lemon and orange groves, and suddenly we were at the bridge over the Litani River. Lebanese soldiers waved us on. A dead horse lay at the side of the road, its neck jerked back at a right angle. It was beginning to swell.

Then we could see the long low curve of Tyre, with minarets sticking up against the sky. I counted 15 ships, from freighters to fishing boats, sunk in the harbor. We went up Ramel Road, where five apartment houses had been hit by Israeli shelling. Two Arab teenagers came over to see us when we stopped, one of them holding the rusting case of a hand grenade.

"They were out in the water and kept shooting," said the first boy, who lived in a six-story apartment house with blue trim and white walls. He spoke in a mixture of English and Arabic. "Then the airplanes came from the other side, shooting." He went around to the back of the house where he had lived, and showed us huge holes in the building's wall. Blue Venetian blinds rattled in the wind off the harbor. The building was abandoned.

"Nobody was killed here," the boy said. "They died down there, in the souk."

In the souk — a casbah of winding narrow streets next to the harbor — there were three shell craters, from 15 to 20 feet wide, filled with brown, stagnant water. A three-story house had fallen into a mess of broken concrete, wood beams, plaster and corrugated iron.

We drove out to the abandoned night club on the edge of the city where the International Red Cross had set up its headquarters. It was right on the beach. A Swiss woman named Nicole (she said her last name "was not important") was running the office.

"We had to move the first aid station into the center of the city, because it was too dangerous for the wounded to come out here," she said. "So now we are just trying to help the refugees locate each other. So many got separated during the shelling and bombing. We have more than 700 messages here. All from people trying to find each other."

Outside her office was the old dining room of the night club. Rain pelted the windows. Out on the veranda a huge Red Cross flag was held in place by rocks. One of the windows had been smashed. The wind made a ghostly sound.

We left the Red Cross building and went back into town to make our way to the UN command post. There were PLO soldiers at the bottom of the hill, most of them sitting aimlessly on piles of rubble. We started up the hill, heading east, and suddenly a man in civilian clothes ran out waving his hands.

"Don't go," he said. "Don't go. Bad there. Shooting."

About 50 yards ahead, we saw PLO soldiers running in our direction. Some dived into ditches beside the road. I could hear the snapping of small arms fire. And then the heavier chung-chung-chung of an automatic. The driver pulled violently off the road, and went to the side of a building, out of the line of fire. We got out and peered around the side. The PLO was firing now, a mixture of carbines and machine guns, but there was no return fire from up the hill.

Then, as quickly as it had begun, the firing mysteriously stopped.

"Lebanese army!" the man in civilian clothes said. "Not UN! Mistake. Small problem. Not UN, not Israeli!"

We looked around the building again and the PLO soldiers were climbing out of the ditches, peering up the road. All the firing had stopped. Later it would be reported, without details, as a minor incident involving a dispute with a local commander of Christian Lebanese troops. But on this road, in the soft rain, it was men shooting at each other with real guns and real bullets. The man in civilian clothes ran up the road, out of sight. A young girl in a yellow dress came out of the bushes across the way, peeling an orange. We never made it to the command post of the United Nations.

III.

The tents were dark blue and wet with the rain and they were pitched in a grove of date palms between the road and the sea. Children ran from tent to tent in the rain. A chicken-wire fence surrounded the enclave, and a PLO soldier stood at the gate, with a Kalashnikov assault rifle under his poncho.

"We are happy you are here," said Labib Androuous, a Lebanese Catholic who was supervising the camp for the civil defense section of the government. "Welcome. Do you want a cigaret?"

Androuous was in his late 30s, with graying, black hair, and he nodded at the PLO soldier and took me into the camp. There were children everywhere, and women in shawls and long gowns, and teenage boys with wrinkled suit jackets that did not match their trousers. These were only a fraction of the estimated 265,000 refugees driven out of southern Lebanon during the brief, savage little war that was fought here last week.

"There are about 1,400 people in this camp," Androuous said. "We have 145 tents and every tent has a number. We know from the number how many people there are in each family, and how much food they need for each meal. They get lunch meat and cheese, some sugar, some rice. We have also set up small gas fires for each tent, so that people can cook. And we have even given them eating equipment, knives and forks."

He was obviously proud of the camp's organization, and moved easily through the milling crowds of women, old men and children.

"Everybody here is Muslim," he said. "Everybody. They are all Lebanese, not Palestinian." His eyes moved uneasily to the PLO guard at the gate. "All of them are very poor. Most of them are farmers. They are without guns. Nobody here has guns."

The rain had turned to a fine drizzle. One of the teenage boys came over with two small plastic cups of dense black coffee. He asked in Arabic where the visitor lived. In New York, he was told. New York?

His eyes brightened, and he yelled to some friends that this stranger was from New York.

"It's like telling him you are from the moon," Androuous said, smiling and sipping the coffee. A group of teenagers crowded around. In New York were the buildings very high, like in the movies? Yes, they were very high. Is it cold there? In the winter, yes, with a lot of snow. Did I know Elvis Presley? No, I said, and besides, he's dead. They nodded gravely as the words were translated. To the left, sheltered under a giant palm tree, a group of women watched in silence. An old man without teeth stood alone, staring at the new arrival.

"Where are the men?" I asked, looking around at the old people, the women, the teenagers and the children.

"Many of them stayed behind," Androuous said. "These people are farmers. . . . When the invasion started, they had to leave. But they could not take the animals. So the fathers stayed behind with the animals. A cow can be the most rich thing in a family. For a week, many of them have not heard from the fathers, and now they are anxious to go back."

He paused, and looked at a line of women waiting at a supply tent where blankets were being issued.

"Of course," he said, "some of them have nothing to go back to."

That was the growing reality of Lebanon. Every day as new refugees came down from the mountains, and reporters moved into the towns they left behind, it had become clearer that the Israeli intention was to wipe some towns off the face of the earth. Their people would then be moved far from the Israeli border. The strategy has hurt, but not destroyed the PLO, and has certainly left a lot of innocent human beings with "nothing to go back to."

One such woman sat in a corner of a tent with a 4-month-old infant loosely cradled in her arms. She had cinnamon-colored skin, and high cheekbones, and hard white teeth. She was 28, but looked 10 years older. She sat there, making a low keening sound, like women in the west of Ireland when they are overwhelmed by grief.

"She is from Abassiyeh," he said, as if that explained everything. Abassiyeh was a hill town behind Tyre, overlooking the coastal plain and the sea. Before the invasion, it contained about 8,000 people. But all reports indicate that it has been completely leveled by Israeli artillery bombardment. The town was bombed one final time from the air, a few hours before the cease fire.

"When the first bombs fell," Androuous explained, "her husband told her to go out of their house, to take the children and go into the country and hide in the fields. He was packing their belongings. She was already outside when the shelling from the boats started. She looked back and there was no more house. She tried to go back, but the house was exploded."

The woman was still squatting there alone, beyond communication, when we walked down to the sea. Over to the left was the stone shell of the old Hotel Saida, long abandoned, but now filled with refugees. At the base of the front steps a group of small boys took turns riding a green tricycle. A mound of orange peels, empty meat cans, and flattened milk cartons was growing at the water's edge.

"We have a doctor now and a nurse," Androuous said. "Some of these people have never seen a doctor. Not once in their life. They are simple people. They are not involved in politics. They want to be left alone with their land."

Another woman, fat and bulky, came up to Androuous talking quietly in Arabic. He listened gravely, nodding his head, his arms folded across his chest. Then he spoke to her for a while and she went away.

"She wanted to leave right now," he said. "With her four children. I told her it would be better to wait a day, until it was safer. Who knows? Maybe her town is gone, too. She wanted to know if the Israelis were leaving, or if they would stay for a long time."

"What did you tell her?"

"I said I didn't know. I said the United Nations troops were here now, and we would know soon if it would be safe."

The sea was pounding hard against the empty beach, drowning the din of the camp. He walked me back to the gate and shook my hand and wished me a good journey. The road was heavy with traffic. Iraqi trucks moved along slowly, their cargoes covered with wet yellow tarpaulins, presumably weapons for the PLO. A truck full of refugees came from the other direction and slowed to look at the camp.

The driver exchanged some words with the PLO guard, shook

his head and moved north. Androuous walked through the crowd, nodding, listening, doing his work. Just past him I could see the woman with the cinnamon-colored skin, cradling her baby, squatting in her tent. She was still crying, for everything.

NEW YORK DAILY NEWS,
March 24, 25, and 26, 1978

NICARAGUA

I.

The phone rings suddenly in the darkness of pre-dawn Managua. Can I be ready in 20 minutes for a trip up north with some of the Sandinista *commandantes?* An hour and a half later, I'm in a small bus with a group of journalists. The announcer on Radio Sandino is exhorting us to defend the revolution, while a young woman hands out sandwiches, cookies and Pepsi-Cola.

Ahead of us, two escort jeeps bristle with automatic weapons. Off the road, a small boy tends a chestnut horse, but doesn't look at the convoy. The radio announcer gives way to Marvin Gaye singing "Sexual Healing."

Then we notice who is driving the Range Rover, directly behind us, with Nicaragua Libre license plate MAY S 177. It's Daniel Ortega. He is the 38-year-old "coordinator" of the nine-man junta that has ruled Nicaragua since July 19, 1979. He's driving almost casually, talking to others, gesturing languidly with a free hand.

"Anybody want another sandwich?" the young woman asks.

Forty-five minutes later, the bus stops abruptly. We've gone a hundred feet past an unmarked dirt road, and the driver has to back up. So do the two jeeps. Standing at the junction with the dirt road are Ortega, Jaime Wheelock, who runs the nation's agrarian reform program, Joaquin Cuadra, chief of staff of the Sandinista army, and junta member Rafael Cordova Rivas. Ortega is moustached, wearing glasses, the corners of his mouth pulled down in a permanently disappointed way.

"They look like they're about to take over a college dorm," someone says, and of course we all laugh with the shock of recognition. The Sandinista *commandantes* are obviously serious men, survivors of combat, prisons or torture. But most of them are children of the '60s; they're the first successful revolutionaries in the world who grew up listening to rock 'n' roll. In an important way, the overthrow of the 45-year-old Somoza dynasty wasn't a victory of the Stalinoid cementheads of the Kremlin; it was the only true victory of the New Left.

We see more of this loose, casual '60s style as the convoy moves up the dirt road and we come over a rise, glimpse three Soviet-built MI-8 helicopters in a field, and rows of barracks with soldiers lounging in the shade. A sign says: "The People of Sandino Are a Victorious Army," but from a barracks radio I can also hear a Spanish version of "The Great Pretender." Ortega strolls over to some officers and soldiers, and starts to chat. Wheelock stretches, smothers a yawn, removes his hat and ruffles his hair. Cuadra says something and Wheelock guffaws. This is not the way Charles de Gaulle arrived at an army base.

Then we are hurrying across a field to the helicopters, bound for a *"Cara al Pueblo"* — literally "Face to the People" — a kind of Sandinista town meeting. A man in civilian clothes, with the grave flat face of an ex-pug, slides behind the mounted AK-47 at the open door. We lift off.

For people my age, I suppose every green countryside seen from a helicopter will always look like Vietnam. On this morning, over this land, the resemblance was uncanny. Down there you could see deep thick jungle, miles of dense valleys winding through mountains. You don't take that kind of country with gunboats or air strikes or rhetoric; you can only take it with infantry.

This was not yet Vietnam, of course; but almost every Nicaraguan I met here fully believes that Ronald Reagan will be reelected and then use some pretext to mount a full-scale invasion. So all over the countryside, in places where Augusto C. Sandino fought the United States Marines from 1926 to 1933, and where the Sandinista National Liberation Front (FSLN) fought Somoza's National Guard from 1961 to 1979, the Sandinistas are stashing arms: machine guns, ammunition, grenades, mortars. Managua might someday soon be carpet-bombed into dust, but the Sandinistas are preparing to fight a guerrilla war in the countryside for the rest of the century.

On this slate-gray morning, we land in a lumpy cow pasture outside a small town called Matiguas. Ortega, Wheelock and the others have landed first, and they wait for us to join them. A line of kids appears behind a barbed wire fence separating the field from a gravel road. Ortega leads the way to the fence, starts talking to the kids. "Are you going to school? How are the teachers? What are you learning?"

Then an aide separates the strands of barbed wire, and Ortega and the rest of us duck through, and the first rain begins to fall. More kids arrive, as Ortega strolls to a small plaza, where trucks and soldiers are waiting. A young girl approaches Ortega with a covered basket of tortillas. He takes some, chats with the girl, the rain pouring down harder, cameras whirring, flashbulbs popping. It is clear now what Daniel Ortega is doing: he will be the FSLN candidate for president in the eventual election, and this morning he is running for office.

We pile into cars and trucks, and then there is a wild jolting 45-minute ride along the gravel road, nothing truly visible through the gray walls of tropical rain, and a sudden lurching halt. *Campesinos* wait on horses, along with more Sandinista soldiers, civilian officials, rural bureaucrats. And then two white horses are brought forward, and Ortega and Wheelock mount them.

There's a moment of hesitation: Wheelock and Ortega look like city boys playing cowboy for a day, the SDS off to a rodeo, and then they start to move. For one absurd moment, it's as if Sandino's army had been resurrected, or we've entered a scene from "Viva Zapata." Here they come, the horses' hooves clattering on stone, and below them in the distance are the people of Rio Blanco.

I can hear their cheers through the rain. It's a shameless act of theatrical hokum, but it works. Wheelock looks down at a lowly foot soldier from the American press and struggles to suppress a smile. It's as if he's saying: Could Fritz Mondale do this? Or the world's master of the manufactured moment, Ronald Reagan?

After that entrance, everything else is anticlimax. Ortega makes a speech, but the wind blows his words around, and the rain falls harder, while the crowd hurries back and forth from the speakers' stand to a nearby shelter.

From the audience, the questions are no airy abstractions. Where is the promised school bus? Why does it take so long to get our milk to market? When will you fix these terrible roads? Soldiers want to know why mail takes so long to be delivered, and why, if they can't have leave to go home, their girlfriends can't come to visit?

Ortega and the others give answers, and then it's over, and on to the next campaign stop. The rain never ends, but the *commandantes,* who lived with rain and worse during the years in the mountains, look as if they infinitely prefer it to the weatherless offices of Managua.

It would be a mistake, of course, to think that the Sandinista leadership is made up of kids on a lark. Ortega was in Somoza's prisons from 1967 to 1974, was jailed numerous times before that, and fought as a guerrilla during the last three years of the revolutionary war. His brother Humberto was also a jungle fighter (and is now minister of defense). His brother Camilo was killed in February 1978, when he was the only FSLN member to join the rebellious Indians in the town of Masaya. Daniel Ortega looks young, but he's not playing at being a revolutionary; he is one.

He is also, of course, a Marxist. Unfortunately, to call someone a Marxist these days is to say very little that is precise; the present governments of France and China, Greece and Albania (among others) could be described as Marxist, since their leaders were certainly shaped by the theories of Karl Marx.

But Ortega and the other FSLN leaders have repeatedly said that for them Marxism is only one tool among many; the core of their revolution is *Sandinismo*. This vague doctrine boils down to an absolute insistence on the sovereignty of Nicaragua. Sandino himself said it this way in 1928: "What motivates us is the desire that the Yankees not have a pretext for continuing to tread upon the soil of our Fatherland, and [the desire] to prove to the civilized world that we Nicaraguans ourselves are capable of solving the problems of a free and sovereign nation."

During the revolution, Ortega was a leader of the *Terceristas* — or Third Force — the segment of the FSLN that was least dogmatic, most broadly based. He is believed to be among the more moderate, pragmatic members of the leadership. But at a casual airport press conference after the trip to Rio Blanco, he said that Nicaragua must have combat airplanes to defend its airspace against reconnaissance flights that are giving logistical aid to the contras. He would get the planes from France, he said, or from the Soviet Union, or from whoever else would sell them to Nicaragua. But he would get them.

After that discussion, the few reporters walked out through the airport lounges, where Crosby, Stills and Nash were singing about Marrakesh. Two weeks later, Daniel Ortega was in Moscow.

II.

The Church of Santo Domingo de Guzman was consecrated on May 4, 1963, but on this bright Sunday morning, as well-dressed people filed into pews for the 11 o'clock Mass, the building felt much older.

The altar was all wood and white cloth, with painted plaster statues of the risen Jesus and a serene Mary. At the foot of the altar stood a huge carved wooden chair, flanked by chairs of diminishing size. This was a church in the old style, serene as Sunday morning, marred only by the round fluorescent lights attached to the wood-panel ceiling.

To the right of the entrance there was a confessional booth upon which was fixed a permanent sign: EXCMO SENOR ARZOBISPO METROPOLITAN MONS MIGUEL OBANDO BRAVO. How extraordinary: In this small church, wedged on a breezy hill above the American and the Soviet embassies, every sinner had the chance to confess his failures of flesh and will to one of the most powerful men in Nicaragua. For this was the church of Managua Archbishop Obando Bravo, the acknowledged leader of the opposition to the Sandinista revolutionaries.

"If he were the candidate in the elections," says Conservative leader Mario Rappaccioli, "he would get 80% of the vote, no contest."

Since 1980, Obando Bravo has warned his flock against the "totalitarian" drift of the revolution, opposed the military draft, urged the Sandinistas to bring the contra leadership into the government. The Sandinistas have reacted in varying degrees of contempt and rage. But their slogan — "between religion and revolution there is no contradiction" — acknowledges their fear of Obando's potential for trouble.

On this day, two thirds of the archbishop's parishioners were female, and seven of these polite, oddly sad women wore pearls. They also wore dresses of muted blues and grays, sensible shoes and expressions that were more baffled than defeated. In Marxist caricature, they were, of course, the hated bourgeoisie, vicious exploiters of the poor, grubby materialists whose souls longed for permanent salvation in Miami. But Nicaragua is not Cuba; there are no mobs scaling the walls of the Peruvian Embassy, no long waits for exit visas; anybody who wants to leave can leave. These people have chosen to stay.

On this day, a young four-piece band in yellow long-sleeved shirts played at the front of the church. They were very good, but all eyes were on the archbishop. He entered forcefully, a squat compact man with gold-rimmed glasses, garbed in purple and scarlet. Everything about him was blocky: hands, features, feet, body, even the powerful tuneless bass in which he did some singing. During the hand-clapping up-tempo tunes, Obando's mouth remained sealed; he would sing only one chorus of "Glory, Glory Hallelujah" through the long morning service.

His sermon was unremarkable, a reflection on Pentecost, an expression of mild bafflement about why his efforts to end the contra war had been so misunderstood, a prayer "for those in prisons, for those who are fighting." His tall peaked archbishop's hat was secure upon the blocky head; he dispensed Communion with paternal ease.

When the Mass ended, his flock walked out into the sunshine, whispering, murmuring, failure clinging to them like dandruff on a suit. I saw only one peasant family in the church: a man with a brown hawklike Indian face, his wife, his children. They sat in the last pew and didn't leave until the last station wagon door had slammed.

Later that day, I went to Mass at the Church of Santa Maria de Los Angeles, a low circular building in the heart of a slum called El Riguero. The 1972 earthquake that moved Archbishop Obando from the ruined cathedral to Santo Domingo also destroyed the old church in El Riguero. This new church is the replacement, and it's not yet finished. One huge mural on the far wall remains incomplete, but against the back wall are murals of what is called here the "Church of the Poor" or "The People's Church."

We see Jesus portrayed as a revolutionary, Sandinistas battling oppression, a portrait of Gaspar Garcia Laviana, a Spanish priest of the Sacred Heart who went off to the mountains in 1977 to fight with the FSLN. His farewell letter to his parish sums up for many the Christian roots of the Nicaraguan revolution:

"The Somoza system is a sin, and to free ourselves from oppression is to free us from sin. With my gun in my hand, full of faith and love for my Nicaraguan people, I will fight to my last breath for the coming of the kingdom of justice in our homeland, that kingdom of justice that Messiah announced to us under the light of the Star of Bethlehem."

Garcia Laviana was killed in combat in 1978, and his name was remembered fondly during a brief talk at these evening services by the Rev. Uriel Molina. This remarkable priest, a native of Matagalpa, is one of the best-known exponents of the "option for the poor," which motivates the pro-Sandinista movement in the Nicaraguan church. He is of the generation profoundly shaped by the style and example of Pope John XXIII, by the reforms of Vatican II in 1962, and most importantly, by the calls for change that came from the 1968 meeting of Latin American bishops in Medellin, Colombia.

"The Sandinista front was born at the same time as Vatican II," Molina once explained. "In 1965, my superiors sent me to the only house we had in Managua, in the El Riguero neighborhood. That was before the earthquake when the old Managua still existed, and El Riguero was quite far from Managua. I ended up there in a little church, with very poor people."

Almost 20 years later, the people of El Riguero are still very poor, and there are more of them; the poor have been crowding into Managua, the birth rate is up and the death rate is down.

On this evening Molina conducted services in a plain white robe, accompanied by a nine-piece band, which alternated up-tempo tunes and melancholy revolutionary songs. The only obvious members of the bourgeoisie were some visiting foreigners. The people themselves were simply dressed in clean clothes, their children freshly scrubbed. Nobody wore pearls.

At the end of Mass, Molina remained beside the altar and slowly removed his priestly garments; he finished in a sports shirt and slacks and then began to talk individually to his parishioners. The moment was oddly moving, part of the process of demystifying the role of the priest and emphasizing his work.

For the priests of Uriel Molina's generation, the most crucial theologian has been a Peruvian priest named Gustavo Gutierrez, whose use of Marxist theory led to his book "A Theology of Liberation." In a way, this has been the most revolutionary book in modern Latin American history, a call for revolt against the traditional church alliance with dictators, land owners, army colonels and industrialists at the expense of the poor. Molina and others who have embraced liberation theology grew up in a state of rage caused by the desperate poverty they saw around them and the indifference of the church. Gutierrez said that the problem was "how to say to the poor, to the exploited classes, to the marginalized races, to the despised cultures, to all the nonpersons, that God is love and that all of us are, and ought to be in history, sisters and brothers."

In the late '60s and early '70s, such present Sandinista leaders as Army Chief of Staff Joaquin Cuadra, Vice Minister of Interior Luis Carrion, agrarian reformers Roberto Gutierrez and Salvador Mayorga, among others, came to El Riguero to work with Molina, to learn from him, to share his "option for the poor." Most were middle-class university students seeking a moral alternative to the repression and corruption of the Somoza regime. Defying the desperate pleas of their parents, most stayed for a few years, sharing the poverty of the ghetto, and then moved on to the FSLN. Certainly the experience deeply marked them all and remains critical to the philosophy of the Sandinistas.

Commandante Alvaro Baltodano once told journalist Margaret Randall:

"We read the Bible, studied liberation theology and discovered that if you really read the Bible with your eyes open, you find that the history of the Hebrew people is a history of their fight for liberation. When you read about the life of Jesus Christ you realize that whether he was or wasn't God, he was a man who was with the poor and who fought for the freedom of the poor."

The history of the split in the post-revolutionary church in Nicaragua has been turbulent.

The division was clearly seen during the visit of Pope John Paul to Managua last year. On the same day, he humiliated a kneeling Rev. Ernesto Cardenal (the priest-poet who is now minister of culture), and then ignored the mourning mothers of 17 Nicaraguan soldiers who had just been killed by contras. This led to angry chants in the Plaza of the Revolution of "Queremos la Paz" ("We want peace") from the pro-Sandinistas and "Viva Obando" from their opponents.

The Sandinistas insist freedom of religion is guaranteed in Nicaragua. But as junta coordinator Daniel Ortega says, "When priests enter a political discussion, rather than a theological one, we feel we have the right and the duty to answer them politically."

Obando insists, "we want a system that is more just, more human, that does away with the enormous gaps between rich and poor. But we believe that Christianity is enough to change the conscience of man and the conscience of society without the need to resort to Marxism-Leninism."

The division remains.

NEW YORK DAILY NEWS,
June 25 and 26, 1984

PRAGUE

Year after year I'd see them in public places: on street corners in Chicago or in Washington parks or standing in the rain outside the United Nations in New York. It was always Captive Nations Week or some great date in a fading national history, and the exiles would chant their anguish and their protests in languages I could never know. The men were gaunt and moustached. The women were plump, with shiny pink skin. The languages in their leaflets had too many consonants, and in my life I was drawn more passionately to lands that were lush with vowels. Usually I sighed and walked on by.

After Hungary in '56, there was a brief time when their existence was recorded in the public prints. This man had fought a Soviet tank with a Molotov cocktail and that man's sister had died hurling a paving stone at a machine gunner; they made words and phrases like *sacrifice* and *freedom* and *in vain* sound like something more than

Fourth of July oratory. But by the time we had plunged into our own anguished '60s, most of us had ceased to care. We could do something about Vietnam. It was our war, waged by our politicians, fought by our armies. We could do nothing about Eastern Europe except exchange missiles with the Russians.

But the exiles kept coming on the appointed days to the United Nations. The numbers dwindled. The men began to look sleeker and were certainly grayer, and the women seldom came at all. Some of my friends in the reporting trade dismissed them with innuendo — their leaders were on the CIA payroll, some of them had collaborated with the Nazis, they were mere props for the addled legions of the American Right. I remember talking to some of them one drizzly morning (for the weather of Eastern Europe often seemed to have immigrated with them). I needed a column for the newspaper I then served, and tried to get them to tell me their solutions to the problems back in the old country. *"Drive out the Russians!"* they said. *"Use the atom bomb!"* Faces flushed, mouths contorted, they split the damp air with their slogans. One balding man literally screamed at me: *"Better dead than Red!"* I never wrote the column.

In '68 we read about the changes in Czechoslovakia under Alexander Dubcek, the lifting of the heavy hand of Stalinism, the exuberant attempt to make "socialism with a human face." In a way, this crack in the Stalinist ice pack seemed to further isolate the exiles outside the United Nations, particularly the Czechs and the Slovaks; they began to look like cranks. Then, on August 20 of that terrible year, one week before the American tribes gathered in Chicago for the Democratic convention, the Soviets and their Warsaw Pact allies invaded Czechoslovakia. The Prague Spring was crushed. In Chicago, through the billy clubs and the tear gas, some young American antiwar demonstrators held signs accusing Mayor Daley of running "Czechago." That year, nobody cared much for exact analogy.

But after that brief flurry, Eastern Europe faded from the American consciousness. The Reagan Right, of course, used its existence to pander for ethnic votes; the fading American Left sometimes spoke wistfully about the Prague Spring. But neither seemed really to care very much. There were other matters to divert us: Watergate, abortion, Iran, drugs, various gurus, the religion of the Leveraged Buyout. Reagan railed at the Evil Empire, invented the contras (degrading the 1956 Hungarian resistance by calling these hired thugs "freedom fighters"), and directed the heroic invasion of Grenada. But there was

never any talk about "rolling back" the Red hordes in Prague or
Warsaw, Sofia or Bucharest, East Berlin or Budapest; and places such
as Lithuania, Estonia, Armenia, and Latvia had long ago vanished
from the map. The attitude was brutally simple: Eastern Europe was
"theirs"; Central American was "ours." *Realpolitik über Alles.* And
every year or so, I'd pass the old exiled stalwarts holding weathered
signs and chanting in the streets, occasionally producing one of their
American children to do a dance in a folk costume from the old
country. If it was a slow news day, the papers maybe even ran a
picture.

But while visiting Prague and East Berlin last December, I kept
thinking about those angry and grieving exiles and felt increasingly
ashamed of myself. I should have listened harder and learned more.
In Prague, there were people like them everywhere, with the same
gaunt faces and ill-fitting clothes, the same grievances against injustice, except that now the world was listening. Their uncontested
leader was the fifty-three-year-old playwright Vaclav Havel, whose
moral authority was based on the years he'd spent in the country's
prisons. But when I first saw him, at a basement press conference in
the Laterna Magika theater, I realized that he easily could have been
one of those men from the sidewalk opposite the United Nations.

He did not speak in slogans. Even when addressing vast crowds,
Havel's language is concrete, precise, nuanced; he does not rant; even
in confrontations with his former jailers, he sounds most reasonable.
But his mission was the same as that of his countrymen: to get the
dead clammy hands of Stalinism off Czechoslovakia and allow its
people to breathe freely. Within a month after Prague police had used
bats, clubs, and gun butts on hundreds of student demonstrators,
Havel and other members of the opposition umbrella group called
Civic Forum managed to force the old hard-line leaders to accept
the first noncommunist government in the nation since before the
communist coup in 1948. Not a shot was fired, not a window broken. It was an amazing process to watch; I woke each morning
charged with an exhilaration I had almost never felt in the minefields
of politics.

This revolution was a triumph of human intelligence. Czechoslovakia, like all countries ruled by totalitarians, was an oligarchy of
the stupid. After 1968 the country's best writers, including such
world-class talents as Milan Kundera, Josef Skvorecky, and Ludvik
Vaculik, were silenced, jailed, or driven into exile. Rock 'n' roll musi-

cians were thrown into dungeons. Only the corniest jazz (white Dixieland, for example, or moldy swing music) was officially tolerated. The brilliant Czech new wave of '60s filmmakers was halted, the best people exiled or cast out of the industry, while the Barrandov film studios ground out witless comedies and historical epics that nobody went to see. Thousands of scientists, engineers, schoolteachers, and scholars were removed from their jobs because they were ideologically suspect, and were then forced to do the most menial labor. In all cases, they were replaced by mediocrities, ass-kissing careerists, and Stalinist hacks. It was the most sustained act of national stupidity since Spain expelled both the Jews and the Arabs within ten years of each other at the end of the fifteenth century, thus ridding itself of its most brilliant artists, architects, mathematicians, and merchants.

For an American, some of this was uncomfortably familiar. We, too, once had a blacklist that prevented writers, directors, and actors from working in movies or television — on ideological grounds. During the McCarthy era, we, too, lost scientists, schoolteachers, and scholars, on ideological grounds. Our religious Right continues trying to impose its party line on everything from abortion to the content of television shows. We have a free press, but the vast majority of our newspapers wouldn't challenge the intelligence of a cocker spaniel. Certainly, in our mass media, we seldom read, see, or hear from American communists or socialists, who are dismissed as a disloyal opposition. In Prague, people showed me bound copies of samizdat, precious hand-typed books passed from person to person because they were banned from the bookstores. In East Berlin I saw a line of almost three hundred people waiting in a freezing rain to buy the first West German books to be sold in the East. But a glance at any American best-seller list, or the shelves of any bookstore in a shopping mall, will show you what most Americans have chosen to do with their freedoms.

Still, we have choice, and until last year, millions of Eastern Europeans had no choice at all. Those who protested, like Havel, were visited by the secret police and taken away in handcuffs. He was a writer, and writers are rememberers or they are nothing. And that made him dangerous. In Czechoslovakia people were told to forget the Prague Spring, to forget the country's democratic past between the world wars, to forget the 1948 coup. The social contract was simple: Let the party make the big decisions and the individuals could make most of the small decisions. If they agreed to give up memory and a critical intelligence, citizens could indulge in small bourgeois pleasures: a cottage in the country, a car, skiing, clothes that made Czech women the most chic in Eastern Europe. In Moscow, citizens wait in line for potatoes; on Parizska Street in Prague, I saw a line outside Christian Dior.

But the basic neo-Stalinist demand was for national amnesia, and that, too, was familiar. It was at the heart of the Reagan era, when Americans were urged by the Great Communicator to forget Vietnam and forget Watergate, and use borrowed money to indulge in mindless pleasures.

This is not to say that the United States is the moral equivalent of a totalitarian state. That's ludicrous. But all human beings, including Americans, are confronted every day by the temptation of the totalitarian solution. Wandering the streets of Prague and East Berlin, I never saw a homeless person, never ran into a junkie, never felt a personal sense of menace. The total state, after all, places order above all human values, including justice. But back home in New York and Los Angeles and other American cities, I've talked to many people over the years who demand those Good Old Draconian Measures to deal with our disorders. They would gladly surrender the Bill of Rights if that meant clearing the streets of drug addicts and gunmen. I even heard this argument from some of the Eastern European exiles on the rainy sidewalks outside the United Nations.

That taste for the draconian certainly hasn't perished from the earth, as we saw in December in Romania and Panama. In the hardest of the old Stalinist states, the end came in blood and destruction, with the ruling family joining that of the czar on the casualty lists of the century's revolutions. In Panama, an American soldier was killed, another soldier's wife was insulted, and the great might of the United States was unleashed on the regime of Manuel Noriega. According to polls, most Americans loved this fierce spectacle. And while such peaceful and historic events as the collapse of the Berlin Wall drew poor television ratings, many cheered the brutality of the Romanian revolution. Apparently, nothing makes American blood quicken faster than the spirit of revenge. If it's history, most of us yawn; if it resembles a movie, we snap to attention.

That was what was so special about the events in Prague. Over and over, Havel and the others sent out the message: *We are not going to do to them what they've done to us.* "That would be the worst corruption of this revolution's ideals," said a filmmaker named

Antonin Masa, who had spent twenty years directing his movies only in his imagination. "We want a country that is generous and decent. And where every man can speak his piece. That's all. Revenge is a debasing emotion." Another quoted Albert Camus, saying how it should be possible to love one's country and justice too.

There are lessons here for all of us. The American Right, after an initial period of bafflement, is claiming a triumph of capitalism over communism. "But that's not what is going on here," said Rita Klimova, who lived in New York as a child from 1939 to 1946, returned to Prague, became an economics professor, was blacklisted after the fall of Dubcek, and earned a marginal living as a free-lance translator. "If people here had to choose a model, it would probably be Sweden. A democratic socialist society, with freedom for the individual. This is a struggle for *choice*." Others noted that in the places where the United States did use physical force in the crusade against communism (Cuba, North Korea, Vietnam), Stalinism was still in power, its authority reinforced by the need (real or imaginary) to resist an outside threat. In Eastern Europe, the more pacific techniques of trade, cultural exchanges, and communications helped bring about the great change. Stalinism eventually fell of its own dumb weight. One Czech friend said to me: "There were two specific factors. One was Gorbachev, who made it clear that he wouldn't send the tanks. The other was the decision to stop jamming Radio Free Europe and the Voice of America. That allowed us to get hard news. We didn't care about the propaganda or the oratory. Just the news. That was *very* important."

He and the others were too modest to mention the one final factor: courage. Men like Havel, who began their lonely fight more than a decade ago, believed enough in their cause to place their bodies before the might of the state. They had no guns. They had no money. And in the end they won. They won for themselves and their families and their friends, for their country, for memory and history. But they also won for those lonely men and women who stood for so many years in the hard rain of strange cities. I wish I could find some of them and say that I am sorry for not listening to them in their separation and solitude. But they're gone now. And that might be the happiest ending of all.

PART V

THE
TALENT IN THE
ROOM

The fulfillment of talent is one of the enduring human mysteries. Nobody can truly explain why a mediocre baseball player can become a brilliant baseball manager. Nobody absolutely knows why a singer of enormous technique can't move an audience or why so many gifted actors don't become stars. At six, some children play the piano with the confidence of Mozart, and at twenty they are working as record store clerks. There were some splendid young painters in my art school classes; almost all have vanished. I've seen young writers arrive in New York, bursting with talent, full of swagger and hubris, and then witnessed their descent after a few seasons into permanent silence. In political clubs, I've met men and women with great political intelligence, wonderful gifts for oratory, and unusual clarity about issues; they didn't make it out of the assembly district. For thousands of talented writers, painters, dancers, athletes, politicians, and actors, talent simply wasn't enough.

Most of these pieces are about gifted people who lasted long enough to allow their talents to fully mature. They started with what *Webster's Third New International Dictionary* describes among its definitions of talent as "the abilities, powers, and gifts" bestowed on certain human beings. At first, those abilities, powers, and gifts were crude and raw. But these people combined them with a vision of the future and then had time to refine them, strengthen them, push against their limitations. Such sustained growth is never easy, particularly in the arts. In my youth, self-destruction was a fashion. Whiskey and drugs carried too many gifted people to early graves — Charlie Parker, Jackson Pollock, Fats Navarro, Montgomery Clift, and Billie Holiday to name only a few. Their aborted lives did not serve as useful guides to conduct for the generations that followed. Rock 'n' roll heaven is jammed with everyone from Elvis Presley (we think) to Brian Jones, Janis Joplin, Jimi Hendrix, Lowell George, and Jim Morrison, among hundreds of others; the latest young recruit is Kurt Cobain. The music didn't kill them. The life did.

Now the plague of AIDS is slaughtering the talented young with the remorseless efficiency of the guns and drugs that destroy so many impoverished kids on the other side of town. On some mornings, the obituary page of the *New York Times* has a peculiar consistency; the dead are either eighty-five or thirty-five. The old have had their shot at life; we can only mourn the young dead. Those young people simply never had the time to go all the way down the road with their talents. We'll never know what they might have added to our shaky civilization.

The talented human beings who do last are very rare. Each is an individual, but they share common characteristics. Most of them are very intelligent, including those without much formal education. Intelligence doesn't guarantee a smooth ride; it certainly didn't help Mike Tyson to sidestep trouble. But without intelligence, most raw talent has no chance at all to develop. The most intelligent people are never content to repeat what came before them; they constantly push against personal boundaries; they make their own discoveries, and are pleased to pass on the results to others.

To be sure, they are often self-absorbed, particularly when young, focusing their intelligence on the study of themselves. This is not empty, self-caressing narcissism; they often don't like what they see in the mirror and struggle to change it, a process common to actors, novelists, and politicians. Most of them also grapple with personal emotions, particularly doubt, fear, and humiliation; that battle doesn't always end with maturity. Most develop a mental toughness; instead of retreating from personal turbulence, they learn to control their emotions with their minds. The best of them obviously channel their emotions into the work. That's why they can touch so many complicated emotions in strangers, emotions that range from hope to pity to absurd laughter.

In most of them, intelligence is annealed to will. Cus D'Amato would have called the latter quality "heart." The word itself has an odor of the sentimental but when prizefighters use it they mean a peculiar kind of courage that accepts pain in order to reach a goal. That's not always a simple victory over another human being; Floyd Patterson called his autobiography *Victory Over Myself.*

They also have a complex sense of time. They can surrender to the moment, forcing everything they know into one painting, one song, one dance. The moment is always charged by the lessons of the past. But they also seem capable of imagining a limitless future, full of things not tried, not even dreamed. The actor longs to play Lear, the politician wants to be president. They don't talk about retiring. Not even the athletes. They have the World Series ring or the championship belt. They want more. To go on and on. To be remembered.

I'm aware that all but one of the subjects in this section are men. I wish that were not so. I wish I'd gone to see Rebecca West while she was alive, and had talked with Martina Navratilova while she was one of the greatest of all champions. I wish I'd somehow found my way to the doors of Katherine Anne Porter, Martha Gellhorn, Flannery O'Connor, or Dorothy Parker. In the early 1960s, before she became a star, I did a piece on Barbra Streisand for the *Saturday Evening Post;* we've remained friends and she, of all people, should be in this company. Over the years, I've written profiles of Jeanne Moreau, Sophia Loren, Brigitte Bardot, Linda Ronstadt, among other accomplished women; that they aren't here is because of me, not them; my work just wasn't worth preserving.

The pieces here are not briefs for the prosecution. In each case, I admired the subjects of my attention. In general, I wasn't interested in showing that they also had feet of clay; every human being does. Besides, there is now an abundance of literary prosecutors abroad in the land to do that work. I'm glad I was around to see these gifted human beings exercise their talents. In the case of Bob Fosse, I was blessed by his friendship and will miss him all my days.

JFK

That day I was in Ireland, in the dark, hard northern city of Belfast. I was there with my father, who had been away from the city where he was born for more than 30 years. He was an American now — survivor of the Depression and poverty, father of seven children, fanatic of baseball — but he was greeted as a returning Irishman by his brother Frank and his surviving Irish friends, and there were many Irish tears and much Irish laughter, waterfalls of beer, and all the old Irish songs of defiance and loss. Billy Hamill was home. And on the evening of November 22, I was in my cousin Frankie's house in a section called Andersonstown, dressing to go down to see the old man in a place called the Rock Bar. The television was on in the parlor. Frankie's youngest kids were playing on the floor. A frail rain was falling outside.

And then the program was interrupted and a BBC announcer came on, his face grave, to say that the president of the United States had been shot in Dallas. Everything in the room stopped. In his clipped, abrupt voice, the announcer said that the details were sketchy. Everyone turned to me, the visiting American, as if I would know if this were true. I mumbled, talked nonsense — maybe it was a mistake; sometimes these things are moved on the wires too fast — but my stomach was churning. The regular program resumed; the kids went back to playing. A few minutes later, the announcer returned, and this time his voice was unsteady. It was true. John F. Kennedy, the president of the United States, was dead.

I remember whirling in pain and fury, slamming the wall with my hand, and reeling out into the night. All over the city, thousands of human beings were doing the same thing. Doors slammed and sudden wails went up. *Oh, sweet Jesus, they shot Jack!* And *They killed President Kennedy!* And *He's been shot dead!* At the foot of the Falls Road, I saw an enraged man punching a tree. Another man sat on the curb, sobbing into his hands. Trying to be a reporter, I wandered over to the Shankill Road, the main Protestant avenue in that city so long divided by religion. It was the same there. *Holy God, they've killed President Kennedy:* with men weeping and children running with the news and bawling women everywhere. It was a scale of grief I'd never seen before or since in any place on earth. John Fitzgerald Kennedy wasn't "the Catholic president" to the people of the Shankill or the Falls; he was the young and shining prince of the Irish diaspora.

I ended up at the Rock Bar, climbing to the long, smoky upstairs room. The place was packed. At a corner table, my father was sitting with two old IRA men. They were trying to console him when he was beyond consolation. For the immigrants of his generation, Jack Kennedy was always special. After 1960, they knew that their children truly could be anything in their new country, including president.

"They got him, they got him," he said, embracing me and sobbing into my shoulder. "The dirty sons of bitches, they got him."

And then "The Star-Spangled Banner" was playing on the television set, and everyone in the place, 100 of them at least, rose and saluted. They weren't saluting the American flag, which was superimposed over Kennedy's face. They were saluting the fallen president who in some special way was their president too. The anthem ended. We drank a lot of whiskey together. We watched bulletins from Dallas. We cursed the darkness. And then there was a film of Kennedy in life. Visiting Ireland for three days the previous June.

There he was, smiling in that curious way, at once genuine and detached, capable of fondness and irony. The wind was tossing his hair. He was playing with the top button of his jacket. He was standing next to Eamon De Valera, the president of Ireland. He was laughing with the mayor of New Ross in County Wexford. He was being engulfed by vast crowds in Dublin. He seemed to be having a very good time. And then he was at the airport to say his farewell, and in the Rock Bar, we heard him speak:

"Last night, somebody sang a song, the words of which I'm sure you know, of 'Come back to Erin, mavourneen, mavourneen, come back aroun' to the land of thy birth. Come with the shamrock in the springtime, mavourneen. . . .' This is not the land of my birth, but it is the land for which I hold the greatest affection." A pause and a smile. "And I certainly will come back in the springtime."

II.

Twenty-five springtimes have come and gone, and for those of us who were young then, those days live on in vivid detail. We remember where we were and how we lived and who we were in love with. We remember the images on television screens, black-and-white and grainy: Lee Harvey Oswald dying over and over again as Jack Ruby steps out to blow him into eternity; Jacqueline Kennedy's extraordinary wounded grace; Caroline's baffled eyes and John-John saluting. We remember the drumrolls and the riderless horse.

But across the years, there have been alterations made in the reputation of John Fitzgerald Kennedy. Those who hated him on November 21, 1963, continue to hate him now. Some who were once his partisans have turned upon him with the icy retrospective contempt that is the specialty of the neoconservative faith. And time itself has altered his once-glittering presence in the national consciousness. An entire generation has come to maturity with no memory at all of the Kennedy years; for them, Kennedy is the name of an airport or a boulevard or a high school.

Certainly, the psychic wound of his sudden death appears to have healed. The revisionists have come forward; Kennedy's life and his presidency have been examined in detail, and for some, both have been found wanting. The presidency, we have been told, was incomplete, a sad perhaps; the man himself was deeply flawed. Some of this thinking was a reaction to the overwrought mythologizing of the first few years after Dallas. The selling of "Camelot" was too insistent, too fevered, accompanied by too much sentimentality and too little rigorous thought. The Camelot metaphor was never used during Kennedy's 1,000 days (Jack himself might have dismissed the notion with a wry or obscene remark); it first appeared in an interview Theodore H. White did with Jacqueline after the assassination. But it pervaded many of the first memoirs about the man and his time.

Some of the altered vision of Kennedy comes from the coarsening of the collective memory by the endless stream of books about the assassination itself. We've had the 26 volumes of the Warren Commission report and dozens of analyses detailing its sloppiness and inadequacy. We've gone back again and again to Dealey Plaza and the Texas School Book Depository and the grassy knoll. In thousands of talk shows, magazine articles, newspaper columns, and books, we've heard the Cuban-exile theory, the Mafia theory, the Castro theory, the J. Edgar Hoover theory, the Jim Garrison theory, the CIA theory, the Texas-oil theory, the KGB theory, the E. Howard Hunt theory, the two-Oswalds theory.

We've seen documentaries and docudramas. We've watched the Zapruder film over and over again. We've heard sound experts tell us that the evidence proves that there was a fourth shot and therefore two gunmen. We've read cheap fiction about the assassination and superb fiction like Don DeLillo's *Libra*. In the end, nothing has been resolved. If there was a conspiracy, the plotters got away with it. Twenty-five years have passed. Kennedy is still dead. And so is Oswald. And Ruby. And so many of the others. And in a peculiar way, the details of Kennedy's death have obliterated both the accomplishments and failures of his life.

At the same time, other tales have helped to debase the metal of the man: the smarmy memoirs of women who certainly slept with him and others who certainly didn't; the endless retailing of the gossip about his alleged affair with Marilyn Monroe, that other pole of American literary necrophilia; the detailed histories of the family and its sometimes arrogant ways. These days, with a renewed public hypocrisy in sexual matters, Kennedy has acquired the dreaded "womanizer" label, complete with half-baked theories about the origins of his supposed Don Juan complex. He was afraid of dying, say the theorizers. He was selfish and spoiled. He was revolting against his mother's rigid Catholicism or imitating his father's own philandering.

He was described in some gossip as a mere "wham, bam, thank you ma'am" character; other talk had him a hopeless romantic. By all accounts, he was attracted to beautiful and intelligent women, and many of them were attracted to him. And during the time he journeyed among us, this was hardly a secret. When I was a young reporter for the *Post* in late 1960, I was once assigned to cover Jack Kennedy during one of his stays at the Carlyle hotel. He had been elected but had not yet taken office. "We hear he brings the broads in two at a time," the editor said. "See what you can see."

There was nothing to see that night, perhaps because of my own naïve incompetence as a reporter, or because I was joined in my vigil by another dozen reporters and about 100 fans who wanted a glimpse of John F. Kennedy. Most likely, Kennedy was asleep in his suite while we camped outside the hotel's doors. But I remember thinking this was the best news I'd ever heard about a president of the United States. A man who loved women would not blow up the world. Ah, youth.

Two other events helped eclipse the memory of Jack Kennedy. One was the rise of Robert Kennedy. In his own brief time on the public stage, Robert understood that Jack's caution had prevented him from fully using the enormous powers of the presidency. If Jack was a man of the fifties, the later Robert Kennedy was a man of the sixties, that vehement and disturbed era that started with the assassination in Dallas and did not truly end until Richard Nixon's departure from the White House in disgrace in 1974. The differences were often a matter of style: Jack was cool, detached, rational; Robert was passionate, wounded (by his brother's death, among other things), emotional. Jack was an Anglophile, a product of Harvard and the London School of Economics; Robert came from some deeper Celtic root.

The murder of Robert Kennedy in 1968 played a part in the revision of the Kennedy legend. In a quite different way, the process was completed by Chappaquiddick. Some who had been drawn to politics by Jack Kennedy at last began to retreat from the glamour of the myth. A few turned away in revulsion, seeing after Chappaquiddick only the selfish arrogance of privilege. Others faded into indifference or exhaustion. At some undefined point about a decade ago, the country decided it wanted to be free of the endless tragedy of the Kennedys. Even the most fervent Kennedy partisans wanted release from doom and death. They left politics, worked in the media or the stock market or the academy. A few politicians continued to chase the surface of the myth, copping Jack Kennedy's mannerisms, his haircut, the "Let us go forth" rhythms of his speeches. Gary Hart, who even played with his jacket buttons the way Jack did, was the most embarrassing specimen of the type; others were in the Bob Forehead mold. They helped cheapen Jack Kennedy's image the way imitators often undercut the work of an original artist.

Out in the country, beyond the narrow parish of professional politics, the people began to look for other myths and settled for a counterfeit. It was no accident that if once they had been entranced by a president who looked like a movie star, then the next step would be to find a movie star who looked like a president.

III.

The mistakes and flaws of the Kennedy presidency are now obvious. Domestically, he often moved too slowly, afraid of challenging Congress, somewhat late to recognize the urgency of the civil-rights movement, which had matured on his watch. He understood the fragility of the New Deal coalition of northern liberals and southern conservatives; he had been schooled in the ways of compromise in the House and Senate and was always uneasy with the moral certainties of "professional liberals." When faced with escalating hatred and violence in the South, Kennedy did respond; he showed a moral toughness that surprised his detractors and helped change the region. But he was often bored with life at home.

Foreign policy more easily captured his passions. He was one of the few American presidents to have traveled widely, to have experienced other cultures. His style was urban and cosmopolitan, and he understood that developments in technology were swiftly creating what Marshall McLuhan was to call the "global village." But since Kennedy had come to political maturity in the fifties, he at first accepted the premises of the Cold War and the system of alliances and priorities that had been shaped by John Foster Dulles.

Even today, revisionists of the left seem unable to forgive the role that Kennedy the Cold Warrior played in setting the stage for the catastrophe of Vietnam. He had inherited from Eisenhower a commitment to the Diem regime, and as he honored that commitment, the number of U.S. "advisers" grew from 200 to 16,000. Kennedy encouraged the growth of the Special Forces, to fight "brushfire" wars. He instructed the Pentagon to study and prepare for counterinsurgency operations. In Vietnam, U.S. casualties slowly began to increase; the Vietcong grew in power and boldness; Diem concentrated his energies on squelching his political opposition in Saigon, and soon we were seeing those photographs of Buddhist monks incinerating themselves, while Madame Nhu and her husband (Diem's brother) became lurid figures in the public imagination.

By most accounts, Kennedy intended to end the American commitment to Vietnam after the 1964 election. But since he'd won in 1960 by only 118,000 votes, he didn't feel he could risk charges by the American right that he had "lost" Vietnam. So the guerrilla war slowly escalated, and such writers as David Halberstam and Neil Sheehan reported from the field the truth that the official communiqués too often obscured: The war was being lost. Kennedy sent his old Massachusetts adversary Henry Cabot Lodge to Saigon as the new ambassador. But events were moving out of control. Diem was assassinated in November 1963 (not, as legend has it, on Kennedy's orders). The quagmire beckoned, and at his death, Kennedy still hadn't moved to prevent the United States from trudging onward into the disaster.

But for most of Kennedy's two years and ten months as president, Vietnam was a distant problem, simmering away at the back of the stove. Kennedy's obsession was Cuba. It remains unclear how much he knew about the various CIA plots to assassinate Fidel Castro. But the two major foreign-policy events of his presidency were the Bay of Pigs invasion of April 1961, and the missile crisis of October 1962. One was a dreadful defeat, the other a triumph.

According to Richard Goodwin and others (I remember discussing this with Robert Kennedy), Jack Kennedy had begun the quiet process of normalizing relations with Castro before his death. Although this, too, was to be postponed until after the 1964 elections, Kennedy had come to believe that Cuba was not worth the destruction of the planet.

Today, Castro is the last player of the Kennedy era to remain on the stage, his regime hardened into Stalinist orthodoxy. In Miami, the exiles have become citizens; young Cuban-Americans think of the old anti-Castro fanatics as vaguely comic figures. If Castro died tomorrow and the regime collapsed a week later, an overwhelming majority of the Miami Cubans would stay in Florida. But there is still a hard belief among the old exiles (and some factions of the American right) that Kennedy was responsible for the defeat at the Bay of Pigs because he refused to supply air cover. But detailed studies of the operation (most notably by Peter Wyden) make clear that even with air cover, the force of 1,400 white middle-class Cubans could never have prevailed against Castro's almost 200,000 militia and regular-army troops. Success had to depend upon a general uprising against Fidel and massive defections among his troops. Neither happened.

Today, it's hard to recall the intensity of the Cuban fever that so often rose in those years. I remember being in Union Square when the Brigade was going ashore. A week earlier, I'd actually applied for press credentials for the invasion from some anti-Castro agent in midtown; with great silken confidence, he told me I could go into Cuba after the provisional government was set up, a matter of a few days after the invasion. But from the moment it landed, the quixotic Brigade was doomed. And in Union Square on the second night, when it still seemed possible that the Marines would hurry to the rescue, there was a demonstration against Kennedy, sponsored by a group that called itself the Fair Play for Cuba Committee. Its members chanted slogans against the president. A year later, a much larger group demonstrated during the missile crisis. In a strange, muted way, these were the first tentative signals that the sixties were coming. And later, after Dallas, when the world was trying to learn something about Lee Harvey Oswald, we all saw film of him on a New Orleans street corner, handing out leaflets. They were, of course, from the Fair Play for Cuba Committee.

IV.

And yet . . .

And yet, across the years, learning all of these things from the memoirs and biographies and histories, understanding that Camelot did not exist and that Jack Kennedy was not a perfect man, why do I remain moved almost to tears when a glimpse of him appears on television or I hear his voice coming from a radio?

I can't explain in any rational way. I've tried. Hell, yes, I've tried. I've talked to my daughters about him, after they've seen me turning away from some televised image of Jack. They've seen me swallow, or take a sudden breath of air, or flick away a half-formed tear. They know me as an aging skeptic about the perfectibility of man, a cynic about most politicians. I bore them with preachments about the need for reason and lucidity in all things. And then, suddenly, Jack Kennedy is speaking from the past about how the torch has passed to a new generation of Americans, born in this century, tempered by war, disciplined by a hard and bitter peace — and I'm gone.

There is more operating here for me (and for so many millions of others) than simple nostalgia for the years when I was young. Nothing similar happens when I see images of Harry Truman or Dwight Eisenhower. Jack Kennedy was different. He was at once a role model, a brilliant son or an older brother, someone who made us all feel better about being Americans. All over the globe in those years, the great nations were led by old men, prisoners of history, slaves to orthodoxy. Not us (we thought, in our arrogance). Not now.

"Ask not what your country can do for you," Kennedy said. "Ask what you can do for your country." The line was immediately cherished by cartoonists and comedians, and Kennedy's political opponents often threw it back at him with heavy sarcasm. But the truth was that thousands of young people responded to the call. The best and the brightest streamed into Washington, looking for places in this shiny new administration. They came to Kennedy's Justice Department and began to transform it, using the power of law to accelerate social change, particularly in the South. They were all over the regulatory agencies. And after Kennedy started the Peace Corps, they signed up by the tens of thousands to go to the desperate places of the world to help strangers. It's hard to explain to today's young Americans that not so long ago, many people their age believed that the world could be transformed through politics. Yes, they were naïve. Yes, they were idealists. But we watched all this, and many of us thought, This is some goddamned country.

Out there in the wider world, people were responding to him as we were. It wasn't just Ireland or Europe. I remember seeing the reports of his 1962 trip to Mexico City, where a million people came out to greet him, the women weeping, the men applauding him as fellow men and not inferiors. I'd lived in Mexico and knew the depths of resentment so many Mexicans felt toward the Colossus of the North. In one day, Kennedy seemed to erase a century of dreadful history. The same thing happened in Bogotá and Caracas, where four years earlier Richard Nixon had been spat upon and humiliated. This was after the Bay of Pigs. This was while the Alliance for Progress was still trying to get off the ground. I can't be certain today what there was about him that triggered so much emotion; surely it must have been some combination of his youth, naturalness, machismo, and grace. I do know this: In those years, when we went abroad, we were not often forced to defend the president of the United States.

We didn't have to defend him at home, either. He did a very good job of that himself. We hurried off to watch his televised press conferences because they were such splendid displays of intelligence, humor, and style. We might disagree with Kennedy's policies, and often did; but he expressed them on such a high level that disagreement was itself part of an intelligent process instead of the more conventional exchange of iron certitudes. He held 64 press conferences in his brief time in office (Reagan has held 47) and obviously understood how important they were to the furthering of his policies. But he also enjoyed them as ritual and performance. He was a genuinely witty man, with a very Irish love of the English language, the play on words, the surprising twist. But there was an odd measure of shyness in the man, too, and that must have been at the heart of his sense of irony, along with his detachment, his fatalism, his understanding of the absurd. He was often more Harvard than Irish, but he was more Irish than even he ever thought.

I loved that part of him. Loved, too, the way he honored artists and writers and musicians, inviting them to the White House for splendid dinners, insisting that Robert Frost read a poem at the inauguration. He said he enjoyed Ian Fleming's books about James Bond; but he also brought André Malraux to the White House, and James Baldwin, and Pablo Casals. Perhaps this was all a political ploy, a means of getting writers and artists on his side; if so, it worked. Not many writers have felt comfortable in the White House in all the years since.

Part of his appeal was based on another fact: He was that rare American politician, a genuine war hero. Not a general, not someone who had spent the war ordering other men to fight and die, but a man who had been out on the line himself. When he first surfaced as a national figure, at the 1956 Democratic Convention, reporters rushed to find copies of John Hersey's *New Yorker* account of the PT-109 incident in the South Pacific. They read: "Kennedy took McMahon in tow again. He cut loose one end in his teeth. He swam breaststroke, pulling the helpless McMahon along on his back. It took over five hours to reach the island. . . ."

Reading the story years after the event, some of us were stunned. Kennedy was the real article. There had been so many fakers, so many pols who were tough with their mouths and avoided the consequences of their belligerence. Kennedy had been there, not simply as a victim but as a hero, a man who'd saved other men's lives. When he was president, that experience gave his words about war and peace a special authority. We also knew that his back had been terribly injured in the Solomons and had tormented him ever since. He had almost died after a 1954 operation, and he wore a brace until the day he died. But he bore his pain well; he never used it as an excuse; he didn't retail it in exchange for votes. Hemingway, another hero of that time, had defined courage as grace under pressure. By that definition, Jack Kennedy certainly had courage.

Grace, wit, irony, youth, courage: all combined to make us admire Kennedy. And there was one more thing: the speeches. Kennedy spoke too quickly; he often failed to pause for applause; his accent was strange to many Americans. But he made some of the greatest political speeches I've ever heard.

Most of them were written by Ted Sorensen (with occasional help from others, including Arthur Schlesinger Jr. and Richard Goodwin). But Kennedy was not a mindless robot, reciting the words presented to him by his handlers. He was actively involved in the process of crafting each major speech, from sketching the broad outlines to changing (and often improving) specific language. Kennedy had written two books *(Why England Slept* and the best-selling *Profiles in Courage)* before becoming president. He originally wanted to be a newspaperman and sometimes mused about buying the Washington *Post* after he left office. He cared about words, and it showed in the speeches.

Looking again at the texts, I can hear his voice still coming to me across the decades, charged with urgency, insistent that the world must be challenged and life itself embraced. He never slobbered. He lifted no phrases out of cheap movies. All the revisionism cannot deny the quality of those words and the tough-minded decency of their message. Some excerpts:

To Baptist ministers in Houston, September 12, 1960:

"I believe in an America that is officially neither Catholic, Protestant, nor Jewish. Where no public official either requests or accepts instructions on public policy from the pope, the National Council of Churches, or any other ecclesiastical source. Where no religious body seeks to impose its will, directly or indirectly, upon the general populace or the public acts of its officials. . . . For while this year it may be a Catholic against whom the finger of suspicion is pointed, in other years it has been, and may someday be again, a Jew or a Quaker or a Unitarian or a Baptist. . . . Today I may be the victim, but tomorrow it may be you."

To the American people, after returning from Europe, June 6, 1961:

"Mr. Khrushchev made one point which I want to pass on. He said there are many disorders throughout the world, and he should not be blamed for them all. He is quite right. It is easy to dismiss as Communist-inspired every anti-government or anti-American riot, every overthrow of a corrupt regime, or every mass protest against misery and despair. These are not all Communist-inspired. The Communists move in to exploit them, to infiltrate their leadership, to ride their crest to victory. But the Communists did not create the conditions which caused them."

Reporting to the nation about the white mob violence attending James Meredith's entrance into the University of Mississippi and the decision to protect him with the National Guard, September 30, 1962:

"Even among law-abiding men, few laws are universally loved, but they are uniformly respected and not resisted. Americans are free, in short, to disagree with the law but not to disobey it. For in a government of laws and not of men, no man, however prominent or powerful, and no mob, however unruly or boisterous, is entitled to defy a court of law. If this country should ever reach the point where any man or group of men by force or threat of force could long defy the commands of our court and our Constitution, then no law would stand free from doubt, no judge would be sure of his writ, and no citizen would be safe from his neighbors."

In a commencement address at American University, about the need to negotiate with the Soviet Union, June 10, 1963:

"What kind of peace do we seek? Not a Pax Americana enforced on the world by American weapons of war. Not the peace of the grave or the security of the slave. I am talking about genuine peace, the kind of peace that makes life on earth worth living, the kind that enables men and nations to grow and to hope and to build a better life for their children — not merely peace for Americans but peace for all men and women — not merely peace for our time but peace for all time. . . .

"So, let us not be blind to our differences — but let us also direct attention to our common interests and to the means by which those differences can be resolved. And if we cannot end now our differences, at least we can help make the world safe for diversity. For in the final analysis, our most basic common link is that we all inhabit this small planet. We all breathe the same air. We all cherish our children's future. And we are all mortal."

To the nation, on civil rights, June 11, 1963:

"We preach freedom around the world, and we mean it, and we cherish our freedom here at home — but are we to say to the world and, much more importantly, to each other that this is a land of the free except for Negroes; that we have no second-class citizens except Negroes; that we have no class or caste system, no ghettos, no master race except with respect to Negroes?"

Receiving an honorary degree at Amherst, October 26, 1963:

"The men who create power make an indispensable contribution to the nation's greatness. But the men who question power make a contribution just as indispensable, especially when that questioning is disinterested, for they determine whether we use power or power uses us.

"Our national strength matters. But the spirit which informs and controls our strength matters just as much. This was the special significance of Robert Frost. He brought an unsparing instinct for reality to bear on the platitudes and pieties of society. His sense of the human tragedy fortified him against self-deception and easy consolation. 'I have been,' he wrote, 'one acquainted with the night.' And because he knew the midnight as well as the high noon, because he understood the ordeal as well as the triumph of the human spirit, he gave his age strength with which to overcome despair. . . ."

V.

Years later, long after the murder in Dallas and after Vietnam had first escalated into tragedy and then disintegrated into defeat; long after a generation had taken to the streets before retreating into the Big Chill; long after the ghettos of Watts and Newark and Detroit and so many other cities had exploded into nihilistic violence; after Robert Kennedy had been killed and Martin Luther King and Malcolm X; after Woodstock and Watergate; after the Beatles had arrived, triumphed, and broken up, and after John Lennon had been murdered; after Johnson, Nixon, Ford, and Carter had given way to Ronald Reagan; after passionate liberalism faded; after the horrors of Cambodia and the anarchy of Beirut; after cocaine and AIDS had become the new plagues — after all had changed from the world we knew in 1963, I was driving alone in a rented car late one afternoon through the state of Guerrero in Mexico.

I was moving through vast, empty stretches of parched land when the right rear tire went flat. I pulled over — and quickly discovered that the rental car had neither a spare nor tools. I was alone in the emptiness of Mexico. Trucks roared by, and some cars, but nobody stopped. Off in the distance I saw a plume of smoke coming from a small house. I started walking to the house, feeling uneasy and vulnerable — Mexico can be a dangerous country. A rutted dirt road led to the front of the house. A dusty car was parked to the side. It was almost dark, and for a tense moment, I considered turning back.

And then the door opened. A beefy man stood there, looking at me in a blank way. I came closer, and he squinted and then asked me in Spanish what I wanted. I told him I had a flat tire and needed help. He considered that for a moment and then asked me if I first needed something to drink.

I glanced past him into the house. On the wall there were two pictures. One was of the Virgin of Guadalupe. The other was of Jack Kennedy. Yes, I said. Some water would be fine.

NEW YORK,
November 28, 1988

SINATRA

I.

One rainy evening in the winter of 1974, I was home alone when the telephone rang. I picked up the receiver, looking out at the wet street, and heard one of the most familiar voices of the century.

It was Frank Sinatra.

"What are you doing?"

"Reading a book," I said.

"Read it tomorrow. We're at Jilly's. Come on over."

He hung up. I put the book down. I didn't know Sinatra well, but despite all the rotten things I'd read about him, I liked him a lot and was sometimes touched by him. We'd met through Shirley MacLaine, who went back a long time with Sinatra. In 1958 Sinatra put her in *Some Came Running,* expanded her part to fit her talents, and made her a movie star. When they occasionally met, it was clear to me that Sinatra admired her relentless honesty, loved her in some complicated way, and was, like me, a little afraid of her.

I took a cab to Jilly's, a seedy time warp of a saloon at the Eighth Avenue end of 52nd Street. The long, dark bar was packed with the junior varsity of the mob; of all the Sinatra groupies, they were the most laughable. They were planted at the bar like blue-haired statues, gulping Jack Daniel's, occasionally glancing into the back room. A maître d' in a shiny tuxedo stood beside a red velvet rope that separated the back room from the Junior Apalachin conference at the bar.

"Yes, sir?" the maître d' said.

"Mr. Sinatra," I said. "He's expecting me."

He turned nervously, his eyes moving past the empty tables at the booths in the left-hand corner against the wall. Jilly Rizzo looked up from a booth and nodded, and I was let through. " 'Ey, Petey babe," Jilly said, coming around a table with his right hand out. Jilly has one glass eye, which gives him a perpetually blurry look. "Hey, Frank," he said, "look who's here."

"Hey, Peter, grab a seat!" Sinatra said brightly, half rising from the booth and shaking hands. He moved clumsily, a newly heavy man who hadn't learned yet to carry the extra weight with grace; he seemed swollen, rather than sleek. But the Sinatra face was — and is — an extraordinary assemblage. He has never been conventionally handsome: There are no clean planes, too many knobs of bone, scars from the forceps delivery he endured at birth. But the smile is open, easy, insouciant. And his blue eyes are the true focal point of the face. In the brief time I'd known him, I'd seen the eyes so disarmingly open that you felt you could peer all the way through them into every secret recess of the man; at other times they were cloudy with indifference, and when chilled by anger or resentment, they could become as opaque as cold-rolled steel.

"You eat yet?" he asked. "Well, then have a drink."

As always, there was a group with him, squashed into the worn Leatherette booths or on chairs against tables. They had the back room to themselves and were eating chop suey and watching a Jets game on a TV set. Sinatra introduced Pat Henry, the comic who sometimes opens for him; Roone Arledge of ABC; Don Costa, one of Sinatra's favorite arrangers; a few other men; and some young women. Sinatra was with a thin blond model in a black dress. He didn't introduce her.

The conversation stopped for the introductions, then started again. Sinatra leaned over, his eyes shifting to the TV screen, where Joe Namath was being shoved around.

"I don't get this team," he said. "They got the best arm in football and they won't give him any protection. Ah, *shit!*" Namath was on his back and getting up very slowly. "Oh, man. That ain't *right!*"

They cut to a commercial, and Sinatra lit a Marlboro and sipped a vodka. His eyes drifted to the bar. "Jesus, there's about 43 indictments right at the bar," he said loudly.

"Present company excluded," Pat Henry said, and everybody laughed.

"It better be," Sinatra said, and they all laughed again. The blonde smiled in a chilly way. The game was back on again, and Sinatra stared at the TV set but wasn't really watching the game. Then the game ended, and Jilly switched off the set. There was more talk and more drinking, and slowly the others began to leave.

"Hell, let's go," Sinatra said. He said something to Jilly, and then he and the blonde and I walked out. A photographer and a middle-aged autograph freak were waiting under the tattered awning.

"Do you mind, Mr. Sinatra?" the photographer asked.

"No, go ahead," he said. The flashbulbs popped. The blonde smiled. So did Sinatra. "Thanks for asking."

Then he signed the woman's autograph book. She had skin like grimy ivory, and sad brown eyes. "Thanks, dear," Sinatra said. We all got into the waiting limousine and drove down the rainy street, heading east.

"What do you think they do with those autographs?" he said. "Sell them? To who? Trade them? For *what?* How does it go? Two Elvis Presleys for one Frank Sinatra? Two Frank Sinatras for one Paul McCartney? I don't get it. I never did."

We drove awhile in silence. Then the chauffeur turned right on a street in the Sixties and pulled over to the curb. Sinatra and the blonde got out. He took her into the brightly lit vestibule. He waited for her to find a key, tapped her lightly on the elbow, and came back to the limo.

"You have to go home?"

"No."

He leaned forward to the driver. "Just drive around awhile."

"Yes sir."

And so for more than an hour, on this rainy night in New York, we drove around the empty streets. Sinatra talked about Lennon and McCartney as songwriters ("That 'Yesterday' is the best song written in 30 years") and George Harrison ("His 'Something' is a beauty"), prizefighters ("Sugar Ray was the best I ever saw") and writers ("Murray Kempton is the best, isn't he? And I always loved Jimmy Cannon"). It wasn't an interview; Frank Sinatra just wanted to talk, in a city far from the bright scorched exile of Palm Springs.

"It's sure changed, this town," he said. "When I first came across that river, this was the greatest city in the whole goddamned world. It was like a big, beautiful lady. It's like a busted-down hooker now."

"Ah, well," I said. "Babe Ruth doesn't play for the Yankees anymore."

"And the Paramount's an office building," he said. "Stop. I'm gonna cry."

He laughed and settled back. We were crossing 86th Street now, heading for the park.

"You think some people are smart, and they turn out dumb," Sinatra said. "You think they're straight, they turn out crooked." This was, of course, the Watergate winter; the year before, Sinatra sat in an honored place at the second inauguration of Richard Nixon. "You like people, and they die on you. I go to too many goddamned funerals these days. And women," he said, exhaling, and chuckling again, "I don't know what the hell to make of them. Do you?"

"Every day I know less," I said.

"Maybe that's what it's all about," he said. "Maybe all that happens is you get older and you know less."

After a while, the limousine pulled up in front of the Waldorf, where Sinatra has an apartment. He told the driver to take me home.

"Stay in touch," he said, and got out, walking fast, his head down, his step jaunty, his hands deep in the pockets of his coat. I remember thinking that it was a desperately lonely life for a man who was a legend.

II.

"I am a symmetrical man, almost to a fault."

— Frank Sinatra

At 64, Francis Albert Sinatra is one of that handful of Americans whose deaths would certainly unleash a river of tearful prose and much genuine grief. He has worked at his trade for almost half a century and goes on as if nothing at all had changed. He is currently in New York making his first feature film in ten years, *The First Deadly Sin*. His first new studio album in five years is in the record stores, a three-record set called *Trilogy*, and despite one astonishing lapse in taste (a self-aggrandizing "musical fantasy" written by banality master Gordon Jenkins), it reveals that what Sinatra calls "my reed" is in better shape than it has been in since the 1960s. In concert halls and casinos he packs in the fans, and the intensity of their embrace remains scary. But his work and its public acceptance are now almost incidental to his stature. Frank Sinatra, from Hoboken, New Jersey, has forced his presence into American social history; when the story of how Americans in this century played, dreamed, hoped, and loved is told, Frank Sinatra cannot be left out. He is more than a mere singer or actor. He is a legend. And the legend lives.

The legend has its own symmetries. Sinatra can be unbelievably generous and brutally vicious. He can display the grace and manners of a cultured man and turn suddenly into a vulgar two-bit comic. He can offer George Raft a blank check "up to one million dollars" to pay taxes owed to the IRS; he can then rage against one of his most important boosters, WNEW disc jockey Jonathan Schwartz, and help force him off the air. In his time, he has been a loyal Democrat and a shill for Richard Nixon; a defender of underdogs everywhere and then a spokesman for the Establishment; a man who fought racism in the music business and then became capable of tasteless jokes ("The Polacks are deboning the colored people," he said on the stage of Caesars Palace in 1974, "and using them for wet suits"). He has given magical performances and shoddy ones. He has treated women with elegance, sensitivity, and charm, and then, in Lauren Bacall's phrase, "dropped the curtain" on them in the most callous way. He acts like royalty and is frequently treated that way, but he also comes on too often like a cheap hood. He is a good guy–bad guy, tough-tender, Jekyll-Hyde.

"Being an eighteen-karat manic-depressive," Sinatra said once, "I have an over-acute capacity for sadness as well as elation."

Over the years, those wildly fluctuating emotions became a basic component of the Sinatra legend — accepted, even demanded by his audience. That audience is now largely eastern, urban, and aging, with New York at the heart of the myth. The hard-core fans are Depression kids who matured in World War II, or part of the fifties generation, who saw him as a role model. In some critical way, Sinatra validates their lives — as *individuals*. He sings *to* them, and *for* them, one at a time. These Americans were transformed by the Depression and the war into unwilling members of groups — "the masses," or "the poor," or "the infantry" — and their popular music was dominated by the big bands. Sinatra was the first star to step out of the tightly controlled ensembles of the white swing bands to work on his own. Yes, he was 4-F (punctured eardrum), but the overwhelming majority of Americans experienced World War II at home, and the 1940s Sinatra was a reminder that Americans were single human beings, not just the masses, the poor, or the infantry. Later, in the 1960s, when crowds once again shoved individuals off the stage of history, he was submerged by musical groups like the Beatles and Rolling Stones and in 1971 even went into a brief retirement. He came back later in the decade, when individual values were again dominant.

"I've seen them come and go, but Frank is still the king," a New Jersey grandmother said at one of Sinatra's weekend performances at Resorts International in Atlantic City. "He just goes on and on, and he's wonderful."

Indeed, Sinatra's endurance has become a rallying point for many people who feel that their sacrifices and hard work are no longer honored, their values demeaned, their musical tastes ignored and sneered at. They don't care that Sinatra got fat; so did they. They don't care that Sinatra moved from the New Deal to Ronald Reagan; many of them did the same thing, for the same basic reason: resentment at being ignored by the Democratic party. They had overcome poverty and survived two wars; they had educated their children and given them better lives; and sometimes even their children didn't care. But it should never be forgotten that Frank Sinatra was the original working-class hero. Mick Jagger's fans bought records with their allowances; Sinatra's people bought them out of wages.

"There's just not enough of Frank's people around anymore to make him a monster record seller," says one Warner Communications executive. "Sinatra is a star. But he's not Fleetwood Mac. He's not Pink Floyd."

Sinatra has never been a big single seller (one gold record — more than a million sales — to twenty for the Beatles), but his albums continue to sell steadily. One reason: Most radio stations don't play Sinatra, so that younger listeners never get to hear him and go on to buy his records. In New York, only WNEW-AM and WYNY-FM play Sinatra with any frequency. As a movie star, he had faded badly before vanishing completely with the lamentable *Dirty Dingus Magee* in 1970. Part of this could be blamed directly on Sinatra, because his insistence on one or two takes had led to careless, even shoddy productions. On his own, he was also not a strong TV performer; he needed Elvis Presley, or Bing Crosby, to get big ratings. Yet Sinatra remains a major star in the minds of most Americans, even those who despise him.

"What Sinatra has is beyond talent," director Billy Wilder once said. "It's some sort of magnetism that goes in higher revolutions than that of anybody else, anybody in the whole of show business. Wherever Frank is, there is a certain electricity permeating the air. It's like Mack the Knife is in town and the action is starting."

That electricity was in the air of Jilly's that night in 1974. But its effect is not restricted to a platoon of gumbahs. The other night, Sinatra came into Elaine's with his wife, Barbara, and another couple. It was after midnight, and Sinatra stayed for a couple of hours, drinking and talking and smoking cigarettes.

I was with some friends at another table. They were people who are good at their jobs and have seen much of the world. But their own natural styles were subtly altered by the addition of Sinatra to the room. They stole glances at him. They were aware that Sinatra's blue eyes were also checking out the room, and unconsciously they began to gesture too much, playing too hard at being casual, or clarifying themselves in a theatrical way. Somewhere underneath all of this, I'm sure, was a desire for Frank Sinatra to like them.

I knew how that worked, because I'd felt those emotions myself. When I first met Sinatra, I was bumping up against one of the crucial legends of my youth, and sure, I wanted him to like me. Growing up in Brooklyn in the forties and fifties, it was impossible to avoid the figure of Frank Sinatra. He was armored with the tough-guy swagger of the streets, but in the songs he allowed room for tenderness, the sense of loss and abandonment, the acknowledgment of pain. Most of us felt that we had nothing to learn from cowboys or Cary Grant (we were wrong, of course). But thousands of us appropriated the pose of the Tender Tough Guy from Sinatra. We've outgrown a lot of things, but there are elements of that pose in all of us to this day, and when we see Sinatra perform, or listen to the records at night, the pose regains all of its old dangerous glamour.

And make no mistake: Danger is at the heart of the legend. At his best, Sinatra is an immensely gifted musical talent, admired by many jazz musicians. He is not a jazz singer, but he comes from the tradition. As a young band vocalist, he learned breath control from trombonist Tommy Dorsey; after work, he studied other singers, among them Louis Armstrong, Lee Wiley, Mabel Mercer, and another performer who became a legend.

"It is Billie Holiday, whom I first heard in 52nd Street clubs in the early '30s, who was and still remains the greatest single musical influence on me," he wrote once, later telling *Daily News* columnist Kay Gardella that Lady Day taught him "matters of shading, phrasing, dark tones, light tones and bending notes." And in the saloons of the time, the young Sinatra learned a great secret of the trade: "The microphone is the singer's basic instrument, not the voice. You have to learn to play it like it was a saxophone." As he matured, Sinatra developed a unique white-blues style, supple enough to express the range of his own turbulent emotions. And like the great jazz artists, he took the banal tunes of Tin Pan Alley and transformed them into something personal by the sincerity of his performance; Sinatra actually seemed to *believe* the words he was singing. But Billy Wilder is correct: The Sinatra aura goes beyond talent and craft. He is not simply a fine popular singer. He emanates power and danger. And the reason is simple: You think he is tangled up with the mob.

"Some things I can't ever talk about," he said to me once, when we were discussing the mandatory contents of his book. He laughed and added, "Someone might come knockin' at my f------ door."

Sinatra is now writing that autobiography and preparing a film about his own life. Alas, neither form seems adequate to the full story; autobiographies are by definition only part of the story, the instinct being to prepare a brief for the defense and give yourself the best lines. And a two-hour movie can only skim the surface of a life that has gone on for six decades. Faulkner says somewhere that the best stories are the ones we are most thoroughly ashamed of; it could be that the best movies are the ones that can't be photographed. No, Sinatra deserves a novel.

The novelist, some combination of Balzac and Raymond Chandler, would recognize Sinatra as one of those rare public men who actually cast a shadow. The shadow is the mob, and who can tell what came first, the shadow or the act? A conventional autobiography will talk about the wives: Nancy Barbato, Ava Gardner, Mia Farrow, and Barbara Marx, one for each adult decade. It might mention, discreetly, all the other love affairs, passionate or glancing: Lana Turner, Juliet Prowse, Lauren Bacall, Kim Novak, Jill St. John, Lady Adele Beatty, Dorothy Provine, and the anonymous brigade of starlets, secretaries, models, stewardesses, and girls from the old neighborhood.

"I loved them all," Sinatra says now, smiling ruefully, reminding you that he is now a grandfather and all of that was long ago. "I really did."

But the novelist can come closer to the elusive truth than an autobiographer as courtly as Sinatra will ever allow himself to do. Both would deal with the public career, the rise, fall, rise again of Frank Sinatra. We can see the high school dropout watching Bing Crosby sing from the stage of Loew's Journal Square in Jersey City in 1933, vowing to become a singer. We can follow him, one of Balzac's provincial heroes, as he wins an amateur contest and crosses the river to appear for the first time on a New York stage at the Academy of Music (now the Palladium) on 14th Street the following year. The hero then sings with a group called the Hoboken Four on the *Major Bowes Amateur Hour* in 1935, plays local clubs, begs in the hallways of WNEW for the chance to sing for nothing on live remotes. And of course there will be the familiar story of the job at the Rustic Cabin on Route 9W in 1939, and how Harry James heard him late one night and gave him a job in the big time. And then how Sinatra went to work for Tommy Dorsey and played the Paramount and became a star.

And because this is a story with a hero, it must tell the story of The Fall. The hero hurtles into love with Ava Gardner, and his career becomes a shambles: He loses his voice, his wife, his children; he gets into public fights; he wins the love goddess; he loses her; he hits bottom. And then there is The Great Comeback: He pleads for the part of Maggio in *From Here to Eternity,* is paid $8,000, gives a stunning performance, wins the Academy Award, and comes all the way back. He leaves Columbia Records for Capitol, then starts his own company, Reprise, and makes his greatest records. At the same time he consolidates his power in Hollywood, investing his money brilliantly, producing his own films, using power with the instincts of a great politician. These are the years of the private jets, the meetings of the Clan on the stages of Las Vegas, the friendships with Jack Kennedy and other politicians, and the house at the top of Mulholland Drive, where the wounded hero heals his ruined heart with girls and whiskey and friends. It's a good story. A sentimental education or a cautionary tale.

But as autobiography it is not enough. We must have some understanding of the shadows. In *The Godfather* Mario Puzo used some of the elements in the singer he called Johnny Fontane; other novels have used Sinatra-like figures in various ways; yet no fictional account has truly defined the man in all of his complexity. We only know that the mob runs through his story like an underground river. He is the most investigated American performer since John Wilkes Booth, and although he has never been indicted or convicted of any mob-connected crime, the connection is part of the legend. And to some extent, Sinatra exploits it. His opening acts feature comedians who tell jokes about Sinatra's sinister friendships; if you cross Frank, the jokes say, you could end up on a meat hook in a garage. In some circumstances Sinatra laughs at the implications; other times, he explodes into dark furies, accusing his accusers of slander and ethnic racism.

"If my name didn't end with a vowel," he said to me once, "I wouldn't have had all this trouble."

But the facts indicate that he did know some shady people. He was friendly with Jersey hoodlum Willie Moretti until the syphilitic gangster was shot to death. He was friendly with Joseph "Joe Fisher" Fischetti, traveled with him to Havana in 1947, where he spent time with Lucky Luciano. A nineteen-page Justice Department memorandum prepared in 1962 said that its surveillance placed Sinatra in contact with about ten of the country's top hoodlums. Some had Sinatra's unlisted number. He did favors for others.

"I was brought up to shake a man's hand when I am introduced to him, without first investigating his past," Sinatra said huffily during the Luciano uproar. The same could be said about the scandal over the photograph taken a few years ago with mob boss Carlo Gambino, backstage at the Westchester Premier Theater. More serious questions have now been raised about Sinatra and that same theater.

A federal grand jury is investigating whether Sinatra, his lawyer Mickey Rudin, and Jilly Rizzo took $50,000 under the table during a May 1977 gig there. Court papers filed by prosecutor Nathaniel Akerman said that the possible Sinatra connection arose during the trial of one Louis "Lewie Dome" Pacella, supposedly a friend of Sinatra's. The court papers state: "The grand jury's investigation was based in part on evidence introduced at Pacella's trial, which showed that in addition to Pacella, other individuals close to Frank Sinatra had received monies illegally. . . ." Once again, Sinatra is afloat on that dark underground river.

"Did I know those guys?" he said to me once. "Sure, I knew some of those guys. I spent a lot of time working in saloons. And saloons are not run by the Christian Brothers. There were a lot of guys around, and they came out of Prohibition, and they ran pretty good saloons. I was a kid. I worked in the places that were open. They paid you, and the checks didn't bounce. I didn't meet any Nobel Prize winners in saloons. But if Francis of Assisi was a singer and worked in saloons, he would've met the same guys. That doesn't make him part of something. They said hello, you said hello. They came backstage. They thanked you. You offered them a drink. That was it."

He paused. "And it doesn't matter anymore, does it? Most of the guys I knew, or met, are dead."

One of them was Salvatore Giancana, sometimes known as Momo, or Mooney. A graduate of Joliet prison, he ducked World War II by doing a crazy act for the draft board, which labeled him "a constitutional psychopath." He rose through the wartime rackets to the leadership of the Chicago mob in the 1950s. During that period he and Sinatra became friends and were seen in various places together. The star-struck Momo later began a long love affair with singer Phyllis

McGuire, and the friendship deepened. In 1962 Sinatra, Dean Martin, and Sammy Davis played a special engagement at a Giancana joint called the Villa Venice, northwest of Chicago. When the FBI questioned the performers, Sinatra said he did it for a boyhood friend named Leo Olsen, who fronted the place for Momo. Sammy Davis was more to the point.

"Baby, let me say this," he told an FBI man. "I got one eye, and that one eye sees a lot of things that my brain tells me I shouldn't talk about. Because my brain says that if I do, my one eye might not be seeing *anything* after a while."

Sinatra's friendship with Sam Giancana was most severely tested in 1963, when the Nevada Gaming Control Board charged that the Chicago hoodlum had been a week-long guest at Sinatra's Cal-Neva Lodge in Lake Tahoe. His mere presence was enough to revoke the casino's gambling license, and Sinatra first said he would fight the charge. When Edward A. Olsen, then chairman of the gambling board, said that he didn't want to talk to Sinatra until he subpoenaed him, Olsen claims Sinatra shouted over the phone, "You subpoena me and you're going to get a big, fat, f------ surprise."

But when the crunch came two weeks later, Sinatra chose not to fight the revocation order. Apparently his friendship with Giancana was more important than his investment in Nevada, and he sold his interests for $3.5 million. In 1975 Giancana was shot to death in the basement of his Chicago home. Phyllis McGuire went to the funeral, but Sinatra didn't. Sinatra is again trying to get a gambling license in Nevada.

"It's ridiculous to think Sinatra's in the mob," said one New Yorker who has watched gangsters collect around Sinatra for more than 30 years. "He's too visible. He's too hot. But he likes them. He thinks they're funny. In some way he admires them. For him it's like they were characters in some movie."

That might be the key. Some people who know Sinatra believe that his attraction to gangsters — and their attraction to him — is sheer romanticism. The year that Sinatra was fifteen, Hollywood released W. R. Burnett's *Little Caesar*; more than 50 gangster films followed in the next eighteen months. And their view of gangsters was decidedly romantic: The hoodlums weren't cretins peddling heroin to children; they were Robin Hoods defying the unjust laws of Prohibition. Robert Warshow defined the type in his essay "The Gangster as Tragic Hero":

The gangster is the man of the city, with the city's language and knowledge, with its queer and dishonest skills and its terrible daring, carrying his life in his hands like a placard, like a club. For everyone else, there is at least the theoretical possibility of another world — in that happier American culture which the gangster denies, the city does not really exist; it is only a more crowded and more brightly lit country — but for the gangster there is only the city; he must inhabit it in order to personify it: the real city, but that dangerous and sad city of the imagination which is so much more important, which is the modern world.

That is almost a perfect description of Frank Sinatra, who still carries his life in his hands like a placard, or like a club. His novel might be a very simple one indeed: a symmetrical story about life imitating art.

III.

"My son is like me. You cross him, he never forgets."

— Dolly Sinatra

Somewhere deep within Frank Sinatra, there must still exist a scared little boy. He is standing alone on a street in Hoboken. His parents are nowhere to be seen. His father, Anthony Martin, is probably at the bar he runs when he is not working for the fire department; the father is a blue-eyed Sicilian, close-mouthed, passive, and, in his own way, tough. He once boxed as "Marty O'Brien" in the years when the Irish ran northern New Jersey. The boy's mother, Natalie, is not around either. The neighbors call her Dolly, and she sometimes works at the bar, which was bought with a loan from her mother, Rosa Garaventi, who runs a grocery store. Dolly Sinatra is also a Democratic ward leader. She has places to go, duties to perform, favors to deny or dispense. She has little time for traditional maternal duties. And besides, she didn't want a boy anyway.

"I wanted a girl and bought a lot of pink clothes," she once said. "When Frank was born, I didn't care. I dressed him in pink anyway. Later, I got my mother to make him Lord Fauntleroy suits."

Did the other kids laugh at the boy in the Lord Fauntleroy suits? Probably. It was a tough, working-class neighborhood. Working-class. Not poor. His mother, born in Genoa, raised in Hoboken, believed in work and education. When she wasn't around, the boy was taken care of by his grandmother Garaventi, or by Mrs. Goldberg, who lived on the block. "I'll never forget that kid," a neighbor said, "leaning against his grandmother's front door, staring into space. . . ."

Later the press agents would try to pass him off as a slum kid. Perhaps the most important thing to know about him is that he was an only child. Of Italian parents. And they spoiled him. From the beginning, the only child had money. He had a charge account at a local department store and a wardrobe so fancy that his friends called him "Slacksey." He had a secondhand car at fifteen. And in the depths of the Depression, after dropping out of high school, he had the ultimate luxury: a job unloading trucks at the Jersey *Observer*.

Such things were not enough; the boy also had fancy dreams. And the parents didn't approve. When he told his mother that he wanted to be a singer, she threw a shoe at him. "In your teens," he said later, "there's always someone to spit on your dreams." Still, the only child got what he wanted; eventually his mother bought him a $65 portable public-address system, complete with loudspeaker and microphone. She thus gave him his musical instrument and his life.

She also gave him some of her values. At home she dominated his father; in the streets she dominated the neighborhood through the uses of Democratic patronage. From adolescence on, Sinatra understood patronage. He could give his friends clothes, passes to Palisades Park, rides in his car, and they could give him friendship and loyalty. Power was all. And that insight lifted him above so many other talented performers of his generation. Vic Damone might have better pipes, Tony Bennett a more certain musical taste, but Sinatra had power.

Power attracts and repels; it functions as aphrodisiac and blackjack. Men of power recognize it in others; Sinatra has spent time with Franklin Roosevelt, Adlai Stevenson, Jack Kennedy, Richard Nixon, Spiro Agnew, Walter Annenberg, Hugh Carey, Ronald Reagan; all wanted his approval, and he wanted, and obtained, theirs. He could raise millions for them at fund raisers; they would always take his calls. And the politicians had a lot of company. On the stage at Caesars Palace, or at an elegant East Side dinner party, Sinatra emanates power. Certainly the dark side of the legend accounts for some of that effect; the myth of the Mafia, after all, is not a myth of evil, but a myth of power.

But talent is essential, too. During the period of The Fall, when he had lost his voice, he panicked; he could accept anything except impotence. Without power he is returned to Monroe Street in Hoboken, a scared kid. That kid wants to be accepted by powerful men, so he shakes hands with the men of the mob. But the scared kid also understands loneliness, and he uses that knowledge as the engine of his talent. When he sings a ballad — listen again to "I'm a Fool to Want You," recorded at the depths of his anguish over Ava Gardner — his voice haunts, explores, suffers. Then, in up-tempo songs, it celebrates, it says that the worst can be put behind you, there is always another woman and another bright morning. The scared kid, easy in the world of women and power, also carries the scars of rejection. His mother was too busy. His father sent him away.

"He told me, 'Get out of the house and get a job,' " he said about his father in a rare TV interview with Bill Boggs a few years ago. "I was shocked. I didn't know where the hell to go. I remember the moment. We were having breakfast. . . . This particular morning my father said to me, 'Why don't you get out of the house and go out on your own?' What he really said was 'Get out.' And I think the egg was stuck in there about twenty minutes, and I couldn't swallow it or get rid of it, in any way. My mother, of course, was nearly in tears, but we agreed that it might be a good thing, and then I packed up a small case that I had and came to New York."

He came to New York, all right, and to all the great cities of the world. The scared kid, the only child, invented someone named Frank Sinatra and it was the greatest role he ever played. In some odd way he has become the role. There is a note of farewell in his recent performances. One gets the sense that he is now building his own mausoleum.

"Dyin' is a pain in the ass," he says.

Sinatra could be around for another twenty years, or he could be gone tomorrow, but the jagged symmetries of his legend would remain. For too many years the scared kid lashed out at enemies, real or imagined; he courted his inferiors, intoxicated by their power; he helped people and hurt people; he was willful, self-absorbed, and frivolous. But the talent survived everything, and so did the fear, and when I see him around, I always imagine him as a boy on that Hoboken street in his Fauntleroy suit and remember him wandering the streets of New York a half century later, trying to figure out what all of it meant.

NEW YORK,
April 28, 1980

GLEASON

Here he comes, "the Great One," in a maroon stretch limousine, its planes and curves glistening in the summer sun. The limousine moves in a stately way down a curving path and stops in front of a huge pile of stone, brick, and mortar that is the centerpiece of the Riverdale estate known as Wave Hill. The Great One steps out of the limousine, blinks in the bright sunshine, glances at the cables, massed trailers, busy extras, grips, and electricians who are part of every movie location. Then he steps into the huge Beaver 36 mobile home that is parked on the shoulder of the driveway.

"Come on in," Jackie Gleason calls behind him. "Have a seat, I'll be with you in a minute."

He's 69, and looks in good shape, given what he has done to the body over the years: the gorging and the pig-outs, the monumental drinking bouts, a broken arm in the forties, a broken leg in the fifties, the crash diets, careening horseplay, billions of cigarettes. He's six feet tall, and large, but he doesn't look fat. He goes to the back of the trailer with a valet, closes the door, and emerges in a black shirt and slacks. The face is now a draftsman's delight: pouches, slashes, the large upper lip sliced by a thin mustache, eyes that alternately sparkle and grieve, a face made for expression. He lights a cigarette, sits back on a couch.

A production assistant leans in through the open door. "Can I get you anything, Mr. Gleason?"

"Yeah," he says, "a couple of broads."

Everybody laughs except Gleason. He blinks in a deadpan way and takes a drag on a cigarette.

Suddenly, it's Gleason time again. The so-called lost episodes of *The Honeymooners* are appearing three nights a week on Showtime; they will go on for a year before joining the classic 39 pieces from 1955–56 already in syndication. Gleason is serving as creative consultant and co-producer of a Broadway musical based on *The Honeymooners*. Membership in R.A.L.P.H. (Royal Association for the Longevity and Preservation of *The Honeymooners*) is soaring as more and more young people discover the great comedies made 30 years ago by Gleason, Art Carney, Audrey Meadows, and Joyce Randolph within a 20-by-30-foot set in the Adelphi Theatre on West 54th Street. When four "lost" episodes of *The Honeymooners* were shown at the Museum of Broadcasting last year, the place was jammed with old fans and new.

"Who couldn't be happy about it?" Gleason says. "To think that something you did 30 years ago can still give people *laughs*: I mean, that's somethin'!"

But the Gleason surge is more than a nostalgia act; he's working harder than he has in years. To begin with, there is the TV movie that brought him to Riverdale on this bright summer day. Producer Robert Halmi managed to bring Gleason together with Art Carney for the first time since 1978 in the only non-*Honeymooners* work they've done since the early fifties. The movie, to be on CBS September 23, is called *Izzy and Moe*; it's about two failed vaudevillians (Izzy Einstein and Moe Smith) who became Prohibition agents in the 1920s and provided grand tabloid entertainment for the duration of the Volstead Act. Gleason worked hard with writer Robert Boris to remove any possible echoes of *The Honeymooners* from the script.

"We didn't want to do Ralph and Norton again," Gleason says. "And this is nothing like them. These are two different guys altogether."

For *Izzy and Moe*, Gleason is supervising the music, most of it in a Dixieland style (he's composed three tunes). After that, he will head out to Hollywood to work with Tom Hanks in a feature film called *Nothing in Common*.

"Yeah, I'm working," Gleason says, and then waves the cigarette. "But what the hell, I *always* worked."

But there is more to this latest Gleason moment than career notes; there's a growing awareness that Gleason has been for many years one of this country's great comic geniuses, on a level, perhaps, with Laurel and Hardy, Buster Keaton, and Chaplin. This doesn't apply to his acting in the *Smokey and the Bandit* movies (although even that work has its own solidity and sense of surprise), or to the straight acting he did in such films as *The Hustler* (for which he received an Academy Award nomination in 1962), *Requiem for a Heavyweight,* or the much acclaimed TV version of *The Time of Your Life.* Gleason deserves the half-mocking title the Great One for his accomplishments on his own television shows — that is, for the work he created or controlled.

"Jackie Gleason is an artist of the first rank," John O'Hara wrote years ago, with uncharacteristic generosity. "An artist puts his own personal stamp on all of his mature work, making his handling of his material uniquely his own. Millions of people who don't give a damn about art have been quick to recognize a creation. Ralph Kramden is a character that we might be getting from Mr. Dickens if he were writing for TV."

That gets close to the heart of Gleason's enduring accomplishment. He was a creator of a vast Dickensian cast of characters: Reginald Van Gleason III, the Poor Soul, Joe the Bartender, Charlie "the Loudmouth" Bratton, Rudy the Repairman, Crazy Guggenheim, Stanley R. Sogg (the late-show pitchman who sold, among other things, a book called *How to Slide Downhill on Your Little Brother*).

And then, of course, there were Ralph and Alice, Norton and Trixie. I first saw them while I was a teenager in Brooklyn in the fifties, sitting in Catherine Rogan's living room. I laughed at them then and laugh at them now. "This was nudge comedy," Gleason says. "When you see Ralph or Ed, or any of the others, you nudge the guy next to you and say, 'Jeez, that's just like Uncle Charlie,' or some guy down the block."

True, but there was more to the show than that. When Gleason first exploded on TV all those years ago, he wasn't just a gifted comedian. He was *ours.* He wasn't just New York; he was *Brooklyn.* When he swaggered onstage to open the show, flanked by gorgeous women, we swaggered with him; when we read about his all-night sessions at Toots Shor's or Eddie Condon's, his gigantic meals, his partying with show girls and prizefighters and Max Kaminsky's band, we ate and drank and partied with him; when we picked up the *News* and *Mirror* in 1954 and read about his $11-million deal with CBS, it was as if we'd signed the deal, too.

So, in Brooklyn in the fifties, we watched *The Honeymooners* in a broader context; it was the continuing story of Ralph and Alice, Norton and Trixie, but it was also part of the Gleason legend. We didn't imagine in those days that *The Honeymooners* would be with us the rest of our lives. And yet here they are, six nights a week, as constant as the stars (each of the 39 episodes has been played more than 200 times in the New York area). Some of us left Brooklyn, others stayed; we made our lives; but Ralph and Norton remain the same, and we know them better now than we did then.

"I guess it lasted for a couple of reasons," Gleason says. "One, the show was funny. That usually helps. Two, you like the people. If the audience likes you, you're home free."

The show was also a triumph of show-business craft. Gleason, with his producer, Jack Philbin, and his crew of writers (Walter Stone, Marvin Marx, Herbert Finn, and others), evolved rules for *The Honeymooners* that contributed to the show's durability. "First, it had to be believable," Gleason says. "Whatever the deal was, you had to believe it *could* happen. Second, the audience had to know what's really going on *before* Ralph does. *That* was the key to the comedy."

In addition, each show was classically constructed, with a beginning, middle, and end ("I see stuff now that stops, but doesn't really *end*"). The situations were quickly, carefully, and lucidly set up, the characters were clearly defined, and the relationships were held together by a rough kind of love. Ralph really did believe that Alice was the greatest (he would never ever *really* try to send her to the moon with a haymaker). Alice loved Ralph in the most confident way, unafraid to slam into him, completely aware of his flaws and faults, his insecurities, his boastfulness, his wild-eyed schemes, but equally clear about his strengths, the most important of which was a heart as big as Bensonhurst. They had no kids (except Ralph), a fact that made the relationship more modern than those in most of the kid-littered sitcoms that first showed up in the fifties. And, of course, Ralph and Norton loved each other, too, without ever stating what they felt. They were as dependent upon each other as Don Quixote and Sancho Panza, whom Ralph, the dreamer, and Norton, the practical man, resemble in other ways.

In his 1956 biography of Gleason, *The Golden Ham,* Jim Bishop reconstructed the story conference that led to the invention of *The Honeymooners:*

> One afternoon Joe Bigelow and Harry Crane were trying to write a sketch with the star, and Gleason said that he had an idea for a sketch that would revolve around a married couple — a quiet shrewd wife and a loudmouthed husband.
>
> "You got a title for it?" asked Bigelow.
>
> "Wait a minute," said Crane. "How about 'The Beast'?"
>
> Jackie got to his feet. "Just a second," he said. "I always wanted to do this thing, and the man isn't a beast. The guy really loves this broad. They fight, sure. But they always end in a clinch."
>
> Bigelow shrugged. "It *could* be a thing."
>
> "I come from a neighborhood full of that stuff. By the time I was fifteen, I knew every insult in the book."
>
> "Then let's try it," said Bigelow.
>
> "But not 'The Beast,' " said Jackie. "That's not the title."
>
> "Why not?"
>
> "It sounds like the husband is doing all the fighting. We need something a little left-handed as a title. You know, this kind of thing can go and go and go."
>
> "How about 'The Lovers,' " said Harry Crane.
>
> "That's a little closer, Harry." Gleason paced the floor. "A little closer, but it could mean that they're not married. We need something that tells at once that they're married."
>
> " 'The Couple Next Door'?"
>
> "No. How about 'The Honeymooners'?"
>
> That was it, and, like a great novelist, Gleason reached back into the early years of his life for his characters. They're still with us; they're still with Gleason.
>
> "I knew a lot of guys like Ralph," he says now, "back there, growing up."

In William Hazlitt's *Lectures on the English Comic Writers,* written in the winter of 1818, there's a line that's true of all of us but seems particularly appropriate to Gleason: "To understand or define the ludicrous, we must first know what the serious is." The serious roots of Gleason's talent go back to the Brooklyn of his childhood, specifically to Bushwick, which was then an Irish and Italian working-class district.

"Everything happened there," Gleason says. *"Everything."*

He was born Herbert John Gleason on February 26, 1916, the second child of Herbert Gleason and Mae Kelly. There was a brother eleven years older than Jackie; his name was Clemence, and he died when Jackie was three. Though Jackie has no memory of him, he took his dead brother's name at confirmation. His father, slim, black-haired, a drinker, worked in the Death Claims Department of the Mutual Life Insurance Company at 20 Nassau Street.

"He had beautiful Spencerian handwriting," Gleason remembers. "And he would fill in the policies with the names. I remember him sometimes doing the work at night at the kitchen table."

Herbert Gleason was paid $35 a week; he sold candy bars on the side. The family moved all around Bushwick, living on Herkimer Street and Somers Street, Bedford Avenue and Marion Street. But young Jackie stayed in the same school, P.S. 73. And he went to the same church, Our Lady of Lourdes. The Gleasons settled at last in the third-floor-right apartment at 358 Chauncey Street, the street where, many years later, Ralph and Alice, Norton and Trixie were to establish permanent residence.

On Friday, December 15, 1925, at ten minutes after noon, Herbert Gleason took his hat, his coat, and his paycheck, left the offices of the insurance company, and was never seen again. The night before, he had destroyed all the family pictures in which he appeared. When Mae Gleason realized that he was not coming back, she took a job as a change clerk in the Lorimer Street station of the BMT. And Jackie started his education on the streets. He was a member of a gang called the Nomads, hung around Schuman's candy store and Freitag's Delicatessen's (as it was pronounced). He went dancing at the Arcadia when he had money, and he learned to shoot pool. About his father, years later, Gleason said, "He was as good a father as I've ever known." But his father did leave him with something: a vision.

"My father took me to the Halsey Theatre, a real dump, a classic," he says. The Halsey featured a daily movie and five acts of vaudeville. "We sat way down front, in the first row. I'd never seen this before, guys coming out and saying funny things, getting laughs. And for some reason, at some point, I stood up and looked out over the audience. That was the moment. I knew I wanted to be like that, facing an audience, the audience facing me. I knew I wanted to do that."

It was a while before he faced an audience again. After his father left, Jackie started hanging out in Joe Corso's Poolroom One Flight Up ("That was the whole name"). He went there with his friend Carmine Pucci, and when they won at pool, they'd buy cheap wine or "loosies" (individual cigarettes). "I was a rack boy when I was ten, and hustling guys already. Graduation day was always the best. On graduation day, everybody'd get these gold pins. And I'd play them for their gold pins. Then I'd take the pins to the hockshop and get maybe $20, and nobody ever asked what a ten-year-old kid was doing with all these gold pins."

When he graduated from P.S. 73, he talked himself into the school play, doing a recital of "Little Red Riding Hood" in a Yiddish accent that tore up the place, and then went on to John Adams High School, supposedly for "vocational training." He never finished the first year, and moved on to his true school: the streets.

"For a while, I worked as an exhibition diver for a guy named Chester Billy: He was the star and the rest of us did all the funny stuff. We had this portable tank that was six feet deep. They greased the bottom so when you dove in you slid right up. The bottom was terrible, disgusting; it stunk of grease. They would fold up the tank after the show with the grease still in it. And all the girls in the show had green hair from the chlorine.

"Anyway, we ended up in Bangor, in some kind of an armory. And Billy was supposed to dive into the tank from some girders. About 90 feet. But this day he was sick — he got loaded the night before or something — and he said to me, 'You do it.' I said, 'Are you kidding?' He said, 'You do it, or you're fired.' So I climbed up in the girders and looked down, and said, 'What the hell,' and dove. Obviously, I lived. But when I pulled myself up on the side of that greasy tank, I said to myself, 'That's it, I quit.' And I did."

Still, it was show business. In Brooklyn, he went with his friends (and his first girlfriend, Julie Dennehy — pronounced Dunnahee, immortalized later by Joe the Bartender) to places called the Bijou, the Gem, the Diamond. "There was an outdoor theater, too, where they couldn't start the picture until it was dark. I got the Poor Soul from the assistant manager in one of those places." And finally he arrived at the Halsey again, where there was an amateur show on Wednesday nights "which was usually guys who played stomach pumps and things like that."

Gleason thought he could do as well as most of the contestants, probably better ("Vanity is an actor's courage; if he doesn't have that, he's finished"). He worked up an act with a friend named Charlie Cretter, who had a soprano voice. Cretter dressed as a girl; Gleason told jokes.

"All the guys from the Nomads, all the people from the neighborhood were all there, and when we came on, they started cheering and shouting. And we were a hit. I guess the guy that ran the Halsey realized we could sell tickets, so he offered me the master of ceremonies job. I took the place of a guy named Sammy Birch, who was a friend of mine. First prize was 50 cents, and second prize was a card that introduced you to the guy that booked the acts, the agent. I must've been a hit, because the guy from the Folly Theater, three stations away, he came and saw me and offered me a job at his theater too. So I worked Wednesday night at the Halsey and Monday and Friday at the Folly. That was the beginning."

During this period, Gleason met a young dancer named Genevieve Halford; years later, he married her. But most of the time, he was going with Julie Dennehy. Sometimes he went to the Myrtle Burlesque, to watch the comics. He remembered seeing an act called Izzy Pickle and His Cucumbers. He was also a fan of Billy "Cheese and Crackers" Hagen. ("A beautiful broad would walk across the stage, and he'd say, 'Cheese and crackers.' That's as dirty as they got.") Two of his friends were working as ushers at Loew's Metropolitan in downtown Brooklyn, and they started writing down the jokes of visiting Manhattan comics for Gleason to use at the Halsey and the Folly. He hadn't yet learned that he was a comedian, not a comic. ("I always like Ed Wynn's distinction," Gleason says. "He said that a comic *says* funny things; a comedian *does* funny things.") But every night, burlesque, vaudeville, saloon humor were working their way into the Gleason style.

Then in April 1935, his mother died of erysipelas. She was just short of 50; Gleason was 19.

"After the funeral, I had 36 cents to my name," Gleason says. "And I was on the stoop, and Mr. Dennehy came along and said I could stay with them. I said, 'No, I got 36 cents, I'm going to New York.' So I went over there on the train. I bought an apple-butter waffle and some apple juice to eat. That left me about 11 cents. Then

I ran into Sammy Birch, from the neighborhood, the guy who was before me at the Halsey. He was staying at the Hotel Markwell, and he let me sleep on the floor."

Within weeks, Gleason had a gig at Tiny's Château in Reading, Pennsylvania, for $25 a week. "Then Sammy got me a job at the Oasis in Budd Lake, New Jersey." He stayed all summer. "The joint's gone now, and Sammy's gone, too. Maybe this is a ghost story. Maybe we're dead."

In September 1935, he moved into the Club Miami on Parkhurst Street in Newark; this was Gleason's graduate school, and he stayed for two years. "It was a real bucket of blood," Gleason remembers fondly. "My job was to introduce the acts and quell the fights. One night, I'm doing the last show and this fat guy is heckling me. I use the usual lines on him, but nothing works. Finally I say, 'All right, *you,* come with *me!*' I start out the side door, taking off my coat, everybody trying to stop me." Gleason takes a drag on a cigarette. "Next thing I know, I'm in the furnace room and they're waving fans over me, and slapping my cheeks, and laying the ice on me. And I say, 'Who was *that?*' And they tell me it's a guy named Tony Galento."

He married Genevieve Halford on September 20, 1936; she was then working as a dancer in a joint called the Half Moon, in Yorkville. Gleason moved her to the Club Miami as part of a four-girl chorus line; they lived in Mother Mutzenbacher's rooming house. He bought the wedding and engagement rings for $60 "from a guy that just got out of the can."

Genevieve expected something like a conventional home life; she was a good Catholic, gave him two daughters, but never got the home life. By 1937, Gleason was moving around, playing the Bally Club and the Rathskeller in Philly, a joint in Cranberry Lake; following Henny Youngman (still his favorite comedian) into the Adams-Paramount in Newark; working the Empire Burlesque; playing for a few weeks at Frank Donato's Colonial Inn in Singac, New Jersey (where he met a young singer named Sinatra). He still made money hustling pool. And in other ways.

"Sometimes I made money 'busking' at fights. I weighed '75, '85 at the time, and what you did busking, you filled in for some guy that didn't show up, or if there were a bunch of quick knockouts and they wanted to fill out the card. You got paid $2 a round and $5 if you won. For that money, there was no sense in us killing each other, I figured, and before the fight, I'd go to the guy and say, 'You know, let's not end up in a *hospital*.'

"Then one night I was in Chicago. Actually, Cicero, where I was playing the 606 Club. I went over to the arena. Anyway, I was fighting some guy named O'Connor, and I go in and hug the guy, and he steps back and gives me a rap. I say, 'What's this? I thought we . . .' And he says, 'F--- you!' " Gleason fingers a scar on his brow. "He gave me this. And that was the end of busking. I was cut, my teeth were loose, I'd had it." He smiles. "Fighting's not that hard. It's going out the dressing-room door that's murder."

The goal was always Manhattan, and the village that was then called Broadway. By 1939, the closest he'd come was playing a place that was always called "the ever popular" Queens Terrace, under the el in Woodside. Gleason now had a personal manager named Willie Webber, and after much pleading, Webber talked Fred Lamb of the Club 18 (across the street from "21") to come out to Queens and look at his new kid. Lamb was impressed, and brought Gleason into the Club 18 on January 20, 1940, for $75 a week. This was what is called a tough room, but after the free-for-all of the Club Miami, Gleason was ready, holding his own with Pat Harrington, Jack White, and Frankie Hyers, the mad comics who were the club's regulars. One night, Jack Warner came in, saw Gleason, and signed him for Warner Bros. at $250 a week.

"I never expected anything from Hollywood," Gleason remembers. "I had no idea of becoming a big star, having a big picture career. I was a kid, I was having a lot of fun, and they were paying me $250 a week in the Depression! Not bad." His first movie was *Navy Blues*. "It had Jack Oakie, Jack Haley, Jack Carson, me, and Ann Sheridan, some of the worst drinkers in the history of show business. Now, across the street from Warners was a joint called My Blue Heaven. And every day when they wrapped, there was a stampede across the street. I mean, a *stampede!* I mean, these were drinkers!"

There were a few more now-forgotten movies, but Gleason kept busy working at Slapsie Maxie's, then a wild club in Hollywood fronted by former light-heavyweight champion Maxie Rosenbloom. And he continued learning, studying the craft of making movies, discovering his strengths and limitations in front of an audience. Most of all, he learned to trust his own instincts.

"I never did a lot of analyzing," he says now. "It was funny or it wasn't. Once you start analyzing it, the mechanics and all that, you're through. It's instinctive. That's why a comedian can be a serious actor, maybe a great actor, but I never heard of an actor becoming a great comedian."

Gleason was turned down for army service (badly healed broken arm, 100 pounds overweight), shuttled back and forth between the coasts. He was separated from his wife, and in New York lived at the Astor or the Edison and did his drinking in Toots Shor's. There were a lot of women. "They were all wonderful," he says. "At one time, I was working at Billy Rose's and there were 22 girls in the chorus and all you had to do was say, 'Would you care to have dinner?' "

Gleason also started working in theater; there was a flop called *Keep Off the Grass,* with Jimmy Durante and Jane Froman; another turkey called *The Duchess Misbehaves,* in which Gleason played, of all things, the painter Goya. He worked awhile in *Hellzapoppin,* did a memorable Foreign Legion bit in *Along Fifth Avenue,* and then in 1945 was in a smash hit, *Follow the Girls.* I have a friend who was at this show on V-E Day, 1945, and she says, "It was the most insane evening in the theater I've ever spent."

In 1949, television called for the first time, and he took the role that eventually would go to William Bendix in *The Life of Riley.* It was the wrong part at the wrong time, and after one season the sponsors canceled. Gleason went back to the clubs. "Who the hell knew what television was?" he says. "Nobody."

He was working in Slapsie Maxie's in June 1950 when the call came from DuMont. This was the fourth television network, and the only one to go out of business. A man named Milton Douglas was producing a weekly variety show called *Cavalcade of Stars,* with rotating hosts, and he offered Gleason two weeks as host for $750 a week. Gleason, who doesn't fly, refused to cross the country for two weeks at $750; he insisted on four weeks. Douglas sighed, and agreed. Gleason took the Super Chief back to New York. He was 34 years old, a bouncer, braggart, pool hustler, failed husband, loudmouth, boozer, squanderer of money and time, a failed movie actor, a middle-level nightclub act, a mediocre radio performer. He was all these things, and when he walked into the studios at DuMont, he was ready. The four weeks became twenty years. From DuMont, he went to CBS, and in one form or another, he was a regular performer on television until 1970.

"Four weeks after I started the DuMont show," Gleason remembers, "I took a broad to Coney Island. We stop at Nathan's for some dogs, and then we're walking around. And I notice three, four people staring at me. Then ten, a dozen. Then, out on the boardwalk, there's maybe 50 of them, and I knew then, the first time, what television was, how powerful it was." He shakes his head, remembering the moment clearly half a lifetime later. "I also knew that I was never gonna be able to walk around Coney Island with a broad again, maybe the rest of my life."

Gleason is sitting in the trailer in Riverdale talking and smoking. Art Carney comes in, dressed in the style of the 1920s. Gleason is asked about the young comedians. "Eddie Murphy is a very good comedian," he says, "but his concert act is frightful. I can't understand why he thinks he needs all the four-letter words. I don't think you need it; it gives you easy laughs, a replacement for dropping your pants." He lights another cigarette. "Murphy has a thing where I do it to Norton!"

Carney says, "I thought we kept that pretty quiet."

"It was only three times," Gleason says.

"Seven."

Deadpan, they go into a riff about great actors they've worked with.

"Olivier was the best I ever saw," Gleason says. "Working with him was a great experience."

Carney says, "Don't forget Hobart Bosworth."

"Or Rex Reed," says Gleason.

"And Monte Blue, one of the all-time greats."

Carney says he first saw Gleason at the Roxy in the forties, "doing the pinball thing." Gleason explains, "The guy comes onstage with a pinball machine, and he moves left, right, the hip, the arms, his back to the audience." Gleason laughs, remembering the character. Both men say they'd prefer working with a live audience to making movies. "We always performed before a live audience on TV," Gleason says. "And I think that's one of the reasons for the show's success. The audience directs you. There was no stopping, no retakes, no cards. We never stopped." Why not do theater? Gleason shakes his head. "Nah. Somebody once asked me when I got tired of doing

Take Me Along. I said, 'About twenty minutes after eleven on opening night.' But also it's hard with three critics in town, three newspapers. You don't have a shot. I remember seeing the show about
Harrigan and Hart, and saying, 'This is a hell of a good show.' They
bombed it right out of Broadway."

Carney says, "They wanted us to do that years ago, remember?"

"Yeah," Gleason says. "That's the only bullet we ever missed."

Carney leaves for makeup. Gleason, who once had two floors at the
Park Sheraton, an apartment on Fifth Avenue, the famous $650,000
round house in Peekskill (with its eight-foot round bed), now lives
on the Inverrary golf course near Fort Lauderdale. He's married to
Marilyn Taylor, the younger sister of June Taylor, whose dancers
were featured on the Gleason variety shows. In the fifties, they were
together for a long time, until she became convinced that Gleason,
the lapsed Catholic, would never divorce Genevieve, and she left him.
When he finally did get a divorce in 1971, he married Beverly McKit-
trick; that lasted three years, and when he was free, he went looking
for Marilyn and married her. She is a soft-spoken, sweet, funny
woman; in New York with him during the shooting of *Izzy and Moe*,
she is protective of Gleason, making certain he doesn't stay out all
night, that he eats properly, gets his sleep. She doesn't have much to
worry about; the New York nights of Gleason's youth are far behind
him. Except in memory.

"Memory is the only money you ever really have," says the man
who once told America that "the worst thing you can do with money
is save it."

The real trouble is that most of his friends are dead. Shor is gone,
and Eddie Condon, and a lot of people from the television shows.
He shakes his head, and then his face slowly brightens.

"I went to Condon's once on Christmas Eve," he says, "and we're
all drinking, and I suddenly realize the band is gone. I say to Condon,
'Where in the hell is the *band?*' So he takes me downstairs, through
one door, into a boiler room, down through another subterranean
passage — I mean *subterranean!* And then another door, and a tunnel, and then he opens the last door . . . and it's Santa's workshop!
Here's the whole goddamned band, stoned out of their brains, working on these little . . . *trains.*"

That led Gleason to another night at Condon's. "Someone in the
band took the strings off Condon's banjo. Just cut them off. And

there was Condon up on the stand, loaded to the gills, playing away, no strings."

Gleason did more than drink with musicians; later, he was to sell millions of albums of his lush arrangements of standard love songs.

"Even the music goes back to Chauncey Street," he says. "I always was sensitive to sounds. At night, lying there in the apartment, I'd hear these sounds: footsteps upstairs, or out on the street; the mice in the walls; the ticking of a clock. I was fascinated by sounds. And years later, I'm working with Tommy Dorsey, and I say, 'I'd like to make some records!' He says, 'Why?' And I say, 'I hear things!' "

Gleason can't read music; his own tunes are hummed or picked out a note at a time on a piano and written down by an arranger. He loves conducting. When he assembled more than 50 French musicians to record the score for a 1962 film called *Gigot,* he had to explain through an interpreter what he wanted. "I say to the interpreter, 'Tell them I want the first note to sound like someone pissing off a cliff into a Chinese teacup.' " A beat. "He tells them." Another beat. "At first, a few of them smile. Then they start looking at each other, and *then* they start to nod. And I tell you, it was *beautiful.*"

Even the romantic music had something to do with Brooklyn.

"I saw Clark Gable in a picture," Gleason remembers. "He's on a couch with a broad. Nothing's happening. Then the music starts, and Gable is the most romantic-looking son of a bitch you ever saw. And I say to myself, 'If *Gable* needs strings, what about some poor schmuck from Brooklyn?' "

More than anyone else, the friend Gleason seems to miss is Toots Shor. "One night in Shor's, the 52d Street joint, Toots was bragging about what a great athlete he was. One thing led to another, and I said, 'You can't play pool, you can't fight — if you did, I'd knock you on your ass!' But I said, 'Maybe you can run!' 'Of course, I can *run,*' says Toots. So we organize a race. But I say to him, 'Toots, if I go outside and the two of us start running, we're gonna draw a crowd, and it'll be terrible, we'll never get it finished. So when we go out, you run towards Sixth Avenue and I'll run towards Fifth, and we'll go around the block — 51st Street — and whoever gets to the bar first wins a grand.' Agreed! So we go out, and Toots starts huffing and puffing towards Sixth Avenue, and I stroll towards Fifth. In front of '21,' I jump in a cab and drive around the block. And when Toots finally gets there, I'm already at the bar with a drink.

He says, 'Aw, you son of a bitch.' And he hands me the grand. We're sitting there another twenty minutes, when suddenly Toots turns to me, the eyes popping out of his head, his veins all straining in his neck, and he yells: '*Wait a minute!*' He roars, '*You never passed me!*' " Gleason is laughing now. "*That* was the greatest double take I ever saw."

All of that was long ago. Gleason moved to Florida in the early sixties, and when I ask him why he doesn't come to New York more often, he just shakes his head and says, "Everybody's dead."

In Florida, he plays a lot of golf and reads. For years, he read the literature of parapsychology, the occult, and books about the world's religions. But now he also reads history. "I don't read fiction," he says. "You know, our *lives* in this business are devoted to fiction."

Did he have any advice for young people who want to get into show business? "Work at everything — weddings, benefits, bar mitzvahs. Play for no money, if you have to. And find out everything. When I was working, I'd listen to the band, talk to the lighting guys, the stage manager, the carpenters, every branch of it. You have to *like* show business. That's the main thing. And you have to *know* everything."

Were there parts he'd wanted to play and didn't, chances that he never got to take? "No," Gleason says. "Almost everything I wanted to do, I've been able to do. And most of it turned out pretty good." A pause. "Everybody's been damned nice to me. I've been very lucky."

And how would he like to be remembered?

"Ah, hell," the Great One says, staring at the smoke from the cigarette. "I'd just like to be remembered."

NEW YORK,
September 23, 1985

FRANZ

ew York was full of swaggering energy in the spring of 1958, when I was living over a secondhand bookstore on Fourth Avenue and Twelfth Street, still trying to be a painter. It was a town where everyone was working, nobody cared about politics, and all things seemed possible. Even for the likes of me.

During the day I studied art at Pratt Institute, and in the chilly evenings I would wander to the Cedar Street Tavern on University Place to nurse a few beers on the thin leftovers of my G.I. Bill money. This was the great bar of the action painters, and of poets too, and visiting cowboys and a few stray seamen and too many rich girls from Bennington who lectured you about Selling Out. I went there because I wanted to see painters in the flesh, to see how they walked and moved and ordered their drinks. I was still something of a kid, unformed and green, and this information was much more important to me than theories of push-pull, color fields, plastic depth, the vital gesture, or the idea of the sublime.

Some insisted, of course, that the Cedar wasn't what it had been; they always say that in Village bars. But about the Cedar they might have been right. In 1958, Jackson Pollock had been dead almost two years; de Kooning was not around much anymore; other regulars were moving uptown, never to return. But look: down past the end of the bar, in the first rough booth in the brightly lit back room: that elegant, beautiful girl is Joan Mitchell. Sitting with Alfred Leslie. And Philip *Guston*. And in that other booth, laughing raucously, that's Grace Hartigan, looking like fifty miles of trouble out of a *film noir*. She's talking to *David Smith*. And that huge fellow with the Zapata mustache: Harold Rosenberg. And over there, that's Larry Rivers — *he draws figures!* — jittery-eyed, junkie-thin, fingers drumming on the table as if in time to a melody nobody else can hear. All were engulfed in a blue nicotine fog, drinking hard, laughing, having a great old time. And among them, every night, was the painter I admired most in the world: Franz Kline.

With Pollock and de Kooning, Kline was the third glittering star in the Big Three constellation. He sat in a booth facing the door, dressed in a camel's-hair coat, with his rough, lumpy slab of a face made oddly elegant by a carefully trimmed mustache. A spear of hair fell across his brow like a brushstroke by that other Franz, Mr. Hals. When women came to the booth he always tried to rise and bow in greeting, like a *boulevardier* from the French films we saw around the corner at the Eighth Street or the Art. Franz was one of those bulky men who look taller sitting down. But when he rose to go to the john, he moved with an athlete's grace, giving off the same muscular aura that emanated from the paintings. We all knew the legend: back home in the coal country of Pennsylvania, he'd played baseball and football, he'd been a boxer. In the age of Hemingway, such credentials were more important than they should have been. As he went by, through the door that Pollock had once torn off its hinges, he had a word and smile for everybody. Everybody called him Franz.

It was not in me, then or now, to fawn over famous men; by the tough code of the '50s, that just wouldn't be hip. But the Bennington girls had no such restraints, and they went for Franz the way sharks go for drowning sailors. So it was hard to be alone with Franz Kline; I suppose that's why he went to the Cedar. But one night a painter friend named Haig Akmajian (he lived in my building) brought me over and introduced me. The great painter smiled and welcomed me to the booth and ordered the first of many beers; he treated me as if I were an established member of The Club. And we talked. And talked. Or rather, Franz talked and I listened. I wasn't a reporter then, I made no notes; but I can hear him now. He had an elaborate, writerly way of speaking, with that rare tone that combines irony with affection. Nothing he said ever sounded bitter, except his references to Walter O'Malley, who had led the Dodgers out of Brooklyn with the Giants following timidly in their wake. "That s.o.b. will find a private place in hell," Franz said of O'Malley. And then laughed, embarrassed by his own bitterness. It was difficult to believe that Franz Kline would send anyone on earth to hell.

He talked about Sugar Ray Robinson and Lester Young, Akira Kurosawa and Brigitte Bardot. He asked me about Pratt, where he had taught a few years earlier (as had Isamu Noguchi, George McNeil, Adolph Gottlieb, and Richard Lindner, among other stars of the New York art world). "You can help teach people how to draw," he said, "but you can't teach them to be *painters*. All you can do is let them know they better love it or get the hell out."

At some point we started talking about cartoonists. His face brightened as he sipped his beer. "I wanted to be a cartoonist when

I started out. I wanted that more than anything." He loved the cartoons of Willard Mullin in the *World-Telegram*. ("I don't know how he does it, day after day, on that level. The guy's a genius.") He was the first man to tell me he was a fan of the amazing Cliff Sterrett, whose surrealistic comic strip, "Polly and her Pals," was usually overlooked by the solemn analysts of popular culture. And of course he paid homage to George Herriman, whose "Krazy Kat" was the highbrows' favorite comic strip. "But you know," he said, "I even like 'Orphan Annie.' The politics are neanderthal. But the man knows how to use blacks."

I was astonished. This was years before pop art was proclaimed by critics as the successor to abstract expressionism. No painter's vision seemed more distant from cartooning than the great bold abstractions of Franz Kline. But as he talked that night, I realized that it was comics that had made him want to be an artist. Born in 1910, he grew up in the '20s with John Held Jr. as his hero. Held's drawings in the old *Life* and *Judge* and *Vanity Fair* made him the most famous cartoonist of his time. In their way, Held's short-skirted flappers and bell-bottomed college boys expressed the hedonism and silliness of the Roaring Twenties as powerfully as the stories of Scott Fitzgerald. But Kline saw form as well as content; he liked the way Held designed a page, placing a number of figures in the space but using blacks to establish a pattern that became the true structure of the drawing.

Kline also talked with affection of certain illustrators and figurative painters. He admired Jack Levine and praised John Sloan and Reginald Marsh, who in different ways had embraced the energy and tension of the city the way the New York School did with pure paint. (Kline once said to Irving Sandler, "Hell, half the world wants to be like Thoreau at Walden, worrying about the noise of traffic on the way to Boston; the other half use up their lives being part of that noise. I like the second half.") As we talked, he was amused, perhaps even delighted, that I knew the work of the British pen-and-ink illustrators — men like John Leech, Donald Keene, and above all Phil May, who tried to turn the city into art.

"Phil May got me to go to England," Kline said. "I wanted to draw like he did, that big open *confident* way." Franz Kline in England? Yes: before the war. After two years at Boston University's School of Fine and Applied Art, he moved to London in 1935 and enrolled in art school. He was apparently not much touched by the political fevers of the day: the Spanish Civil War, the threat of fascism, the romance of communism. Instead, he absorbed the look of architecture, trains, bridges, ships, theaters, music halls. He spent hundreds of hours drawing the figure and mastering the principles of composition. He walked the streets that once teemed with Phil May's ragamuffins. He looked hard at the drawings of the Frenchmen: Daumier, Steinlen, and Forain. In London, the dream of a career as a cartoonist gave way to the desire to be an illustrator.

London also had a certain logic for the young man who became Franz Kline. With the grand exception of Turner, it had produced great draftsmen rather than colorists (Hogarth, Rowlandson, Tenniel, du Maurier, Gillray, Phiz). For Franz, London must have been a gloriously dark indoor city of black and white. I often wonder what his art would have been like if he'd gone instead to Venice or Mexico.

"I had a good time there," he said of London. "I was never so hungry in my life. But I really *did* learn to draw."

When I mentioned that I'd spent a year in art school in Mexico, his eyes brightened and he laughed. "When I came back from London, everybody around was trying to be Orozco or Siqueiros, except the guys who wanted to be Mondrian." He and his wife (whom he'd met in England) moved to Manhattan in 1938, with Franz now determined to be a fine artist. He missed being part of the great brawling fraternity of New York artists who worked for the WPA, but he slowly got to know most of them in the bohemian bars of Greenwich Village. "Some of them liked the Mexicans because of the politics," Kline said. "Some, like Jackson, for the size of the work." He shrugged. "I didn't care for all of them, but I liked the attempt, you know? They could all draw. They had power. They were trying to do something *big*."

Listening to Kline talk at the height of his fame, in a voice whose confident baritone seemed to match the blacks of his paintings, I felt something else brewing under the polished, generous surface. I was too young to identify it, but I think now that he probably knew his own huge achievement was only provisional. He'd done Something Big too. But now there were dozens of kids at Pratt belting out "Klines" (or Pollocks or Rothkos or de Koonings) and talking in the opaque codes of the new art theorists. Rebellion was undergoing its familiar transformation into orthodoxy.

The young hadn't struggled through the rigorous art schools of the '30s, hadn't been challenged by the Depression or the war, hadn't been forced to support themselves by doing murals for bars (as Kline had done at Minetta's and the Bleecker Street Tavern). Not one of them would have done a mural for an American Legion Post, as Kline had done in 1946 back home in Lehighton, Pennsylvania, four years before he broke through into the style that made him famous.

For Kline's generation, the work of the artist could be defined not simply by what he did, but what he refused to do. They had struggled to make an art that was uniquely American: not pseudo-European, neo-Mexican, or some additional knockoff of Picasso. They wanted to be as American as the comic strip or jazz. The best of them certainly didn't want to be rich or famous; if anything, they shared a romantic view of the clarifying power of poverty. They wouldn't pander to an audience, or shape their work to please collectors or museum directors or even critics (although Harold Rosenberg and Clement Greenberg did have an enormous influence on the artists who came right *after* the first generation). They hated glibness and facility; they thought the American artist had a special responsibility to be original (the worst epithet was "derivative"). They expected the artist to live or die in every brushstroke (they'd have hung the likes of Mark Kostabi from a lamppost on Eighth Street), to paint as if he or she might die before morning.

It was a heroic enterprise. Macho: yes. Self-destructive: sometimes. Safe, timid, conniving, calculated: never. And they'd accomplished much of what they'd set out to do, shifting the center of Western art from Paris to New York. But by 1958, other words were being spoken: exhaustion, repetition, mannerism. And Franz must have heard them too.

"It's closing time, isn't it?" he said one night, gazing around at the almost empty Cedar. And then he led a few of us up to Fourteenth Street for a nightcap at his studio. I'd never been in a real painter's studio before. That dark loft was clearly a place of work. I could see rolls of canvas, buckets of paint, large house-painters' brushes, cans of turpentine, baking pans caked with paint. The floor looked like a Pollock. There were small painted drawings scattered around, some of them on the floor, proof that Franz knew what he was going to paint when he approached the canvas. The public image of the action painters was, of course, a crude cartoon. In their work, they could express anger, serenity, anxiety, a contempt for the slick and the sentimental. But for men like Franz Kline, painting was never mere performance or raw therapy. They were making art.

Most of the sketches were on heavy paper, but about a half-dozen were done on classified pages of the *Times*. I was staring down at one, a shape like a machine gun, done in lavender paint, when Franz came over and handed me a beer. "I like the grayness, that texture," he said of the *Times*. "It looks like a sidewalk. Besides, someday soon I might need a job."

He laughed, handed out more beers, turned on a radio (in my beer-blurry memory, it was Symphony Sid on WEVD). I walked around the dark studio, the way I've since seen actors prowl on empty stages or young ballplayers walk into Yankee Stadium, imagining myself in this loft, struggling heroically with paint and canvas. Stacked against the walls were paintings tacked on frames. Someone asked to take a look. Franz smiled: "Sure, why not? But they're not all finished."

He switched on some lights. And then we saw them, all mauves and greens and yellows and blues, with great bold structures on this canvas, more delicate and lush coloring on that one. Some had matte surfaces, thinned with much turpentine, the color as layered and luminous as Tintoretto. Others were glossy, the voluptuous color premixed before going on the canvas, scraped with palette knives or sticks. A few were bright, but most had a dark brooding power.

"The gallery doesn't want me doing them," he said. "They want the *real* Franz Kline. Black and white, black and white . . ."

He shook his head and smiled in a sad way and sipped a beer. He was pleased that we liked what we saw, but insisted that he wasn't finished with many of them. He probably wouldn't show them at the Sidney Janis Gallery show scheduled for May. "They're not there yet," he said. Then he turned off the lights and we went back to drinking beer and talked for a while about prizefighters before we all went home through the gray New York morning.

Some of the paintings in color were shown at the Janis show, but most people were impressed by the ferocious *Crow Dancer*, which was another version of the mounted machine gun, a picture that I think now was called *Siegfried*. In later years, I saw different versions of what I saw that night, the shapes altered or refined, the colors overpainted. Among them, I'm sure, were the great painting *Shenandoah Wall*, along with *Horizontal Rust* and *Andrus*. Franz certainly didn't intend to move through the '60s or '70s repeating what he had done in the '50s. He had added color to his artistic weaponry. Like Guston (and in different ways, Richard Diebenkorn and Wayne

Thiebaud), he might have returned to the figure. Franz was a man who loved to draw.

But like the Cedar Tavern, Franz Kline didn't make it very far into the '60s. In the spring of 1962, Kline, along with Mark Rothko and Andrew Wyeth, was invited by President Kennedy to a dinner at the White House in honor of André Malraux. The date of the dinner was May 11, a Friday. Kline didn't make it. A week before, he suffered a heart attack and was taken to New York Hospital. While he was there, Janis opened a group show that included *Scudera,* Kline's last painting, all deep rich blues, with some red and a broken black square. On Sunday, May 13, Franz Kline died, just short of his fifty-second birthday.

That night, I was working at a newspaper when the word arrived on the AP wire. I was first shocked, then filled with a kind of remorse. In my few encounters with Franz, he'd offered the same hand of friendship that he'd given to so many others. But out of stubbornness or empty vanity, I'd never really taken it. He was too famous and accomplished for us to enter as equals that private conspiracy called friendship. And I was too proud to serve as anyone's acolyte. By 1962, I'd put painting behind me, with sorrow but no regrets, and gone my own way, into the world of words.

But when the night shift was over, I didn't go home. At eight in the morning I walked up Rector Street to a newspaper bar called Page One and starting drinking beer. Around eleven, I went to the pay phone and called the *World-Telegram* and asked for Willard Mullin. When the great sports cartoonist answered, I told him my name.

"I don't know if you saw the paper yet," I said, "but Franz Kline, you know? The painter? He died yesterday. And he was a fan of yours. I just wanted to tell you that."

"No kidding?" A beat. "What was his name?"

"Kline," I said. "Franz Kline."

There was another pause, then: "Oh, yeah. Franz Kline. He did those big black and white things, right?"

"Yeah."

"You know," the cartoonist said, "I bet that guy could've learned how to draw."

ART & ANTIQUES,
May 1990

KEITH

It is morning in the clubhouse at Huggins-Stengel Field in St. Petersburg and Keith Hernandez is moving from locker to locker, handing out schedules. He is the player rep of the world champion New York Mets; this is one of his duties. Still dressed in street clothes and sneakers, he says little as he hands the sheets to each of the players. At 33, he is young in the world of ordinary men; in baseball, especially on this young ball club, he is middle-aged. Kids and veterans nod and study the mimeographed sheets, which tell them when the bus will leave for the afternoon game and how many tickets they can expect for wives and friends. Hernandez explains nothing; he was out late the night before with a woman down from New York. "Too much goddamned wine," he says. And besides, he has been here before, through 13 major league seasons; this is a time for ease, the careful steady retrieval of the skills of the summer game.

"It's all about getting back in a kind of groove," Hernandez says. "Not about getting in shape. Most of the guys are in shape, or they get in shape before coming down. I worked out with weights all winter, the first time I ever did that, 'cause I'm getting old." He smiles, shakes his head. "At the Vertical Club in New York. Jesus, don't go there at five o'clock. It's fucking insane, a social — No, this is about getting your stroke right. About getting back your concentration. I don't worry about it much until the last 10 games before the season starts. If I'm having trouble *then,* then I worry."

In the clubhouse, Hernandez wanders among those who have made it to The Show and those who desperately want to. They all move with that coiled and practiced indolence that is unique to baseball, the style of a game where the most exciting action seems to explode out of the greatest calm. A large table is spread with food; there are boxes of Dubble Bubble and sugarless gum. Some players nibble as they dress; others knead and work new gloves, bad-mouth each other, talk about women, read newspapers and sports magazines, all the while stripping off street clothes and pulling on jocks and T-shirts and uniforms.

Kevin McReynolds, new to the team after a winter trade from San Diego, stares into space. Darryl Strawberry isn't here yet (two weeks before the great alarm clock rhubarb); neither is Dwight Gooden. Hernandez leaves the mimeographed sheets on the small benches in front of their lockers and moves on. When he's finished, he dumps the leftovers in a trash can, sits down at his own locker, lights a Winston and reaches for the *New York Times* crossword puzzle.

"We'll talk later," he says, takes a drag, and stares at the puzzle while unbuttoning his shirt. Hernandez examines the words the way fans examine stats. His own stats are, of course, extraordinary. One of the most consistent hitters in the game, in three full seasons as a Met, he has averaged .311, .309, and .310. Against left-handed pitching last year, he hit .312; against right-handers, .309. He hit .310 at home and .311 on the road. Last year, he had 13 game-winning RBIs, and his career total of 107 is the most in National League history.

It seemed that every time you looked up last season, Hernandez was on base; this wasn't an illusion; he tied with Tim Raines for the lead in on-base percentage (.413), with 94 walks added to 171 hits. Although he has never been much of a power hitter (his career high was 16 home runs for the Cardinals in 1980), when there are men on base there is nobody you'd rather have at bat. "I can't stand leading off an inning," he says. "It's so goddamned boring." Hernandez hit safely in 10 of the 13 postseason games. That's what he's paid to do.

"Keith is the kind of consistent clutch hitter who relies on 'big' RBI production as compared with 'multi' RBI production," says the astute Mets announcer Tim McCarver in the new book he wrote with Ray Robinson, *Oh, Baby, I Love It!* "As an example, a lot of one-run games are won by key hits in the middle innings rather than by big three-run home runs late in the game. Keith is a spectacular middle-inning hitter. . . . You've heard the baseball adage, 'Keep 'em close, I'll think of something'? Well, the something the Mets think of is usually Keith Hernandez."

The fielding stats are even more extraordinary. Last year, he won his ninth straight Gold Glove Award at first base — the most of any player in history — with only five errors in the season, for a .996 average. Those stats don't even begin to tell the story of what Hernandez does on the field; like all great glove men, he makes difficult plays look easy.

But more important, Hernandez can still dazzle you with the play that follows no rule. In the 12th inning of a game with Cincinnati last July 22, the Reds had runners on first and second with none out. Carl Willis dropped a splendid bunt down the third base line, and suddenly, there was Keith, all the way over from first. He threw to Gary Carter, who was playing third, and Carter went back to first for the double play. The Mets won 6-3 in the 14th inning. McCarver, who calls Hernandez "the Baryshnikov of first basemen," writes: "Baseball is a game where, if you do the routine things spectacularly, you win more games than doing the spectacular things routinely — because few athletes have the talent to do spectacular things routinely. Keith has that kind of talent."

In spring training, of course, all players spend their mornings doing the routine things routinely. And on this day, after the cigarette and the crossword, Hernandez is suited up. He makes a quick visit to the john. And then he joins the other players as they move out onto the field. To a visitor who believes the phrase "spring training" is the loveliest in the American language, the view is suddenly beautiful, the bright blue and orange of the Mets' uniforms instantly transforming the great sward of fresh green grass.

After more than 130 days without baseball, it's beginning again. The wan sun abruptly breaks through the clouds and the young men jog out to the far reaches of the outfield and then back. They line up in rows, and then an instructor leads them through 15 minutes of stretching exercises. There is something wonderfully appealing about the clumsiness of the players during this drill; thrown out of their accustomed positions and stances, they don't look like professional athletes at all. Instead, the field now looks like part of some peculiar kind of boot camp, stocked with raw recruits. Jesse Orosco glances at Doug Sisk to see if he's doing the exercise correctly; Lenny Dykstra says something to Carter, who laughs; Backman does a push-up when the others are twisting through sit-ups. Hernandez leads with his left leg when everyone else is leading with the right. You can see more athletic workouts at the New York Health & Racquet Club.

But then it's over and they're all up and reaching for gloves. The players pair off, playing catch, loosening up, while the sun begins to dry the wet grass. Hernandez is throwing with Roger McDowell. The ease and grace and economy of movement are obvious; it's as if he is on a morning stroll. He chatters away with other players (as he does with opposing players who reach first base during the season, a tactical matter that is less about conviviality than it is about distracting the enemy). Dykstra slides a package of Red Man from his hip pocket and bites off a chunk and Hernandez says something we can't hear and Dykstra tries to laugh with his mouth shut. On the sidelines, Davey Johnson has emerged to watch his charges. His coaches — Buddy Harrelson, Bill Robinson, Vern Hoscheit, Sam Perlozzo, and Mel Stottlemyre — are on the side, glancing indifferently at the players, talking about famous assholes they've known. The list is fairly long and each new name brings a guffaw and a story. Harrelson turns to a visitor and says, "That's *all* off the record." And laughs. On the field, Hernandez is working out of a pitcher's windup. He throws a strike. "You think Mex can make this team?" Perlozzo says. Stottlemyre smiles. "He already did."

Then the players amble over to the batting cage, where Perlozzo will be throwing. There's a wire fence beside the cage and fans have assembled behind it, some wearing Mets jackets, caps, and T-shirts. A few are old, the stereotypical snowbirds of spring training; but more are young. They've arranged vacations to come down to see the ballplayers. A few are screaming for autographs. Hernandez waits to bat, says, "Jesus Christ, *listen* to them. . . ." The kids among them seem in awe, and are not screaming. "These are supposed to be *grown-ups*." Two of the middle-aged fans are waving baseballs to be signed. I mention to Hernandez what Warren Spahn had said at a banquet the night before in St. Petersburg: "Baseballs were never meant to be written on. Kids ought to play with 'em. They ought to throw 'em, hit 'em. I hope someday they develop a cover you can't write on." Hernandez says, "Ain't that the truth."

But the fans are persistent and I remember waiting outside Ebbets Field with my brother Tom one late afternoon long ago and seeing Carl Furillo come out, dressed in a sports shirt. His arms looked like the thickest, most powerful arms in the known universe. I wanted to ask him for an autograph but didn't know how; a mob of other kids chased after him and he got in a car with Jackie Robinson and Roy Campanella, and I wondered how he had ever been able to sign the petition at spring training in 1947 saying he couldn't play with a black man. Years later, I learned that Leo Durocher told the protesting players (Dixie Walker, Hugh Casey, Kirby Higbe, Bobby Bragan, Furillo, among others) to go and "wipe your ass" with the petition. Durocher was the manager and Robinson was on the team and there was nothing else to say except play ball. Standing at the batting cage, while Hernandez took his swings and the fans demanded to be authenticated with signatures, I realized again how much of the adult response to baseball is about the accretion of memory and the passage of time.

"Christ, I hate spring training," Hernandez said at one point. "It's so goddamned *boring*."

But for the rest of us, spring training is something else: the true beginning of the year, a kind of preliminary to the summer festival, another irreversible mark in time. On the field and in the clubhouse, kid players come over to Hernandez. "Hey, Mex, lemme ask you something. . . ." They are talking to him about the present and the future. But we who don't play also see the past; it helps us measure accomplishment, skill, potential. Don Mattingly is another Musial; Wally Backman is another Eddie Stanky. At spring training, somewhere in the Florida afternoons, we always hear the voice of Red Barber and know that in a few weeks we'll be playing the Reds at Crosley Field and the Cardinals in Sportsman's Park and we could lose one in the late innings if that goddamned Slaughter lifts one over the pavilion roof. This is not mere sentiment; it's history and lore, part of the baggage of New York memory.

New Yorkers don't easily accept ballplayers. They almost always come from somewhere else, itinerants and mercenaries, and most of them are rejected. We look at Darryl Strawberry and unfairly compare him to Snider, DiMaggio, Mays, Mantle. We question his desire, his heart, his willingness under pressure to risk everything in one joyful and explosive moment. Since he is young, we reserve judgment, but after four seasons, he still seems a stranger in the town. Those who are accepted seem to have been part of New York forever. Hernandez is one of them.

II.

He was born on October 20, 1953, in San Francisco. Although his teammates call him Mex, he isn't Mexican at all. His grandparents on his father's side immigrated from Spain in 1907; his mother's side is Scotch-Irish. Keith's father, John, was a fine high school player (hitting .650 in his senior year) and was signed by the Brooklyn Dodgers for a $1000 bonus in 1940. According to William Nack in *Sports Illustrated*, John Hernandez was badly beaned in a minor league night game just before the war; his eyesight was ruined, and though he played with Musial and others in some Navy games, when the war was over, John Hernandez knew he couldn't play again. He became a San Francisco fireman, moved to suburban Pacifica, and started the process of turning his sons, Gary and Keith, into the ballplayers he could never be. They swung at a balled-up sock attached to a rope in the barn; both playing first base, they learned to field ground balls, thousands of ground balls, millions.

From the time Keith was eight, he and his brother were given baseball quizzes, questions about tactics and strategy, *the fundamentals*. His mother, Jackie, took home movies at Little League games, and they would be carefully studied, analyzed for flaws. John Hernandez was not the first American father to do such things; he will not be the last. But he did the job well. Perhaps too well.

"My father taught me how to hit," Keith says. "He made us swing straight at the ball, not to undercut it, golf it. A straight swing, an even stroke. He really knew."

But Nack, and other writers, have described the relationship of father and son as a mixed blessing. In brief, John Hernandez is said to be unable to leave his son alone; Keith is one of the finest players in the game, an acknowledged leader of a splendid world championship team, the father of three daughters of his own; but too often, his father still treats him as if he were the kid behind the barn, learning to hit the slider. When Keith goes into a slump (and he has one almost every year, usually in midseason), his father is on the phone with advice. As Nack wrote, "Keith knows that no one can help him out of a slump as quickly as his father can, and so, throughout his career, he has often turned to his father for help. At the same time, he has felt the compelling need to break away from his father and make it on his own, to be his own man."

Obviously it would be a mistake to think that Keith Hernandez is the mere creation of his father. His brother, Gary, was trained the same way, went to Berkeley on an athletic scholarship, but didn't make it to the majors. Keith had his own drive, his own vision. At Capuchino High (where he hit .500 one season), he also starred on the football and basketball teams, and says that football was particularly good training. "I was a quarterback, and I had to make choices all the time, to move guys around, read the other teams' defenses. But I was 5-11, 175 pounds then and that was too small, even for college. I went down to Stanford for a tryout, saw the size of these guys, and decided baseball was for me."

Major league scouts were watching him in high school, but in his senior year he quit the team after an argument with the manager. Most of the scouts vanished. Until then, it had been expected that Keith would be a first-round draft pick in the June 1971 free agent draft; instead, he was chosen by the Cardinals in the 40th round. He had always been a fairly good student, and was accepted at Berkeley, but when the Cardinals offered a $30,000 bonus, he decided to head for professional ball.

There are hundreds of stories about minor league phenoms who burn up the leagues and fizzle in the majors; Hernandez had the opposite experience. He has always hit better for average in the majors than he did starting out in A ball at St. Petersburg in 1972 (.256) or AAA ball at Tulsa in the same year (.241). He found his groove in Tulsa in '73 and '74, and was brought up for 14 games in St. Louis in 1974. He hit .294 in those games, was soon being described as the next Musial, started the 1975 season at first, couldn't get going, was sent down again, and brought up again the following year, this time to stay.

That first full year with the Cardinals, he hit .289, the next year .291. Still, he didn't feel secure. In 1978, the year he met and married Sue Broecker, he slumped to .255. "I didn't feel I was *really* here until '79," he says. That year, he hit .344, with a career-high 210 hits. He won the batting championship, and shared the Most Valuable Player award with Willie Stargell, who hit .281.

"Yeah, you get better," he said one afternoon in St. Petersburg. "You know more. You watch, you see, you learn. You know something about pacing yourself too. One of the most important things about the minors is learning how to play every day. In high school, college ball, you play maybe twice a week. You don't know what it's like to do it day in and day out. . . . In the majors, you're seeing guys over and over. You look at a guy like Steve Carlton for 11 or 12 years. You know how hard he throws, you know how his breaking ball is, you know how he likes to pitch you. And you know the catchers too, how they see you, what kind of game they like to call."

Hernandez is one of those players who seem totally involved in the game. On deck, his concentration is ferocious. After an at-bat, including those in which he fails ("a great hitter, a guy who hits .300, fails seven out of 10 times"), he is passing on information about pitchers.

"I look for patterns," he says. "I usually only look at the way a pitcher pitches to left-handed hitters. I don't pay much attention to the right-handed hitters. What does he like to do when he's in trouble? Does he go to the breaking ball, or the fastball, does he like to come in or stay away? I look for what you can do to hurt him. There are very few pitchers that are patternless. Of course, there are a few guys — Seaver, Don Sutton — who don't have a pattern. They pitch you different every time. That's why they have 500 wins between them, why they're future Hall of Famers."

Hernandez is known as a generous player; he will talk about hitting with anyone on the team "except pitchers, 'cause they might get traded." Pitchers themselves are a notoriously strange breed (a player once described his team as being made up of blacks, whites, and pitchers), and though Hernandez is friendly with all of them, and was amazingly valuable to the young Mets staff in the 1984 season (Gary Carter didn't arrive until '85), he still maintains a certain distance.

"Most pitchers . . . can't relate to hitting because they can't hit, they've never hit. They don't know how. And there's very few that know how to *pitch*. But it's not so simple. Some guys you can hit off, some you can't. I was always successful against Carlton, and he was a great pitcher. And then there's some sub-.500 pitcher, and you can't get a hit off him. It's one of the inexplicable mysteries of baseball."

Hernandez clearly loves talking about the craft of baseball. But there are some subjects he won't discuss. One is his ruined marriage to Sue Broecker. There have been various blurry published reports about this messy soap opera. How Keith played around a lot after the marriage, particularly on the road. How they broke up after the All-Star game in 1980, then reconciled and had a baby. How Keith liked his booze after games, and later started dabbling with cocaine. She got fed up, one version goes, and then demanded most of his $1.7 million a year salary as reparations. In my experience, the truth about anybody else's marriage is unknowable; thousands struggle to understand their own.

Hernandez, by all accounts, loves his children; he dotes on them when he is with them, even took a few days out of spring training to take them to Disney World. Marriages end; responsibility does not. Hernandez says that he would like to marry again someday and raise a family, but not until he's finished with baseball. One sign of maturity is the realization that you can't have everything.

He also won't discuss cocaine anymore. At one point, he told writer Joe Klein what it was like around the major leagues in the late '70s. "All of a sudden, it was everywhere. In the past, you might be in a bar and someone would say, 'Hey, Keith, wanna smoke a joint?' Now it was 'Wanna do a line?' People I'd never met before were offering; people I didn't know. *Everywhere* you went. It was like a wave: it came, and then people began to realize that cocaine could really hurt you, and they stopped."

Nobody has ever disputed Hernandez's claim that his cocaine use was strictly recreational; he never had to go into treatment (as teammate Lonnie Smith did); his stats remained consistent. But when Hernandez was traded to the Mets in June 1983 for Neil Allen and Rick Ownbey, the whispering was all over baseball. Cards manager Whitey Herzog would not have traded Hernandez for such mediocre players if the first baseman didn't have some monstrous drug problem. It didn't matter that Hernandez almost immediately transformed the Mets into a contender, giving them a professional core, setting an example for younger players, inspiring some of the older men. The whispering went on.

Then, deep into the 1985 season, Hernandez joined the list of professional ballplayers who testified in the Curtis Strong case in Pittsburgh, and the whole thing blew open. In his testimony, Hernandez described cocaine as a demon that got into him, but that was now gone; he had stopped well before the trade to the Mets. He wasn't the only player named in the Strong case, but he seemed to get most of the ink. When he rejoined the team the next day in Los Angeles, he did the only thing he knew how to do: he went five for five.

When the Mets finally came home to Shea Stadium, Hernandez was given a prolonged standing ovation during his first at-bat. It was as if the fans were telling him that all doubt was now removed: he was a New Yorker forever. Flawed. Imperfect. Capable of folly. But a man who had risen above his own mistakes to keep on doing what he does best. That standing ovation outraged some of the older writers and fans but it moved Hernandez almost to tears. He had to step out of the box to compose himself. Then he singled to left.

Last spring, as Hernandez was getting ready for the new season, baseball commissioner Peter Ueberroth made his decision about punishing the players who had testified in the Strong case. Hernandez was to pay a fine of 10 per cent of his salary (roughly $180,000, to be donated to charity), submit to periodic drug testing, and do 100 hours of community service in each of the next two years. Most of the affected players immediately agreed; Hernandez did not. He objected strongly to being placed in Group 1, those players who "in some fashion facilitated the distribution of drugs in baseball." In the new afterword to his book *If at First . . .* , Hernandez insists: "I never sold drugs or dealt in drugs and didn't want that incorrect label for the rest of my life."

There were some obvious constitutional questions. (Hernandez and the other players were given grants of immunity, testified openly, and were punished anyway — by the baseball commissioner — even though they had the absolute right to plead the Fifth Amendment in the first place.) There was also something inherently unfair about punishing a man who came clean. Hernandez threatened to file a grievance, conferred with friends, lawyers, his brother. After a week of the resulting media shitstorm, Hernandez reluctantly agreed to comply, still saying firmly, "The only person I hurt was myself."

Last year, he took a certain amount of abuse. A group of Chicago fans showed up with dollar bills shoved up their noses. Many Cardinal fans, stirred up by the local press, were unforgiving. And I remember being at one game at Shea Stadium, where a leather-lunged guy behind me kept yelling at Hernandez, "Hit it down da white line, Keith. Hit it down da white line." Still, Hernandez refused to grovel, plead for forgiveness, appear on the Jimmy Swaggart show, or kiss anyone's ass. He just played baseball. The Mets won the division, the playoffs, and the World Series, and they couldn't have done it without him. When *The New York Times* did a roundup piece a few weeks ago about how the players in the Pittsburgh case had done their community service, Hernandez was the only ballplayer to refuse an interview. His attitude is clear: I did it, it's over, let's move on. He plays as hard as he can (slowed these days by bad ankles that get worse on Astroturf) and must know that the Drug Thing might prevent him from ever managing in the major leagues — and could even keep him out of the Hall of Fame.

"I like playing ball," he says. "That's where I'm almost always happy."

III.

Now it's the spring and everything lies before him. The sports pages are full of questions: what's the matter with Gooden and why isn't Dykstra hitting and will the loss of Ray Knight change everything and why does McReynolds look so out to lunch. Nobody writes much about Hernandez; his career and his style don't provoke many questions. He will tell you that he thinks Don Mattingly is "the best player in the game today," but admits that he seldom watches American League games and isn't even interested in playing American League teams in spring. The next day, for example, the Mets are scheduled to play the Blue Jays in nearby Dunedin. "I'd rather not even go," says Hernandez. "It's a shit park and we're never gonna play these guys, so why?"

In the clubhouse, nothing even vaguely resembles a headline; Hernandez does talk in an irritated way about Strawberry, as if the sight of such natural gifts being inadequately used causes him a kind of aesthetic anger. "Last year, he finally learned how to separate his offense from his defense and that's a major improvement," Hernandez says. "Before, if he wasn't hitting, he'd let it affect his fielding. Not last year."

His locker is at the opposite end of the clubhouse from that of Gary Carter, who is the other leader of the club. I'm told that some players are Carter men, some Hernandez men. There could not be a greater difference in style. Carter is Mister Good Guy America, right out of the wholesome Steve Garvey mold. You can imagine him as a Los Angeles Dodger — but not a Brooklyn Dodger. He smiles most of the time and even his teeth seem to have muscles; he radiates fair-haired good health; if a demon has ever entered him, he shows no signs of the visit.

You can see Carter on a horse, or kicking up dust with a Bronco on some western backcountry road or strolling toward you on the beach at Malibu. Hernandez is dark, reflective, analytical, urban. Through the winter, you see him around the saloons of the city, sometimes with friends like Phil McConkey of the Giants, other times with beautiful women. His clothes are carefully cut. He reads books, loves history, buys art for his apartment on the East Side. Carter is the king of the triumphant high-fives; Hernandez seems embarrassed by them. In a crisis, Carter might get down on a knee and have a prayer meeting; Hernandez advocates a good drunk. Between innings, Carter gives out with the rah-rah on the bench; Hernandez is in the runway smoking a cigarette.

They are friendly, of course, in the casual way that men on the same team are friendly. But it's hard to imagine them wandering together through the night. Hernandez speaks about his personal loneliness and fear; Carter smiles through defeat and promises to be better tomorrow. Both are winners. In some odd way, they were forever joined, forever separated, during the Greatest Game Ever Played (well, one of them): the 6th playoff game against Houston. In the 14th inning, Billy Hatcher hit a home run off Jesse Orosco to tie the game. There was a hurried conference on the mound. Hernandez later said he told Carter, "If you call another fastball, I'll fight you right here." Carter insists that the words were never uttered, telling Mark Ribowsky of *Inside Sports:* "Keith *never* said that, he just told the press that he did out of the tension of the game. I call the pitches and *I* decided not to throw anything after that but Jesse's slider, his best pitch. Let's get that straight once and for all."

That was last season. This is the new season, and in the cool mornings of the Florida spring, they are all still thousands of pitches away from the fierce tests of August, the terrors of September. There will be crises, dramas, fights, slumps, failures, disappointments, along with giddy joyous triumphs. There are perils up ahead. The Cardinals might get themselves together again; the Phillies had a great second half last year and could come on strong. When you're a champion, you have to defend what you've won. But for now, they are all months away from discussions of such arcane phenomena as the All Important Loss Column. Up ahead lies the season of the summer game and it remains a mystery, a maybe, a perhaps.

On another morning, Hernandez was waiting to take his swings, 10 hits apiece, and two young women were standing behind the fence, chewing gum. "They've gotta be from New York," Keith said. "Every girl in New York chews gum. Everywhere. All the time. In restaurants. In bed. Drives me crazy." He laughs. He looks at a foam rubber pad he wears in BP to protect his left thumb, which was hurt when Vida Blue jammed him in a game years ago. Then he steps in and takes his swings, the straight level strokes his father taught him, always making contact, intense in his concentration. That day, he wasn't playing in the team game, and the field was almost empty. When he was finished hitting, he and Backman helped pick up all the balls and handed them to Perlozzo. Dave Magadan was ready to hit. Hernandez leaned down and touched his toes. "I'd like to go back to bed," he said. "But I can't do that anymore. I'm getting old. . . ."

With that he walked out onto the empty field, and then began to jog easily and gracefully through the lumpy grass, and then to run, out around the edges of the field, under the palm trees beside the fence, a lone small figure in a lush and verdant place.

VILLAGE VOICE,
April 7, 1987

CUS

In those days, you had to pass a small candy stand to get to the door of the Gramercy Gym on East 14th Street. The door was heavy, with painted zinc nailed across its face and a misspelled sign saying "Gramacy Gym," and when you opened the door, you saw a long badly lit stairway, climbing into darkness. There was another door on the landing, and a lot of tough New York kids would reach that landing and find themselves unable to open the second door. They'd go back down the stairs, try to look cool as they bought a soda at the candy stand, then hurry home. Many others opened the second door. And when they did, they entered the tough, hard, disciplined school of a man named Cus D'Amato.

"First thing I want to know about a kid," Cus said to me once, on some lost night in the '50s, "is whether he can open that door. Then when he walks in, I look at him, try to see what he's seeing. Most of them stand at the door. They see guys skipping rope, shadowboxing, hitting the bags. Most of all, they see guys in the ring. Fighting. And then they have to decide. Do they want this, or not? If they want it, they stay, they ask someone what they should do. Most of them are shy, for some reason. Almost all fighters. They whisper. You tell them to come back, and you'll see what can be done. They have to spend at least one night dealing with fear. If they come back the second time, then maybe you have a fighter."

I wasn't a fighter, but I came up those stairs almost every day in the late '50s and early '60s, and in some important ways I learned as much from Cus D'Amato as the fighters did. I was living then on 9th Street and Second Avenue, working nights at the *Post,* and I'd wake up around three in the afternoon and walk to 14th Street and hang out with the fighters. My friend José Torres was then the hottest young middleweight in the city and one of Cus D'Amato's fighters. He had lost by one point to Laszlo Papp in the finals of the '56 Olympics in Melbourne, and when he came to New York from Puerto Rico he placed his career in the hands of Cus.

"I didn't know anything about New York," he said. "I didn't know very much about boxing. Most of all, I didn't know anything about life. So I learned about everything then from Cus."

Cus, who died last week at 77 after a long struggle with pneumonia, was one of the best teachers I ever met. He was a tough, intelligent man who was almost Victorian in his beliefs in work and self-denial and fierce concentration. For years he'd lived alone in the office of the gym, accompanied only by a huge boxer dog named Champ; there were books on the shelves (he loved the Civil War and essays on strategy and tactics and almost never read novels, although he admired W. C. Heinz's *The Professional*) and a gun somewhere and a small black-and-white TV set and a pay phone on the wall. After Floyd Patterson became champion in 1956, Cus took an apartment over a coffee shop on 53rd Street and Broadway and bought some elegantly tailored clothes and a homburg; but, talking to him, I always sensed that his idea of paradise was that room and the cot in the office of the Gramercy Gym.

"You can't want too many things," he said to me one wintry evening, after the fighters had gone, the speed bags were stilled, and we stood at the large gym windows while snow fell into 14th Street. "The beginning of corruption is wanting things. You want a car or a fancy house or a piano, and the next thing you know, you're doing things you didn't want to do, just to get the *things.* I guess maybe that's why I never got married. It wasn't that I didn't like women. They're nice. It's nice. It's that women want *things,* and if I want the woman, then I have to want the things she wants. Hey, I don't want a new refrigerator, or a big TV set, or a new couch. . . ."

Cus wanted his fighters to be champions, to have money and glory; but he truly didn't seem to want much for himself. Once a bum made his way to the Gramercy from the White Rose bar across the street;

Cus gave him a dollar; the next day, five bums showed up, and the day after that, almost 40. The fighters laughed, as Cus dispensed singles; and then Cus said, "That's it, that's all! You want to come back here, bring trunks!" He was a sucker for old fighters. Once when Cus had the shorts (he had to declare bankruptcy in 1971) Ezzard Charles came around to see him; the great light-heavyweight and former heavyweight champion was a broken man, confined to a wheelchair; he needed a thousand, and Cus borrowed the money, gave it to the old champion, and never heard from Charles again. When Patterson won the championship by knocking out Archie Moore on November 30, 1956, Cus used his share of the purse to make Floyd an elaborate $35,000 jewel-encrusted crown; a few years later, Patterson wouldn't even talk to Cus. Cus once quoted Gene Fowler to me: "Money is something to throw off the back of trains."

He loved style in fighters and in writers, too. His favorite sports writers were Jimmy Cannon, Dick Young, and Dan Parker, all of whom took shots at him in print from time to time ("I don't mind, they gotta job to do and I'm not perfect"), but he also said that the sports writer who moved him most consistently was the elegant Frank Graham of the *Journal-American*. Later, when Torres became friends with Norman Mailer, Cus started to read his work, as if inspecting it for signs of moral decay. "The guy is really good, isn't he? He's like a Robinson, he can box, he can punch. . . ."

He cherished great fighters — Ray Robinson, Joe Louis, Muhammad Ali, Sandy Saddler, Willie Pep, Tommy Loughran — but sometimes, late at night, sitting over coffee, he'd talk about the fighter that didn't exist: the perfect fighter, the masterpiece. "The ideal fighter has heart, skill, movement, intelligence, creativity. You can have everything, but if you can't make it up while you're in there, you can't be great. A lot of guys have the mechanics and no heart; lots of guys have heart, no mechanics; the thing that puts it together, it's mysterious, it's like making a work of art, you bring everything to it, you make it up when you're doing it."

Toward the end, he thought perhaps that he had the perfect heavyweight at last in young Michael Tyson, who has now knocked out all nine of his professional opponents, six in the first round. "He's strong, he's brave, he's in condition, and most of all, he's got that other thing, the mysterious thing," Cus said, the last time I saw him. "I have no doubt he'll be a champion. But more than that, he might be a great fighter."

There were a lot of good fighters at the Gramercy in the late '50s: Joe Shaw, a fierce-punching 140-pounder; light-heavyweight Jim Boyd, who'd won the gold medal in Melbourne; two more light-heavyweights, named Sylvester Banks and Paul Wright; a wonderful southpaw featherweight named Floyd Smith; and some fine amateurs ranging from bantamweight Georgie Colon to light-heavyweight Simon Ramos. But as Cus became more involved managing Patterson and Torres, the day-to-day training was left to Joe Fariello (now educating Mark Breland). Cus was away at camp with Patterson; he was up at Stillman's with Torres, to find experienced professionals for sparring partners. And during the same period, Cus was waging his wars with the International Boxing Club and Madison Square Garden. Some people thought he grew increasingly paranoid.

"If this goes down instead of up," he said to me one day as we stepped into an elevator in a midtown office building, "we're in trouble."

He laughed, but Cus meant it, too. The Mob was all over boxing when Cus brought his first good fighters out of the Gramercy Gym. The hoodlums cut into fighters, arranged tank jobs, fixed judges. Frankie Carbo was called the underworld's commissioner of boxing, a vicious punk who lived off other men's sweat and controlled a number of managers. Carbo was friendly, sort of, with Jim Norris, a rich bum with a hoodlum complex who ran the IBC out of the old Garden on Eighth Avenue and 50th Street. There's no room here to relate the details of Cus D'Amato's sustained contest with Norris, Carbo, and the Garden. Certainly he was on the moral high ground, but the terrible thing was that his personal crusade also hurt his fighters.

We'll never know how good Patterson and Torres might have become if they'd been fighting more often, battling those fighters who were controlled by the IBC and the Garden. Certainly Torres would have made more money. I remember one main event he had to take in Boston, when he was still a hot fighter in New York. The total purse came to $28.35. Joe Fariello said, "Joe, you take the $20, I'll take the $8, and we'll send the 35¢ to Cus." Patterson did get rich, and Torres did become champion years later than he should have, and in the wrong division (he was one of the greatest middleweights I ever saw, but had to settle for the light-heavyweight championship in 1965). But the competitive fire of Shaw withered from lack of action; the others drifted away.

"It breaks my heart sometimes, thinking about those kids not fighting," he said to me once. "But I don't see any other way."

That was the problem. From 1959 on, Cus never worked a corner for any of his fighters; he didn't even hold a manager's license, as a result of the botched promotion of the 1959 Patterson-Johansson fight, when it appeared (but was never proved) that Cus helped bring Fat Tony Salerno in as a money man. The fighters did their best, and for some fights Cus would come to camp, work with them, talk strategy and tactics. But Patterson broke with him, and Torres was forced to go with another manager (Cain Young) to get his chance at a title. Around the time Torres retired, Cus moved upstate, far from the gyms of the city. "I like it up there," he said once. "I like the clear skies, the lake, where I go fishing. It's beautiful. Beautiful." Did he miss the gym on 14th Street? "Yeah," he said. "Sometimes. . . ."

The last time I saw him was almost exactly a year ago, on the 57th floor of the World Trade Center. We were there to watch Torres be sworn in as chairman of the New York State Athletic Commission, the first professional fighter and the first Puerto Rican ever to hold the job. "I'm so proud of José, I can't explain it," Cus said. We talked about Tyson and other things. And then I asked him if he'd ever gone back to the Gramercy Gym since he sold it in the '70s. "No," he said, and looked up at José, who was standing with Mario Cuomo at the front of the room. "No, I don't like to look back."

And so I did the looking back, sitting in the packed, brightly lit conference room, remembering Cus talking to me when I was 20 about the uses of fear, the meaning of courage, the need to concentrate energy and purpose in all things, and how I'd tried and failed so often to follow his lessons. I'd modeled a character on Cus in one of my novels, and he'd liked the book but objected when he saw the TV movie; on the screen, John Cassavetes stood on a ring apron talking to a fighter and smoking a cigarette. "What manager would *do* that? What kind of *example* would he be showing to a kid?" I remembered that conversation, and after José was sworn in, I turned to Cus and said, "Listen, Cus, I want to thank you for everything." He squinted suspiciously at me. "What do you mean?" he said, and I said, "For letting me climb the stairs."

He nodded, turned away, and said, "You goddamned writers."

I'm sorry I never got to explain.

VILLAGE VOICE,
November 19, 1985

TYSON

An artificial Christmas tree stands in a corner of the waiting room, with a bunched-up bedsheet at its base feigning snow. Unmatched pieces of cheap furniture, some wicker, some plastic, are arranged awkwardly around the edges of the room. It could be the antiseptic lobby of a second-class motel except for the view through the picture windows behind the Christmas tree: two parallel steel-mesh fences topped with barbed wire and a slope of sour lawn rising toward blank walls and tan-brick buildings. The complex is called the Indiana Youth Center. But it's not a place where schoolkids play checkers or basketball on frigid afternoons. The barbed wire makes it clear that this is a jail.

So does the posted rule against bringing drugs or alcohol on visits; so does the order to place wallets and handbags in a locker in the far corner, along with all cash in excess of five dollars, any pens, notebooks, tape recorders, books, all hats and overcoats; and so does the stamping of your hand with invisible ink, the emptying of pockets into a plastic tray, the body search, the passage through a metal detector.

The rules of entrance obeyed, I walk down a long, wide ramp into the prison, pause at a sign forbidding weapons beyond this point, and wait for a steel-rimmed glass door to be opened. Up ahead there are other such doors, with guards and a few prisoners moving languidly along a corridor that is lit like an aquarium. The door in front of me pops open with a click. I turn right to a guard's booth, where I hand over my pass and am told to thrust my right hand into a hole in a wooden box. An ultraviolet light certifies the stamp. I am then instructed to go through the door to the left, into the visitors' lounge, and give the pass to the guard behind the high desk in the corner. I do what I am told and wait. In the lounge a dozen couples sit facing each other on thick plastic-covered chairs, maintaining space and privacy, drinking soda bought from machines, trying hard to be loose, glancing tensely at the clock, conscious of time. Behind them a wall of picture windows opens upon a vista of gray grass and blank, tan walls. The Indiana sky is the color of steel.

Then, suddenly, from another door, Mike Tyson appears. He smiles, gives me a hug, and says, "How are ya, buddy?"

Twenty-two months have passed since he vanished from the nightsides of cities, from the bubble of champagne and the musk of women, from the gyms where he prepared for his violent trade, from the arenas that roared when he came after an opponent in a ferocious rush, his eyes hooded, gleaming with bad intentions. Twenty-two months have passed since he was convicted of raping an eighteen-year-old beauty-pageant contestant who consented to leave her own Indianapolis hotel room at nearly 1:30 in the morning, who moved around the streets for a while with Tyson in his rented limousine, who then went to Tyson's suite in the Canterbury Hotel, where she sat on the bed with him, went to the bathroom and removed her panty shield, on the way passing the door that led to the corridor and the possibility of flight. Twenty-two months since the jury believed Desiree Washington lay helpless while Tyson had sex with her. Twenty-two months since the jury believed that it was perfectly normal for a rape victim to spend two more days taking part in the Miss Black America pageant of 1991. Twenty-two months since Michael Gerard Tyson, twenty-five-year-old child of Amboy Street, Brownsville, Brooklyn, was led away — refusing to express remorse for a crime he insists he didn't commit — deprived of his freedom, his ability to earn millions, his pride.

But if there is anger in him or a sense of humiliation, neither is visible on this gray morning. He is wearing jeans and a white T-shirt — with his prison number, 922335, hand-lettered over his heart — and to a visitor who first met him when he was sixteen, he looks taller somehow. In the TV-news clip that plays every time his name is mentioned, Tyson weighs about 250 pounds, swollen and suety in a tight-fitting suit as he smiles in an ironic way and holds up his cuffed hands on his way to a cell. Now, a few days before his second Christmas in prison, he is about 220, the belly as flat as a table, the arms as hard as stone. He looks capable of punching a hole in a prison wall.

"Yeah, I'm in good shape," he says, "but not boxing shape." He works out in the prison gym every day, a self-imposed regimen of calisthenics, weights, running. "No boxing," he says, the familiar whispery voice darkened by a hint of regret. "They don't allow boxing in prison in Indiana." He smiles, nodding his head. "That's the rules. Ya gotta obey the rules."

We walk over to the chairs, and Tyson sits with his back to the picture windows. His hair is cropped tight, and he's wearing a mustache and trimmed beard that emphasize the lean look. Then I notice the tattoos. On his left bicep, outlined in blue against Tyson's ocher-colored skin, is the bespectacled face of Arthur Ashe, and above it is the title of that splendid man's book *Days of Grace*. On his right bicep is a tattooed portrait of Mao Tse-tung, with the name MAO underneath it, in cartoony "Chinese" lettering. I tell Tyson that it's unlikely that any other of the planet's six billion inhabitants are adorned with *that* combination of tattoos. He laughs, the familiar gold-capped tooth gleaming. He rubs the tattoos fondly with his huge hands.

"I love reading about Mao," he says. "Especially about the Long March and what they went through. I mean, they came into a village one time and all the trees were white, and Mao wanted to know what happened, and they told him the people were so hungry they ate the bark right off the trees! What they went *through*. I mean, *that* was adversity. This . . ."

He waves a hand airily around the visiting room but never finishes the sentence; he certainly feels that the Indiana Youth Center can't be compared to the Long March. I don't have to ask him about Arthur Ashe. For weeks Tyson and I have been talking by telephone, and he has spoken several times about Ashe's book.

"I never knew him," Tyson said one night. "I never liked him. He was a *tennis* player, know what I mean? And he looked like a black bourgeois, someone I couldn't have nothin' to do with. Just looking at him I said, '*Yaaagh*, he's *weak*.' That was my way of thinking back then." A pause. "But then Spike Lee sent me his book, and I started reading it, and in there I read this: 'AIDS isn't the heaviest burden I have had to bear . . . being black is the greatest burden I've had to bear. . . . Race has always been my biggest burden. . . . Even now it continues to feel like an extra weight tied around me.' It was like *wham!* An extra *weight* tied around me! I mean, wow, that really *got* me, and I kept reading, excited on every page."

On the telephone, with the great metallic racket of prison in the background, or here in the visiting room of the Indiana Youth Center, Tyson makes it clear that he doesn't want to talk much about the past. He doesn't encourage sentimental evocations of the days when, as a raw teenager from a reform school, he learned his trade from the old trainer Cus D'Amato in the gym above the police station in Catskill, New York. He doesn't want to talk about his relationship with Don King, the flamboyant promoter whose slithery influence many blamed for Tyson's decline as a fighter and calamitous fall from grace. He is uncomfortable and embarrassed discussing his lost friends and squandered millions. He has no interest in retailing the details of the case, like another Lenny Bruce, endlessly rehashing what happened on July 19, 1991, in room 606 of the Canterbury Hotel or the astonishingly feeble defense offered by his high-priced lawyers or his chances for a new trial. He wants to talk about what he is doing now, and what he is doing is time.

History is filled with tales of men who used prison to educate themselves. Cervantes began *Don Quixote* in a Spanish prison, and Pancho Villa read that book, slowly and painfully, while caged in the Santiago Tlatelolco prison in Mexico City more than three hundred years later. In this dreadful century, thousands have discovered that nobody can imprison the mind. In the end, Solzhenitsyn triumphed over Stalin's gulags, Antonio Gramsci over Mussolini's jails, Malcolm X over the joints of Massachusetts. From Primo Levi to Václav Havel, books, the mind, the imagination, have offered consolation, insight, even hope to men cast into dungeons. I don't mean to compare Mike Tyson to such men or the Indiana Youth Center to the gulags; Tyson is not serving his six-year sentence for his ideas. But he understands the opportunity offered by doing time and has chosen to seize the day.

"Sometime in that first month here," he said one night, "I met an old con, and he pointed at all the guys playing ball or exercising, and he said to me, 'You see them guys? If that's all they do when they're in here, they'll go out and mess up and come right back.' He said to me, 'You want to make this worth something? Go to the library. Read books. Work your mind. Start with the Constitution.' And I knew he was right."

And so Tyson embarked on an astonishing campaign of exuberant and eclectic self-education. Early on he read George Jackson's prison classic, *Soledad Brother,* "and the guy knocked me out. It was like any good book: The guy sounded like he was talking directly to me. I could *hear* him, I can hear him *now*. He made me understand a lot about the way black men end up in prison, but he didn't feel *sorry* for himself. That's what I liked. I got so caught up with this guy, he became a part of my life."

Tyson has been reading black history too. He is fascinated by the revolution in Haiti in the early nineteenth century, "the only *really* successful slave revolt, because blacks took *power.*" He can quote from John Quincy Adams's defense of the slaves who mutinied on the Spanish ship *Amistad* in 1839 off the coast of Cuba and sailed for fifty-five days all the way to New York. "They landed in Long Island," he says. "Imagine! Long *Island.*"

The process of self-education did not begin smoothly. In his first weeks in jail, Tyson enrolled in a school program, then quickly dropped out. "You know, I'm out on the streets, I'm out there, or I'm training, or I'm in the bars, I'm chasing these women. Then I come to this place after not going to school since I was what? Sixteen? Seventeen? They hit me with this thing, they said, 'Bang! Do this, do this work. . . .' It was like putting a preliminary fighter in with a world champion."

Dispirited, angry at the teachers and himself, he dropped out for a while. "Then I started very gradually studying on my own, preparing for these things. Then I took that literacy test — and blew it out of the water."

He went back to classes, studying to take a high school equivalency examination, and met a visiting teacher from Indianapolis named Muhammad Siddeeq.

"He was just talking to the other kids one day and said, 'Does anybody need any help? If so, I'll help you in the school process.' And I said, 'Yeah, I need help.' So he showed me things, in a simple way. . . ."

One thing Tyson learned quickly was the use of percentages and decimals. "I never learned that before," he says, still excited. "It's a small thing, maybe, something I shoulda learned in grammar school. But you come from a scrambled family, you're running between the streets and school, missing days, fucking up, and you end up with these *holes.* One thing never connects to another, and you don't know why. You don't know what you didn't learn. Like percentages. I just never learned it, it was one of the holes. I mean, later on I knew what a percentage was, you know, from a $10 million purse, but I didn't know how to do it myself. That was always the job of *someone else.*" He laughs. "One thing now, I can figure out how to leave a tip. There's restaurants out there where I should eat for free for a couple of years."

He isn't simply filling those gaping holes in his education that should have been bricked up in grammar school. He reads constantly, hungrily, voraciously. One day it could be a book on pigeons, which he raised with great knowledge and affection in the Victorian house where he lived with D'Amato and D'Amato's longtime companion, Camille Ewald, whom Tyson calls "my mother." But on other days he could be reading into the history of organized crime, thrilled to discover that the old Jewish gangsters of Murder Inc. hung out near Georgia and Livonia avenues in Brownsville, walking distance from his own childhood turf. He discovered that Al Capone was from Brooklyn and went west to Chicago. And there were black gangsters too.

He talks about Lucky Luciano, Meyer Lansky, Bugsy Siegel, Frank Costello — some of the Founding Fathers of the Mob — with the same intensity and passion he gave as a teenage fighter to Ray Robinson, Mickey Walker, and Roberto Duran. The old gangster he's most impressed by is the gambler Arnold Rothstein. "He was smart — Damon Runyon called him the Brain — and figured out everything without ever picking up a gun. He helped teach these younger guys, like Lansky and Luciano, you know, how to act, how to dress, how to behave. In *The Great Gatsby* — you know, by this guy F. Scott Fitzgerald? — the gambler called Meyer Wolfshiem, he's based on Arnold Rothstein. I mean, this guy was *big*."

In one way, of course, studying such histories is a consolation; in a country where the percentage of young black males in prisons is way out of proportion to their numbers in the general population, it must be a relief to learn that the Irish, Italians, and Jews once filled similar cells. But Tyson's study of organized crime is part of a larger project.

"I want to find out how things *really* work. Not everything is in the history books, you know." A pause. "Some of those guys didn't like blacks. They sold drugs to blacks. They poisoned black history. They didn't respect us as human beings. But most of them couldn't read and write. The first ones came to this country ignorant, out of school, making money. They didn't have any kind of morals. They wanted to be big shots and they wanted to be respected by decent people. They tried to be gentlemen, and that was their downfall. When you try to be more than what you really are you always get screwed up."

He emphasizes that gangsters are not heroes. "You can read about people without wanting to be like them," he says. "I can read about Hitler, for example, and not want to be like him, right? But you gotta *know* about him. You gotta know what you're talking about. You gotta know what *other* people are talking about before you can have any kind of intelligent discussion or argument."

So it isn't just gangsters or pigeons that are crowding Tyson's mind. He has been poring over Niccolò Machiavelli. "He wrote about the world we live in. The way it really is, without all the bull-shit. Not just in *The Prince*, but in *The Art of War, Discourses.* . . . He saw how important it was to find out what someone's motivation was. 'What do they want?' he says. What do they *want,* man?"

And Voltaire. "I loved *Candide*. That was also about the world and how you start out one thing and end up another, 'cause the world don't let you do the right thing most of the time. And Voltaire himself, he was something, man. He wasn't *afraid*. They kept putting him in jail, and he kept writing the truth."

He has recently read *The Count of Monte Cristo* by Alexandre Dumas, aware that the grandmother of the French writer was a black woman from Haiti. "I identify with that book," he says. "With Ed-mond Dantès in the Château d'If. He was unjustly imprisoned, too. And he gets educated in prison by this Italian priest." He laughs out loud. "And he gets his *revenge* too. I understand that; I feel that. Don't get me wrong, I don't want revenge against any person. I don't mean that. I mean against fate, bad luck, whatever you want to call it."

He is familiar with the Hemingway myth that so exhilarated ear-lier generations of Americans: Hemingway the warrior, Hemingway the hard drinker, Hemingway the boxer. But he talks most passion-ately about Hemingway the *writer*. "He uses those short, hard words, just like hooks and uppercuts inside. You always know what he's saying, 'cause he says it very clearly. But a guy like Francis Bacon, hey, the sentences just go on and on and *on*. . . ."

Obviously, Tyson is not reading literature for simple entertain-ment, as a diversion from the tedium of prison routine. He is making connections between books and writers, noting distinctions about style and ideas, measuring the content of books against his life as he knows it. But he is not taking a formal course in literature, so I asked him one night how he made the choices about what he reads.

"Sometimes it's just the books that come to me. People send them and I read them. But sometimes, most of the time, I'm looking. For example, I'm reading this thing about Hemingway and he says he doesn't ever want to fight ten rounds with Tolstoy. So I say, 'Hey, I better check out this guy Tolstoy!' I did, too. It was *hard*. I sat there with the dictionary beside me, looking up words. But I like him. I don't like his writing that much because it's so complicated, but I just like the guy's way of thinking."

Along with literature, Tyson has been reading biographies: Mao, Karl Marx, Genghis Khan, Hernán Cortés. In casual talk, he scatters references to Hannibal, Alexander the Great, Oliver Cromwell. "When you read about these individuals, regardless of whether they're good or bad, they contribute to us a different way of thinking. But no one can really label them good or bad. Who actually knows the definition of good or bad? Good and bad might have a different definition to me than it may have in *Webster's Dictionary,* than it may have to you."

He knows that for *his* life, the models in books might not always apply. But in all such books, he insists that he finds something of value.

"I was reading Maya Angelou," he said one evening, "and she said something that equates with me so much. People always say how great a writer she is, and people used to say to me, 'Mike, you're great, you could beat anybody, you don't even have to train.' But you know how hard it is for me to do that? To win in ninety-one seconds? Do you know what it takes away from me? And Maya Angelou said about herself it takes so much from me to write, takes a lot out of me. In order for me to do that, she says, to perform at that level, it takes everything. It takes my personality. It takes my creativity as an individual. It takes away my social life. It takes away *so much*. And when she said that, I said, 'Holy moley, this person understands me.' They don't understand why a person can go crazy, when you're totally normal and you're involved in a situation that takes all of your normal qualities away. It takes away all your sane qualities."

In prison Mike Tyson is discovering the many roads back to sanity.

One of those roads is called Islam. Tyson was raised a Catholic by his mother, Lorna, and during the upheaval in that time before he went to jail, he was baptized as a favor to Don King in a much-photographed ceremony presided over by Jesse Jackson. But water, prayer, and photographs didn't make him a born-again Christian.

"That wasn't real," he says now. "As soon as I got baptized, I got one of the girls in the choir and went to a hotel room or my place or something."

Now he has embraced Islam. In a vague way, he'd known about Islam for years; you could not grow up in the era of Muhammad Ali and know nothing about it. "But I was avoiding it because people would press it on me. I always avoided what people pressed on me. They wanted me to do the right thing — and Islam, I believe, is the right thing — but all these people wanted me to do the right thing for the wrong reason."

In prison, through his teacher, Muhammad Siddeeq, Tyson started more slowly, reading on his own about the religion, asking questions. He insists that Siddeeq is not a newer version of Cus D'Amato. "He's just a good man," he says, "and a good teacher." Nor does Tyson sound like a man who is making a convenient choice as a means of surviving in jail. He admits that "there are guys who become Muslims in jail to feel *safe* — and give it up the day they hit the streets again." Tyson might do the same. But in repeated conversations, he sounded as if he'd found in Islam another means of filling some of those holes.

"I believe in Islam," he told me one night. "That's true. It's given me a great deal of understanding. And the Koran gives me insight into the world, and the belief of a man who believes that God has given him the right to speak his word, the prophet Muhammad, peace be unto him. I look at Islam from different perspectives, just as I look at everything else. I find it so beautiful because in Islam you have to tolerate *every* religion, you know what I mean? 'Cause everyone has different beliefs. Most so-called religious leaders are bullshit. Voltaire knew that, knew organized religion was a scam. Their object is power. They want power."

Tyson's skepticism about organized religion includes some of the sects and factions within Islam. He pledges his allegiance to none of them.

"One guy says, 'I believe in Islam, I live out of the Koran.' Well, I believe in *that* but *other* than that, please. . . . They got a sect here and a sect there. Unbelievable. I just don't understand that. How can *I* be a Muslim and *you* be a Muslim, but we have two different beliefs?"

Tyson thinks of Islam as not simply a religion but a kind of discipline. He says he prays five times a day. The Koran is a daily part of his reading (but obviously not the only reading he does). "And you know, I got a sailor's mouth," he laughed. "But I've cut down my cursing at least 50 percent." He clearly needs to believe in something larger than himself, but his choice of Islam is entwined with a revulsion against certain aspects of Christianity.

"If you're a Christian," he says, "and somebody's a Christian longer than you, they can dictate to you about your life. You know, *this* is what you should do, and if you don't do *this*, you're excommunicated. I just found that bizarre . . . in conflict with human qualities, you know what I mean? I couldn't understand why a person couldn't be a human and have problems and just be dealt with and helped. In Islam there's nobody who can put you in your place. They can let you know this is wrong, you need help on this. But the only one that can judge you is Allah."

I asked Tyson how he could reconcile his embrace of Islam with the fact that many of the slave traders were Muslims. The horrors of the Middle Passage often began with men who said they accepted Allah. Tyson answered in a cool way.

"Look, everyone in Arabia was a slave, know what I mean? They had white slaves, black slaves, Arab slaves, Muslim slaves. Everybody there was a slave. But the slave traders were contradicting Islam and the beliefs of Islam. The prophet Muhammad, he wasn't a slave trader or a slave. As a matter of fact, the Arabs were trying to kill him, to enslave him. People were people. But Europeans took slavery to a totally different level. Brutalized, submissive, abhorrent. But you can't condemn all the Jews or all the Romans because they crucified Christ, can you?"

Tyson emphasizes one thing: He's a neophyte in his understanding of Islam and has much to learn.

"Being a Muslim," Tyson says, "is probably not going to make me an angel in heaven, but it's going to make me a better person. In Islam we're not supposed to compete. Muslims only compete for righteousness. I know I'm probably at the back of the line. But I know I'll be a better person when I get out than I was when I came in."

For the moment, jail is the great reality of Tyson's life. Unless a court orders a new trial or overturns his conviction, he will remain in prison until the spring of 1995. The Indiana Youth Center is a medium- to high-security facility and looks relatively tame compared with some of the others I've seen in New York and California. Boredom is the great enemy. "I get up and eat and go to class," he says, explaining that he doesn't eat in the prison dining room, because "the food is *aaaccch*," but goes to a commissary where he can buy packaged milk, cereals, and other food, paying from a drawing account called the Book. He works out in the gym every day, shadowboxing, doing push-ups, running laps to keep his legs strong and lithe. "There's nothing else to do," he says. "You gotta keep busy so you don't go crazy."

But it's still prison. For now it's the place where Mike Tyson is doing time, using all of his self-discipline to get through it alive.

"I'm never on nobody's bad side," he says. "Even though there's guys in here just don't like the way you walk, the way you look, or whatever, I just — I'm never on nobody's bad side. I don't like to be judgmental, because we're all in the same boat. I have to remember to be humble. But sometimes I get caught up with who I was at one time, and I must remind myself my circumstances have changed."

There are still a lot of hard cases on the premises, including Klansmen and members of the Aryan Brotherhood. Tyson laughs about their swastikas, shaved heads, white-power tattoos. "They talk back and forth," he said. "But they realize once they're in prison, no one gives a fuck about them."

More dangerous are people who seem to crack under the stress of doing time. "A couple of days ago, this guy who never bothered nobody just cracked a guy on the head with a lock in his sock," he said in an amazed tone. "And there are other guys — they'll do something disrespectful to some guy, and they'll walk around with their headphones on, acting like they didn't do anything, jamming, dancing, then, next thing you know — *ka-pow!* — they get clocked."

In the bad old days, Tyson might have empathized with such people; he is, after all, the man who as champion once socked an off-duty heavyweight named Mitch Green in Harlem at 4:00 in the morning. But in prison, he is at once part of the general population and detached from it because of his celebrity. "When I get out, I have a future," he says. "A lot of these guys don't." Sometimes he even volunteers for a form of solitary confinement ("to be alone, to focus, to meditate, to read, *to get some fucking sleep*"). But he also looks with compassion on his fellow prisoners.

"They send some guys to prison that don't necessarily have bad records," he says. "Instead of rehabilitating him, they *de*habilitate him by sending him to prison. Without him even being attacked or molested, just from what he witnesses, some things that are so taboo to his humanity. It could totally drive him insane."

Among the scarier aspects of prison these days is AIDS. "They are falling like flies in here," Tyson said. "And some of these guys keep boning each other over in the dorms." There are other people for whom prison is life itself. "There's one guy here who's been inside for thirty-one years. Not in *here* but in other prisons. There are other guys with so much time. . . . I watch them adapt. This is their home. You don't go in their door without knocking."

Tyson said that much of what he has seen is sad and comic at the same time.

"You see a guy, he's doing all the time in a lifetime, he's talking to a girl on a phone. I mean, he's doing *ninety years*. And what's he saying? 'Don't go out tonight, baby. Don't go out tonight, baby. Don't go out tonight, baby.' "

Tyson laughed in a sad, rueful way.

"Most guys that are in here, they got a lot of time, so they lose hope. They get caught up in the sideshows, like homosexuality, drugs, you know what I mean? It's very difficult for me to think about participating in the things these guys do. You talk to the guys, and to me they seem rather sane. But to see their conduct, some of them, they're in a totally insane frame of mind. The fact is, prison is like a slave plantation. We have no rights which the authorities respect. I wasn't a criminal when I got put in here. I didn't commit no crime. But we become the problem *out there*, because we're not aware. We become the problem because out there we're robbing, we're stealing, we're selling drugs, we're killing. I hear people talk about revolution. They mention Castro, Mao, Lenin, the Black Panthers. But how can you have a revolution when you have crime, when you have people selling drugs, you have people murdering? There's no collective ideas there."

I asked Tyson if the young prisoners from Indiana resembled the young men from his Brooklyn neighborhood. He said that many of them did. When he was champion, Tyson refused to offer himself as a role model; he certainly doesn't see himself as one now. But he does understand the Brownsvilles of America.

"At the age of ten or fifteen, you become very influenced by what you see," he said. "You see these guys looking good, with fly cars, nice girls on their arms. You think this is what you want to be. But any kind of proper success has to do with education, unless you're an athlete, and everyone's not going to be Michael Jordan or Muhammad Ali. You fall in bad company. You see drug dealers and gangsters with all their bullshit. You know *they* didn't go to school. So you don't fill the *holes*. You go after the wrong shit. The thing I've noticed in here, with the white kids and the black kids and the Latin kids and the Asian kids — the only thing they have in common is poverty."

I asked him if drugs were another common factor. Tyson himself was never a druggie in the conventional sense; his drugs were liquor and celebrity. He whispered, "Of course.

"Drugs and women," he said. "You know, we all run through the same complexities in life."

Among those many complexities in American life is racism.

"It's very difficult being black," he said one evening. "These reporters came to interview me from South Africa, and one of them asked me was I racist. And I said, 'Yes, I am a racist — to people who are racist toward me.' I never liked to believe that I'm a racist because of the way I was brought up, both from my mother and from Cus and Camille. But, you know what I mean, sometimes things are in the air and people say or do things detrimental or hurtful towards you. You strike back at them. That's what I meant in that interview. Not *all* white people. Shit, no. *Those* people. Those specific people. I just want to be treated the way I treat people."

Behind many of these feelings are jagged memories of that Brownsville childhood. "Too many guys, too many black people, men and women, *hate* themselves. They see the shit around them and they give up before they ever start. They get one or two little tastes of power — sticking a gun in somebody's face — and then it's over."

He was in jail when the riots erupted in Los Angeles, and he hated what he saw on CNN.

"It could have all been prevented if people believed in fairness and equality. But you have to understand: The things that people do and what they *should* do are totally different. We should live like every man is equal, every woman is equal. But how we *do* live is, You get yours, I get mine, fuck you." He talked about Rodney King. "Some guys in here, they heard Rodney King and they laughed. But what he said was powerful, man. Why *can't* we live together? Why the *fuck* can't we all live together?"

In jail Mike Tyson is engaged in an admirable attempt to find out who he is, to discover and shape the man who exists behind the surface of fame and notoriety. There is no Cus to explain the world, to tell him what to do. In the end, there's only himself. And because he is in prison, this is no easy process.

"You have good days, and you have bad days, but you just think to yourself, *This isn't the end.* You say, 'I was kind of wild out there; maybe I was heading for something more drastic.' Which is all a part of playing head games so you won't get insane."

Like anyone in prison, Tyson misses life on the outside. He misses certain people, and in most of our talks he circles back to Cus D'Amato. "A lot of things Cus told me, they are happening now," he says. "But at that time, I didn't keep them in mind, because I was just a kid. Cus tried to store everything in my mind so fast. He didn't think that he was gonna be around. He tried to pack everything in at one moment, you know what I mean? I'm trying to be a fighter, I'm trying to have some fun on the side, and I'm just running crazy. Now I think about him all the time. Like, damn! Cus told me that. And God! He told me *this* too. And, oh! He told me that.

"He was always saying to me, before I was anything: 'What are you gonna do? Look how you talk to me *now,*' he said. 'Look how you act. How you gonna act when you're a *big-time fighter?* You're just gonna dump me.' I said, 'I'm not gonna do that, Cus. I'm not gonna do it.' And I didn't." He laughs. "I used to say, 'Cus, I'll sell my soul to be a great fighter.' And he said, 'Be careful what you wish for, 'cause you might get it.'

"I miss him still. I miss him. I think about him. No, I don't dream about him; I don't dream much in this place. But I miss Cus. I still take care of him, make sure nothing bad happens, 'cause I promised Cus before he died to take care of Camille. I was young, I was, like, eighteen, and I said, 'I can't fight if you're not around, Cus.' And he said, 'You better fight, 'cause if you don't fight, I'm gonna come back and haunt you.'"

The ghost of Cus D'Amato doesn't haunt Tyson; if anything, the old manager instilled in the young man a respect for knowledge and a demand for discipline that are only now being fully developed. "Cus had flaws, like any man," Tyson says. "But he was right most of the time. One thing I remember most clearly that he said: 'Your brain is a muscle like any other; if you don't use it, it gets soft and flabby.'"

Other things do haunt Tyson. One of them is that fatal trip to Indianapolis. "I had a dick problem," he admits. "I didn't even want to go to Indianapolis. But I went. I'm in town with the best girl [rapper B Angie B] that everybody wants. And I had to get this — why'd I have to do that, huh, man? Why'd I have to do that? I had a girl *with* me. Why'd I have to make that call? Why'd I have to let her come to my room?"

He has his regrets too, and says that he is trying hard to acquire some measure of humility, leaning on the Koran.

"Remember, when I accomplished all that I did, I was just a kid," he says quietly. "I was just a kid doing all that crazy stuff. I wanted to be like the old-time fighters, like Harry Greb or Mickey Walker, who would drink *and* fight. But a lot of the things I did I'm so embarrassed about," he says. "It was very wrong and disrespectful for me to dehumanize my opponents by saying the things I said. If you could quote me, say that anything I ever said to any fighters that *they* remember — like making Tyrell Biggs cry like a girl, like putting a guy's nose into his brain, like making Razor Ruddock my girlfriend — I'm deeply sorry. I will appreciate their forgiveness."

He isn't just embarrassed by the words he said to fighters. "I have girls that wrote to me and said they met me in a club," he says. "And I said something crazy to them. And I *know* I said that, you know, 'cause that was my style. And I say, wow, what was going through my *mind* to say that? I don't dwell on it too much. But I just think: *What the* hell *was I thinking?* To say this to another human being?"

Tyson tries to live in the present tense of jail, containing his longing for freedom through a sustained act of will. But when I pressed him one evening, he admitted that he does yearn for certain aspects of the outside world.

"I miss the very simple things," he says. "I miss a woman sexually. But more important, I miss the pleasure of being in a woman's presence. To speak to a woman in private and discuss things. Not just Oh! Oh! Oh! More subtle than that. I just want to be able to have privacy, where no one can say, 'Time, Tyson! Let's go!' You miss being with people. I miss flying my birds. They're not gonna know me, I'm not gonna know them, 'cause there're so many new ones now 'cause of the babies. I miss being able to hang out. Talk to Camille. Laugh. I miss long drives. Sometimes I used to just get in the car and drive to Washington. I miss that a lot. I miss, sometimes, going to Brooklyn in the middle of the night, pulling up in front of the projects and one of my friends will be there, shooting baskets. I'll get out of the car, and we'll talk there, like from 4:00 in the morning until 9:00 or 10:00. People are going to work, and we're just talking." A pause. "I miss that."

He insists that he doesn't miss what he calls the craziness. "It was all unreal. Want to go to Paris? Want to fly to Russia? Sure. Why not? Let me have two of those and three of them and five of those. Nobody knows what it's like — fame, millions — unless they went through it. It was unreal, unreal. I had a thousand women, the best champagne, the fanciest hotels, the fanciest cars, the greatest meals — and it got me here."

He does have some specific plans for the future. "I want to visit all the great cities, I want to see the great *libraries*," he says. "One of the few things I did that impressed me was going to Paris that time and visiting the Louvre. I was *devastated* by that place, man. I want to see all of that, everywhere."

Yes, he said, he will box again. He will be twenty-eight when he returns, the same age as Ali when he made his comeback and certainly younger than George Foreman when he made his. He asks repeatedly about active fighters and how they looked in their latest bouts, because he only sees brief clips on CNN. "I'm a fighter," he says. "That's what I do. I was born to do that."

He wants to make money; nobody knows how much Tyson has left, not even Tyson, but his return to boxing could be the most lucrative campaign in the history of sport. "I want to have money for a family," he says. "In the end, that's how you can decide what kind of man I was. Not by how many guys I knocked out. But by the way I took care of my kids, how I made sure they went to college, that they had good lives and never wanted for nothing. And what I taught them. About the world. About character."

Tyson would even like to try college himself. "I'd like to go to a black college that's not well-known," he says, "to study and learn. But also to have some kind of exhibitions, too, fights to benefit the college. I don't have to fight benefits for a church or a mosque. But the black colleges, *that* I want to do. . . ."

In the end, of course, all education is self-education, and Tyson is clearly deep into the process. The faculty of Tyson's university includes Cus D'Amato and Alexandre Dumas, Machiavelli and the prophet Muhammad, Dutch Schultz and Ernest Hemingway, and dozens of others. Part of the curriculum includes what some academics call life experience. There are millions of college graduates who don't know what Tyson knows. About writers and thinkers. About life itself.

"A lot of people get the misconception that by being free that you're *free*," he says. "That's not necessarily true. There's people on the outside who are more in prison than I'll ever be in here." He chuckles. "You know, it's human to fall. But it's a crime to stay down and not get up after you fall. You must get up."

In the visitor's lounge at the Indiana Youth Center, he smiles when a woman offers to buy him a soda. "Sorry, thank you, but I don't drink soda." He looks at his hands. Twenty-two months earlier, he'd come to this elaborate cage like a man knocked down. When he started school, he got to one knee. Now he's standing up.

"I know this," he says. "When I get out, I'm gonna be in charge of my own life. I used to leave it to others. I'd say, 'Hey, I'm the boss.' But then I'd leave it to people, to Cus, to Don King, whatever. But that's what you do when you're a kid. You can't do that when you're a man."

I utter some banality about the dangers that might still confront him on the outside, how powerful the pull of the ghetto spirit might be when the bad guys from the neighborhood come calling on him again.

"Well, that's no problem anymore," he says and laughs. "They're all dead."

He turns and glances at the picture window. Fat white snowflakes are now falling from the steel-colored sky, out there in the world of highways, car washes, diners, and motels. Another prisoner's name is called, and a black man rises and touches his woman's face. Time is running out.

"Sometimes I get so frustrated in here, I just want to cry," says the fighter who once described himself as the baddest man on the planet. "But I don't. I can't. Because years from now, when this is long behind me, I want to know I went through it like a man. Not to impress anyone else. But to know it *myself*, know what I mean?"

A departing visitor nods, recognizing Tyson, and he nods back, a look granted like an autograph. He turns to me again, his hands kneading each other, his right leg bouncing like a timepiece.

"When you die, nothing matters but the dash," Tyson says abruptly. "On your tombstone, it says 1933–2025, or something like that. The only thing that matters is that dash. That dash is your life. How you live is your life. And were you happy with the way you lived it."

A guard calls Tyson's name now. Time is up. Tyson rises slowly. He tells me to send his best to friends in New York. He promises to stay in touch. We embrace awkwardly. He looks as if he wants to freeze the moment, freeze time itself. Then he turns and nods politely to the guard and flashes a final goodbye grin to his visitor.

"Take care," number 922335 says, and returns to the world of rules, to sleep another night where the snow never falls.

ESQUIRE,
March 1994

MADONNA

Of this we can be certain: Madonna is the greatest artistic force of the AIDS generation. As a sex symbol, she is all we have, but she is a lot more than that. It doesn't matter that she can't sing very well, that she's an ordinary dancer, that there are many women of more refined beauty. She is the triumphant mistress of her medium: the sexual imagination. In an age when real sex can lead to horror and death, here is Madonna — reckless, bawdy, laughing and offering us all the consolation of outrageous illusions.

In almost every version of her public self, Madonna appears as a fearless sexual adventurer, sharing sex with strangers, colliding with rough trade, risking pain or humiliation to break through to pleasure beyond all conventional frontiers. With music, dance and, above all, image, she challenges organized religion, the middle class that spawned her, political hypocrisies and what George Orwell called "the smelly little orthodoxies." Follow me, ye weak of heart, she says. Up ahead lies the big O! Nirvana! Fearless fucking! Just roll the dice.

What saves this performance from preposterous narcissism is a simple corrective: There's a wink in the act. While Madonna presents her latest illusion, a hint of a smile tells us that we shouldn't take any of it too seriously. She always hedges her bet with camp, elegant caricature and a style appropriated from the gay underworld on the eve of AIDS.

That style was part of the exuberant rush that accompanied gay liberation, when the doors of many closets flew open and out came leather and chains and whips, every variety of mask, anonymous multiple couplings and a self-conscious insistence on sex as performance. Before she became a star, Madonna moved through that world in New York. Today she presents it as a glossy nostalgia, tempered with irony and served up to everyone from suburban teenagers to aging baby boomers. They all seem to love it.

Without that ironic wink, of course, she would be as square as Jesse Helms. But Madonna is hip to something huge: AIDS made sexual freedom a ghastly joke. At the point where the sexual revolution had triumphed for everyone, the most ferocious sexually transmitted disease of the century arrived, wearing a death's-head from some medieval woodcut. Every artist was forced to confront it, just as 19th century artists were hammered into dealing with syphilis. Some artistic responses to AIDS were moving and tragic; too many were runny with self-pity. But Madonna came roaring into the room in a spirit of defiance. She would not go gentle into that good night.

But she also knew that the only completely safe sex is the sex you can imagine — that is, an illusion. If you can't have something you desire with every atom of your flesh and blood, you must be content with a gorgeous counterfeit. That insight became the armature of her work. And she elaborated on it with a shrewd understanding of sexual psychology: The most reliable erogenous zone is the human mind, and the libido feeds on images, not ideas.

Like Michael Jackson, Madonna vaulted to stardom with videos, a form thick with imagery that sometimes triumphs over the banality of lyrics. Jackson's images were charged with rage, Madonna's with frank and open carnality. But as the Eighties went on, as the graves filled with the young dead, as AIDS defied a cure, Madonna's images became more obviously infused with a dark comic spirit. It was as if she were saying: I know this is a lie and you know this is a lie, but it's all we have.

This surrender to illusion is at once daring and sad. Most American performers spend their careers trying to convince us that their lies are the truth. Madonna is braver than most and more original: She says openly that her lies are lies. She asks you only to admire the form of the lies. This was itself a breakthrough for a pop artist. Until Madonna, the basic task of any performer was to persuade the audience to suspend its disbelief. Frank Sinatra or Billie Holiday wanted us to believe that their grieving lyrics and aching tones expressed the pain and hurt of the performers themselves. A millionaire such as Mick Jagger wanted us to believe he was a working-class hero or a street fighting man. But Madonna says something else. Don't suspend your disbelief, she implies. Disbelief is the basic point.

I went to the publication party for her book, *Sex,* and, like the book, the party was a celebration of the counterfeit. Scattered around Industria, the city's hottest photo studio, were many extraliterary diversions: actresses dressed as nuns pretending to offer blasphemous pleasures; peroxide blond androids languidly flogging each other with strips of licorice; black dancers in chains and leather; writhing gym-toned bodies; many undulating bellies; much bumping and grinding. Everything, in short, except actual fucking. And that, of course, was the point: This wasn't real and the audience knew it wasn't real.

Madonna's video *Erotica* was playing continually, shot in the grainy black-and-white style of Forties porno films. But it wasn't a real porno film. It was fake porno. Ah, yes: I remember Paris. The Germans wore gray and you wore nothing. Nostalgia remains the most powerful of all American emotions.

Sex went on to become the number-one best-seller in the nation, assisted by the hype but also driven by the genius of Madonna. And that might tell us something about America.

Books have taught us that love is an illusion but sex is real. For millions of Americans, that old formulation appears to have been reversed. You can experience love, but anything more than the illusion of sex is too dangerous. The possibility of death is always a marvelous corrective to human behavior. But if such an immense change is, in fact, under way, its poster girl is Madonna. Sometimes life really does imitate art.

PLAYBOY,
April 1993

FOSSE

osse was dead and after the urgent calls and the logistics of death, there seemed nothing really to do about it except go for a walk along Broadway in the midnight rain.

This was the square mile of the earth Bob Fosse cared for more than any other. Up there on the second floor at 56th Street was the rehearsal hall where I'd met him years ago. Around the corner was the Carnegie Deli, where he'd have lunch with Paddy Chayefsky and Herb Gardner, trading lines, drinking coffee, smoking all those goddamned cigarettes. On the 11th floor of 850 Seventh Avenue, he and Chayefsky and Gardner had their separate offices, and from Paddy's they would often gaze in wonder across the back courtyard of the Hotel Woodward, at the man in underwear who was always shaving, no matter what the hour. A few blocks away was the building where Fosse lived the last decade of his life.

And down the rain-drowned avenue was the sleazy hamlet I always thought of as Fosseville: all glitter and neon and dangerous shadows. This wasn't Runyon's fairy-tale Broadway; it was harder, meaner, as reliable in its ruthlessness as a switchblade. Yet even in his most cynical years, Fosse insisted on seeing its citizens as human, observing their felonies and betrayals not as a journalist or a sociologist but as the fine artist he was. "I see a hooker on a corner," he said to me once, "and I can only think: there's some kinda story there. I mean, she was once six years old. . . ." On this late night, I could see Fosse in black shirt and trousers, standing in some grimy doorway, looking out at his lurid parish; he had been young here and almost died here and sometimes fled from the place and always came back. In Fosseville the gaudiest dreams existed side by side with the most vicious betrayals; everything was real but nothing was true. And, of course, he believed in some dark way that all could be redeemed by love.

Nobody loved harder. He loved his wives: Mary Ann Niles, who danced with him in the last years of the nightclub era (and who died a year after Fosse), Joan McCracken, who died on him when they were both young, and Gwen Verdon, who was with him when he lay down for the final time on the grass of a small park in Washington. But Fosse wasn't one of those men who can be married; the emotional core of his masterpiece, *All That Jazz,* is not so much the romantic attraction of death, but the impossibility of fidelity. There were simply too many beautiful women in this world, with their grace and style and intelligence and mystery; the demand of monogamy was like ordering a man to love only one Vermeer.

And so he loved many women; most were dancers and actresses, because in the world where he worked they were the women he met. He treated all of them with the same grace. I saw him most often when he was between women; he was then usually engulfed by a bleakly romantic sense of loss (although the only remorse he ever expressed was about Gwen). When he met a new woman, when he was swept away, he would vanish from his usual precincts; no male friends were as important as a woman or the possibility of love.

It was no accident that he always celebrated women in his work, although he was hardly an illustrator of feminist dogma. In the '50s and '60s, half the men I knew were in love with Gwen Verdon, who on stage combined humor, vulnerability, toughness, and sensuality in shows designed, choreographed, directed by Fosse. She always moved the tough guys most of all. "Every time I see her," the sportswriter Jimmy Cannon said of Gwen, "I want to run away with her." When *Damn Yankees* was in its long run, Paul Sann, the greatest newspaperman I ever knew, said of Gwen one night: "You better go see her now, kid, 'cause you ain't gonna see anything like her again on Broadway for the rest of your fucking life." About Gwen Verdon, as about so many things, Sann was absolutely right.

But if it's forever impossible to separate Fosse from Gwen, he was also a fine director of other women. Liza Minnelli, Valerie Perrine, and Anne Reinking did their best work with Fosse. He was one of the few directors to see *King Kong* and recognize that Jessica Lange could be a superb actress; later they would become lovers, and he would cast her as the Angel of Death in *All That Jazz.* It was entirely appropriate, of course, that Fosse would imagine death as a woman, thus merging his two most passionate obsessions.

But he loved other things too: almost all forms of music; nightclub comics; cheap vaudeville jokes (Q. "Do you file your nails?" A. "No, I throw them away . . ."); the New York Mets; good food (he spent hours cooking in the huge kitchen of the house in Quogue, bringing his perfectionism to the details of the simplest meal); Fred Astaire (there were no pictures of himself in the Quogue house and two of Astaire); air hockey; children; *New York Post* headlines; boxing and football; his daughter Nicole; good wine, margaritas, and brandy; his cat, Macho, a stray discovered beaten-up and bloodied in the Quogue grasslands and nursed to plump domesticity; and, of course, those goddamned cigarettes.

After family and lovers, he admired writers more than anyone else. Among his friends were Gardner and Chayefsky, E. L. Doctorow, Peter Maas, and Budd Schulberg. Although he liked to affect the I'm-only-a-song-and-dance-man pose, Fosse was a careful, intelligent reader. His writer friends knew how high Fosse's own standards were (whether he failed or succeeded, he never set out to manufacture crap) and they often responded to his subtle urgings that they do better. Some writers who worked with him were angry at the end, as he demanded from them what he could more easily demand from a dancer; those who didn't work with him had easier friendships.

Yes, Fosse was competitive, and cared (perhaps too much) about the way he stood in relation to other directors. In 1974, after he had his first ferocious heart attack, Gardner and Chayefsky were summoned to Fosse's hospital room to serve as witnesses to his will. There were two lawyers waiting. Fosse was in critical condition in his bed, silent and trapped in a ganglia of tubes and wires. The lawyers asked the two writers to sign the will; Gardner did so immediately. But Chayefsky insisted on reading the text. He discovered that Fosse hadn't left him anything, so he turned to the silent Fosse and said: "Fuck you, *live!*" Fosse started to laugh; all measuring devices began to go wild; the lawyers blanched; a platoon of nurses arrived to save Fosse's life. Finally, all was calmed down again. Chayefsky resumed reading the will, while Fosse lay silent. Then Paddy came to a provision that reserved $20,000 for a party for Fosse's friends. Hey, that's great, Chayefsky said, it's just what Josh Logan did. For the first time, Fosse spoke.

"How much did Logan leave for the party?" he said, in a thin weak voice.

"Twenty thousand," said Chayefsky.

"Make mine twenty-five," said Fosse, falling back, as Chayefsky and Gardner dissolved into laughter. That visit probably saved his life.

Quite simply, Fosse wanted to be the best at what he did. In that impossibly romantic quest, he drove dancers hard (although never harder than he drove himself) and kept demanding more from his stars. He worked hard at understanding actors, studying with San-ford Meisner, reading the basic texts from Stanislavski to Harold Clurman. And he developed his own ways to get his actors to do their best work.

"He could act incredibly humble when he wanted something from you," said Roy Scheider, who believes his own best work was in *All That Jazz*. "When he met someone he wanted for the first time, he knew everything about you. He'd done research, he'd seen your movies or plays. He'd say, 'You know, you were very good in that part, hey, wait, you got a nomination, didn't you? You *won*.' And there'd be a pause, after he did all this praising. And then he'd say how *that* was nothing compared to what lies ahead in your work with me. And he made you *believe* it. And then he *did* it. . . . After three, four meetings you'd be thoroughly convinced that you were not capable of giving him what he wanted. And then he would begin to build your confidence, making you feel that your *reflowering* would take place in *his* show." Scheider laughed. "You see, for him, it was always being done for posterity. Every time out of the chute, it was for history."

Because he worked so hard, and because he knew how much pain was involved in the making of a show or a movie, Fosse generally despised critics. He thought they saw too much and, as a result, their sensibilities were blunted, making them unable to respond to amazing theatrical moments in the way an audience might. They were all too glib, dismissing (or praising) two years of another's work in a review dashed off in an hour. He thought critics were primarily responsible for the failure of *Star 80* (based on Teresa Carpenter's brilliant article for the *Voice*); when *Big Deal* opened to lukewarm reviews last year and then closed after 100-odd performances, he was disheartened.

"Maybe all they want are Eddie Murphy movies or sets that sing," he said. "Maybe all they want is shit. Maybe it's over for people like me."

But he was still working at the end; trying to choose between a movie about Walter Winchell, a movie version of *Chicago*, probably with Madonna, or something completely new. During the summer, we talked a few times about his experiences during the Second World War, when he was a 17-year-old sailor working in an entertainment unit in the South Pacific; he was with the first Americans to enter Japan at the end of the war and was still horrified at the scale of the destruction in Tokyo and the stupidly brutal way so many American soldiers treated the Japanese, particularly the women. "It still makes me sick," he said. "That was the first time I was really ashamed to be an American." The contrast between the idealism of fighting the war and the morally corrosive realities of victory was a splendid setup for a Fosse movie, but Fosse was uneasy about it. "That world is gone, that music, the way people were. . . . Most of the country wouldn't know what I was talking about."

Now we'll never know. The night after we all got the news, there was a small gathering at Gardner's apartment, a kind of secular wake. Some wept; others told the old stories, with examples of Fosse's dark humor; all were in shock, because Fosse had been looking better than at any time in years. Later, wandering through Broadway in the rain, I thought that for Fosse, who so perfectly expressed a certain vision of New York, the worst thing about dying in Washington might have been that he closed out of town.

VILLAGE VOICE,
November 3, 1987

PART VI

POSITION
PAPERS

These are pieces about certain aspects of American society in the last decade of the century. They were written by an American liberal who had come to distrust all dogma, including liberal dogma. For me, liberalism must be tolerant, generous, intelligent, and humane or it is no longer liberal. If social systems created by liberals — the welfare system, for example — no longer function for the good of human beings, it is stupid to defend them simply because they have been entered into some aging liberal catechism. They must be changed, gradually and humanely, and replaced with something better.

It is also foolish for liberals to refuse to recognize uncomfortable truths. They need to look at racism as it exists now, not as it did while Martin Luther King was marching in the streets of the American South. They must identify and condemn white racism *and* black racism. They must separate the race hustlers from those seriously concerned about growth and progress. They must move beyond habits of complaint and blame to the creation of enduring solutions.

Above all, they must reject grim sectarianism, whether practiced by radical feminists, the Christian Coalition, or Louis Farrakhan. They must be wary of exclusively legalistic solutions to deep societal problems. They must laugh at any insistence that an individual human being can be completely explained by the group to which he or she belongs. Liberals can't be the thought police or the speech police or the gender police. They can't go around all day telling strangers to put out their cigarettes. They can't call the district attorney to solve problems of manners. They have to lighten up. They have to recover the confident, exuberant style of the liberal America that once believed we could have justice and the racetrack too. They have to do it soon. The other guys are at the three-quarter pole and pulling away.

BLACK AND WHITE AT BROWN

When I was young and laboring as a sheetmetal worker in the Brooklyn Navy Yard, I sometimes imagined myself as a student on a college campus. This impossible vision of the Great Good Place was constructed from scraps of movies and magazine photographs, and was for me a combination of refuge and treasurehouse. The hard world of tenements and street gangs was replaced in my imagination with buildings made of red brick laced with ivy, and a wide, safe quadrangle where ancient oaks rose majestically to the sky. There was an immense library, offering the secrets of the world. The teachers were like Mr. Chips, at once stern, wise, passionate, and kind. And, of course, there were impossibly beautiful women, long of limb and steady of eye, talking about Fitzgerald or Hemingway, walking beside me on winter evenings with snow melting in their hair.

I never made it. I went to other schools of higher learning: the Navy, Mexico, newspapers. I had absolutely no regrets. But when I walked onto the campus at Brown University recently, that old vision came flooding back. There before me were the buildings, the trees, the open quadrangle that I had ached for as a boy. There were the lights, like molten gold, in the library. There were the fine young women. I wondered how anyone here could be unhappy.

But I knew that at Brown, and on many similar campuses around the nation, the malignant viruses of the outside world had proved impossible to resist. The worst of these was that ancient curse: racism. Last year, the Justice Department reported racial incidents on seventy-seven campuses, from state universities to the most elite academies, ranging from jokes to full-scale brawls. This was an increase of almost 50 percent over the year before, and Brown, the most liberal of the eight Ivy League schools, was not immune. This struck me as a heartbreaking phenomenon. I grew up believing that racism was a consequence of ignorance. But 80 percent of the students at Brown had finished in the top 10 percent of their high schools. If they were racist, the nation was doomed. I went to take a look.

At the Wriston Quad, everyone I saw was white. At the other campus, called Pembroke (it was once a separate school, for young women), blacks chose to "hang" with blacks. On a visit to a cafeteria, I noticed blacks generally sat with blacks, whites with whites. I heard tales (from whites) of pledges from one of the black fraternities marching around campus in paramilitary style ("They look like the Fruit of Islam, for Christ's sake"). I heard blacks complain about white "insensitivity," or outright racism (shouts of "nigger" from white fraternity houses, watermelon jokes). Whites who called themselves liberals complained about black separatism, symbolized by the hermetic clustering of blacks around the college's Third World Center. One white student said, "It's self-segregation, and they've chosen it, not us." One black student said, "When the whites see more than two blacks at a time, they think about calling the cops instead of saying hello."

None of this, of course, was like Mississippi in the '50s, when the White Citizens Councils owned the night. But it wasn't trivial, either. Many of the discussions here referred to two distinct series of events: The Incidents and The Attacks. The Incidents took place last spring. In April racist graffiti appeared in the West Andrews residence hall on the Pembroke campus. The message NIGGERS GO HOME was found in an elevator, MEN and WOMEN were crossed out on lavatory doors and replaced by WHITES and NIGGERS. Racist words were also written on the doors of minority students' rooms and on posters.

Then, on April 28, a flyer appeared on a bathroom mirror, again in West Andrews. It said: "Once upon a time, Brown was a place where a white man could go to class without having to look at little black faces, or little yellow faces or little brown faces, except when he went to take his meals. Things have been going downhill since the kitchen help moved into the classroom. Keep white supremecy [sic] alive! Join the Brown chapter of the KKK today."

Brown president Vartan Gregorian reacted the next day with righteous fury. He addressed a crowd of 1,500 students on the Green, threatened to expel anyone guilty of spreading racism or homophobia, and said, "There are many outlets for racism and bigotry in this country. Brown will not be one of them, I assure you of that." By all accounts, it was a tough, persuasive performance. Students later presented Gregorian with that quintessential element of the '60s, a List of Demands. He answered them the following week, and although his petitioners weren't completely satisfied, the racist graffiti stopped. The identity of the faceless yahoo was never discovered.

In the fall, The Attacks started. Within a period of three months, twenty-seven students were assaulted in the streets immediately adjacent to the Brown campus. All but four of the victims were white. All of the attackers were young blacks. Seven of the assaults were accompanied by robberies, but the others appeared to be simple cases of underclass black kids arbitrarily beating the crap out of rich white kids. On one level, they were a variation on traditional town-gown conflicts. But the racial factor was impossible to ignore. Gregorian was angered again, called for help from the Providence mayor and police chief, beefed up campus security, but was reluctant publicly to characterize The Attacks as racially motivated. "Until we have clear evidence one way or the other," he said in a letter to parents, "we are treating them as what, in all cases, they clearly were — assaults or assault and battery."

But on campus, there was a continuing discussion of the racial context of the violence. Some black students said that the outsiders were aware of The Incidents in the spring and The Attacks were their way of striking back at racism. This interpretation — the Mugger as Freedom Fighter — infuriated other students. Some whites noted that the organized black students were quick to complain about words directed at blacks, but were generally silent when punches were directed at whites.

"The blacks don't want to admit that there's black racism," one white student told me. A black student seemed to confirm this: "There can't be black racism, it objectively can't exist. When a man fights back against his oppressor, that's not racism."

Out there in the real world, of course, there is as much evidence of black racism as there is of white racism. I've met West Indian blacks who look down upon American blacks, light-skinned blacks who can't abide dark-skinned blacks, southern blacks of the old Creole aristocracy who are uneasy with (or terrified by) the homeboys from the housing projects, and blacks of all classes and pigments who hate whites because they are white. Racism is a grand refusal to see individuals as individuals, each responsible for his or her own actions. No race is immune to the virus.

But at Brown, there are some specific institutions that seem to exacerbate the wounds they are intended to heal. All freshman minority students are invited to come to the campus three days early to take part in the Third World Transition Program (TWTP). The intention of the program is honorable: to help minority students feel comfortable in this new environment, where whites are in the majority. Hearing about it from some minority students, I realized that if I'd ever made it to a place like Brown, I might have been singled out for the same kind of help, as a Catholic among Wasps, as a semihood from Brooklyn among the gentry. I also knew that I would have resisted with full fury any attempt to register me in the Street Punk Transition Program. I'd have held off anybody who draped a fatherly arm over my shoulder to tell me I had been so severely maimed by poverty that I needed special help.

So I found myself agreeing with much of the criticism of the TWTP at Brown. It is race-driven; it assumes that nonwhites are indeed different from other Americans, mere bundles of pathologies, permanent residents in the society of victims, and therefore require special help. "They're made to feel separate from the first day they arrive," one alumnus said. "And they stay separate for the next four years." During those three intense days of TWTP, critics say, friendships are forged within a group that excludes whites. By the time white students arrive on campus, defensive cliques have already been formed, racist slights or insensitivities are expected (perhaps even welcomed as proof of the victim theory), and the opportunity for blacks to know whites more intimately (and vice versa) is postponed during a long process of testing that is sometimes permanent.

The term *Third World,* as used at Brown, is itself laughable; I can't believe that even a semiconscious professor would allow such slovenly usage in the classroom. The grouping includes, for example, Japanese and Japanese-American students in an era when Japan is virtually the center of the First World. It also includes those minority students from financially privileged backgrounds who came down the track of prep schools and grew up infinitely more comfortable than most whites. Alas, at Brown, *Third World* is not used to describe people from developing nations (or from economically deprived sectors of the U.S.); it is a racial concept that includes everyone who is not Caucasian.

That some forms of racism exist at Brown and other campuses is undeniable; they are American institutions, after all, and there is racism in American society at all levels. But after I talked with students, faculty, administrators, and a few alumni, the deeper reasons for the emergence of campus racism remained vague and provisional. In one report, Gregorian suggested some possibilities: "The economic dislocations of the 1980s, a shared sense of 'brotherhood and risk,' ignorance of the civil rights struggles of the '60s and '70s, rampant consumerism, cynicism, narcissism." The Reagan years.

There are other possibilities. Many of today's college students were born in the '60s. The more radical students might have a certain nostalgia for that era, when the goal of every young American wasn't limited to the service of greed. There could be other factors: the growing stupidity of all Americans, the decay of high schools, a reaction to twenty years of affirmative-action programs that are perceived by some as giving blacks unearned advantages, a spreading reaction to the disorder of the underclass. I don't have a single explanation for the phenomenon of campus racism, and I don't think anybody else does, either.

But walking around campus, talking to students, I found my own reactions shifting between anger and envy. In their desire to be what Brown students call P.C. (politically correct), some of these privileged young people seemed to be denying themselves the fullest experience of the social and intellectual feast at which they were guests. Too many black students were postponing (perhaps losing) the chance to learn to function in the country Out There, where blacks make up only 13 percent of the population and where, for good or bad, true power is attained through compromise and connection. Instead of getting to know white people (thus demystifying them, forging alliances with them on the basis of a common experience), the separatists substitute too much '60s-style oratory about empowerment for hard thought. They waste precious hours on such arcane matters as whether the words *black* or *African American* are P.C.

Worse, by insisting upon being special cases, by institutionalizing the claim of victimhood, by using imprecise nomenclature ("white America," whatever that might be), they become perfect foils for true racists. On campus, those whites who might start with a vague prejudice against blacks find easy reasons to give it a hardened form. White liberals, committed to integration, throw up their hands (often too easily) and give their energies to other matters. News of this is both infuriating and sad. If anything, black students with true pride in themselves and their race should be commanding the destruction of the patronizing, self-limiting concept of a Third World ghetto on campus. That would take some courage. But in an era when all of Orwell's "smelly little orthodoxies" are being swept away, nobody should waste a single precious hour on being politically correct. There's too much to do Out There.

That was the basis for my feelings of envy. These young people were the most fortunate of all Americans. While some of them continued arguing the gnarled social issues of the postwar period, *their* century was being shaped by the great change sweeping across the Soviet Union and Central Europe. The wasteful ideological contests that had mauled my generation were swiftly becoming obscure. That meant these young people were free to enter a new century that might be infinitely better than the dreadful one now coming to its exhausted end. And they could only make that exciting passage with the intellectual tools they acquired at places like Brown. With any luck, in *their* time even the new idiocies of racism would become a wan memory.

So I envied them that splendid prospect as I did their certainties, and their passion, and yes, the red-brick buildings and those libraries, and all the fine young women coming across the quad in the wintry light with snow melting in their hair.

ESQUIRE,
April 1990

THE NEW RACE HUSTLE

That morning, my wife and I drove across the Brooklyn Bridge, listening to talk radio. We could have been in any of a hundred other cities in America because, on the radio, the Legion of the Invincibly Stupid was already hammering away at the remnants of our common civility. Whites slandered blacks and blacks returned their oratorical volleys, while the host fueled the ugly duel. As we plunged deeper into Brooklyn, news bulletins fed the talkers: The trials of two whites charged with killing a black youth in Bensonhurst moved toward verdicts; a black boycott of two Korean grocery stores continued into its fifth month; a Vietnamese man was in critical condition, his head broken by a black kid who called him a "Korean motherfucker" while beating him senseless with a claw hammer. Ah, the melting pot. O ye gorgeous mosaic.

We parked beside the second-oldest church in the city, its Dutch stolidity and simple, combed lawns summoning images of a time long gone, and then walked a few blocks to the boycotted Korean store. My wife, Fukiko, was uneasy. She is a Japanese writer; if Vietnamese could be mistaken for Korean, so could Japanese. There have been signs that Asians are increasingly becoming targets of various forms of American resentment. In 1982 two Detroit autoworkers beat to death a Chinese American named Vincent Chin, thinking he was one of those terrible Japanese who had "ruined" the American auto industry. All through the '80s, other patriots burned crosses or tossed bombs at the homes of Vietnamese in Texas, Florida, and California. Cambodians have been attacked in Boston. Last year, in Stockton, California, a man walked into a school yard with a machine gun, murdered five children from Southeast Asia, and wounded many more. If you're Asian, it can get scary out there.

But on this morning, there was more posturing and rhetoric than danger. About fifteen picketers were in the gutter outside the Red Apple grocery store. They were protesting because one of the Korean shopkeepers had quarreled with a fifty-two-year-old Haitian woman over the price of some plantains and limes and then — the woman claimed — assaulted her. The picketers occasionally chanted slogans ("Koreans out! Shut 'em down!"), screamed at blacks who were breaking the boycott ("Traitor! Traitor!"), glowered for TV cameras, and refused to speak to reporters, including my wife. "They think all reporters are racists," said a black TV reporter. "Even me." The racism charge was amusing — in a ghastly way. The black picketers had spent weeks shouting slogans about chopsticks and fortune cookies at their Korean targets; they had called them "yellow monkeys"; one of their major supporters was a race hustler named Sonny Carson, a convicted kidnapper who insisted last year that he wasn't antisemitic, he was anti*white*. The Legion of the Invincibly Stupid is an equal-opportunity employer.

And yet none of this was surprising. Any student of American history knows that nativist and racist movements have been part of our social fabric since the mid-nineteenth-century heyday of the xenophobic Know-Nothing Party. And when "real" Americans didn't blame Catholics, Jews, Italians, Greeks, or Irishmen for their own inadequacies, they blamed Asians. First the Chinese, then the Japanese. I thought of all those old hurts, insults, and humiliations as my wife and I talked to the Koreans about their lives. They told stories as old as the immigrant tradition: how they arrived without language, full of hope, first laboring for others in the same immigrant group, finally buying their own businesses, starting families, working. And working. And working.

"I buy a book, with English word," a man named Kyung Ho Park said, after explaining that his average workday (before the boycott) was fifteen hours long. "No time for school. . . ."

When I was growing up, Italians, Eastern European Jews, and Greeks told these stories. There were resentments then too from the Legion of the Invincibly Stupid; ethnic quarrels; even more brutal racism than now. But well into the 1950s, cities like New York were still manufacturing centers, and there were jobs for almost anybody who wanted to work, including people like my father, an immigrant with an eighth-grade education. The city's traditional liberalism was made possible by an economy in which more than 30 percent of the jobs were in manufacturing; that figure has dropped to 10 percent, and the town's great generous liberal spirit is as frayed and tattered as an old coat.

One result: Immigrants like Kyung Ho Park are working in a city obsessed with fixing blame for its social and economic woes. New York is home to people of immense wealth, and they live well-defended lives in the gaudy canyons of Manhattan. But in spite of the Reagan-era economic boom, New York also contains 840,000 people who live on welfare, more than every man, woman, and child in San Francisco. They don't often see millionaires in their neighborhoods; they do see immigrants. And in the American tradition, the wrath of some is falling upon the newest arrivals, of whom the Koreans are the most visible. Sadly, the Asian immigrants frequently look upon those customers who are welfare clients with more contempt than pity.

"I work," one Korean said to me on Church Avenue. "They don't work. Why do I must feed them?"

That is to say, why must I pay taxes, why must I work long hours at a difficult job, while so many will not do what I do? For years, the children and grandchildren of older immigrants have sung the same blurry refrain: We made it, why don't *they?* Now you begin to hear it from the Koreans too. "You don't like my store," one angry Korean immigrant said to me, "then go to your own store. But they don't have store. Too hard. Too much work."

Such complaints can't be dismissed glibly as the latest examples of newcomers picking up the American racist virus. On the crudest level (down on the streets), they have a certain validity. In New York, as in other American urban centers, the Third World city within the larger city depends upon the taxes and energies of others for its food, clothing, housing, education, medical care, police, fire, and sanitation services. This year's budget for New York City is more than $27 *billion,* and some estimate that fully half of that immense sum is used for servicing the poor. It's inconceivable to think of this happening in Tokyo or Seoul or Singapore.

The persistence of the virtually permanent welfare-supported underclass is the most disgraceful measure of the decline of America's once all-powerful manufacturing plants. But most Americans don't want to talk anymore about root causes; they just see people sitting on the stoop while they go to work. Even the most orthodox liberals now understand that welfare degrades those who receive it and infuriates those who pay for it. So it is no surprise that some poor Americans mutter paranoid theories while others look for scapegoats. More and more these days, our favorite scapegoat is the Asian.

Cheap politicians blame Japan for the nation's economic decline; *they* work too hard, *they* save too much money, *they* close certain markets. Lee Iacocca growls in commercials that Americans make better cars than *they* do. Idiots like Donald Trump bellow, "The Japanese are ripping us off!" In movies like *Rambo,* Asians are mowed down by the hundreds while audiences cheer. And as usual in this country, what we are describing as a race problem is really one of class.

On Church Avenue in Brooklyn, you could feel the seething class bitterness of the black demonstrators. Earlier, they claimed that their anger wasn't simply about the incident that set off the protest. They told various auditors that Koreans — *all* Koreans! — were rude to blacks, suspecting them of shoplifting, acting curt with them, refusing to touch their hands when making change. "Fuckin' people don't know how to *treat* people," one exasperated black man said to me. "They act like every African American is a thief."

Even some Koreans will admit that this perception has some truth to it. A few will cite cultural differences as the heart of the matter (among Koreans, they say, smiling is discouraged, direct eye contact is considered aggressive, and women are taught not to touch strangers). Others blame bitter experience in underclass neighborhoods, which led them to make racial assumptions. A harder truth is that the success of the Koreans in New York is a form of humiliation for many African Americans. You can see a cartoon version of the relationship (*and* the problems with manners) in Spike Lee's sad movie, *Do the Right Thing*. I hear it on black talk radio and in conversations with black friends. With amazing speed, the Koreans have become Haves, while too many blacks, born here, speaking English, remain Have-Nots.

The Koreans only began coming to the United States in significant numbers after the 1965 Immigration and Nationality Act finally ended the racist restrictions against immigrants from Asia. Today more than two hundred thousand Koreans are believed to be living in New York, and they own 9,500 small businesses. The Korean greengrocer has become a widely admired (if stereotypical) figure in the city's life. And in spite of language problems and immense cultural differences, the newcomers have leapfrogged over the city's blacks on what used to be called the ladder of economic success.

"Don't try an' tell me that Koreans work harder than we do," a black man named Virgil Hills said to me a few blocks from the boycott site. "They just got advantages we don't have." Again, some truth here. Certainly, it's extremely difficult for American blacks to open their own grocery stores (or other retail businesses), because so many banks redline them, refusing to provide start-up loans. But the *real* advantages the Koreans have are not those talked about on the street. Back home, almost all of the Koreans were middle class; that is, urban, well educated, goal oriented, imbued with the Confucian ethic. In a 1987 essay on New York's Koreans, the sociologist Illsoo Kim cited one survey of 560 Korean householders in New York showing that 86 percent were married and living with spouses. Some 67 percent had finished college back home. Another study showed that 40 percent of Koreans who arrived in the mid-1970s had professional or technical backgrounds. American blacks with the same backgrounds have no need to open grocery stores; they have access to higher levels of American society.

But these educated Koreans — blocked from American corporate or professional life by the language barrier — have made great use of their abilities. In the greengrocer business, they have analyzed the American systems of purchase, distribution, and marketing, and made their own improvements. In addition, they get up early and stay late, usually the only formula for success. The Koreans have also expanded the sense of family beyond the essential base. In New York alone, there are twelve Korean banks, six daily newspapers in Korean, several cable channels with Korean programming, and at least three radio stations. There are almost three hundred Protestant churches in the Korean community and a burgeoning number of business groups and "prosperity associations." This network helps bind Koreans together, allowing them to learn from one another about the sometimes scary new world in which they are living. In a way, of course, this is another version of the old "self-help" philosophy that helped older immigrants become Americans. It had its failings; many immigrants were injured or exploited by their own kind. But that system worked a hell of a lot better than state welfare. Talk to Koreans, and they tell you they would rather starve than go on welfare; that would be a loss of face. They absolutely refuse to enter the dependency culture in which so many of the American poor find themselves trapped. Those blacks who sense a certain contempt from Koreans are probably reading the signals correctly. In the Korean grocery stores, *all* members of the family work; most often, the business itself was set up by the pooled savings of several family members. In underclass areas, where the Korean grocer is often paid with food stamps, the American family is in disarray or doesn't exist at all.

As it is to most working people everywhere, pride is important to the Koreans; it also shapes their reactions to trouble. Because they work so hard, they are understandably furious when kids steal from their stands. "I pay for what I eat," one Korean told me. "They don't want to pay. Just take." Since many of the stores are in ghetto or marginal areas, the kids are usually black, and that shapes the way some Koreans see *all* blacks. In a more perfect world, they would make finer distinctions; unfortunately, they live in this world. They are also frustrated by the lack of interest American police and courts have in such petty crimes. So they often deal with shoplifters themselves. In the past two years, I've witnessed three separate incidents of Korean grocers chasing kids through the streets. They didn't catch them, but when I asked for their reactions, they just shook their heads, full of contained fury. I saw the same look on the Koreans who were objects of the boycott, as they gazed out at the protesters and the TV cameras.

"I don't understand this kind of problem," Man Ho Park (brother of Kyung Ho) told my wife that day on Church Avenue. "So much anger. So much time doing nothing. Why not work? Why not use time for, for . . . improve life?"

Later, driving back slowly from the boycotted stores, we passed many other Korean groceries, wedged among the video shops and record stores and fast-food joints. Black women shopped. Children cried in strollers or gazed at the colorful displays of oranges and mangoes, bananas and grapes, yams and tomatoes. On the corners, knots of young black men talked, laughed, watched passing cars, sipped from beer cans. As we stopped for a light, one of them saw my wife looking out the window. He stared at her for a long moment. The light changed, and then slowly, almost as a matter of duty, he gave her the finger.

ESQUIRE,
September 1990

A CONFEDERACY OF COMPLAINERS

One rainy morning this past spring, Colin Powell went home at last to Morris High School in the South Bronx. He had been gone for thirty-seven years. But now Powell was one of the most famous generals in recent American history, thanks to the crisp poise and tough intelligence he displayed on television during the seven months of Operation Desert Shield/Storm, and he was proving that, for at least a morning, you can go home again. He stepped briskly from a limousine into a tight cocoon of security men and school officials, wearing his new celebrity lightly. He smiled. He shook hands. He ignored the small crowd of black and Latino men across the street, huddled in front of a methadone clinic. And he didn't seem to notice the abandoned hulks of gutted buildings down the slope of Boston Road. As a man tempered by Vietnam, he has taught himself to ignore the defeats of the past. He glanced up at the school entrance, shook his head in an ironic way, and went in. I walked across the street to talk to the junkies.

"What the hell *he* know about bein' down?" said a man named Roderick. "I seen him on the TV. That man's whiter than George fuckin' Bush! Talk so pretty! Man got everything he want, college boy, all that shit."

Another joined in, then a third and a fourth, and soon the familiar rap was flowing. They'd drawn the wrong hand in life; they were poor and black, or poor and Hispanic, or poor and luckless, and therefore never had a chance in a World They Never Made. Their fathers had run off when they were young, or their mothers, or their girlfriends. They'd been locked up by bad cops, beaten up or flunked out or sneered at by racist schoolteachers, abused by mean Army sergeants or heartless welfare investigators or cruel bosses. Look at us, they said: Look what has been done to us. By Vietnam or racism or capitalism. I stood there for a few minutes, listening to the old familiar litany, and then fled across the street to see Powell talk to some kids.

The chairman of the Joint Chiefs of Staff was impressive. The core of his twenty-minute talk, delivered in a gymnasium with a broken roof, was made of platitudes: Stay in school and get a diploma; don't take drugs, because that's *stupid*. But such bromides were given some renewed power because Powell now spoke with the authority of success. In addition, he was a black man who'd come from Kelly Street, down at the bottom of the broken tundra of the South Bronx, one of the worst slums under the American flag. Certainly Powell had arrived here with luminous cards of identity. But then, after the clichés, he delivered what was probably the morning's most important message — and its most subtle.

"If you're black, if you're Puerto Rican or Hispanic," he said, "be proud of that. But don't let it become a *problem*. Let it become somebody *else's* problem."

Thus spoke a man who clearly has spent his life refusing to become a victim.

To hear Colin Powell that morning was refreshing, even moving, because we live now in a nation that is sick with what I call victimism. Since the collapse of communism and the continuing mistrust of capitalism, victimism might now be the dominant American ideology. Many whites insist that they are innocent victims of vengeful blacks, who are portrayed in their fearful fantasies as marauding bands coming to get their wives, sisters, mamas, or selves. Meanwhile, Hispanics in big cities claim to be the victims of whites *and* blacks, while I've heard blacks claim that AIDS was invented to kill blacks and crack cocaine was invented as part of an antiblack conspiracy set up by the CIA and the Medellín cartel, both of which are pumping it into the ghettos to debase black society.

At the same time, all sorts of people say they are victims of Asians, from the professional Japan-bashers in Washington to those on the street who believe the Korean greengrocer must be engaged in some nefarious plot that will end with a takeover of America. And there are Asians among us who believe they are victims, too; they are angry because someone once called them the Model Minority; they're mad because some universities are creating quotas to keep out Asians and Asian-Americans; in the *Miss Saigon* uproar, they were furious because the part of a Eurasian went to a Caucasian.

This peculiar American capacity for anger seems without limit. Millions of women claim to be the victims of men, while men cite alimony laws and stake claims to their own status as victims of feminist hypocrisy ("How can they claim I'm oppressing them," one divorced friend said, "and then take my money?"). The American day seems to begin with one long and penetrating whine: *Look what they are doing to me!* And "they" are Catholics or Protestants or Jews, liberals or conservatives, northerners or southerners, eastern bankers or western oilmen, members of the NAACP or the NRA, slaves to the AFL-CIO, with occasional believers in the remaining power of the International Communist Conspiracy or the Trilateral Commission. Life in these semi-United States often seems to be an illustration of Jean-Paul Sartre's dictum that hell is other people.

In the end, all adherents of victimism have a few things in common. Most of them are miserable. They hate their jobs, their wives, their husbands or kids or dogs, the cities in which they live, the food they eat, the politicians who lead them, the newspapers, Peter Arnett, their mothers and fathers, and almost all foreigners. For a few brief weeks, they were happy hating Saddam Hussein. But then they noticed that people *they* hated also hated Hussein, so they retreated back into life as gray, throbbing muscles of resentment.

More important, victimism has one overriding slogan, the response to almost all questions about the source of their misery and victimhood: *It's not my fault!* Dropped out of high school? Not my fault. Started shooting heroin or smoking crack when others passed up both? Not my fault. Married the wrong people, got caught robbing stores, crashed the car with a load on? Not me, man, not my *fault.* Victimism implies that nobody is personally responsible for the living of a life. The defeats, disappointments, and failures that were once thought to be part of each human being's portion on this earth are not only unacceptable now, considered soul-killing, career-bruising, life-threatening, but they are always the fault of *somebody else.*

I've heard the endless complaint on all levels of society. In a ghetto, I see a woman point to a hole in the bathroom wall and demand to know why the landlord won't fix it. Well, I ask, how'd it get there? It just appeared, she says. Why doesn't she fix it herself? What? *What?* Are you crazy? *It's not my fault!* This could be explained as the heritage of fifty years of welfare. But I hear the echo out in East Hampton on a summer afternoon, where one of those captains of industry is complaining about the Japanese. We shouldn't even let their cars *in* here! Why not? Because the Japanese are *unfair.* In what way? He mumbles about rice, cigarettes, other items not easily admitted to Japan, and how the Japanese won't let Americans into the construction business, and how they insist on writing their documents in Japanese, the crafty buggers. I say, What does all that have to do with *car* sales? The captain of industry glowers: Well, he says, what would *you* do about our car sales? Make better cars, I suggest. He looks at me, eyes widening. What? Don't you understand? The Japanese are *giving us the shaft!* We are falling behind, but hey, fella, get on the team! *It's not our fault!*

On the silliest level, victimism disguises itself with the sophomoric rigidities of political correctness. Surely, the demand for PC is one of the more comical developments in American life. We have people eating out of garbage cans while humorless brigades of ignorant kids are combing language, literature, and the corner bar for evidence of expression that will offend, hurt, or enrage *somebody*. They warp, bend, fold, spindle, and otherwise mutilate words that they find offensive, and in the process throw out all notions of freedom of speech. The slogan of these incipient Stalinists seems to be: I'm offended, therefore I am.

But the sad comedy of victimism usually plays on a wider stage, and in some cases the scripts are straight out of the theater of the absurd. The drug raid on three University of Virginia fraternity houses was partly in response to complaints that the local cops only went after drug dealers and users in the black part of town. In Los Angeles, one accused drug dealer is claiming that his arrest in a sweep of dealers working near public schools was a "separate and unequal" prosecution, targeting minorities. Both charges are loony; imagine the outcry if the police *stopped* policing minority neighborhoods, leaving the crack dealer to operate under the commandments of laissez-faire capitalism. Victimism insists that the police can never be decent; if they do the job, they are hurting and offending people; if they refuse to do the job, they are contributing to genocide. God bless America; it's a laugh a minute around here.

But there is a darker, more dangerous aspect to victimism. It can be used as a license. Bernhard Goetz was a statue in the park of Victimist theory. So are all the other nerds who shoot first. All they need is the perception of being victims. In the past few years, we have seen a number of cases in which battered wives have burned, shot, or stabbed their husbands and then been acquitted on the grounds that *they* were the victims. I have no doubt that many of these women were abused by the idiots they married. Was murder really the only solution? At what point does the claim to victimhood serve as a license to kill?

Watching Colin Powell, I thought about the world in which he was young and how hard he must have worked to make the journey of his life. He graduated from Morris High School in February 1954, a few months before *Brown* v. *Board of Education*. He didn't need the Supreme Court to get him into college; he'd already been admitted to the City College of New York, where you needed a 90 average to get in. But Colin Powell didn't brag to the assembled students, and though he reminded them that they had greater opportunities than he did, he didn't whine about the timing of his life. He was another tough guy who didn't need to show how tough he was as he played the hand he was dealt. So he'd already learned some lessons from his parents about work and struggle. And he must have been free of self-pity, that most corrosive of human emotions. He was shaped by forces now almost forgotten: the immigrant work experience, the Depression, the tradition of hard work.

I'm not sure when — or more important, *why* — self-pity was elevated into the great all-encompassing American whine. One possible explanation is the presence in our collective imaginations of two gigantic twentieth-century events: the Holocaust and Hiroshima. These were real, with millions of true victims, but they also live in most of us on the level of hallucination and nightmare. They were not problems of manners. They were not offenses of language. Even today, it's difficult for many people to deal with them. There is a valid argument that no words, no pictures, no movies can ever fully express the horror of the Holocaust or the atom-bombing of Hiroshima and Nagasaki. But an awed silence can't satisfy everyone. Some Americans might be adapting the robes of the victim in solidarity with the victims of this century's horrors; others might don them in annoyance, saying in effect, Yeah, that's terrible, but *I have my own problems.* And some might be trying to relieve some tangled feelings of national guilt; for the incineration of so many Japanese civilians, for failing to act to save the European Jews when it was clear that the Holocaust had begun.

I don't pretend to have the answers to such cosmic questions. But I do know that Americans, who once worshiped in the church of self-reliance, have moved to another house of worship, where they are in the grip of a fever of victimism. Its whining propagandists insist upon respect without accomplishment, while its punitive theory of society is enforced by lawyers. The amount of energy consumed by the furies of victimism is extraordinary. The wasted lives of those who buy its premise add up to a genuine tragedy that is made worse by being a self-inflicted wound. In this state of mind, the nation can never heal itself; it is too busy blaming others to look into its own heart. But all of us, including the most damaged, would be helped by a moratorium on self-pity. We need less Freud and more Marcus Aurelius, less adolescent posturing and more stoic maturity, less weeping and gnashing of teeth and more bawdy horselaughs in the face of adversity.

In all the cities of America, the young are now being introduced to the world through the shaping ideology of victimism. How sad. I wish Colin Powell could talk to all of them, black, white, or Latino, male or female, of every class and religion, and tell them: Be proud, live life in your own skin, and whatever is bothering you, hey, man: Make it someone else's problem.

ESQUIRE,
July 1991

LETTER TO A BLACK FRIEND

Though you are black and I am white, we have been friends now for most of our adult lives. All friendships are difficult, but until the last few years, ours endured some of the most terrible strains of the past three decades. Somehow, for all that time, it didn't matter that I was the son of bone-poor Irish immigrants and you the descendant of African slaves; we usually saw the world the same way, were enraged by the same atrocities, amused by the same hypocrisies, celebrated together the often paltry evidence of human kindness or generosity.

Yes, the accident of race was always an unavoidable presence in our friendship; after all, I met you in 1955, the year that Emmett Till was murdered in Mississippi for the terrible crime of whistling at a white woman. As the years passed, there was even more awful evidence of man's apparently infinite capacity for stupidity and murder. But for each of us, our racial and cultural differences were a mutual enrichment, uniquely American. The country was an alloy or it was nothing. And between us there was a splendid exchange: Yeats for the blues, Joyce for Charlie Parker, O'Casey for Langston Hughes; both of us claimed Willie Mays. Somehow, we remained optimists. As young men, we had read our Camus, and we believed that it was possible to love our country and justice, too. That simple faith, with its insistence on irony, was at the heart of our friendship.

But America is older now and so are we and something has changed between us. Now irony isn't enough. Nor is bebop. Nor

Camus. There is no longer any sensible way to avoid a bitter truth: in the past few years, a shadow has fallen on the once sunny fields of our friendship.

The heart of the matter is the continued existence and expansion of what has come to be called the Underclass. You know who I mean: that group of about five million black Americans (of a total of thirty million) who are trapped in cycles of welfare dependency, drugs, alcohol, crime, illiteracy, and disease, living in anarchic and murderous isolation in some of the richest cities on the earth. As a reporter, I've covered their miseries for more than a quarter of a century. Moving among them, from the rotting tenements to the penal corridors of public housing to the roach-ridden caves of welfare hotels, I've seen moral and physical squalor that would enrage even Dickens. I've spoken to the damaged children. I've heard the endless tales of woe. I've seen the guns and the knives and the bodies. And in the last decade, I've watched this group of American citizens harden and condense, moving even further away from the basic requirements of a human life: work, family, safety, the law.

For years I chose to ignore the existence of a permanent Underclass, dismissing it as the fevered dream of neoconservatives and apostate liberals; there were too many signs of genuine racial progress in this country, and I was certain that what Langston Hughes called "a dream deferred" could not be deferred forever. I believed that because you had convinced me of it. Now we both recognize the existence of the Underclass, in all its fierce negative power, but you refuse to look at this ferocious subculture for what it is: the single most dangerous fact of ordinary life in the United States.

Instead, you have retreated defensively into the clichés of glib racialism. Your argument is simple: the black Underclass is the fault of the white man. Not some white men. *All* white men. You cite various examples of a surging white racism: the antibusing violence in liberal Boston, the Bernhard Goetz and Howard Beach cases in liberal New York, a resurgent Klan in some places, continued reports of whites using force to keep blacks from moving into their neighborhoods, white cops too quick to arrest, abuse, or shoot down black suspects, persistent examples of racial steering in middle-class housing, the Al Campanis controversy. Certainly racism continues to be real in the United States; only a fool would deny it.

But I insist on stating that in the course of our lives much has changed. When I was a kid in the Navy, stationed in Pensacola in 1954, the Supreme Court ruled on *Brown* v. *Board of Education* and banned segregation in the public schools. At the time, if you possessed the Congressional Medal of Honor and were black, you could not swim at the white beaches of Florida. Throughout the South, you could not sit in just any seat on just any bus; you could not walk through the front door of any American movie house, sit at any counter in just any American restaurant. There were separate washrooms and drinking fountains for blacks and whites. The White Citizens Councils seemed to own the night. In many places blacks were denied the right to vote through poll taxes, gerrymandering, or terrorism. Blacks could not attend "white" public schools, including white state universities that they helped support with taxes. Blacks and whites could not marry each other in many states and could not even fight each other in boxing rings in others. Radio stations segregated black music. Blacks seldom appeared on television and were cast in movies as domestics or feets-get-movin' buffoons of the Stepin Fetchit variety. When I tell this to my children, they find it hard to believe.

This you must admit: your children and mine have grown up in a different United States. And, for all its flaws, a better one. De jure segregation is a memory (which is not to say that it doesn't persist in a de facto form in housing and education). For the first time in American history, there is a substantial and expanding black middle class. As I write to you, the leading contender for the Democratic nomination for President is a black man named Jesse Jackson. Bill Cosby stars in and produces the highest-rated entertainment show in the country, Oprah Winfrey hosts the most popular talk show. Bryant Gumbel is at the top of the heap on the *Today* show. Eddie Murphy is one of the most successful stars in Hollywood feature films, and Michael Jackson, Lionel Richie, Whitney Houston, and Tina Turner sell millions of records to white fans as well as black. From 1977 to 1982 the number of black businesses increased almost 50 percent, from 230,000 to 340,000. They grossed $12.4 billion in 1982. More important, in 1964 there were 280 black elected public officials in the United States; today there are more than five thousand, over 60 percent of them in the South. The mayors of Los Angeles, Atlanta, New Orleans, Newark, Detroit, Washington, Philadelphia, and Chicago are black. Last year the nomination of Robert Bork to the United States Supreme Court was rejected because of the crucial opposition of white southern senators who were afraid of offending their new black constituents. *True* black power is being achieved.

But this was not accomplished without help. Twenty-five years have passed since James Baldwin shook the nation with *The Fire Next Time,* twenty-three years since Lyndon Johnson called for a War on Poverty, twenty years since the murder of Martin Luther King. Whatever its motives, white America (if it can be called that) was not indifferent. Billions of tax dollars have been spent by federal, state, and local governments to repair the injuries of racism. You might reply that the sum was a pittance in comparison with the gross national product; certainly far more dollars have been poured down the insatiable maw of the defense racket than were spent to reduce poverty. But the fact remains that those billions *were* spent. Few countries in the history of this planet have made such an effort for their most damaged citizens; it doesn't matter if the motives were guilt, fear, or (as you believe) a cynical form of bribery to head off full-scale revolt. What does matter is that the effort was made. And continues.

But we have come to understand one terrible truth: for the black Underclass, life in the United States is infinitely worse. For them, King, Malcolm, and the rest have died in vain.

Yes, there is a white underclass and an expanding Hispanic underclass. But the first is relatively contained; the fall into poverty, homelessness, welfare is generally temporary. Hispanics are a separate category too, for the indexes of their poverty reflect some of the traditional problems of immigrants: the lack of knowledge of the English language, larger family size, a dependence upon agriculture or nonunion industries for jobs.

But most black Americans are not recent arrivals. Blacks speak the American language. Millions of American blacks have long since left behind the bondage of the farm. The old Jim Crow unions are gone (even in the building trades there is a begrudging acceptance of blacks). But in the past decade American cities have witnessed a new phenomenon: newly arrived Koreans, Pakistanis, Cubans, Haitians, Greeks, Vietnamese, Russian Jews, West Indians, even Afghans are moving past American blacks. Japanese-Americans — whose parents were thrown into American concentration camps during World War II — are winning disproportionate shares of college scholarships and moving to the top in many professions. And the black Underclass seems incapable of progress.

Need I recite the sad statistics? I must. I realize that such numbers have as much to do with the dailiness of human lives as a box score has to do with a ball game. But we need to know them. They tell us about our failure — mine *and* yours.

Almost 30 percent of *all* black American families are now living below the federal poverty line of $10,989 a year for a family of four (compared with 8 percent of whites). In New York City it is estimated that 60 percent of black youths never finish high school, in a time when even a high school diploma is barely sufficient to function in the job market. The national infant-mortality rate is 50 percent higher among blacks than among whites; eleven thousand black infants died in 1984, and in New York last year, after the advent of crack, infant death increased by *20 percent.*

The living face even greater hazards. One third of black New Yorkers between the ages of five and nineteen are victims of homicide, and nationally the leading cause of death for black men between the ages of sixteen and thirty-four is murder. Not smallpox. Not tuberculosis. Not influenza. Not one of the ancient plagues of the earth. *Murder.*

Last year, AIDS killed more black junkies in New York than it did homosexual men, and nationally blacks now account for 24 percent of all AIDS cases (roughly twice the proportion of blacks in the general population). Blacks account for half of the heterosexual AIDS cases. Half the female AIDS victims are black; two of three infants born with AIDS are black. According to the Centers for Disease Control, a black woman is thirteen times more likely to contract AIDS than a white woman. Of the fifty thousand women in New York City who are infected with the AIDS virus (but as yet free of the symptoms of the disease), 80 percent are black or Hispanic. Doctors expect that eventually all will die. AIDS researcher Beny J. Primm said at last year's national convention of the Urban League: "My friends are afraid that they will be called racist if they cite these statistics. But I have said it is better to be called a racist now than to be called a conspirator in a conspiracy of genocide five or ten years from now, when many, many blacks will die because of your silence today." In a speech last year, Dr. Donald R. Hopkins, then deputy director of the CDC, summed it up: "This disease is the fifth horseman of the Apocalypse in our nation's minority communities."

But the extraordinary hazards of black life in the Underclass are not limited to murder and AIDS. Blacks have more heart disease than whites, more cancer, more cirrhosis. Fifty percent of older black women are obese (compared with one third of the whites), and blacks have hypertension and strokes at twice the rate of whites. As you might expect, whites live about six years longer than blacks.

The grim numbers go on and on. In the late 1950s, 30 percent of poor black families were headed by women; today it is more than 70 percent. In 1959 only 15 percent of black births were out of wedlock; by 1982 it was 57 percent (five times the white rate). In 1960, 42 percent of babies born to black teenagers were illegitimate; by 1983 it was 89 percent. From 1970 to 1984 the number of black families headed by women increased 108 percent (it was 63 percent for whites). Of the 27,178 families with children living in projects run by the Chicago Housing Authority, only *8 percent* are headed by a husband and wife.

What goes on here? When you and I were growing up in the slums of New York, this simply didn't happen very often. If a young man got a young woman pregnant, her father, brothers, or uncles would come knocking on his door. Today, in the urban wilderness of the Underclass, too many young black men apparently think nothing of getting women pregnant and then moving on, leaving the children's care, feeding, clothing, and housing in the indifferent hands of the paternalistic state. After all the work done by blacks and whites to destroy the stereotype of the shiftless, irresponsible black man, here come these characters.

"There is, even now, a lot of anger within the black community toward the young black man," said black psychiatrist Alvin F. Poussaint (an adviser to *The Cosby Show*) in a recent issue of *The Black Scholar*. "And increasingly, if he continues to deteriorate in his ability to function well, he is going to be rejected by black women. That is happening already. Even low-income black females perceive the black male as a loser, as trouble: dangerous and violent. . . ."

Poussaint believes that some young black males are compensating for feelings of inferiority in the larger society. "Sometimes, if you feel impotent in terms of society, you react by stressing your sexual role. That's why many of them will see getting someone pregnant as proof of manhood, rather than having a child and being a responsible father to that child."

Since 1981, unwed motherhood has replaced marital breakup as the leading cause for welfare eligibility (among blacks *and* whites), but the true cause might be incomprehensible ignorance. In the past few years, I've interviewed black women who can't remember the full names of the fathers of their children and others who can't spell their kids' names. Many of these women seem to learn nothing from the experience of the first illegitimate child. They just have more babies. One result, in the words of the *Chicago Tribune,* is "mothers in their early teens, grandmothers in their late twenties, and great-grand-mothers in their early forties."

I remember you telling me several times that this was part of the heritage of three centuries of slavery, a theory most frequently offered by black intellectuals and white liberals in response to the 1965 Moynihan Report. In the days before emancipation (say such theorists), black families were purposefully broken apart by the slaveholders, who feared uprisings by men and women who didn't want their children born into slavery. As a result, there has been a psychological fracture in the black family ever since.

But this secular belief in predestination — insisting that human beings are prisoners of history and not its makers — has been refuted by the stirring history of black Americans themselves, from Frederick Douglass to Martin Luther King Jr. and many millions in between. To insist that only black Americans are permanent prisoners of the past, unable to shape their own lives, is itself a form of racism.

Common sense alone tells us that if it had been true, then the trauma would have affected *all* blacks; obviously it hasn't. And the post-slavery history of the black family indicates that this particular consequence of "the peculiar institution" was in fact soon left behind. In his brilliant new book, *The Truly Disadvantaged,* black sociologist William Julius Wilson shows that in 1940, the last year of the Great Depression, only 17.9 percent of black American families were headed by women, and the reason was usually that the husbands were dead. Today, the percentage is 43 and rising, but widowhood is no longer the cause. The men are in the wind. This has had an obvious economic effect; of black families earning $25,000 a year, only 8 percent are headed by women; of those earning $4,000 and less, 80 percent are headed by women. And that raises the essential question in refuting the theory: How could slavery have a greater corrosive effect on the black family *today,* almost half a century later, than it had in 1940? The question contains its own answer; it couldn't.

Alas, we have difficulty even now — in the midst of the catastrophe — discussing such matters. You and I have been asked for a generation to suspend all criticism of the personal behavior of blacks in the Underclass. We would give aid and comfort to racists. Or erode the already uncertain self-image of blacks. To hold blacks responsible for their lives, we have been told (most eloquently by William Ryan), is "blaming the victim." Before such arguments, liberals fell silent; and the crisis of the Underclass deepened.

At last, the long silence seems to be coming to an end. Both the NAACP and the Urban League have begun to speak about the need to break the trap of welfare dependency. Last year, Michael Lomax, chairman of Atlanta's Fulton County Commission, publicly discussed the failure of the black establishment to deal with AIDS among blacks. He saw that failure as part of a larger pattern:

"It is a matter of coming to terms, at last, with the fact that there are problems within our community that were not imposed upon us by white society. Intravenous drug use, teenage pregnancy, and sexual promiscuity are behaviors that are pathological in our own community, and we must come to grips with that, to take responsibility."

That last word is the key. You were responsible for your family, I for mine. But if the typical Underclass family is matriarchal, who is responsible? To blame the system, or Whitey, or history is to embrace a gigantic self-deception.

Coming out of this drastic deterioration of the Underclass black family are multiple pathologies. You know the most obvious one: the staggering rate of violent crime. Black Americans are murdering, raping, assaulting, and robbing each other at alarming rates. Blacks make up about 13 percent of our country's population, but 50 percent of all those arrested for murder are black, as are 41 percent of the victims. Black women are three times more likely to be victims of rape than are whites. Yes, too many white cops shoot too many black suspects. Yes, there might be an element of racism involved. But in any given year, white cops don't kill as many blacks as blacks do on some big-city weekends.

Again, we must go back to the numbers. According to a Justice

Department survey, 46 percent of the nation's prison population is black; by 1984, the rate of imprisonment for blacks was six times that for whites. National mayhem rates are bad enough; they are even worse in large inner-city ghettos. In Chicago in the 1970s, eight of every ten murderers were black, as were seven of every ten victims; 98 percent of black killings were committed by other blacks. In 1984, 61 percent of those arrested for robbery were black, as were 41 percent of those charged with aggravated assault.

I remember talking to you one night last year when you were furious with Benjamin Ward, the black police commissioner of New York City. You were angry with Ward because he had described black-on-black crime as "our dirty little secret" to a Columbia University forum sponsored by the New York Association of Black Journalists.

"We provide the victims and we provide the perpetrators," Ward said. "We should not be ashamed to say that. We should not try to hide it. We have to speak out about it. . . . Most of the crime in this city is by young blacks under thirty. I think the young black male has always been perceived in this city by whites, and by blacks as well, as being a more dangerous person than a white. And I believe that just as many black women in this room tend to cross the street when they see some of those kinds of people coming down the street as whites do. And I believe blacks are victims. But we're generally the victims of some other black committing crimes against us."

By most accounts, the audience of students hissed Ward's remarks; black nationalists seemed to dismiss him as "a white man's nigger." Or as another Oreo cookie. But he was not hissed a few nights later when he continued the discussion at a meeting of two hundred black ministers in Bedford-Stuyvesant in Brooklyn, where the Underclass rules the street.

"When you go home tonight," Ward said, "if your place is burglarized, it probably would have been one of your neighbors. . . . If you stay here late tonight and then go outside, it might be a young black man that will hurt you." Ward was once the city's corrections commissioner and said, "It broke my heart [to see so many young blacks in jail]. You go to upstate New York, our state prisons, and that's what you see — the fruit of our community serving time behind those walls." Then he added: "I'm sending as many there as I possibly can, seventy thousand perhaps this year for peddling drugs. And I don't regret it one minute. Because *they* are committing the genocide against the blacks, they are ripping off the neighborhoods. . . ."

In Brooklyn, before a black audience, Ward's remarks were punctuated by a chorus of "amens." Certainly the statistics supported his words. New York City is 24 percent black, but in 1986, 52.8 percent of all those arrested were black. Blacks accounted for 55.4 percent of the murder and manslaughter arrests (a total of 644), 65.2 percent of the forcible rape arrests (966), 69.3 percent of the robbery arrests (15,944), and 55.7 percent of the arrests for aggravated assault (13,079). After Ward's statement was made public, state director Hazel Dukes of the NAACP said: "What he is saying is real and must be addressed. It makes you think."

It certainly does. These numbers don't tell the full story, of course; they are the statistics of arrests, not convictions. But only a fool would insist that life in big cities is better now than it was thirty years ago. You and I are not old men, but it's hard to explain to our children that in New York when we were young, it was possible on hot summer evenings to sleep in parks or on rooftops or fire escapes. Exhausted by a hard day's work, we slept unmolested to the end of subway lines. Like you, I grew up in a poor neighborhood; my front door was never locked, and neither was yours.

Most city people don't talk about their apprehension anymore. They have simply altered their behavior. In the big cities, blacks and whites live behind iron barricades: locks, bars, gates. When we walk down a street at night, we follow the pattern described by Ward, peering over our shoulders, always alert to danger; if a group of the black young is seen, we cross the street or reverse direction.

What all of us have learned is that the fear of the Underclass is about class, not race. This has much precedent in American history; at various times in our big cities, the middle class often felt threatened by the crime and moral disorder of the Irish, Jewish, and Italian poor. But there are three elements of the current catastrophe that were not present among previous generations: drugs, television, and welfare.

You too have seen the ravages of drugs. Heroin has been with us since the 1950s; in New York alone we have 220,000 heroin addicts — the equivalent of eleven army divisions. We had friends who died of overdoses; together we mourned Charlie Parker and Fats Navarro and Billie Holiday; we saw others virtually decompose before our eyes, their teeth rotting, arms scarred or abscessed by tracks, stealing from their families, hurrying always from one connection to another. Heroin was one of the first plagues we saw together. But other drugs are everywhere now in the ghettos of the Underclass: pot and pills and most of all these days, crack. Every day, thousands of girls turn tricks to get their share of this superpotent, highly addictive, easily smokable form of cocaine; for their supply, teenagers bash old men on the heads. These stupid kids seem to have no grander ambition than to get high. Crack, we are told, gives them illusions of power; heroin smothers their pain. There seems to be no vision that includes working toward power, or confronting personal pain like men and overcoming it. Instead we hear the steady whining complaint about Whitey and the System and the Man.

"Racial issues get a big reaction in the press," says black congressman Floyd Flake of Queens, New York, "but it's drugs that is bringing us down."

Every day we see young people from a proud, tough race, nodding out on sidewalks or in public parks, wandering the streets at all hours, frequently homeless, or joined in the numb Fraternity of the Lost, in shooting galleries, abandoned houses, empty lots. We should not be surprised. These are kids who have been shaped in whole or in part by welfare or television. That is to say, to the habit of passivity and dependence, where nothing requires work. To read a book, to absorb it, to agree with it or quarrel with it: this takes work. But according to a 1986 Nielsen Media Research survey, blacks watch TV 39 percent more than all other American households. That means they are consuming a steady diet of slick crap, charged with violence, crawling with cheap emotions. The cumulative message of TV is that solutions should be easy. After all, if the Equalizer can confront a crime, overcome villains, come up with a solution in less than an hour, why should anyone have to master trigonometry?

Television is also the favored medium of the illiterate. Older generations of poor Americans learned to read in order to entertain themselves; some never got past dime novels, some discovered the glories of the world's literature and history. The poor no longer must read to be entertained. Television provides entertainment easily and seductively. And while transmitting its grand distractions, the medium inevitably provides models for behavior. In television shows, virtually nobody is ever shown *working* — except cops. And even in cop shows, the emphasis is on action, not the tedious process of analysis and deduction.

So I'm no longer surprised when black high school students tell me they have never heard of James Baldwin, Richard Wright, Jean Toomer, or Ralph Ellison, to mention only a few extraordinary black writers. They don't know that Alice Walker wrote *The Color Purple*. They have never heard of Romaire Bearden or Max Roach or Dizzy Gillespie or Charlie Parker. They don't even know Aesop's fables or the Old Testament or the tales of the Greek gods. Go to a jazz club and listen to Wynton Marsalis: the audience is white. Young blacks are listening to the puerile doggerel of rap music. I find many white kids equally ignorant these days, but most of them don't have to fight their way out of the Underclass. Hundreds of thousands of black American kids are growing up in complete ignorance of the basic elements of Western culture *and* the culture of black America. Increasingly, they are not even acquiring the tools required to cure the ignorance.

The black high school dropout rate in large cities is approaching 60 percent. Many such kids can't speak a plain American language, never mind aspire to the eloquent mastery of Martin Luther King or Malcolm X. For a while some tried to make this a virtue; they argued that black English was a separate language of enormous strength and value and should even be codified and used in school. Alas, that was just another elaborate rationalization. Obviously, the American language has been enriched by black English and the argot of music and the street. But it will not lead the way to MIT. In a recent article in *Harper's,* Julian Bond remembered: "My little girl brought a note home from school that said, 'Julia be late too often.' What kind of teacher wrote that note? Is he teaching *my* daughter how to read and write? I'm talking about a public school in Atlanta. . . ."

You and I have met such teachers in New York; they exist all over the country now, passing on their own incomplete skills to the young. And the young are leaving. Wilson cites the appalling situation in the Chicago public schools. Of 25,000 black and Hispanic students who enrolled in the ninth grade in 1980, only 9,500 finished four years later; of these, only 2,000 could read at the twelfth-grade level. In the predominantly black and Latino New York public-school system, 39.7 percent of all sixth graders failed to meet the standard in reading, and 43.7 percent failed mathematics. By the time these kids get to eighth grade, the failure rate is 60 percent. One third of the city's one million students drop out before graduation (the percentage is much higher among blacks and Hispanics). Those who do graduate are often not much better off. They aren't ready for the real world of the last decade of the twentieth century, and nobody knows this better than the corporations in the city itself.

The New York Telephone Company reports that only 16 percent of the applicants for entry-level jobs are able to pass simple exams in vocabulary and problem solving. When J.C. Penney and Mobil Oil announced they were moving their corporate offices out of New York, they cited the lack of a quality work force as one of their major reasons. More than *half* the freshmen entering City University from public schools fail the writing and math courses. Last summer, four New York banks reserved 250 jobs for high school graduates from disadvantaged backgrounds. They were to be given crash courses in job preparation and had to pass some entry-level tests simple enough for a "bright sixth grader." Only one hundred of these high school graduates could pass the tests, which included such rigorous questions as, "How many quarters are there in seventeen dollars?"

So in a time when the old barriers to blacks have fallen, when the doors of the establishment have at least partially opened, we are seeing that too many young blacks can't even walk in the door. There was a time when some of us thought that the education problem could be solved by integration; that is no longer possible in most big-city schools because there simply aren't enough white students to integrate with. In New York, white public-school enrollment declined more than 45 percent from 1968 to 1980; in Chicago it was 60 percent, in Detroit 75 percent. Much of this exodus was the result of white flight, which superficially resembles racism; alas, it's more complicated than that.

Again, the issue is class. White parents pull their kids from the public schools, placing them in parochial or private schools (or leaving the city for its suburbs) because they want their children to be educated. It's as simple as that. The black middle class does the same thing for the same reason. They don't feel they can educate their children in schools that are violent, drug-ridden, seething with anger, or dominated by the anti-intellectual ethos of the Underclass.

You blame the schools and their administrators. So do I, to some extent. There are too many incompetent teachers, too much flab in the curricula, too slovenly a set of standards for students. But in the end, a school can't educate a human being; an education is not something "given" to somebody like a suit of clothes. You cannot absorb learning passively, as if it were the check arriving every two weeks in the mailbox. You must *work* at an education, generally for your entire life; like anything worth having, you must earn it. You must *take* it. Humble origins are no excuse for surrender. The mother of Camus was illiterate; he won the Nobel Prize for Literature.

So I've come to believe that if there is to be a solution to the self-perpetuating Underclass, it must come from blacks, specifically from the black middle class. Blacks might have no other choice.

Whites — liberal or otherwise — have not been emotionally committed to the cause of black Americans since the triumph of the civil rights revolution, which culminated in the Voting Rights Act of 1965. Around the same time, white liberals were pushed out of the movement by the Black Power crowd; the ignorant lies of black anti-Semitism drove out other whites, depositing some in the chilly precincts of neoconservatism; the preposterous visions of black separatism convinced others that it was time to take a walk. To equate "black pride" with the hatred of whites was reverse racism; it was dumber politics.

So whites will pay taxes, which in turn will support welfare and rotten schools and second-rate hospitals; whites will see to it that the police and the firemen and the sanitation men do their work in the ghettos. But it might be a long time before whites will cry again the way they did for Emmett Till or the little girls who died in the Birmingham bombing. Or for Medgar Evers. Or Malcolm. Or King.

So salvation (if it's possible) will be up to the black middle class — for several reasons. One simple reason is that the departure of the black middle class from the ghetto helped intensify and concentrate the Underclass. In one sense, that exodus was itself the most obvious symbol of the triumph of the civil rights movement. For more than a decade, middle-class and working-class blacks have been heading downtown (or uptown, or out of town, depending upon the city), renting better apartments, buying houses or condos, seeking out better and safer schools for their kids, less melodramatic lives for themselves. According to a study by Reynolds Farley and Walter Allen, some 13 percent of black families now have incomes over $25,000; 44 percent of that group own their own homes; 8 percent are headed by a college graduate (compared with 19 percent of whites), 17 percent hold managerial or professional jobs. Middle-class blacks have not yet achieved parity with whites, but in a very important way, they are part of a splendid success story.

But they have left behind the growing catastrophe. You know this to be true. In the bad old days, when you were young, the ghettos were populated by a broad range of black Americans. There were black doctors and lawyers, clergymen, and musicians to be seen — and emulated — by the young. You know that Harlem was never paradise (to mention the most famous black ghetto); it always had its share of unemployment, alcoholism, drug addiction, broken marriages, and welfare. But when you and I were young, the middle class was still there, serving as what William Julius Wilson calls "a social buffer."

The young saw every day that there was great diversity in black life, socially and economically, and plenty of reason for pride. As writer Nicholas Lemann has pointed out, there were healthy role models for the young: people who worked, didn't commit crimes, use drugs, or aim only to get high on a Saturday night, thousands who were not reduced to welfare (except as temporary relief) and thought of it as a shameful condition. These people didn't wait for the landlord to sweep the stoop or change a light bulb; they didn't have to be dragged in protest to school or a library; they didn't sneer at "dead-end" jobs. Such families wouldn't give racists the satisfaction of seeing them in degraded conditions. They were too proud for that. And too proud to depend upon the kindness of strangers. A true man was someone who housed, clothed, and fed his family. There was no other definition.

And because such people lived in the ghetto, everybody gained. This was the ironic by-product of the racism that created the ghetto in the first place. You remember how you got your first jobs: someone heard they were hiring at American Can, or there was a slot open at the A & P, or the bottling plant needed help. The news came from people you knew on the streets or who lived in the same building, men and women who were working themselves and knew of other jobs. The barbershop was a communications center, or the candy store, or the corner bar, or the church. In addition, there were black people in the ghettos who could inspire the young. This kid stayed in school and studied hard because he wanted to be like that lawyer. We will never know how many kids in Harlem were inspired to play music by the regal sight of Duke Ellington walking on Lenox Avenue or Art Tatum getting out of a new car in front of Minton's. We can't count the number who wanted to speak like Adam Clayton Powell. Or be as hip as Miles Davis or as elegant as Sugar Ray Robinson.

Well, the middle class left the ghetto and that, of course, was their right, perhaps even their obligation. But for the kid in the Underclass, today's role models are a harder sort: crack dealers, pimps, stickup men. In spite of a tentative move toward gentrification in places such as Harlem, bad guys are the only visible symbols of black success. There is no stigma to welfare. Even prison holds no terrors; it functions as part of a puberty rite, the institution where the bad blades and homeboys receive their higher educations on their way to early graves.

You ask the immemorial question: What is to be done?

There are no simple answers. We are seeing the culmination of fifty years of American history, the consequences of some social policies that succeeded and many that failed. The Underclass has been a long time forming, since about the time that the great black migration to the North began during and after World War II. This was caused by the mechanization that changed the economy of the South; where once a hundred black men toiled in a cotton field, now there was one machine and ten men and all the others were heading north. But when they arrived in places like New York and Chicago, they soon discovered that there might be jobs at Young & Rubicam, but not any were for men and women who'd spent their lives chopping cotton. By the late 1950s, the jobs that supported my father and other European immigrants began to vanish, too, jobs in small factories, jobs that didn't require much formal education. Soon welfare became the dismal alternative to all those glittering visions of renewal. Soon despair was general.

I would like to see the black middle class return in great waves to the urban ghettos to attack the roots of that despair and to work at the restoration of genuine pride and lost dignity. I am speaking here of you and your friends, of course, along with all those younger than you, the bright young men and women with their M.B.A.'s and BMWs. Obviously, I don't mean that you must move your family back to the ghetto. Or that your friends should do the same. That simply isn't going to happen in the immediate future. But in important ways, such a drastic commitment isn't necessary. After all, back in the 1950s, it wasn't necessary for the freedom riders to live permanently in the South, either. But just as the sit-ins and freedom rides were directed from the North against the institutions of the segregated South, this campaign would come from the outside, from the suburbs, from downtown, and yes, from the South.

It would help to consider the Underclass as a Third World country within the borders of a First World nation. Members of the black middle class are now citizens of that First World country. But if Bob Geldof can help Ethiopia, you and other suburban and downtown blacks can surely help those who've been left behind in the Third World. To begin with, you could mount the most widespread private literacy campaign in the history of this country, drawing on the experiences of Cuba and Nicaragua, utilizing all the skills you have gained in the wider world of business, communications, journalism, marketing. You could force Eddie Murphy to make some TV commercials about the importance of reading, thus redeeming himself for once bragging to Barbara Walters that he never reads (given the nature of the catastrophe in the black Underclass, this was surely the most disgusting single public statement by a black man in the past decade). You could publicly destroy a hundred or so TV sets to symbolize the need for the Underclass to remove itself from the hypnotic glow of the tube and begin functioning again as active participants in life instead of as a passive audience.

You could teach black teenagers about birth control — clearly, graphically, intelligently — and then supply birth-control devices to everyone. You could make clear to young black men that they aren't men at all if they abandon their women and children. You could instruct young women that when they make the momentous decision to have a child, they must be prepared to support it for the rest of their days and not leave that awesome task to the state. You could demand through lawsuits, demonstrations, sheer moral force, and the use of the media that the police round up the crack dealers and smack peddlers. These vicious bastards should then be tried and jailed, instead of being sent back to the streets where they smirk at the impotence of the law and wink at the unwary young. This would require cooperation with the police and an end to the incessant knee-jerk portrayal of the police as the enemy.

But your main target should be the welfare system. This seems to an outsider the single most degrading and corrupting fact of life in the Underclass, and the goal should be its virtual destruction. Human beings must work. It is as necessary to life as food and drink, sex and rest. You would have to stop the nonsense about "dead-end" jobs. There are no "dead-end" jobs for people who want to make something of their lives. When I was a kid I worked as a messenger, a delivery boy, a bank teller, a lowly assistant in an advertising agency's art department, a sheet-metal worker in the Brooklyn Navy Yard. I didn't make a career of any of those jobs, but they taught me how to work. That is, they taught me how to get up in the morning when I wanted to sleep another few hours. They taught me how to perform tasks that didn't personally interest me. They taught me how to understand the needs of other people and their expectations of me. I say this as a man of the Left, knowing that the dogmatists will accuse me of collaborating with the neocons and other dogmatists of the Right. I can only answer that social justice must be based on work, not welfare. To demand the expansion of the welfare system, instead of its elimination, is to consign the Underclass to permanent darkness.

Where would the jobs come from? Obviously, many of them at the beginning would have to come from the government. There is an extraordinary amount of work to be done in the United States, repairing the collapsing physical infrastructure of streets, bridges, highways. This is work that does not require a high school education. In every major city, in those places where the Underclass resides, there are hundreds of abandoned buildings, structurally sound but gutted by fire; they could be reclaimed through the use of sweat equity, converted into condominiums for a resurgent black and Hispanic working class. The current generation might never be able to enter the high-tech world of the modern service industries, but they can work, men and women alike, with the sweat of their backs and the power of their hands to make certain that their children will be able to function in the twenty-first century. The money now being wasted on welfare could be used for the creation of jobs; if that is called "workfare," so be it. You must start somewhere.

The time to begin is now. Waiting will only worsen the disaster. You cannot, for example, wait for a day-care system to be created; somehow my mother raised seven kids and worked all her days; my father lost a leg in his twenties and kept on working. They didn't have day-care centers. They didn't take welfare, either. Too busy for self-pity. They had no more advantages than anyone else (my mother arrived as an immigrant the day the stock market crashed in 1929), unless you insist that being white was some immense privilege. If it was, it did them no good. All they knew was that in America, they would have to work.

In the best of all possible worlds, of course, the federal government would help fund this immense project, including the building of day-care centers. To say that the richest nation on earth can't afford this is ludicrous. As just one example, they could scrap the idiotic Star Wars program and use that trillion dollars (over ten years) to guarantee full employment, even at the risk of fueling inflation. Jobs are everything. A job for one man could take four people off the dole. Jobs would take more pistols out of the hands of young men than another hundred thousand police. Any sensible citizen knows that the Underclass is a greater threat to our national security than the Russians. The Russians aren't killing people on the streets of our cities. They aren't spreading AIDS. They aren't presiding over the deaths of American infants.

But the War on Poverty taught us that bureaucrats are not very good at repairing holes in the human spirit. That is why the most important part of this must be up to you and to the rest of the black middle class. In the end, out of self-interest, white America will pay the price for domestic tranquillity. But there is very little now that whites can do in a direct way for the maimed and hurting citizens of the Underclass. For two decades, you have called them brother or sister. You have said they are family. If you believe these sentiments, you must go to them now. They need you more than they need white pity. Or white social workers. Or white cops. They need someone to love them. Soon. If you do not go, neither will anyone else. And then they will surely be doomed. So, in a different way, will all of us.

ESQUIRE,
March 1988

THE NEW VICTORIANS

Here they come, with their steel faces and inflamed eyes, their fearful visions and apocalyptic solutions: the New Victorians. The Cold War is over and Americans are desperate for a new enemy. The New Victorians have found one and, as usual, it is other Americans.

Look there, in a museum, there are photographs by Robert Mapplethorpe. Of naked men! Of sex! And in magazines and movies and video stores, nothing but smut and filth and degradation! The New Victorians tremble at the terrifying sight of the naked female breast, the curly enticements of pubic hair, the heart-stopping reality of the human penis. Disgusting. Degrading. Moral collapse! And if the republic is to be saved, the enemy must be cast into eternal darkness. Or at least returned to the wonderful iron hypocrisies of the 19th century.

The collective public face of the New Victorians is made up of the usual suspects: Senator Jesse Helms, Pat Buchanan, the television Bible-whackers. But in the past few years, these yahoo crusaders have increasingly found themselves marching with unfamiliar allies. For there, at the front of the parade, loudly pounding the drums, is a small group of self-styled radical feminists. Sexual crusades indeed make strange bedfellows.

The unlikely Lenin of the feminist wing of the New Victorians is a 46-year-old lawyer named Catharine MacKinnon. She is a tenured professor of law at the University of Michigan, but that is a blurry job description. Basically, MacKinnon is a professional feminist. That is to say that, like a priest, a theologian or a romantic revolutionary, she is exclusively dedicated to the service of a creed. MacKinnon's feminist vision is not limited to the inarguable liberal formulas of equal pay for equal work, complete legal and political equality and full opportunity to compete with men. Like Lenin, she doesn't want mere reform. She wants to overthrow the entire system of what she sees as male supremacy. During the past decade, when the country shifted to the right and millions of American women rejected the harder ideologies of feminism, MacKinnon labored on with revolutionary zeal.

That zeal was shaped by the social and sexual upheavals of the

Sixties and Seventies. MacKinnon was born in Minnesota, where her father was a federal judge, a major player in the state's Republican Party. Like her mother and grandmother, Catharine MacKinnon attended Smith College. In the Seventies she went to Yale Law School, worked with the Black Panthers and rallied against the Vietnam war. But when many of her classmates moved on to the real world and its dense textures of work and family, she stayed on in New Haven and found both a focus and an engine for her life in an almost religious embrace of the women's movement. MacKinnon's basic formulation was simple: "Sexuality is to feminism what work is to Marxism: that which is most one's own, yet most taken away."

At Yale, MacKinnon created the first course in the women's studies program but was never given tenure. For a decade she served as an itinerant lecturer or visiting professor at the best American law schools, including Yale, Chicago, Stanford and Harvard, delivering sermons on the problems of women and the law. As a legal theorist, she is credited with defining sexual harassment and was frequently cited during Justice Clarence Thomas' confirmation hearings. As a public speaker, dripping with scorn and cold passion, she was always in demand. The elusive guarantee of tenure was finally granted at Michigan in 1989.

But for all MacKinnon's passion and occasional brilliance, even some feminists and legal scholars who applaud her work on sexual harassment find the rest of her vision indefensible. She dismisses them all, firm in her belief that she has discovered the truth. In a series of manifestos and lawsuits, MacKinnon has defined the legal agenda of the New Victorians. Their common enemy is that vague concept: pornography. MacKinnon's basic legal theory is that pornography is a form of sex discrimination. She says that it's made by men for men, but it is harmful only to women. Therefore, women should have the right to sue those who produce it and sell it. Pornography, in Mac-Kinnon's view, is a civil rights issue.

Andrea Dworkin (author of *Intercourse* and *Pornography: Men Possessing Women*) functions as Trotsky to MacKinnon's Lenin, providing rhetorical fire to her analytical ice. Dworkin came to speak before one of MacKinnon's classes at the University of Minnesota in 1983 and the women have been friends and allies ever since. Here's an example of Dworkin's style: "Know thyself, if you are lucky enough to have a self that hasn't been destroyed by rape in its many forms; and then know the bastard on top of you."

Together, MacKinnon and Dworkin have had some limited successes. Hooking up at various times with such odd fellows as antifeminist Phyllis Schlafly, local opponents of the Equal Rights Amendment or various mountebanks from the religious right, they drafted antiporn ordinances for Indianapolis; Bellingham, Washington; Cambridge, Massachusetts; and Minneapolis and supported them with articles, interviews and public hearings. These proposed laws were either defeated by the voters, vetoed by local politicians or ruled unconstitutional by the courts. But the New Victorians did not surrender.

Last February, Canada's Supreme Court ruled that MacKinnon's basic theory on pornography was correct. It upheld a law suppressing "obscene" material that "subordinates" women, stating that "materials portraying women as a class as objects for sexual exploitation and abuse have a negative impact on the individual's sense of self-worth and acceptance." Yes, the court admitted, this decision limits freedom of expression. But there was a superseding need to halt "the proliferation of materials which seriously offend the values fundamental to our society."

This obviously was a major victory for the New Victorians and for MacKinnon herself; she had worked with a Toronto women's group on the drafting of a brief that supported the Canadian bill. The Canadian court's decision also provided a legal model for what the New Victorians want to see done in the United States. They are now trying to pass similar legislation in Massachusetts.

MacKinnon told *The New York Times:* "It's for the woman whose husband comes home with a video, ties her to the bed, makes her watch and then forces her to do what they did in the video. It's a civil rights law. It's not censorship. It just makes pornographers responsible for the injuries they cause."

That is the heart of this grim little crusade. They want pornographers to disappear under the threat of civil lawsuits. But Massachusetts obviously is a limited target, the focus of parochial attention. They have grander plans for us all. Like the wonderful people who brought us Prohibition (and the Mob), MacKinnon and her allies among the New Victorians want to impose their vision and their rules on the entire country. The likes of Orrin Hatch, Arlen Specter and Alan Simpson moved Senate Bill 1521 out of committee, thus urging their colleagues in the Senate to make the furious, fear-driven visions of MacKinnon and Dworkin the law of the land.

The bill is officially called the Pornography Victims' Compensation Act, and it would allow victims of sex crimes to sue producers and distributors of sexual material if the victims can prove the material incited the crimes. The legislation has been nicknamed the Bundy Bill, after mass killer Ted Bundy, who claimed on the eve of his execution that pornography made him do it. If it passes and is upheld in the current right-wing Supreme Court, Bundy's final victim will surely be the First Amendment.

MacKinnon believes that in America the law is the essential tool of social change. In a narrow sense, this is certainly true. The civil rights of blacks, for example, were more radically altered by *Brown vs. Board of Education* than by many years of prayer, argument and human suffering. But she goes on to insist that the law is not neutral but male, conceived by men to serve the interests of male power. Today, MacKinnon insists, the law serves the interests of male supremacy. And to change the present power arrangements in the United States, the law must be used against itself.

"Our law is designed to . . . help make sex equality real," MacKinnon has written. "Pornography is a practice of discrimination on the basis of sex, on one level because of its role in creating and maintaining sex as a basis for discrimination. It harms many women one at a time and helps keep all women in an inferior status by defining our subordination as our sexuality and equating that with gender."

Surely, that assigns far more power to pornography than it could ever have. But even if you agree with its claims, the question is whether more laws are needed. MacKinnon knows that if a woman is coerced into making a porno film, the people who abused her are subject to a variety of charges, including kidnapping, assault, imprisonment and invasion of privacy. But MacKinnon and Dworkin insist the present laws are not enough. In a discussion of Minneapolis' proposed antiporn ordinance, they said of pornographic acts: "No existing laws are effective against them. If they were, pornography would not flourish as it does, and its victims would not be victimized through it as they are." In other words, because the present laws don't work, add another law. Maybe *that* will work.

The world as MacKinnon sees it is now "a pornographic place" and, as a result, women are being held down, tied up and destroyed. "Men treat women as who they see women as being," MacKinnon writes. "Pornography constructs who that is. Men's power over women means that the way men see women defines who women can be. Pornography is that way. . . . It is not a distortion, reflection, projection, expression, fantasy, representation or symbol, either. It is a sexual reality."

Of course, common sense tells us otherwise. The vast majority of men simply don't use pornography to "construct" women, because the vast majority of men don't ever see much pornography. And the vast majority of men don't spend their days and nights dreaming of inflicting cruelties on women and then carrying them out. If they did, Americans would be up to their rib cages in blood. There are violent men and there is violent pornography (estimated by one study at about five percent of the total produced in the United States). But MacKinnon isn't attacking only the violence she says suffuses the "pornotopia"; she is after pornography itself, as she and her allies define it.

The word that names that concept, as Walter Kendrick points out in his 1987 history of the subject, *The Secret Museum,* can be traced back to the Greek *pornographoi* ("whore-painter"), apparently coined by the second-century writer Athenaeus and promptly forgotten. The word was revived, appropriately, during the Victorian era, and by 1975 the *American Heritage Dictionary* was defining it as "written, graphic, or other forms of communication intended to excite lascivious feelings."

The inequality of women and men in this poor world goes back at least to the late Neolithic Period, long before the creation of pornography or its naming. But MacKinnon and the radical feminists insist that such inequality was "constructed" by pornography. And obviously, the current usage of the word was too mild to serve their purposes. They needed to make it more specific. In *Pornography and Civil Rights,* a 1988 pamphlet that MacKinnon wrote with Dworkin, it is defined as follows:

> Pornography is the graphic, sexually explicit subordination of women through pictures and/or words that also include one or more of the following: (i) women are presented dehumanized as sexual objects, things or commodities; or (ii) women are presented as sexual objects who enjoy pain or humiliation; or (iii) women are presented as sexual objects who experience sexual pleasure in being raped; or (iv) women are presented as sexual objects tied up or cut up or mutilated or bruised or physically hurt; or (v) women

are presented in postures or positions of sexual submission, servility or display; or (vi) women's body parts — including but not limited to vaginas, breasts or buttocks — are exhibited such that women are reduced to those parts; or (vii) women are presented as whores by nature; or (viii) women are presented being penetrated by objects or animals; or (ix) women are presented in scenarios of degradation, injury, torture, shown as filthy or inferior, bleeding, bruised or hurt in a context that makes these conditions sexual.

The use of men, children or transsexuals in the place of women in [the acts cited in the paragraph] above is also pornography.

Obviously, in spite of the specifics, this is a great vague glob of a definition. MacKinnon would most certainly ban *Playboy,* which she says reduces women to mere objects for the use of men. But her definition of pornography limned in *Pornography and Civil Rights* could cover everything from the latest Madonna video to the novels of Henry Miller, Al Capp's Moonbeam McSwine and Gustave Flaubert's *Salammbô,* acres of surrealist paintings, the Koran and James Cagney hitting Mae Clarke with that grapefruit. We would see the last of *Black Bun Busters,* but we could also lose *Don Giovanni.* The great flaw in the antiporn agitation is that it's based on a mystery: the elusive nature of sexuality.

MacKinnon and Dworkin assume that descriptions of sexual cruelty incite men. They write: "Basically, for pornography to work sexually with its major market, which is heterosexual men, it must excite the penis." And "to accomplish its end, it must show sex and subordinate a woman at the same time."

And they follow with an immense leap of logic: "Subordination includes objectification, hierarchy, forced submission and violence."

None of this elaboration solves the basic mystery of sexual excitement. Across the centuries, men have been excited by everything from high heels and nuns' habits to veiled faces and the aroma of rose petals. Some find erotic inspiration in Rubens, others in Giacometti; in the complex mesh of sexuality, there are no rules. Some men may get excited at written or visual images of women being subordinated, others may see those images as appalling and many would be indifferent to them.

But to think that banning pornography will bring about the political goal of eliminating human inequalities or hierarchies is absurd.

The world has always been composed of hierarchies: the strong over the weak, the smart above the dumb, the talented above the ordinary. MacKinnon may not like the existence of those hierarchies (nor the liberal project of protecting the weak, the dumb and the ordinary), but they are unlikely to be changed by a municipal ordinance banning *Three-Way Girls*. Some feminists would tell you that just being a wife is a condition of subordination. There have been hundreds of novels written by literature professors that relate sexual affairs between male teachers and female students; are such works automatically pornographic? The boss-worker equation has been examined in hundreds of thousands of novels, short stories, movies and cartoons. Does that mean that their relationships include "objectification, hierarchy, forced submission and violence"? And if, heaven forbid, they have sex, are they actors in pornography?

MacKinnon and Dworkin allow no room for such questions. Pornography, as they define it, is everywhere around them, the defining presence in American society. They write:

> Pornographers' consumers make decisions every day over women's employment and educational opportunities. They decide how women will be hired, advanced, what we are worth being paid, what our grades are, whether to give us credit, whether to publish our work. . . . They raise and teach our children and man our police forces and speak from our pulpits and write our news and our songs and our laws, telling us what women are and what girls can be. Pornography is their Dr. Spock, their Bible, their Constitution.

If that torrid vision were true, you would be forced to lose all hope for the nation; there would be almost nobody left who is not part of the pornographic lodge. But common sense tells us that the assertion is not true. It is an almost clinically paranoid view of reality (try substituting "communists" or "Jews" for "pornographer's consumers"). Perhaps more important, it is based on a profound ignorance of men.

Like most men I know, I haven't seen or read much hard-core pornography. I gave up after 90 pages of *The 120 Days of Sodom*, the alleged masterpiece by the Marquis de Sade. I found the anonymous Victorian chronicle *My Secret Life* as repetitive in its sexual scorekeeping as a sports autobiography. *Deep Throat* and *The Devil in Miss Jones* held my attention more than the average Doris Day movie ever did, but I thought Eric Rohmer's *Claire's Knee* was far more erotic. That's me. One person.

But in a lifetime as a man, growing up in a Brooklyn slum, as a sailor in the Navy, as a student in Mexico, as a reporter who moved among cops and criminals, schoolteachers and preachers, musicians and athletes, drunks and bartenders, I have never heard anyone celebrate pornography as defined by MacKinnon and Dworkin. Men talk about sex, of course; though the men who talk the most are usually getting the least. And they talk about women, too; but not so often as women think they do. Most S&M books (and acts) are dismissed by most men as freak shows. Even by the bad guys. Every criminal I've known (there are many) has told me that in prison the rapist is the most loathed of all prisoners, except, perhaps, those jailed for abusing children. Pornography simply wasn't central to their lives and usually wasn't even marginal.

I'm hardly an innocent about the realities of sexual violence. As a reporter for more than three decades, I've seen more brutalized bodies of men and women than most people. But their degradation certainly does nothing at all for my penis. I don't think there is any such animal as a "typical" man. But most men I've known are like me: They have no interest in this junk.

My own lack of interest in the hard-core is based on another critique: The people are not people, they are abstractions. In all pornography, men and women are reduced to their genitals.

Oddly enough, that is precisely the way MacKinnon, Dworkin and most of the New Victorians see human beings: as abstractions. They speak of generalized women who are given names and faces only when they are victims. And over and over again, MacKinnon speaks about men as if they all behaved in the same way and were sexually excited by the same imagery. But which men are they talking about? Read this chilly prose and you are asked to believe that Seamus Heaney and Michael Jordan, Sean Connery and François Mitterrand, Gabriel García Márquez and Arnold Schwarzenegger, along with auto mechanics, bread-truck drivers, carpenters and guitar players, are all fully covered by the same word, respond to the same stimuli and are equally dedicated to the subordination of women. That is absurd.

But this sectarian narrowness does help define their vision of human life in this world. That vision is descended from a basic Victorian assumption: All men are beasts and all women are innocents.

Women fall into vice or degradation only at the hands of cruel, un-scrupulous, power-obsessed men. They have no free will and never choose their own loss of grace. Men only see women the way they are presented in pornography and use pornography as a kind of male instruction manual to maintain all forms of supremacy. Women are never brutal, corrupt or evil and they never truly choose to make porno films, dance topless, pose for centerfolds, work as secretaries or, worst of all, get married. Original sin was the fault of men. Eve was framed.

These women claim to know what billions of other women were never smart enough, or enlightened enough, to understand: Sexual intercourse is the essential act of male domination, created by a sinis-ter male cabal to hurt and humiliate all women and thus maintain power over them forever. As Maureen Mullarkey has written in *The Nation:* "In the Dworkin-MacKinnon pornotopia, there are only the fuckers and the fuckees. The sooner the fuckers' books are burned, the better." She doesn't exaggerate. According to Dworkin, all women are "force-fucked," either directly through the crime of rape or by the male power of mass media, by male economic power or by the male version of the law.

It doesn't matter to the New Victorians that the vast majority of women, even many proud feminists, don't see the world the way they do. With the same amazing knowledge of the entire human race that allows her to speak so glibly about men, MacKinnon dismisses their viewpoints as well.

At a 1987 conference organized by Women Against Pornography, MacKinnon was blunt about the pro-sex feminists who had formed the Feminists Against Censorship Taskforce. That group included such women as Betty Friedan, Adrienne Rich and Rita Mae Brown. "The labor movement had its scabs, the slavery movement had its Uncle Toms," MacKinnon said, "and we have FACT." In another enlightening speech she simply dismissed her feminist opponents as "house niggers who sided with the masters."

Today, absolutely certain of their rectitude, totally free of doubt, equipped with an understanding of human beings that has eluded all previous generations, MacKinnon, Dworkin and their allies have been shaping a Victorian solution to their Victorian nightmares. That solution is, pardon the expression, paternalistic. As MacKinnon writes: "Some of the same reasons children are granted some specific legal avenues for redress . . . also hold true for the social position of women compared to men." Since women are, in the MacKinnon view, essentially children, they must be shielded from harm, corruption and filthy thoughts. The savage impulses of the male must be caged. And women must be alerted to the true nature of the beast.

"If we live in a world that pornography creates through the power of men in a male-dominated situation," MacKinnon writes, "the issue is not what the harm of pornography is but how that harm is to become visible."

That's it: Simply make harm visible and we shall live happily ever after. Common sense and wide experience count for nothing. They know that men are loathsome and are clear about how to tame them. Once tamed, they can be subverted, their powers over women will vanish and the grand utopia of complete equality will arrive for all. That bleak vision of human nature has its own escalating logic, just as Lenin's sentimental abstraction of the proletariat led inevitably to the gulag. In her bizarre 257-page book *Intercourse,* Dworkin repeats the theory that MacKinnon and other academic feminists accept as proven: Gender is a mere "social construct," enforced, in Dworkin's elegant phrase, by "vagina-specific fucking."

Once more, the Victorian sense of sexual horror permeates the discussion. If men are the source of all savagery to women, then sexual intercourse with men is itself a savage act. Women who claim to enjoy heterosexual lovemaking are, says Dworkin, "collaborators, more base in their collaboration than other collaborators have ever been, experiencing pleasure in their own inferiority, calling intercourse freedom."

Forget whips, chains and handcuffs. *All* heterosexual intercourse is disgusting, an act of physical and psychic invasion. As Dworkin writes: "The woman in intercourse is a space inhabited, a literal territory occupied literally: occupied even if there has been no resistance, no force; even if the occupied person said yes please, yes hurry, yes more."

Obviously, this is a total denial of any biologically driven sexual need. To follow the logic to its inevitable conclusion, the only pure feminists, the only noncollaborators with the enemy, would be celibates or lesbians. Alas, billions of human beings, male and female, from Tibet to Miami, don't see the world — or the nature of sexuality — that way. They keep on doing what men and women have been doing since before history or the invention of religion. To the New Victorians this must be infuriating. And so they will attempt an act of hubris that even the old Victorians, in their imperial arrogance, did not try. They will correct human nature.

As Americans, MacKinnon, Dworkin and their allies have one major roadblock to their crusade: the Constitution. In their attack on "First Amendment absolutism," the New Victorians want to discard a basic tenet of our lives: It doesn't matter what we say, it is what we do that matters. That is a mere sentimentality, beloved of the hated liberals and the American Civil Liberties Union. Feminism first, says MacKinnon, the legal theorist, the law second. Or put another way: "The bottom line of the First Amendment is that porn stays. Our bottom line is that porn goes. We're going to win in the long term."

For the past few decades there has been a growth in the making and distribution of pornography. The reasons are complicated: the liberalizing of obscenity laws, the development of cheap offset printing and desktop publishing, the triumph of the VCR, the fear of women among some males that was caused by the ferocious oratory of the early days of the feminist movement itself and, lately, the fear of AIDS.

But there is no proof that pornography — even as defined by MacKinnon and Dworkin — causes all human beings to act upon the bodies of women. As MacKinnon herself points out, pornography is essentially an aid to masturbation. And as Gore Vidal once wrote, masturbation is "normal" sex, in the sense that it is surely the most frequent practice among all the world's billions. Certainly the old Victorian belief that masturbation itself is a loathsome evil, a mortal sin, underlies much of the public rhetoric about pornography. But there is one effect that it may have that the New Victorians can't admit. Rather than inspire men to loathsome acts, pornography may actually prevent them. For every rapist who is discovered to have pornography at home, there may be a thousand men who are content to look at the pictures, read the text, whack off and go to sleep. Nobody can prove this, but MacKinnon can't prove that pornography creates monsters, either.

At the various public hearings she and Dworkin have staged, MacKinnon has brought forth a number of women to relate tales of horror. Some were forced into the making of pornography, others were forced by lovers or husbands into imitating the sex acts described by pornography. Those stories were painful and heartbreaking, and their narrators were clearly damaged by their experiences. But it is unlikely that any future hearings will present balancing testimony from a man who says that he lives a perfectly respectable life, except when he gets off a few times a week in private with a copy of *Water Sports Fetish.* As far as I know, even Geraldo hasn't done a show on the joys of masturbation and its amazing social values.

The Meese Commission on Pornography, called into existence by the antiporn forces of the Reagan administration, asserted in 1986 its belief that pornography causes sex crimes. But the fine print in its 1960-page report showed that it couldn't prove it. Six of the 11 commissioners were committed to the antiporn position before studying the evidence and they still could not make a convincing case. They heard from many experts, including MacKinnon. But even an examination of those incidents where pornography was found in the homes of rapists couldn't prove the longed-for assumption.

The reason wasn't elusive. It is a classic error in logic — heightened into an ideological certainty by the New Victorians — to confuse correlation with causality. A survey may discover that 97 percent of heroin addicts consumed white bread in grade school, but that would not prove that white bread caused heroin addiction. Pornography, as defined by MacKinnon and Dworkin, may inspire a small percentage of men to experiment with more elaborate forms of their own preexisting sexual deviances. But it is just as likely that if they had never seen the material, they would have committed sexual crimes anyway. Alcohol is probably involved in more sex crimes than pornography is, and there have been many cases where religious or social repression led to the explosion, particularly among the young.

But one legal and social principle that the Bundy Bill and other New Victorian legislation casts aside is one of the most cherished conservative beliefs: personal responsibility. In a court of law, you can't go free by saying that your upbringing made you do it, or your environment, your mother, father or friends. Still, many try to make that case. Whining has become one of the most widespread characteristics of Americans, even among criminals. In my experience, the classic excuse of the amateur American murderer has been "God made me do it." Guys shoot up post offices or obliterate entire families and claim that God was in the getaway car giving orders. Charles Manson said he was inspired by the Book of Revelations. John Hinckley said he knew he had to shoot President Reagan after reading *The Catcher in the Rye,* and though J. D. Salinger is God only to a small number of fans, the reasoning is the same. When Ted Bundy said that pornography made him do it, the New Victorians cheered. But he was still only copping a plea. *He* did it. Nobody else. Murderers are responsible for their murders. And in every country on earth, rapists do the raping, not some collective called men.

The legal theory that endorses pornography-made-me-do-it, if accepted, would have no limits. Someone could claim that his family was destroyed as the result of published feminist theories attacking the family, and that feminist writers and their publishers must pay for the damage. Environmentalists could be sued for articles and speeches that place the spotted owl above the jobs of loggers.

And it could go beyond such possibilities. Violence permeates American society, and most of its victims are male. If the producers of *Debbie Does Dallas* can be held responsible for the crimes of someone who watched the video, why can't the same be done to the producers of *Terminator 2* or *Halloween 5* or *The Wild Bunch?* You could go after the Road Runner cartoons, too, or *Hamlet* or the opera *Carmen.* In order to cleanse the American imagination, you would need to eliminate the works of Hemingway and Faulkner, along with hundreds of thousands of other novels and theoretical works that could make violence socially acceptable, thereby causing murder and mayhem. You would end up abolishing boxing, hockey and football. You would be forced to censor all war reporting, perhaps even the discussion of war, on the grounds that *Nightline* is the theory and war is the practice.

Obviously, this is pushing the argument to the frontiers of the absurd. But there is an absurd assumption behind the suppressionist argument: that men are a kind of collective tabula rasa on which the pornographers make their indelible marks. An innocent lad from Shropshire picks up a copy of one of the books that MacKinnon cites — say, *Enemas and Golden Showers* — and goes rushing out into the night, enema bag in one hand, cock in the other. That might have made a glorious scene in a John Belushi movie, but common sense tells us that it doesn't happen very often in what we laughingly call real life.

One minor problem with this theory of human behavior concerns MacKinnon and Dworkin. They've obviously pored over more pornography than the ordinary man sees in a lifetime. "Look closely sometime," MacKinnon writes, "for the skinned knees, the bruises, the welts from the whippings, the scratches, the gashes." If human beings are so weak and pornography so powerful, why aren't Mac-Kinnon and Dworkin playing the Krafft-Ebing Music Hall with the rest of the perverts? There are two possible answers. The first is that MacKinnon and Dworkin (and other researchers for the New Victorians) are morally superior to all men and most women and are thus beyond contamination. The second is more likely: The material is so vile that it is a psychological turnoff to all human beings except those with a preexisting condition. Those people do exist. They have been shaped by many variables, none of which are excuses for what they do. But from the experience of the Victorian era, we know that if such people can't find their preferred reading at adult bookstores, they will not give up their sexual fantasies. The fantasies will simply fester in the dark. And they will use what such people use in countries where pornography is now banned — their imaginations.

In such countries — say, Saudi Arabia, Ireland or Iran — the equality of women hasn't been established by banning pornography, but I'm certain that the sexual impulse, and the instinct to dominate, remains alive. Those instincts are part of human nature, and in spite of centuries of effort by archbishops and commissars and even a few philosophers, they are not truly alterable by the power of the state. The sexual impulse, including sexual fantasy, is not subject to the force of reason. Recent history teaches us that most tyrannies have a puritanical nature. The sexual restrictions of Stalin's Soviet Union, Hitler's Germany and Mao's China would have gladdened the hearts of those Americans who fear sexual images and literature. Their iron-fisted puritanism wasn't motivated by a need to erase sexual inequality. They wanted to smother the personal chaos that can accompany sexual freedom and subordinate it to the granite face of the state. Every tyrant knows that if he can control human sexuality, he can control life. In the end, every tyrant fails.

MacKinnon, Dworkin and their allies in the American right insist that they speak for freedom, for the liberation of women from the demeaning or disgusting images of pornography that motivate the male ruling class. They would not be the first human beings who limited freedom while proclaiming allegiance to its virtues. All of these utopians would benefit from a study of the first Victorian era. There was a legal ban on pornography, but women had no rights at all (they were later won by a coalition of brave suffragist women and liberal men). Pornography certainly existed, but it was rarefied, expensive and available only to rich "gentlemen." Official London adhered to the supermoral antisexual codes, but in *real* London syphilis and gonorrhea were rampant. Some 80,000 women were engaged in prostitution, virgins were sold to the highest bidders and the most infamous character of the era rose from the festering sexual underground and called himself Jack the Ripper. What reasonable man or woman would go back to that future?

In a way, the work of MacKinnon and Dworkin is some of the saddest writing I've ever read. It's narrow and sectarian, often vicious and totalitarian in its insistence on submission by other feminists. But it is also thoroughly without joy or wonder. In this bleak house, nothing else matters except the cruelties of sex and power. Not laughter. Not love. Not the simple luminous pleasure of a summer afternoon. There is no room in this dark vision for Fred Astaire or Buster Keaton, for Lucille Ball or Maria Callas, for Betty Comden or Willie Mays. There is no fantasy or magic, no awe in the presence of human beauty, no desire for spiritual or carnal union. Nobody closes the door for a night of joyous, heart-busting, time-bending, mind-obliterating full-out human fucking. Nobody goes to the racetrack, either. Nobody dances at the midnight hour. Nobody plays the blues. In this airless, sunless world, we don't encounter the glorious moment when a child learns to walk or to read. We hear nothing of decent husbands and loving fathers, of families that have triumphed over poverty, or mothers who have lived hard lives with their intelligence, heart, sensuality and pride intact. Such people exist, in the millions, but they are not in this fiercely correct world of rules and anathemas. Above all, in the sad and bitter world of Catharine MacKinnon, there is no wide tolerant understanding of a species capable of forgiving our endless gift for human folly. There are only the lacerated and the harmed and the odor of the charnel house. I don't envy their dreams. And I hope I'm never forced to live in their fearful new world.

PLAYBOY,
January 1993

ENDGAME

I.

As this dreadful century winds down, its history heavy with gulags and concentration camps and atom bombs, the country that was its brightest hope seems to be breaking apart.

All the moves toward decency, excellence, maturity, and compassion have been made. They seem to have come to nothing. Everyone talks and nobody listens. Boneheaded vulgarians are honored for their stupidity. The bitterly partisan debate on the crime bill in the U.S. Senate is remembered only for Al D'Amato's rendition of "Old MacDonald Had a Farm." The Christian Coalition commandeers the Republican state convention in Virginia, and among the slogans on the wall is one that says WHERE IS LEE HARVEY OSWALD WHEN AMERICA REALLY NEEDS HIM? The American social and political style has been reduced to the complexity of a T-shirt. Outta the way, asshole: Give us gridlock, give us *Beavis and Butt-head,* give us room, man, give us *respect,* and get outta my fuckin' face!

We are approaching Endgame, the moment when the chessboard is clear and victory is certain. Victory over everybody. The reduction of the opposition to rubble.

American civil society, long founded on the notion of "from many, one," *e pluribus unum,* is being swept away by a poisonous flood tide of negation, sectarianism, self-pity, confrontation, vulgarity, and flat-out, old-fashioned hatred. Politics is an ice jam of accusation and obstruction, the hardest vulgarians honored for their cynicism, its good men fleeing to tend private gardens. Pop culture both feeds and reflects the larger society, and as evidence of collapse, it is chilling. Snoop Doggy Dogg and Al D'Amato have triumphed over Wynton Marsalis and George Mitchell. Good taste lies up the block with an ax in its back.

Day and night, from millions of car stereos and boom boxes, gangsta rappers and skinhead semi-demi-quasi-neo-Nazis give the nation its most persistent, defining soundtrack. Some call for the killing of cops, the raping and abandonment of ho's and bitches, the battering of whites or blacks or one another. Rob the weak, they croon. Stomp the soft. Rap videos are pathetic fantasies of force and power, visual tributes to the cult of the Big Gun and the Big Dick. There is no past and no future, only the eternal American present tense. Suburban white kids happily buy the CDs and lean into the lash. There is no room in the music for lyricism, melody, or wit. The only acceptable human emotion is rage.

The fake, the illusion, the performance, are everything. The truth? Hey, buddy, I got your truth, right *here.* At *The 1994 MTV Video Music Awards,* Michael Jackson walks on with his bride, the daughter of Elvis Presley. They hit their marks. They engage in a rehearsed kiss. Jackson whispers some clumsy joke about how nobody thought this would last: marriage as Special Material. They get a standing O. Of course. Nobody mentions that Jackson had to pay an estimated $20 million to settle a child-molestation rap in California. Hey, man, lighten *up.* The man's got a multimillion-dollar career to save! Who cares if we're watching a big press-agented lie? He paid for his sins. Cold cash. Now he's redeeming himself with *access.* And if he *acts* as if he wants redemption, that *is* redemption.

So shut up, asshole, and listen to Roseanne deliver her spontaneously written opening remarks: "I'm not upset about my divorce. I'm only upset I'm not a widow. . . ." Pay attention to Kennedy. You know, the veejay. Look what she's doing. She's standing behind New York mayor Rudy Giuliani, sucking off the microphone! Is that hip or what? You know the gag. Kennedy is a *right-winger,* man. That's why Roseanne said she saw Kennedy backstage and "she asked me to leave because she was blowing Rush Limbaugh." But Kennedy doesn't take any crap. Later on, she tells the audience: "I was backstage giving Rush Limbaugh a hummer. That's a [simulates fellatio] in case you guys didn't know. . . . I have to concede to Roseanne. He said that she gives a much better blow job. So the Prozac's working." But here comes Roseanne right back: "I would like to respond to Kennedy. I'm no longer on Prozac, bitch. Rush Limbaugh told me you swallow."

God bless America.

But if Rodgers and Hart are long gone, so are Edmund Wilson and Ralph Gleason and James Agee. The greatest critics loved the subjects of their examinations: literature, music, movies. They celebrated quality and dismissed the fraudulent, examining each new object of art the way a master watchmaker looks at another man's watch, admiring the accomplishments, pointing out the flaws. There were always literary ax murderers among them. But in a way, the best of them were attorneys for the defense. They've been replaced by prosecutors. And the penalty they demand for imperfection is death. Behind them have arrived the successmeisters, those who rank artists as if they were entrants in the National Football League, failure the unforgivable sin. Book didn't work? Record didn't make it? Movie opened on Aeromexico? That's it: Arraign him, convict him, get him outta my sight. Sentence him to teach. Book him as a lounge act. Make him an usher. Drop him off the gibbet.

In sports, the style established thirty years ago by Muhammad Ali has been appropriated by his inferiors, who emphasize the "dissing" but leave out the irony and the humor. (Only Charles Barkley really gets it.) Prizefighters learn how to demean a man before they've mastered the uppercut. Reggie Miller isn't satisfied with playing better than most men in the NBA; he has to make choke signs and grab his crotch and keep up a torrent of trash talk. No football player seems able to carry a ball for a touchdown without following up with some taunting dance in the end zone. Goodbye, Jim Brown; farewell, Gale Sayers; hello, Neon Deion. No baseball player since Don Baylor has been able to endure the occupational hazard of a knockdown pitch without charging the mound in retaliation. In all sports, grace is treated like a character flaw. Athletes snarl and mock in triumph — and whine in defeat.

But they have one large excuse: They are only part of this America, the torn, violent country where everybody now plays for keeps. The nation approaching Endgame.

Everybody seems infected with the virus of argument and the need for triumph. Leaders of tiny sects are granted huge television audiences, provided their messages are sufficiently drastic, violent, or stupid; more people know about Louis Farrakhan, of the Nation of Islam, than know about Octavio Paz or Isaiah Berlin. Hour after hour, across the day and deep into the night, talk radio spews forth a relentless message of contempt for democratic institutions, from the presidency, the Congress, and the Supreme Court to the governors, state legislators, and mayors. Rush Limbaugh is the master of this electronic genre, but his imitators make him sound like Henry Adams. They have none of Limbaugh's gift for brittle humor and venomous sarcasm. Anyone with compassion is a target. Anyone with a sense of complexity is scorned. Callers with accents are jeered. Complicated issues are reduced to cartoons. Maybe it's an act. Maybe it's just cashing in on Limbaugh's success. But the drumbeat from these electronic kraals is ominous: Hate Washington, hate the media, hate the liberals, hate the blacks, hate the dark-skinned and their babies, hate democracy. All disguised, of course, as a love for America.

In the rest of the media, virtually all public activity is treated as a fight in an alley. If the subjects of stories are not shooting down opponents, they usually don't get covered. Murder is the best story, of course, but even the more tedious stories can be treated like homicides. Health care, welfare reform, GATT, NAFTA: Answer me, baby, who struck John?

In the freest country on the planet, democratic political campaigns are a ghastly joke. The ideal candidate is a cipher, devoid of personal history. The handlers write the scripts, build the drama, concoct the spin, and get famous themselves. Nobody expects them to *believe* any of this bullshit; *oye, compadre,* get *real.* The job is done with a wink, a curled lip, a bony cynicism. None of this 1960s idealism, for chrissakes. The greater the cynicism, the greater the rewards. Hey, look at James Carville. Full of all that Vince Lombardi stuff about winning being everything. He got Clinton from Little Rock to the White House, didn't he? It was the economy, stupid. And Mary Matalin! She's got the knife out, fighting for George Bush. Destroy the Democrats! Save the republic! Naturally, Carville and Matalin get married. Hey, man, don't laugh. The script is everything. It's a Tracy-Hepburn movie. It's a *book deal!* Maybe it's . . . *a fucking network series.*

Meanwhile, in every state, in major cities, in contests for the Senate or the school board, the public discourse is all heat and no illumination. The attack ads come rolling forth, reducing opponents to agents of Lucifer. Vote for me, not the other guy. He's bad, guilty, corrupt, and stupid; therefore, I'm good, I'm innocent, I'm honest, I'm smart. He's got a wife and kids? He has an ailing mother? Hey, don't bother me with details, pal, we're playing hardball here! Quick, my flack, hand me a label: womanizer, flip-flopper, liar, and, uh, *liberal. Brrrrruuuuupppppp.* Who's next?

Most of the American news media have been debased, too. Newspaper, magazine, and television editors *and* their audiences have been powerfully altered by forty-five years of television drama. The average American household now watches about seven hours of television a day, an appetite for entertainment unknown in human history. The result: The American imagination is jammed with the structures of melodrama. Not analysis, not cool judgment, not the humanizing imagery of high art. Drama. Most of it *bad* drama. And as it has been since the time of Aristotle, the essence of drama is conflict.

Even the conflicts of the so-called *real* world — the nonfiction world of news and society — must be simple, easy to follow through meals and other domestic activities, and preferably violent. Following the style of the television tabloid shows, even some network magazines are using feature-film gimmicks: music to tell the viewer what he should feel; ominous photography or bright, happy lighting to make emotional points. *Don't think* is the message; *feel*. In all media, the best-played stories now are the ones that most resemble movies. Give us good guys and bad guys, white hats and black hats, and for chrissakes, don't give us talking heads! Action, baby. Bang-bang. *Conflict*.

In the name of egalitarian vulgarity, the newspapers and the television shows fill up with O. J. Simpson, Lorena Bobbitt, her moronic husband, Amy Fisher, the Menendez brothers; serial killers and heroic cops; priests who corrupt kids and kids who kill parents; drug warriors, gun nuts, and politicians caught getting laid. They in turn become subjects for fictional docudramas of invincible stupidity.

Every day, the American vision becomes cruder, narrower, more parochial. In most newspapers, foreign news gets little play unless Americans are involved. The major newspapers still employ foreign correspondents of immense gifts, but even the greatest reporters must battle for space against the tremendous force of the general parochialism. The mass-circulation newspapers don't even bother. Unless Americans are concerned, most foreign news seems to be about Princess Di.

To be sure, there are exceptions to the tide of simple-minded stupidity. C-Span has become a wonderful window into some areas of the society; it allows us to see the boring parts of the craft of governance. Court TV has the potential to educate more Americans about the law than any medium in the country's history. CNN does a splendid job, in many ways, bringing the audience closer to the outside world than newspapers ever could. But the emphasis remains on conflict, drama, present tense, bang-bang: *Crossfire* is hardly the forum for thoughtful analysis. Maybe nothing is. The networks were positioned to cover the armed invasion of Haiti; when Jimmy Carter made his deal, most returned to the soap operas and talk shows, or cut back, with a sigh of relief, to the O.J. hearings. Who the hell wants to cover a *peaceful* intervention?

As we move toward Endgame, consider this: We live in a country that has never made a movie about Leonardo da Vinci and has produced three about Joey Buttafuoco.

II. US AGAINST THEM

In the wider society, true to the principles of conflict, an often bewildering variety of social factions batter at one another for position and victory (or, as the jargon goes, "hegemony"). Their purpose isn't to make a better society, a place where that illusive American goal, harmony, is possible. The goal is therapy. The goal is dominance. The goal is vengeance: to take no prisoners and, in Murray Kempton's phrase, shoot the wounded.

The unraveling process can have many names: fragmentation, disunification, atomization, balkanization, disintegration. Thoughtful men and women — among them Arthur M. Schlesinger Jr., Gertrude Himmelfarb, Michael Walzer, Allan Bloom, the late William A. Henry III, Robert Hughes — have looked at the battlefield from different positions. They offer their own analyses of the causes of and remedies for the Endgame psychology of permanent division and confrontation. But most agree about the symptoms.

One of the most obvious is also the most disheartening: Almost a hundred years after the last great immigration wave changed the face of American society, vast numbers of Americans — including, sadly, the best-educated — are again being taught to identify themselves with the qualifying adjectives of race, religion, ethnicity, and gender. The idea of the melting pot is dismissed as cultural genocide, replaced by a social worker's version of predestination. American identities, state the clerics of the new dogma, are not shaped by will, choice, reason, intelligence, and desire but by membership in groups. They are not individuals but components of categories, those slots and pigeonholes beloved of sociologists, pollsters, and the U.S. Census Bureau. And such categories, they believe, are destiny.

The ferocious logic of the adjective insists that the individual take sides. To refuse is to betray the larger group, your own flesh and blood. In America now, it is always Us against Them and Them against Us. And to display its anger, its innocence, its righteousness, our side must be in conflict with their side. It's not enough to be an American; you must despise, attack, diminish, and empty the guts of those millions of other Americans who are not like you. Every grave must be pried open by scholarship, every smashed bone waved in triumph like a relic, every ancient crime posted on the schoolhouse door.

The result is a society in apparently permanent, teeming, nerve-fraying conflict: blacks against whites; straights against gays, gays against priests, priests against abortionists; sun people against ice people; citizens against immigrants; Latinos against Anglos; people who work against those who don't; town against gown; blacks against Jews; the orthodox against the reformers; cops against bad guys, lawyers against cops, Crips against Bloods. Good guys and bad guys. Oppressors and oppressed. White hats and black hats. And vice versa. Us against Them. Them against Us. And get outta my fuckin' face.

But there are additional confusions. All the victimized ethnic categories contain *men*. And the feminist rhetoric of the Endgame insists that men are themselves a group of oppressors — brutal, insensitive, selfish, murderous. Catharine MacKinnon and others use the word *men* in the same generalized, blurry way that *women* is used. This astonishingly broad category — men — is defined all too easily by people who believe that the same state of victimhood is endured by the Wellesley graduate and the woman grinding corn in the hills of Chiapas, by Billie Holiday and Katharine Graham, by Jean Harris and Ilse Koch. The existentialist philosophers of my youth insisted that existence preceded essence, that you were born and *then* you forged your identity; the philosophers of gender and ethnicity insist that essence precedes existence.

The ideologues of gender don't care much about making distinctions among men *or* women. Common sense and experience tell us that among the earth's billions, there must be some women who are happy and free and others who are brutal and evil. Common sense and intelligence tell us there are millions of black Americans who are not trapped in lives of welfare, violence, illegitimacy. But common sense is in disrepute. The examination of healthy lives is too often dismissed as sentimentality or "anecdotal" gossip, unverifiable under the cold-eyed scrutiny of such exact sciences as sociology or anthropology. The Endgamers of race and gender will limit their investigations to their own kind, the victims. They will define the group by its pathologies and defeats, not its triumphs. Like all believers, they begin with the truth and find evidence to support it. They adhere to a faith, abstract and rigid, full of iron certainties, free of the century's only useful lesson: doubt.

But doubt is unsettling. And the overriding educational goal these days is to make students — in particular, minority students — feel better about themselves. Unless they *feel* better, the argument goes, unless they acquire greater "self-esteem," they can't learn. The need to *think* better, with greater subtlety and lucidity, is seldom mentioned. And of course nobody — black, white, or Latino; middle-class or poor — should be forced to work very hard. Not at school. Not after school. Kids need time to watch television. They need time to hang out. They need time to work on their *images*.

They are in much trouble, and so are we. The notion of education as therapy has led to the distortion of history, the reduction of standards, and, in the new-fashioned American style, the creation of enemies. The examination of an *American* identity is made subservient to the word before the hyphen. Obviously, the accomplishments of American blacks, Latinos, other minorities, and women should be made known to *all* Americans, not to make them feel better but to make them know more about their own country and the world of which it is a part. Alas, that is not the goal.

The endless, energy-sapping debate over "multiculturalism" is an example of the more general problem. The word itself is an oxymoron. Every bookshelf is multicultural. Every library is multicultural. Every educated man and woman is multicultural. *Culture* is multicultural.

But the most rigid advocates of this form of the hyphen aren't really talking about the multiple, the plural, or about the natural human movement toward synthesis. They don't want to add to the fund of individual knowledge. They are insisting upon indoctrination, on the replacement of the many with the singular. There is only one road to Rome — and they know what it is.

Afrocentrism, for example, is not multicultural. As preached by men like New York's City College professor Leonard Jeffries Jr., it is a segregation of the mind. It is also a fraud. As Václav Havel said in 1990, as part of his struggle against the Endgame impulses of Communists and anti-Communists: Lying can never save us from another lie.

In the raging battle over education, Endgamers like Jeffries are now demanding the right to peddle lies. Literature and history have common intentions: to discover the truth about human beings. They can't be shaped by a creed, an ideology, or a thesis; they can't be wrapped in the straitjackets of political fashion. Stalinist novels were not novels; they were tracts. Hitler's movies were not art; they were propaganda. Mao's poetry is the stuff of wall posters. There have been great Marxist historians, including our own Eugene D. Genovese, but they didn't alter the facts to prove the thesis. In the end, history should be history, not an alibi.

"If some Kleagle of the Ku Klux Klan wanted to devise an educational curriculum for the specific purpose of handicapping and disabling black Americans," wrote Arthur M. Schlesinger Jr., "he would not be likely to come up with anything more diabolically effective than Afrocentrism."

Most purveyors of this therapeutic nonsense attack their critics as racists. But the basic trouble with infusing kids with racial or ethnic chauvinism is that it doesn't even work as therapy. Instead of feeling better about themselves, most of these kids come out of the process seething with bitterness. And this being the United States, anger and rage are followed by the need to blame. Hell, it can't be *my* fault.

The demands for reparations and revision go on and on, spilling into the newspapers, then amplified by talk radio and television. As presented, there is no solution, because the apocalyptic demand is for the alteration of the past or a surrender of intelligence or an assumption of guilt by the living for the crimes of the dead. But resolution really isn't the point of all this sound and fury. Fragmentation is the point. Segregation is the point. Conflict is all. We're Americans. We have been conditioned to prefer conflict to boredom. We prefer violence to talk. We prefer war to peace. We prefer lies to the truth. Clear the board, citizen: We're reaching Endgame.

III. PROFESSIONAL CYNICS

The Endgame culture of cynicism and bitterness is, of course, best observed in Washington. The genius of the American system has been its ability to compromise. We learned from the fratricide of the Civil War that a failure to compromise could unleash the darkest, bloodiest impulses in the American character. Over the years, we developed in Washington a nonideological style that helped us avoid direct conflict. Sometimes you won, sometimes you lost; politics was a long season, like baseball, in which even the greatest hitters failed six times out of ten. Most of the time, the system worked. Slowly. Tediously.

There were human reasons for this. The state was founded on a document, not evolved through a long, shared common history; its principles and promises were abstract. But after 1890, the nation was populated by huge numbers of Europeans who were different from the original British settlers. They were Catholic or Jewish; they often spoke languages other than English or were illiterate farmers. In one big country, they joined the survivors of the slaughter of the Indians, liberated slaves, conquered Mexicans. To meld them into a unified nation required immense efforts of mediation and compromise on the part of the agents of the state. The greatest task was to make the idealism of the Constitution real for every citizen; the alternative was the kind of deep, abiding cynicism that eventually eroded the Communist states, which also had idealistic constitutions. This wasn't easy. Along the way, there were unspeakable crimes against the newcomers, uncountable social offenses, bloody riots, and the horrors of the Civil War. But slowly, decent, intelligent men and women created a living nation from the abstract principles of the state.

That agonizing process created the twentieth-century American political style. The most effective politicians — Sam Rayburn, Everett Dirksen, Lyndon Johnson, Robert Taft — employed a basic courtesy in dealing with their opponents. They disagreed on many things. They were capable of immense vanity. They knew that in the end, politics was about power. But they didn't think it necessary to destroy the enemy. The enemy was over there: Hitler, Tojo, Stalin. Those who swung the broadswords of racism or ideology at other Americans — the Joe McCarthys, the Bilbos and Eastlands — accomplished nothing. They were cheap, vulgar men — ignorant, parochial, and cynical. They never rose to higher office because the American people would not have them. The tougher men who truly changed the country, who moved it along, who made it *better,* did so with a clarity of vision and a certain amount of grace. They were mercifully free of the utopian instinct. They were always willing to settle for half a loaf. And they each in their own way did think about what was best for the country. They were, after all, Americans before they were Texans or Ohioans or Democrats or Republicans. They respected the contract. They respected the presidency.

That era is behind us, perhaps forever.

Look at what is being done to Bill Clinton.

I don't think Bill Clinton is the greatest president we've ever had. But I know he is certainly not the worst. This is a country, after all, that elected Warren G. Harding once and Richard Milhous Nixon twice. But from the moment of his election, Clinton has been subjected to the most sustained campaign of *personal* abuse of any president in memory. No rumor, no allegation of promiscuity, goes unprinted. Jerry Falwell, an alleged man of God, peddles videos that virtually accuse Clinton of murdering Vincent Foster Jr. A newspaper for which I used to work ran a series of stories about the same case that put quote marks around the word *suicide*. The implication was clear: If Foster didn't kill himself, he must have been murdered. Aha! A movie plot! Melodrama!

While reporters were chasing around after Whitewater, Gennifer Flowers, various state troopers, Paula Jones, and God knows who else, Clinton was actually accomplishing a few things as president. The Republicans linked arms in a spirit of mindless obstruction, led by Dole, but Clinton somehow managed to get an economic plan through Congress, cutting the deficit for the first time in a generation, creating more than four million new jobs. He got NAFTA passed, doing so in opposition to organized labor *and* Ross Perot. He finally won passage of his crime bill, too, directly challenging the National Rifle Association. He lost on health-care reform, overwhelmed by the Endgamers who spent millions on attack ads and refused to join the process of compromise. He couldn't overcome the Republican filibuster on campaign reform and lost that, too; Dole continued to make the world safe for lobbyists and cynicism. But in some real ways, the country was in better shape than it had been on the day he took office. Unemployment was down. The economy was stronger. The stock market was healthy. In the Middle East, South Africa, Northern Ireland, the forces of peace and conciliation were winning the day, supported by American policies and actions.

And yet Clinton is the most hated president in memory.

His reluctant intervention in Haiti was an example of the process. Jimmy Carter, Colin Powell, and Sam Nunn worked out a deal that would allow American troops to go into Haiti without shooting. The junta of Raoul Cédras would give up power on October 15. The deposed president, Jean-Bertrand Aristide, would return to power and serve out the term to which he was elected in the only free election in that nation's agonized history. For a few hours, most sane people thought this was a rational solution to a miserable situation. At least American soldiers wouldn't have to go in shooting. And some of them wouldn't have to die.

But before anybody could know how this would work out, the attacks started. The Republicans, who cheered for intervention in Grenada, Panama, and the Persian Gulf, suddenly developed the white wings of doves. Bob Dole sounded like George McGovern, stating that Haiti was not worth a single American life. The radio chatterers unleashed ferocious barrages, attacking Clinton for ducking Vietnam and now putting Americans in harm's way, dismissing Aristide as an anti-American Marxist nutcase. Joe Klein in *Newsweek* called the intervention "a bizarre Caribbean adventure" while also stating that Clinton "did the right thing" and sneering at Carter as "the Prince of Peace." Michael Kramer in *Time* wrote that "Bill Clinton at war has the disquieting countenance of Bill Clinton at peace; few principles seem inviolate; indiscipline and incoherence are the norm; careful planning falls to last-minute improvisation; steadfastness is only a tactic."

Journalists are not cheerleaders, of course; they must maintain an adversarial stance with politicians. But the vehemence of the attacks on Clinton seems more a reflex than thought and analysis. A line has developed on Clinton, and to swerve from it entails risks, most of them social and professional. Few people like to face the question, "Are you fucking *kidding?*" My objection here isn't with the facts or the implications of disaster but with the venomous tone.

In modern times, that slashing, lacerating use of language came into the discourse with Vietnam. It was first employed against Lyndon Johnson (I used plenty of it myself), then Richard Nixon, justified by the endless slaughter of the war and then by Watergate. Irony was lost, along with a sense of shared tragedy. What mattered was the casting of anathemas. The Left used the tone first, then the Right picked it up; now it comes easily to almost everybody. The tone is sometimes apocalyptic and always judgmental, and its essential component is the sneer.

These days, most members of the Washington press corps wear a self-absorbed sneer. They sneer at any expression of idealism. They sneer at gaffes, mistakes, idiosyncrasies. They sneer at the "invisibility" of national-security adviser Anthony Lake but sneer at others for being publicity hounds. They sneer at weakness. They sneer at those who work too hard, and they sneer at those who work too little. They fill columns with moralizing about Clinton and then attack others for moralizing. The assumption is that everyone has a dirty little secret, and one's duty is to sniff it out.

Lost in this rancorous process is any regard for the great American art of compromise. Clinton, a professional politician, obviously believes in it and is sneered at for being an incessant placater of his opponents. Give us the whole loaf or nothing, comes the intolerant call. Make me feel better. Make me happy. Make life perfect. If you don't, then give us term limits. Get rid of the professional pols and give us amateurs. Oliver North. Ross Perot. Don't tell me the world is complicated.

Pericles couldn't govern that polity. What chance can Clinton have? Domestically, he's indicted for being too liberal or too conservative, too soft or too callous, too indifferent to public opinion or too desirous of consensus. In foreign affairs, his most poisonous critics remain in thrall to Ronald Reagan's Hollywood worldview, the Big Dumb Ox theory of foreign engagement, using naked power to get your way.

After all, if a president won't smash his domestic opponents, if he won't kill foreigners with icy dispatch, how can he deal with the blacks and the Mexicans and the immigrants and the feminists and the Cubans and the poor and the rich and the disabled and the pornographers and the liberals and the guys with the hyphens in their names? How can he be a *leader?* How can he be a *man?*

If this goes on, escalating by the hour, the country is doomed. It will remain a state, of course, a geographical entity; but it won't be a nation. We are in the midst of the largest immigration wave since the turn of the last century. If we have already succumbed to our own jagged forms of tribalism, we can't hope to absorb and assimilate the new arrivals. If we tell the new immigrants that to be an American is to insist on status as a victim, to hate the president and the government, to fear one's neighbor, to reduce all discourse to the most primitive level, then our twenty-first century will be a horror. *E pluribus unum* was not intended to be a gigantic mockery. It's time for all Americans to think about what we're doing to ourselves. It's time to ostracize the sectarian swine who, in Yeats's phrase, multiply through division. It's time to honor good taste, hard work, and all those men and women who cherish human decency.

The gulags are gone. The concentration camps exist only in memory. Nobody worries much anymore about atom bombs. But fear is a habit like any other. So is the need for an enemy. And as the great cartoonist Walt Kelly said long ago, "We have met the enemy and he is us." We can't allow that to replace *e pluribus unum* as the American national slogan. We have to learn how to pipe down and back off. We have to stop shouting for a little while and learn again how to listen.

Otherwise, it's black hats and white hats.

Us against Them.

Me against you.

Endgame.

ESQUIRE,
December 1994

PART VII

ROLLING THE DICE

These are personal pieces, about living and about not dying. With any luck, they won't be the last about either subject.

I have arrived at last in that peculiar zone where I am no longer young and not yet old. This stage of a human life is called, of course, middle age. Alas, even that familiar phrase is inaccurate; at fifty-two, I am not in the middle of my life, for there is little chance that I will live to 104. But I am certainly in the middle of my *adult* life, and this sometimes causes personal astonishment. In the course of my time here, I have seen much of the world, loved women, fathered children, worked at several trades, committed cruelties and engaged in folly, had fine meals and good times, drowsed through summer afternoons and heard the chimes at midnight. That is to say, I have lived a life. I am far from finished with that splendid accident, but there is one enormous fact attached to the condition called middle age: I know now that the path is leading inexorably through the evening to the barn. And not far away, up ahead, perhaps over that next lavender hill, lies death.

Above all, the acceptance of certain death is what distinguishes this age of man. For some, the imminence of death creates remorse about the waste of time and opportunities; for others, fear; for a few, relief; for many, a sense of urgency. This is the time of life when men throw over careers to try painting in the South of France; they leave wives for ballerinas; they hole up in mountain cabins to read Proust; they gaze at the shotgun on the wall of the den and see only the quarry of the self. *I am going to die,* the man whispers to himself. *Sooner than later.* This dramatic sense of the inevitable doesn't resemble the fatalism of the combat soldier, who knows that if he lives, he will still be in command of his youth. Nor does the vision of death have the dark romantic glamour it has when you are young. If you have reached middle age, you have already chosen to live. But the warning signs of decline and decay are as unavoidable as sunset. The most obvious are physical.

One summer, after a grueling winter of work, I discovered I had grown a paunch. A bathroom scale told me that I had gained only ten pounds, but the suety paunch, noticed suddenly in the window of a store, made me look like another person, some chunky middle-aged stranger going about his mundane business. The paunch would not go away, and I have been unable to summon the force of my dormant adolescent vanity to work it off. At the same time, white patches appeared in my beard and a few white hairs mysteriously sprouted from my scalp. Because I do not shave, and thus don't engage in morning ablutions, I see my face less frequently than I did when young; these changes were sudden reminders of the inevitable.

Three years ago, I awoke with a terrible pain in my left shoulder; the day before, I had been lifting free weights just to see what I could do; I was sure I had merely pulled a muscle. But the pain went on for months, ruining sleep, aching at all hours. I assumed comical positions in bed, searching for stillness. I found myself unable to pitch quarters into the receptacles at toll booths. I thought: I might live the rest of my life with this pain. I was wrong, of course; the pain was cured with a few shots of cortisone. But the hard, invincible body I thought I possessed when young is gone.

Sometimes I hear my own labored breathing and instantly remember the emphysemic sounds of my father's final years. Fifteen years ago I discovered with alarm that I could not read a scoreboard without glasses; now I don spectacles to watch the evening news. In my twenties, I once worked seventy-three hours straight without sleep, belting down waterfalls of coffee, smoking too many cigarettes, listening through the nighttime hours to Symphony Sid. What I then lacked in craft I made up for with energy. Now I take naps in the afternoon. I have been a fortunate man, free of diseases, with few physical injuries. But now I go each year for the physical examination by the doctor and dread the first appearance of blood in the stool or the spot on the X ray.

Some of the minor warning signs are mental. I cannot, for example, remember any additional names or numbers. I am introduced to a stranger at a dinner party and the new name breaks into letters and flies around the room like dead leaves in an autumn wind. In the past year, I have moved with my wife into a small city apartment and a house in the country; I must carry the telephone numbers and the zip codes in my wallet. Once I hauled around in my head the batting averages of entire baseball teams; now I must search them out each day in the newspaper. My memory of the days and nights of my youth remains fine; it is last year that is a blur. It's as if one of the directories in my brain has reached its full capacity and will accept no more bytes.

None of these small events is original to me, of course. I'm aware that some variation of them has happened to all aging human beings from the beginning of time. As a reporter I've witnessed much of the grief of other human beings, the astonishing variety of their final days. And I knew, watching my father get old and then die, that aging was inevitable; it had happened to him, and I'd seen it happen to my friends. Still, it was a cause of some wonder to undergo changes that had not been willed, that hadn't enlisted my personal collaboration.

To acknowledge the inevitability of death, however, is not to fear it. I was more afraid of death at thirty-five than I am now. My night thoughts that year were haunted by visions of the sudden end of my life. Images of violence, carried over from my work as a reporter, roamed freely through my dreams. Before sleep, I would act out imaginary struggles with the knife-wielding intruder who was somewhere out in those shadowed streets. I did a lot of drinking that year. I slept too often with the light on.

In middle age, I recognize that most of my fear at thirty-five came from a sense of incompletion. That age is a more critical one for American men than is fifty, because the majority of us have grown up obsessed with sports. At thirty-five, a third baseman is an aged veteran, a football player has been trampled into retirement, a prizefighter is tending bar somewhere, wearing ridges of old scar tissue as the sad ornaments of his trade.

But at thirty-five, I often felt as if I was only beginning to live (and of course I was right). I wanted more time, and the prospect of death filled me with panic. There were still too many books that I wanted to write and countries to see and women to love. I hadn't read Balzac or Henry James. I had never been to the Pitti Palace. I wanted to see my daughters walk autonomously in the world. This is the only life I will ever lead (I murmured on morose midnights at the bar of the Lion's Head), and to end it in my thirties would be unfair.

Today, I accept the inevitable more serenely. I know that I will never write as many books as Georges Simenon or read as many as Edmund Wilson. Nor will I enter a game in late September to triple up the alley in center field and win a pennant for the Mets. But my daughters live on their own in the world. I have read much of Henry James and the best of Balzac and have walked the marbled acres of the Pitti Palace. Middle age is part of the process of completion of a life, and that is why I've come to lose the fear of death. I've now lived long enough to understand that dying is as natural a part of living as the falling of a leaf.

And yet, sometimes I wake up in the mornings (usually in an unfamiliar room in a strange city) and in the moments between sleep and true consciousness, I am once again in the apartment on Calle Bahia de Morlaco in Mexico City when I was twenty-one, full of possibilities, with my whole life spread out before me. When I realize where I truly am, and that I am fifty-two and no longer that confused and romantic boy, I am filled with an anguished sadness.

In the three decades since I left Mexico (I was a student of painting there on the GI Bill), I have committed my share of stupidities. The first time around, I was a dreadful husband. I tried to be a good father but made many mistakes. As a young newspaper columnist, drunk with language, I occasionally succumbed to mindless self-righteousness, coming down viciously on public men when I could not bear such an assault myself. I treated some women badly and failed others. There were other sins, mortal and venial.

But in middle age, you learn to forgive yourself. Faced with the enormous crimes of the world (and particularly the horrors of this appalling century), you acquire a sense of proportion about your own relative misdemeanors. You have slowly recognized the cyclical nature of society's enthusiasms, from compassion to indifference, from generosity to meanness, liberalism to conservatism and back, as the pendulum cuts its inexorable arc in the air. And you know that such cycles are true of individuals too. Each of us goes from the problems of others to the problems of the self and back again, over and over, for the duration of our lives. And most often, we measure our own triumphs and disasters, errors and illusions, against the experiences of others. In middle age, I know that it is already too late to agonize over my personal failings. As Popeye once said, "I yam what I yam an' that's all I yam." The damage of the past is done; nothing can be done to avoid it or to repair it; I hope to cause no more, and I'm sometimes comforted by remembering that to many people I was also kind. For good or ill, I remain human. That is to say, imperfect.

And yet I would be a liar if I suggested that I have no regrets. It is that emotion (not guilt or remorse) that comes to me in half-sleep. I wish I hadn't wasted so much of my young manhood drinking; I had some great good times, but I passed too much time impaired. A few of those years are completely lost from memory, and memory is a man's only durable inheritance (I retired from drinking in 1972, with the title). I've employed too much of my talent at potboiling, executing other men's visions for the movies or television, in order to feed and clothe and house my children and to ward off a slum kid's fear of poverty; at twenty-one, growing up in the '50s when the worst of all sins was "selling out," I could not foresee any of that. Through sloth or absorption in work, I allowed some good friendships to wither. I too rashly sold a house I loved and years later still walk its halls and open all of its closets.

I also regret the loss of the illusions of my youth. This is so familiar a process, of course, that it is a cliché. Better men than I, from the anonymous author of the Book of Ecclesiastes to André Malraux, have acquired the same sorrowful knowledge. It's difficult to explain to the young the heady excitement that attended the election of John F. Kennedy or the aching hole his death blew through this country. More impossible still to tell them that there actually was a time, when I was young, when Americans thought that change could be effected through politics. When Fidel Castro triumphed over Fulgencio Batista on New Year's Day in 1959, I cheered with all my friends; now poor Fidel is just another aging Stalinist. Once I embraced the hope for a democratic socialism. There was so much injustice in the world, from Harlem to Southeast Asia, that I wanted to believe in the generous theory of the creed. As Robert Louis Stevenson wrote in one of his essays, "When the torrent sweeps the man against a boulder, you must expect him to scream, and you need not be surprised if the scream is sometimes a theory."

But soon that theory shriveled away, as I read both Marx and history and witnessed the spectacle of "socialist" tanks in Czechoslovakia, the atrocities of Pol Pot, the crushing of Solidarity in Poland. There might again be a time when young Americans will be moved by political idealism or faith in a theory; alas, I won't be able to join them.

For any truly conscious middle-aged American must recognize that belief is the great killer of the century. Political belief has slaughtered millions. Religious belief has slaughtered the rest. *Agree with me or die* has been the essential slogan of the believers, at home and abroad, and you could fill every line of every page of every newspaper in the world with the names of their victims and still not have sufficient room. And yet we cannot seem to ever get free of them; charlatans pose as wise men; hustlers offer themselves as redeemers. And in come the brawny young men with the shovels, to turn the earth and bury the dead.

So in middle age, I am permanently secular. Television preachers provide inexhaustible entertainment, on screen and in motel rooms. And I am moved to outbursts of crazy laughter at the irrational gibberish of the New Age pitchmen, whose public appeal so perfectly mirrors that of the Swaggarts and Bakkers. Both represent some peculiarly American mixture of political exhaustion and the fear of death. Here (they say): grip this crucifix or this crystal and place your faith in the unseeable. Don't worry about the homeless, the starving, the injured, the humiliated; this life is a mere vestibule through which you must pass to greater happiness on the other side of death. Great stuff. But when they start running for the presidency or proclaiming on *The Oprah Winfrey Show* that they are God, I begin to check the locks on my door.

The basic question in middle age might be this: How can I live the rest of my life with a modicum of grace?

For many men, the heart of the matter sometimes becomes sexual desire. In spite of the Leather Elbow School of American Literature (aging professor with leather elbows sewn on his corduroy jacket falls in love with hot sophomore), I'm convinced that most middle-aged men aren't interested in involvements with very young women. It is not that sex has lost its power; if anything, the drive is stronger, because you know what you are doing at last, you have the accumulated sensations of a lifetime packed within you.

But very few young women can join middle-aged men in the exacting voyage of a love affair, never mind embark on the ardent passage of a marriage. Sensible men know this. Unless they have recently emerged from monasteries, middle-aged men simply know too much for young women — about sex, about themselves, and about the world. And most such men are not yet old enough to be cast in the role of sage. In the last years before I married again (fifteen years after my first marriage ended), I met some enchanting young women. They possessed a fresh beauty. They were intelligent. They had common sense. But I couldn't bring myself to explain again who Sandy Koufax was, or Flattop, or to recite the lyrics of "Teach Me To-night." I couldn't describe the rules of stickball or nights at Birdland. None could believe that there was once a world without television and that I had lived in it. Their myths were not mine.

So, like most sensible middle-aged men, those who have learned to adjust their emotional thermostats, I let them pass by. Their young, taut bodies were delightful to gaze upon, but they only re-minded me of the serrated flesh of my own aging carcass. They were of an age when they could still expect ecstasy, some gigantic removal from the planet in the union of love and sex; I envied this blind romantic faith but I also knew better. I also did not want to become a comic figure, the dirty old man of song and story, who gets older and older while the women remain the same age. And I suppose, too, that I feared an inability to perform; all aging men do. Was it possible (I asked myself at the midnight hour) that I once made love eight times in a single day, to two different women? And answered: yes, but no more.

But if my own experience can stand for that of others, then sexual desire certainly does not wane as you move into middle age. It *does* assume its proper part in the larger drama of the completion of a life. And any life is obviously more than sexual bliss or its denial. I have friends who have been searching in vain for two decades for some simple explanation of the meaning of life. I'm convinced that there is no such meaning. I don't ask for the meaning of the song of a bird or the rising of the sun on a misty morning. There they are, and they are beautiful, and I embrace them when I can. They are part of living, and living does have a value. When we're gone, the world vanishes forever. We lose baseball and Vermeer, the poetry of Yeats and the moves of Fred Astaire, wives and children, brothers and sisters, the smell of dogs in winter and the sound of bees on a summer afternoon.

Knowing what you will soon lose makes living even more pre-cious, and the middle-aged man becomes infinitely more concerned with time. I find myself more conscious of light, because light is the most primitive measure of time; I spend as many hours as possible in the country, where the movement of the sun is so much more obvious and poignant than it is in the city. I arrange my social life in different ways, avoiding whenever possible the brittle chatter of cocktail parties, the strained social performances at formal dinners.

I try to avoid all fads and fashions and to be skeptical of flattery. I seldom read books when they are published and find myself drawn back to the classics, to a few books that I first read years ago and failed to understand and that now seem to be about my own time on earth. More frequently now, I read history, biographies, memoirs, and journals because they have the effect of lengthening my life backward into the past, and because the complicated stories of other lives layer and multiply my own.

And because living seems more extraordinary than ever, I sleep less. In this, among so many other things, I resemble my father. In the last thirty years of his life (he died at eighty), he rose before dawn, rattling teacups, furious in some inarticulate way if his sons slept late. He never said so, but I'm certain now that the fury was about the waste of living. We have these dwindling hours and days to savor and use; it is almost sinful to occupy them with death's sweet brother, sleep. And so I am awake. Look (I say to my wife, her hand warm in the chilly dawn): the snow is melting in the fields outside the house. The trees are noisy with birds. The lake is making churning sounds, as the ice breaks and the bass stir at the bottom. In a few more weeks, they'll be playing the first games of another season, and we can watch a fresh new rookie try to hit the curveball. The world will soon be green again. We'll read Trollope beside the pond. And around these parts, fruit always ripens in the autumn.

ESQUIRE,
June 1988

REPRIEVE

That evening, when I returned to the hotel room in Miami, the message light was blinking on the telephone like an extra pulse. I sat down wearily on the edge of the bed and dialed the operator. My wife had called. And two sources for the story I was reporting. And my doctor . . . my doctor? Calling me from New York? The weariness vanished. In fifteen years, he'd never once called me anywhere unless I'd called him first. A week earlier I had submitted to my annual physical. All was normal. But here he was, calling me in a hotel in Miami. I glanced at my watch: a few minutes before 7:00. Probably gone home, but I called his office anyway. He was still there. And he went straight to the point.

"Last week's chest X ray?" he said. "Well, we looked at it again and there's something on it we don't like. . . ."

I laughed out loud. I'd been expecting some variation of this sentence for years. After all, I was a three-packs-a-day man, and at fifty-something, each year's physical was a kind of lottery. When it was over, and I was declared healthy, I always thought: Okay, got away with it again. Now, a few days after granting me my latest pass, the doctor was suddenly taking it back.

"What don't you like?"

"It's small, a dot really, on the upper part of your right lung."

"What is it?" I asked.

A pause, and then the doctor said: "When are you coming home?"

I flew home the next day and soon began a new rhythm of days and nights. I had no symptoms of anything: no cough, no rebellious blood, no weakness, no pain; but I swiftly entered the strange and private universe of the sick. My doctor sent me to another man, who specialized in the lungs. He in turn dispatched me to NYU Medical Center for a CAT scan. That propelled me down many bland new corridors to a series of desks where I was asked to pay first and be tested later. This was something new to me in my life in America, and oddly original; it was like a restaurant extorting payment before serving me food. At every step of this process, money came first. There was a wonderfully cynical assumption behind the most elemental contact in this new world: You are all potential deadbeats.

So I paid to have blood taken from my arms, to breathe into various machines, to swallow and be injected with chemicals. The good doctors and the excellent technicians hadn't devised the system of stand and deliver, of course; it must have evolved over the past few decades in the grand republic we all share with the boys from HUD, the S&L's, and the Medellín Cartel. Nobody else I told was surprised. But all of this was new to me. I'm one of those fortunate human beings who are almost never physically sick. Over the previous thirty-five years, I had been in a hospital only three times as a patient: for the repair of a broken hand and then a broken cheekbone (both sustained while serving my apprenticeship as a young idiot); and finally for the removal of a small cyst over my right eye. As a reporter, of course, I'd been in dozens of hospitals, in pursuit of the usual portion of human folly and calamity; over the years, I'd served emergency-room death watches on shot cops and raped nuns and wounded presidents of the United States. But such duties were really only paid tours in the region of melodrama. The attendant pain, fear, and odor of death were part of my craft, but not my life. Now I was on a private tour.

"What are you looking for?" I asked at an early point in this process.

The doctor shrugged, smiled, and said: "The truth."

He meant the truth about the spot on my lung, of course, not some grander insight into the meaning of the world. But even this limited truth wasn't easy. The spot was the size of a bread crumb and it was high up behind a rib. There were four possibilities: 1) lung cancer, caused by smoking an estimated 780,000 cigarettes over the previous three decades; 2) a fungus unique to the American Southwest and northern Mexico, both regions that I'd visited in the past two years; 3) a tumor caused by the asbestos I'd worked on for two months in the Brooklyn Navy Yard when I was sixteen; 4) tuberculosis. I am a fatalist about most things. Naturally, I was certain it was cancer.

"I don't think so," said my wife.

"Well, we'll soon find out."

It wasn't that easy. For all of the modern technology, the various experts couldn't decide precisely what was in my lung. They did one test to see if I'd been exposed recently to tuberculosis; the result was negative. The same was true about the fungus. The asbestos remained a possibility. So, obviously, did cancer. The big possibility. But, still, the doctors weren't certain. They wanted . . . the truth. They asked me to undergo a bronchoscopy. This meant I'd stay overnight at the hospital, and then, with a local anesthetic, a tube would be passed down my throat into my lung to get as close as possible to the Thing. I agreed.

In the hospital for the bronchoscopy, I noticed something odd about myself: I had no fear. I'm no braver than the average man, but none of this made me tremble or weep or fall into pools of self-pity. I lost no sleep, either to a runaway imagination or to bad dreams. Of course, a bronchoscopy was hardly a major operation, but it wasn't a day off either. And it might tell me that I had *cancer,* a word that seems to fill most Americans with dread. But instead of fear, regrets, or remorse, I found myself living almost entirely in the present tense: This happens, this happens, and this happens. If anything, the lack of fear made me sad. A lifetime of reporting had done its work; I'd been cheated of a basic human reaction.

Early one morning, I was wheeled down corridors on a gurney. I held my wife's hand before vanishing into the operating room. I gazed up, seeing faces distorted by my point of view and by drugs. They entered my throat. I woke later from an exhausted sleep.

"We couldn't get close enough," the doctor said. "I'm sorry."

"You mean the bronchoscopy was for nothing?"

"Not exactly. But —"

"But you still don't know what's in my lung. . . ."

A pause. "Yes."

"So. . . ."

"I want you to see a man . . . he's the best thoracic surgeon in New York."

"You have to operate?"

"Maybe."

I was learning that doctors are reporters, too; some operations are diagnostic, explorations of the unknown; they are done in order to discover the facts. I took a few more tests, and while waiting for results, went away for ten days to stop smoking (that is another story). But because of the location of the Thing (behind a rib, high in the lung), nothing was clear; only a surgeon, opening my right lung with his knife, could give me that clarity. I had to choose: undergo the chest operation immediately or wait and see what happens in the uncertain future. If the Thing was indeed a tumorous cancer, it could be removed in this same operation, along with a larger section of my lung that might be cancerous. I would lose about 20 percent of my lung capacity, but there was a good chance, given the size of the Thing and the fact that we'd found it at an early stage, that I could live a reasonably long life. On the other hand, if I waited, we might discover that the Thing wasn't cancer. It might remain at its present size; it could even vanish. So I was also learning that much of medicine, like so much of life, is best described in the subjunctive.

In the end, I couldn't bear the possibility of months of uncertainty, waiting to see whether the Thing got larger. I talked it over with my wife. I took a few walks around the block. Finally, I called the doctor.

"Okay," I said. "Let's do it."

A few days later, I was in the hospital, with more demands for payment, more papers to sign. They even took money for the telephone and use of a TV. God bless America. From one side of the room I could see the Chrysler Building, still the most elegant in the city, from the other, the East River. I stacked books beside the bed, along with a folder full of letters to be answered. "This might even be fun," I said to my wife, who looked dubious. "I haven't had any time off for almost twenty years. . . ."

"Why don't you get some sleep?" she said.

Late that night, alone in a drowsy fog, I began to think for the first time about death. Hell, this goddamned thing probably was cancer. Maybe it was worse than they were saying. Maybe something would go wrong on the operating table, some stupid failure of my body or their skill; it had happened to men I knew (such as John D. MacDonald); it could happen to me. But I didn't begin to summarize my life, searching for its meaning or drafting some imaginary farewell. Instead, I began to think about the people I would miss if my life ended: my wife and daughters, my brothers and sister and my friends. Their faces moved in and out of my consciousness; I spoke to some and hugged others. Then I saw and heard some of those other people, places, and things that made my life a life: Ben Webster and Cuco Sanchez, Hank Williams, Max Roach and Ray Charles; tabloid headlines, the poems of Yeats, and the faces of gangsters in the paintings of Jack Levine. I saw light spilling down the valleys of Mexico. I was reading Carlos Fuentes and Octavio Paz, Elmore Leonard and García Márquez. I sat in the Lion's Head and the Plaza Athénée and John's Pizzeria on Bleecker Street. It seemed absurd, even outrageous, to think that I'd never again see *Casablanca,* read Hemingway or Rebecca West or V. S. Pritchett, never again look upon the paintings of Tamayo, never, goddammit, finish Proust. If I died now I'd never know whether Tyson could really fight. I'd never see another World Series. And what about the books I hadn't written? The places I hadn't visited out there in the scary world? What would happen to my library? And the cabinets full of files? And what about all the words I hadn't written (or said) to the people I truly cared about, people I often didn't see much because I was so busy working? As soon as this was over, I had to call Fred Exley. I had

to write to my friends Sam Pilch and Tim Lee. I had to track down
. . . I was thinking such things, and certain I could hear Billie Holiday
singing "Miss Brown to You," when I fell into a dreamless sleep.

Early in the morning, a nurse gave me some pills; another injected
me with some nameless drug; a man who looked like John Coltrane
shaved my chest and pubic hair. My wife looked concerned. I made
some bad jokes as they moved me onto a gurney. I made a few more
on the way down the hall. Then I thought this was a kind of dumb
Ronald Reagan act and shut up. I kissed my wife's hand. They
wheeled me into the operating room. They placed something over
my face and I was gone.

From that long, drugged morning, I remember only a vision of
Cardinal O'Connor in a gray sweat shirt, playing handball at one of
those Coney Island courts that seem to have been painted by Ben
Shahn. The good cardinal was sweating hard, great dark blotches
staining his shirt, and he said nothing as he batted the small black
ball against the unyielding wall. I'm not a religious man and don't
know O'Connor, but his cameo appearance in my delirium certainly
cheered me up. I was suddenly awake. My wife smiled and kissed
me. There were feeding tubes in my arms, two tubes draining my
slashed lung, other tubes carrying away wastes. And I hurt. Oh, yeah,
I hurt. Not a sharp, stabbing pain. It was more generalized, as if
some giant had lifted me up and then slammed me viciously to the
ground. This was not a trip to the beach. I hurt. I fucking well hurt.

"Not cancer," my wife whispered. "Tu-ber-cu-lo-sis. . . ."

I have a memory of someone shouting, "Not cancer! Not cancer!"
while I was under. But I don't trust that memory as a fact. I must
have invented it later. I remember nothing of my time on the operating table, although I was there for more than three hours, with
another four in intensive care. The surgeon made an incision from
under my right pectoral muscle across my back. About twelve inches
long. He cut delicately into the lung and found the Thing. Then they
all waited while it was analyzed.

And it wasn't cancer.

The nodule, shaped like a tiny Cheerio, was a necrotizing granu-
loma, caused by tuberculosis. It was not contagious, being already
dead. They sewed me up.

I smiled (she told me) and fell asleep. Later I would talk to friends about the epidemic of TB that is moving through American cities, passed along by our derelict armies. "They cough," the doctor told me, "and twenty minutes later you can walk through it, and. . . ." Later, I would make jokes with visitors and eat ice cream and smell the great garlands of arriving flowers. A lovely nurse from Haiti would wash me, soaping my face, arms, genitals — a Catherine Barkley without the sentimentality — but every last erotic impulse, alas, was erased by pain. After midnight, the man in the next bed ripped at the *trache* in his throat, the strangled sounds *(uh, uh, uh, uh, uh, uh, uh)* rose from him in agonized protest while his wife screamed at him in Yiddish. Later, I would at last have my '60s experience all in one night, drugs lifting this old whiskey drinker into distended bands of time and color and sound while the words of friends and strangers mixed together in the slippery mist of a ruptured consciousness.

But for that long moment, coming back from the anesthetized emptiness, those two words seemed the most lucid and important of all.

Not cancer.

"Not cancer," my wife said again.

"Hand me the dice," I said.

ESQUIRE,
January 1991